LAST MOUNTAIN DANCER

LAST MOUNTAIN DANCER

Hard-Earned Lessons in Love,
Loss, and Honky-Tonk Outlaw Life

Chuck Kinder

CARROLL & GRAF PUBLISHERS
NEW YORK

LAST MOUNTAIN DANCER
Hard-Earned Lessons in Love, Loss, and Honky-Tonk Outlaw Life

Carroll & Graf Publishers
An Imprint of Avalon Publishing Group Inc.
245 West 17th Street
11th Floor
New York, NY 10011

AVALON
publishing group incorporated

Copyright © 2004 by Chuck Kinder

First Carroll & Graf edition 2004

The names of some people and places in this book have been changed.
Everything else is as literally true as the Bible.

Library of Congress Cataloging-in-Publication Data is available.

ISBN: 0-7867-1406-9

Book design by Paul Paddock
Printed in the United States of America
Distributed by Publishers Group West

This hillbilly book goes out to my mountain beauties—
Diane, Daisy, Pearl, Eileen, Nancy Beth, Morgan Ann,
Amy Beth, & little Lulu

CONTENTS

PLANET WEST VIRGINIA

Back in 1994, before I blew out of town to begin my sabbatical leave, I had informed my bemused dubious academic colleagues that I intended to disappear into the hills of my home in West Virginia, immerse myself, as it were, among the lives of mountaineer characters, both the quick and the dead, among both my family members and strangers, whose stories I wanted to write, fascinating, famous brave survival tales I tended to portray as being so wrenchingly parallel to my own. I planned to converse with my people in the secret old language of the mountains, wherein the ancient word for "bone" and "seed" was the same. I intended to bear holy witness to their magical everyday world of devils and angels. Mountain incantations, spooky spells, moany keens, the musical sighs of hill spirits, and the abiding ghost hymns of Hank Williams and Saint Elvis would inform the soundtrack for my twangy tall tale, I would mention. I would mention that my stylistic mode would be oracular in nature and pure High Hillbilly.

I found myself prevaricating mightily like I hadn't done since my Stanford days about my simple but stouthearted coalminer-cum-moonshiner-cum-mountaineer roots, and announcing to any interested ear that I had only been disguised as a deputy professor petrified with longing as he taught at a city-campus university and wrote artsy-fartsy fiction all these lost years. Where exactly had I been derailed in my quest to be bolder and more famous than my old Dad? was one big question I hoped to answer back home, I told folks. Boldly I quoted Flannery O'Connor to those sophisticated, citified, politically correct, deconstructed, Frog-thought theorymongers: "To know oneself is to know one's region. It is also to know the world, and it is also, paradoxically, a form of exile from that world."

Let me say a few things straightaway about that wild, wonderful world called West Virginia, gentle reader.

For one thing, West Virginia is populated by regular, respectable, upstanding, hard-working, everyday folks just like the folks you can find in any part of America. And West Virginians become defensive when outsiders characterize them as ignorant, incestuous, dangerous, armed-to-the-teeth hicks and hillbillies. West Virginians want the world at large to know they can be as bland and boring and ordinary as anybody else in this television-leveled land called homogenized America. But there is little romance, not to mention mythos, in the mundane for me, and this is, after all, my book about West Virginia and how it shaped my own rise to fame and final exile.

My own personal sense of that fabled place called West Virginia is admittedly a folktale state of mind, a mostly imagined interior landscape populated by mythic beings: legendary mountain dancers, moonshiners, stupendous marijuana farmers, snakehandlers, blood-feudists, mystery midgets, mothmen, horny space aliens who drop into my home state as regular as clockwork in order to engage in extraterrestrial sex with a multitude of juicy West Virginia majorettes and to purloin farm animals for bizarre mutilation rituals, and other interesting folk of that ilk. In my admittedly melodramatic, renegade vision of West Virginia, what interests me are the bloody mine wars, the ritual disappearance of revenuers and scabs, unsolved mountain murders, mysteriously vanished hitchhikers whose body parts are found scattered beside twisty backcountry roads, jailbirds, jailbreaks, outlaws on the run, doomed and despairing barroom brawlers, deep mine disasters, and the souls of lost buried miners rising like smoke from mine-ventilation holes in the hills. The lonesome whistles of coal trains passing forlornly in the night figure prominently in my personal romantic sense of West Virginia, as does white-line fever, roadhouse romance, the sad slow dance of jukebox heartbreak, the high-lonesome sounds of old Bill Monroe, George Jones (the old Possum of Pain), Patsy Cline and sweet dreams, the buttkicking ballads of Johnny Paycheck, and, of course, the essential songs of Saint Elvis and Uncle Hank.

What interests me is that haunted West Virginia, famous for howls of loss and longing and hoots of otherworldly laughter that are known to descend from the hills during nights long enough for two or three moons. Not to mention wild, albeit beloved, legendary hogs running in the woods, storied witches in the woods, the ghosts of beheaded coeds stumbling blindly in the woods, ghost lights on forsaken ridges, sacred spectral animals once thought extinct that come down from the hills on full-moon nights.

An extraordinary filmmaker named Jacob Young, who made the famous prize-winning "Different Drummer" series of documentaries featuring weird West Virginians, has suggested that one reason why West Virginia is so famous for its congregation of eccentrics is because of the nature of the people who originally settled in those hills. They were, Jacob Young asserts, ". . . people who simply wanted to be left alone. People who were outcasts, totally individualistic, totally noncon-formist, the rugged individuals who say: 'We don't need no neighbors. We don't need no fucken town.' "

My own bald bizarre ugly brother-in-law is in many ways typical of the often-weird inhabitants of West Virginia and their ragged hopes. Once he mailed me an item he had clipped from the local paper about what it meant to be a *Real West Virginian*.

The piece was entitled: *You Might Be A Real West Virginian If . . .* (and listed several clear qualifications). You might be a Real West Virginian if your front porch collapses and more than six dogs are killed was one clear qualification; or if you consider a six-pack and a bug zapper quality entertainment; or if your wife or mother has ever been involved in a fistfight with an official or another spectator at a high school sports event; or if your wife or mother keeps a spit-cup on the ironing board; or if your wife or mother doesn't remove the Marlboro from her mouth when she tells the state trooper to kiss her ass; or if you prominently display the gift you bought at Graceland; or if there is a stuffed possum mounted anywhere in your house; or if you think a Volvo is a part of a woman's anatomy. You might be considered a Real West Virginian if you had a toothpick in your mouth when the wedding pictures were taken; or if you've ever carried a bottle of beer to a job interview; or if most of your Saturday nights end up in a famous parking lot fistfight.

I had decided straightaway that I, for one, met enough of the qualifications to be certified as a genuine West Virginian-American. But I wondered about some other folks who laid claim to being bona fide citizens of my home state, outsiders who had crossed the state line and for curious reasons of their own attempted to reinvent themselves as one of us, as though our captive land was a miraculous catchall place where you could always land on your feet. "Lord Jesus, save us from them fucken outsiders," is one common prayer in my home state.

There's the famous former Governor and current Senator Jay Rockefeller, for instance, who had come into West Virginia several decades ago as a Vista Volunteer, and had lingered to get into politics. Now Jay Rockefeller passes himself off to the world at large as a genuine West Virginian-American, and on numerous occasions over the past thirty-five-plus years he has spent conspicuous fortunes convincing mountain-state voters to tell him ceremonially his reinvention is really so, pumping a reputed record cool ten million into one campaign alone to roost and rule. And, speaking of famous parking lot fistfights, I'll tell you more about this seemingly feckless, four-eyed, prep-school, rich-boy, New York Yankee Jay Rockefeller character directly.

West Virginia reinvented its-own-self as the thirty-fifth state of the Union on June 20, 1863, two weeks before the battle of Gettysburg pretty much settled the issue of that war, when it seceded from the Confederate state of Virginia to rejoin the Union, a secession within a secession, a sort of opening of Chinese boxes of rebellion. It wasn't so much that West Virginians sided with the dour righteous Yankees, as that they did not approve of those lowland, rich, racist (to put it mildly), prissy plantation owners dictating who they should rebel against. Besides, mountaineers, being mostly a fierce, wilderness, warrior people prone to independence and hardheadedness, held little sentiment for the lazy decadent institution of slavery.

Geographically and historically, West Virginia defies easy classification. On the map, West Virginia's amoebic squashed road-kill shape can put one in mind of any number of unusual things, depending upon the hour of the long night, and what manner of chemicals are raging through one's bloodstream. Sometimes, and don't ask me why exactly, when I gaze at a map of West Virginia at maybe three or four in the morning, I think of a more or less anatomically correct representation of a lumpy, damaged human heart, its *superior vena cava* a panhandle jutting sixty-four miles due north of the Mason-Dixon line, further north than the Yankee stronghold of Pittsburgh, in fact, its eastern panhandle a pulmonary artery running almost as far east as the nation's capital, its rounded southern boundaries not unlike the dual ventricles of the human heart (or perhaps a soft underbelly, or scrotal sac, say, depending . . .), hanging deeper south than even the old Confederate capital of Richmond.

Many Yankees and other assorted outsiders have formed their mostly misguided impressions of West Virginians, and hillbillies in general, for that matter, from movies such as *Deliverance,* which starred the famous Burt Reynolds and Jon Voight, and was based upon a novel written by the famous late neo-Beowulfian poet James Dickey. The film concerned these four fellows, basically southern, moral-flotsamy, town-boy types, who decide to canoe down a wild whitewater river back in the mountains before it is dammed up, in order to test their rather dubious, idle, civilized concept of real manhood before it is too late. The hillbillies they encounter in those isolated, plum-scary mountains have clearly been inbreeding for generations, judging from their banjo-plucking but crosseyed, drooling, idiot children, and the perverse propensity of their menfolk to capture outsiders back in the woods in order to encourage them to participate in such activities as anal intercourse at gunpoint.

That purported propensity for forbidden hellish backwoods embrace notwithstanding, bona fide West Virginian-Americans (at least the ones who interest me the most) may be better characterized as basically folks who have come to more or less relish what they can't help being anyway, namely fugitive survivors who dwell in a sort of perpetual dream of siege and populate the closest thing to another planet you can probably find in America, and who inhabit the sort of life that just seems to keep taking on a life of its own, no matter how eccentric or crazy or dangerous or dead-end, or just plain old fun.

You can imagine West Virginia as one of the final frontiers, I informed clearly bored and mostly besotted folks at a faculty cocktail party I attended just before my departure from Pittsburgh back in 1994. My colleagues rolled their eyes and chuckled as they attempted to politely duck and dodge and just generally distance themselves from my presence at that party. Where even today, I maintained boldly, there is a great nostalgia for the habits and customs and old ways of life in the mountains, which, like life on the old Western Frontier, were often crude and violent and utterly carnivorous, with a great predilection for drinking to excess, and fighting and feuding and fornicating to excess, not to mention dancing wildly until the cows came home at dawn, and risking all for love or revenge, and discharging guns into the air simply to express feelings of arrogance or despair, confusion or joy, or simply for the general old-timey luxurious frontier fuck of it. I was going back to that land where I truly belonged, where I fit in, that country which quickened my hillbilly heart. That country where that old-timey free, wild-as-the-wind, rough-and-tumble, fun-loving, sexual spirit survives deep in the scary hills of West Virginia, lingers there yet to this day in pockets peopled mostly by my own rowdy relatives. I, for instance, would forsake my university professorship in a heartbeat if I thought I could make a decent living grazing hogs in the woods. And I drink whiskey, I reminded those city slickers, following them around the room if necessary to make my points, as they scurried away from me like right-wing Republican rats utterly uninterested in rational Democratic discourse.

I intended to rent me a furnished doublewide in a trailer park by a creek in a hollow near Madison, or Milton, or Welch, or Williamson, or Wherever, West Virginia, I further informed one of my erstwhile colleagues I cornered by the refrigerator in the kitchen, an attractive, untenured young thing with short pinkish punk hair and multiple piercings, who was basing her academic career on the legitimacy of those idiotic French theories concerning the nonexistence of the author. A trailer park just down the blacktop two-lane from a friendly little tavern by the river, I added. And exhausted in the evenings after slaving since the crack of dawn over the stories I had stolen in my frequent forays into the hills of my home state and was making my own, and exhausted also after struggling mightily to set straight all those personal stories that made up my myth of self as I relentlessly wrote my meta-memoir and mythopoetic travelogue to Almost Heaven, I would amble on down to purchase me a possumburger with fried sweet yeller onions for supper at the bar, and drink exactly three longneck bottles of Budweiser (I'd be locally famous for drinking until I dropped only on Saturday nights) while I listened to the half-hour of country tear-jerkers I'd punch on the old jukebox by the door.

As this attractive pierced young assistant professor ducked under my arm and flung herself to my mind in exaggerated panic from the kitchen, I barked at her lovely bare and exotically tattooed back that when I'd pass by the pay phone in the hallway on my way to take a leak, I would not break down and call anybody long distance no matter how much I missed them. Whereupon, after jawboning briefly with my new best Saturday-night barfly buddies, I would stroll through the rainy night back to my old dented trailer where the tiny black-and-white television didn't work and the only station I could get on the ancient radio was purely gospel, and I would lie down on the creaky bed in the dark and sip smokey moonshine from a mason jar and listen to the melancholy escaped sound of rain on the metal roof, while just trying to imagine a better life than that, a sweet miracle of calm resolve and remembrance.

book one

FAMOUS OLD DADDY

THE GIRL WITH NO FACE

I don't know how many folks outside of West Virginia remember Dagmar any more, but once she was famous. Back in the early and mid-fifties, Dagmar had been black-and-white teevee's version of Marilyn Monroe, or, maybe more accurately, of grade-B movie queen Jayne Mansfield. Dagmar was the resident dumb blonde with big breasts on the old Milton Berle *Texaco Theater*, where she cultivated a funny, startled, deceptively stupid look. She also appeared on the teevee variety show *Broadway Open House*, and even had her own short-lived *Dagmar's Canteen* in 1952, where Frank Sinatra was once a guest.

Dagmar had been my own first hope and inspiration for a future beyond the ordinary. Dagmar had become the source of all my earliest discovery and flight and fame fantasies. But I let Dagmar and her famous big breasts slip through my fingers.

Dagmar's real name was Virginia Ruth Egnor, and she was born in 1924 in Huntington, West Virginia. When I was a boy, Dagmar's folks had lived three doors down from us on Waverly Road in Huntington for several years. There were no fences around the small frame houses on our road in those days, and we kids darted in our games like free-range chickens across that little prairie of back yards. In Dagmar's folks' back yard there was a spreading old oak we often used as homebase, where I relished the role of being "it" during hide-and-seek. Being "it" meant that I could hover about that homebase old oak, where it was only a matter of time until one day Dagmar would discover me. Someday Dagmar would be visiting her folks, maybe sitting out at the kitchen table sipping coffee one morning with her mom, when through the back window she would spot a swift,

3

singular, beautiful boy fearless at his play, and with a mere glance Dagmar would recognize the shining of his inner star.

Dagmar would stub out the cigarette she had been languidly smoking, while trying to explain the enigmatic nature of fame to her old mom, and she would rush out the back door to that special splendid boy, rush to enfold him in her fame, not to mention extraordinary bosom, her famous nipples fiery red through her filmy clinging negligee (I loved those words: *nipples, negligee, nipples, nipples, nipples,* which were among those magically learned juicy words of my childhood I would roll around on my tongue like holy cherry LifeSavers).

And then it really happened. Dagmar had actually shown up at her folks' home on Waverly Road the summer I was ten. We awakened one August Saturday morning into all the ordinariness of our own lives to discover an enormous car parked in front of Dagmar's folks' little house. It was a *Cadillac*! It was a Cadillac *convertible*! It was *yellow*! I loved that yellow Cadillac convertible with all my heart. The neighborhood was abuzz. One of Dagmar's prissy little nieces kept sashaying out of the house to preen and prance and keep everybody abreast of the radiant blonde being within. Apparently Dagmar had brought her latest husband home to meet her folks for a real low-key downhome family visit. I skulked and lurked about the little frame house like all the rest of the obscure neighborhood minions that Saturday morning hoping to get at least a peek at the inscrutable face of fame, but to no avail.

Around noon my Dad, or *"Captain,"* as everybody called him, piled as many neighborhood kids as would fit in his old battered green Plymouth station wagon, as was his Saturday afternoon custom, and hauled us all down the road to a public swimming pool called Dreamland. Dad was called Captain because he had been the captain of the Second World War, which he had apparently won pretty much single-handedly. He was famous for this far and wide. When he had mustered out of the Army at the end of the war as a hero, some folks had encouraged him to get into politics. Captain was a big, gregarious fellow with an easy booming laugh, a fullblown sort of character folks always declared was a dead ringer for John Wayne, and it was true. Some folks even declared that

Captain would be a natural for governor of West Virginia, although he was by nature neither a drunk nor a crook. Captain, who was a generally unemployed hero, hauled all us rowdy kids out of the neighborhood on weekends so that my mom, who was an emergency room nightshift nurse, and who pretty much brought home the proverbial bacon in our house plus cooked it up, could collapse in peace.

I recall Dreamland as a vast pool of wavy, faintly bluegreen water splashing with sunlight, air thick with the pungent puzzling sweetness of chlorine and suntan lotion, joyful screams and squeals strangely echoey, smooth oiled teenage girls parading imperiously with their movie-star sunglasses and implicating smiles and the sweet shadowy secrets of their shaved underarms. Music was always blasting from a huge white-stucco two-storied clubhouse trimmed in blue, and blue, onion-shaped domes rose above dressing rooms on a knoll at the far end of the long pool. Dreamland was a Taj Mahal of a swimming pool I both loved and feared, a site of excitement for me and profound failure.

Dreamland was where I learned to swim my first spastic strokes, and where I failed repeatedly to muster courage enough to attempt swimming out to the deep end. I was not afraid of drowning in the deep end. It wasn't that. It was, for one thing, my fear of not looking cool and sleek swimming around like the older boys, but dopey as a duck as I thrashed about in the water of the deep end. I was afraid of being embarrassed if I swam out to the huge circular concrete island in the deep end where the older boys hung out as they strutted and flexed their fulsome brown muscled bodies. Mostly, though, my fear of the deep end was because of the bad dreams.

We piled out of Captain's old Plymouth station wagon that Saturday and charged for the ticket counters, bouncing about impatiently as we inched along in one of the two endless lines. And then I spotted her, in the next line, the famous monster girl with no face. I had seen her maybe two or three other times, and it was always a shock. She was a monster girl whose face had no features. It was like looking at a blur of a face. You got the impression of holes here and there for what could have been perhaps nostrils and a mouth maybe, and eyes, like unaligned marbles amid folds and flaps of flesh and hair that looked like fur and feathers. There were rumors that the girl had been born that way, or that her face had burned off in a fire, or been cut to ribbons in a terrible car wreck or by an escaped crazy man with a knife. Her blur of a face was at an angle to me, and I stared at it. I couldn't help it. I blinked my eyes trying to somehow adjust them, to get them into focus, to compose something recognizable as the regular human face of a girl amid that pulpy mess of skin. Suddenly the monster girl turned her head in my direction and I jerked my eyes away. But she knew I had been staring. I could feel she knew I had been staring, and my neck burned with shame and embarrassment for her exotic horribleness. I couldn't think of anything worse than being her, a person whose face could never show her sadness, or happiness, if she ever had any, whose only expression would be *horribleness*. How could a girl with no face ever leave the safety of a dark room? How could a monster girl ever crawl out from under her rock?

—Let's head for the deep end, soldierboy, Captain said to me the minute we laid out our towels on a grassy slope above the pool that Saturday. —Let's go kick that deep end's ass, Captain added, laughing that bold confident winner-of-the-Second-World-War laugh of his, and he gave my shoulder a poke with his finger that about knocked me down. I was this boney kid who had at best a baffled sense of balance. Then Captain gave me a snappy salute, which meant that I, his little soldierboy, was supposed to snap him a salute back, a little private father–son comradery thing he had initiated when I was maybe one. I knew what this meant in a heartbeat. This meant that my cowardly ass was grass and the Second World War was the mower. I hated the Second World War with all my heart. This also meant Mom had ratted me out to Captain about the deep end and my cowardliness, and I resolved at that moment to keep my heart hidden from everybody forever.

At noon each day when I came home from playing or school for lunch, there would be two pans heating on the stove. One pan contained simmering Campbell's tomato soup. I loved Campbell's tomato soup.

A syringe and needle were being sterilized in the other bubbling pan. After I had enjoyed my Campbell's tomato soup, which I slurped with infinitely slow appreciation while nibbling with elegant slowness upon the crumbs of saltines, Mom would lead me upstairs trudging forlornly behind her like the proverbial prisoner going to the gallows. I would lie face down on my bed with my butt bared, until such time as I had worked up enough courage to gasp into my pillow a feathered, fluttering little birdy whimper of that word: *"now."* Whereupon Mom would deliver into my shivery littleboy butt via that needle the approximate size of a harpoon my daily dose of raging male hormones (I had had a little undescended testicle problem that took four visits to the famous Mayo Clinic to eventually make all better).

While I was working up the courage to say *now,* Mom would let me jabber my head off, as I stalled. If I sensed Mom growing impatient with me, I would attempt to distract her with entertaining albeit inscrutable stories. Sometimes I would be forced to pretend to confide in Mom, telling her what I hoped would pass as truthful, private things, making my revelations as puzzling and painful as possible to engage her interest and sympathies. Hence I had told her more truthfully than I meant to about my fear of the deep end, and then I had told her about the nightmares I had had for years that as I was swimming along happily, something horrible, some horrible scary creature who lived on the bottom of the deep end would awake and see me up above on the surface of the water. Whereupon in my nightmares I would feel something grab my feet from below, and pull me screaming down under the water to be eaten raw.

So there was Captain treading water in the shivery bluegreen water of the deep end, throwing salutes my way and hollering above the pool racket to jump on in, soldierboy, the water's right. But soldierboy just stood there looking down at toes curled like scared worms over the pool's edge. —You can swim like a fish, soldierboy, just jump on in and swim to your old dad, son. I'm right here, son, nothing will happen. You

7

won't drown, soldierboy, hollered Captain. But soldierboy knew he wouldn't drown. That wasn't it. Soldierboy stood there trembling. Like a cowardly leaf. Soldierboy wanted more than anything to be under the water of his beloved shallow end, holding his breath in the currents of uncomplexity at its bottom where nobody could see him.— Come on now, soldierboy, Captain implored, gritting his teeth. I stared at my worried worms.—Come on now, Goddammit, Chuck, jump! Captain encouraged me and slapped the water with a cupped hand. It sounded like a shot. I flinched violently.

—Why don't you go ahead and jump, chickenshit, a neighborhood boy said from behind me and hooted with laughter. They were all around me, the neighborhood boys and girls, all those creepy kids with their giggles, their laughter. I spun around and ran. I pushed my way relentlessly through hooting human beings who knew me.

I skulked around that lake of a pool and slipped into the shameful shallow end on the far side, among the comforting presence of strangers, where I felt at home. I bobbed about in the shallow water, a floating head, keeping a wary eye out for Captain or any of the evil neighborhood kids, while I plotted my revenge. If only I could transform this once-sweet Persian dream of a pool into a lake of acid. Or have schools of gigantic piranha churn the waves into a foam of blood. If only the creature of the deep end awoke while Captain was swimming out there all alone, when suddenly it would happen, and with but a shudder of his great muscles Captain would be pulled down into the deep end, and although my old man would wrestle heroically with the groping tentacles, for he was such a big brave fellow, they would slowly entangle him, pulling him into the dark water toward the deep end monster's huge yellow crazy eyes and great bloody maw.

Then I heard an announcement over the clubhouse's loudspeakers. They announced that we were all honored to have Dagmar, the famous star of screen and television, as a special guest that day at Dreamland. I stood up in the shallow end and looked around wildly. *Dagmar, man oh man*! I saw a crowd passing slowly along the side of the pool by the clubhouse stairs toward the picnic area on the same slope where we had our stuff laid out. In a momentary parting of the excited throng, I was certain I caught a glimpse of utter blondeness. For a moment I considered returning to the slope where we had our blanket, where all the neighborhood kids were hanging out, swallowing my pride in order to get a better look at that famous blonde person and her wondrous breasts up close. But I didn't. I *had* my pride. I turned and dogpaddled with dignity to the concrete island in the shallow end, where I pulled myself up and sat with my back to Dad and Dagmar and all they meant.

At some point, I began jumping over and over again into the pool. Time and again, I would run and hurl myself belly first from the island painfully into the choppy water. Then I would drag myself back up on the island and do it again. I didn't care. I didn't care if I knocked myself out and drowned shamefully at the bottom of the shallow end. I pictured Captain standing over where they had drug my pitiful drowned body onto the deck of the pool, bluegreen water draining from my mouth and nose and ears and eyes. I tried to picture Captain crying his heart out, but I couldn't. The only thing I could make come alive in my imagination was Captain carrying my limp dripping body up the clubhouse stairs while some sad song like "Endless Sea" blasted on the loudspeakers, and all the evil neighborhood kids were standing around wondering out loud if I would come back from the dead and fuck with them, which, buddy, you can bet I would.

Then I pictured Dagmar swimming toward me under water. Like a wondrous waterplant's blooming, her beautiful blond hair floated about her head as her face came toward my own until it filled my vision. Whereupon, in the moment before I lost consciousness, I felt Dagmar's soft white arms enfold me. I was only ten years old, but I imagined myself being deliciously smothered in the immensity of Dagmar's blond breasts as she delivered the drowning soldierboy safely to the surface.

So there I stood on the shallow end island trying to catch my breath after a particularly painful bellybuster, when a kid came directly up to me out of the basic blue and excitedly said these exact words: —Dagmar saw you, boy! *Dagmar saw you, boy!* That kid said exactly that. I swear it! I spun around like an insane top. I looked everywhere. I looked in the water around the island. I scanned the far sides of the pool, and the

9

grassy slopes. *Dagmar saw you, boy.* When I looked back for the kid, he was gone. But that boy had been real, and he had said those exact words full of more wonder than any other words of my childhood. I swear it.

Dagmar had spotted me. That much was clear. I believed that with all of my heart. I believe it to this day. Somehow my fierce painful brave bellybusters had caught Dagmar's attention. Perhaps her blue famous eyes were settled upon me at that moment. They could be. They were. I sprang into action. I threw myself from the concrete island like a virgin into a volcano. I exploded into that violence of water and began to swim frantically for the island in the deep end. I thrashed my arms and kicked my feet wildly. I chopped across the rough surface of the deep end, choking, my eyes burning, toward the distant island. The deep end's water strangled into my throat with each ragged stroke, and it dawned on me that I might never make it. It dawned on me that I might actually drown like a rat. And for what? Fame? Fame wasn't worth it, I realized. Fame wasn't worth drowning like a rat.

But at that epiphanic moment, I felt strangely calm. I closed my eyes and simply kept chopping, blindly, but unafraid, trance-like, and then suddenly I touched concrete. I slapped an astonished hand onto the surface of the island in the deep end and held on for dear life. I had not drowned like a rat after all. I had a second chance at everything, including fame. I was coughing and spitting and my sore arms trembled nearly out of control. I wiped water off my face with my free hand and pushed my hair out of my eyes. I was there. Soldierboy had made it. Soldierboy was at the island in the deep end where he had always really belonged. Soldierboy loved that concrete island with all his heart. He gripped the edge of the island and looked around to see who had witnessed this amazing feat. He looked for the evil neighborhood kids. He looked for Captain, his dad. Soldierboy looked around for Dagmar.

And then suddenly somebody emerged from the water right beside me and grabbed the edge of the island. It was the famous girl with no face, who is the real star of this little story. I took one look at her and screamed. I screamed and screamed and fell back into the water, flapping my arms like crazy wings.

TOWN BOY

In a nutshell, this book is about trying to grow up as famous as my old dad in the dark hills and hollows of West Virginia, and then, having failed in that dubious endeavor, seeking fame far away from home, for all the good that got me. Whereupon, having fallen flat on my face miserably at that enterprise too, meaning the acquisition of renown in the wide world, I returned finally to the hallowed home ground of Almost Heaven to attempt to come to some sort of understanding of the nature of fame, at the very least.

How in the world could anybody aspire to grow up famous in a Godforsaken place like West Virginia? outsider skeptics may ask. Well, the truth is that many famous people besides Dagmar have arisen out of the Godforsaken dark hills and hollows of West Virginia. The famous basketball great Jerry West was born at Cabin Creek on the Kanawha River in West Virginia, not five miles from where I was born in Montgomery. Jerry is a third cousin of mine. The famous aviator, my fifth cousin Chuck Yeager, is from West Virginia. He broke the sound barrier before anybody else in the world. He was a man made of the right stuff to become famous. The famous actress Joanne Dru was born in 1923 in Logan. Peter Marshall, famous for hosting more than 5000 shows of *The Hollywood Squares,* was born in 1927 in Clarksburg. Famous for his pie-in-the-face humorous antics, Soupy Sales was born in Huntington. My own personal famous hero, my second cousin Don Knotts, a.k.a. Barney Fife of the old *Andy Griffith Show,* was born in Morgantown in 1924.

A look-alike younger brother of Don Knotts worked as a clerk in the state liquor store in Morgantown when I lived there as a student at West

Virginia University. I visited this gentleman often. He was a quiet, nervous, enigmatic man, who I often seemed to confuse while I was in line by confessing things of a personal nature he clearly didn't care to hear. My wife thinks I'm a fat, smelly boozehound and that I don't have a shot at fame, I would inform Don Knotts' brother as he made change. I implored him to pass these secrets along to his famous brother in order to provide them with a broader significance. My cousin Don never called to pass comment on these personal matters.

All of these aforementioned famous people from West Virginia are, because of generations of inbreeding, cousins of mine, and they served as role models and inspirations to me in my own quest for that escape from the mundane called fame.

I once entertained a certain fame simply by being from West Virginia. It was during my Stanford days in the early and mid-'70s. When I had arrived on that august campus a poor fellowship boy feeling stricken with otherness and perfectly hicky, I soon discovered that in those days of *The Whole Earth Catalog* and the famous Truck Store in Menlo Park, it was amazingly cool to play *closer to the Earth than thou*. What I had discovered was a multitude of these peculiar rich kids clomping around under the palms in haute hillbilly work boots and Dickie coveralls pretending to be rubes, as though their parents had been farmers instead of ruling-class country club snobs. Because I had pissed in a couple of mine portals and worked road construction and had worked up in the steel mills in Cleveland, and had stumbled about blindly more than once thanks to old mister moonshine, I found I could affect that good-ole-boy, redneck ruse with a little more bucolic bluster than kids whose parents owned estates off the 18th hole at Pebble Beach. Hence I reveled in my rude, loutish lack of polish and played the hip hick to the hilt. I commenced telling tall tales of daring fulltilt moonshine-runs over midnight back-country *thunderroads*. I began chewing godawful Red Man tobacco for further effect until my teeth turned brown and my first wife quit kissing my mouth or ever holding me at night.

Stanford, like Berkeley in those days, was also a hotbed of revolutionary fervor, and the most ravishing albeit hairy underarm girls were hippie-cum-commies. I didn't have a political bone in my body, but I commenced lamenting to my comrades about mine strikes and tent cities I had known as a poor, suffering coalminer's child, about the bloody shootouts with Baldwin-Felts Detective gun-thugs my old daddy had had fighting to organize the union down in them dark, dangerous hills. It had been a ready-made, undemanding, redneck, revolutionary role and form of refuge I had relished in my youth. We would play the Stones' "Street Fighting Man" over and over and pop pills to get into a proper revolutionary fervor, my comrades and I, before we took to the streets to battle the pigs. I found I was adept at this, and I had once been rewarded for my street fighting aptitude with the opportunity of making twisted, neurotic Marxist love to a beautiful, radical Jewess after a particularly paroxysmal Berkeley demonstration, burying my face in thick black commie-princess hair heady and lovely with the lingering aroma of tear-gas.

Actually, if the truth be told, I had grown up a town boy. I had been a big fan of *The Beverly Hillbillies* and of *The Real McCoys,* however, but about the only thing I knew personally about real "country" or "hill" people was that they rode school buses and hung out at the dark dangerous south end of the first floor hall in our junior high school, real tribal and as fascinatingly foreign as gypsies. (It seemed as though most of them simply vanished after junior high school and rarely arrived on those rickety nearly-empty yellow buses at Huntington High.) The running joke was that they were all brothers and sisters or at best inbred kissing cousins, and that they all used lard in bed to prolong if not facilitate love. The guys all had long greasy hair with sideburns and home-carved tattooes on their big biceps, and the girls wore thick eyeliner and dime store perfume and they wore beehive hairdos and often entertained serious albeit exotic body odor. They were simply this high school subculture called *school bus rurals,* who were looked down on as these poor rustic rubes who could have been from another planet for all we cool towncats knew or cared. And then there was Charlie Wilkes.

Charlie Wilkes was this rangy mountainboy badass character who had once cold-cocked the hero halfback of the varsity football team with a left jab. Charlie Wilkes, who used shop class to fashion exquisitely carved billyclubs, was legendary for once having tossed an ex-Marine toughguy teacher out of a second story window after being asked to please quit scaring the girls during study hall and put his dick back in his jeans.

No nuts . . . no nuts . . . no nuts. . . .

Charlie Wilkes did not say it all that loudly. He was just nodding at me and saying it over and over. We were in the shower room after gym class. Other boys gathered around. I kept my back to them and continued to dress as though nothing was amiss. Maybe I had my undershorts on by then.

No nuts . . . no nuts . . . no nuts. . . .

Charlie Wilkes did not even say this with any real meanness in his voice. He was simply standing there bareass, wet from the shower, being muscular and nonchalantly comfortable as guys with the balls of bulls and whose dicks hang down to their knees can be naked. I minded my own important business, namely getting my goddamn clothes on. Then Charlie Wilkes began flipping his towel at the bare backs of my skinny, hairless legs. Everything grew so still around me. Sounds only of Charlie Wilkes's words, so quietly spoken and almost friendly-sounding somehow, and the sound of the snap of the towel as he cracked it expertly through the air like a whip. I had my shirt on by then, I think. Then I bent slightly, hopped to one foot to pull on a leg of the stupidkid corduroy trousers that my mother insisted I wear. The shove was a light one, a mere pressure of fingers. But off-balance, the tile floor slick as wet shells, still barefoot, I rolled over as quickly as I could, trying to complete pulling on my pants. I really wanted to get those pants on. Everybody was laughing by then. I could feel the wetness soaking up into my underwear from the floor. From ear to ear I made with the old goodsport shit-eating grin. And then everybody began to take up the little chant: No nuts . . . no nuts . . . no nuts. . . .

Whereupon some insane boy I didn't know flew through the air screaming and swinging and kicking and clawing at Charlie Wilkes. I wondered who that crazy boy was who somehow had landed on top of Charlie Wilkes down on the wet floor with his teeth sunk into Charlie Wilkes's neck so deeply he could taste blood. And then I felt myself being lifted up into the steamy air and tossed like a rag doll to slide across the slick floor until I came to rest in a heap of bewildered insane boy against the far benches. Then Coach towered above me glaring, smacking a paddle against his enormous, hairy thigh, a special-made paddle, two feet long with quarter-inch holes drilled in parallel lines down its surface that never failed to produce interesting patterns on bare flesh.

Coach was a short man, fat and bald, with a flattened nose and small unblinking snake eyes that "never miss a trick so it was no use trying to pull no wool over them." Played second string on some country high school football team. Cut in his sophomore year from some small state college football roster, but hung on as an assistant manager gofer. Unmarried at maybe forty. Bought a brand new red Ford convertible every other year, which he washed and waxed daily and always decorated with a huge pair of purple parafoam dice dangling from the rear-view mirror. Always wore white socks with colored stripes at their tops, even with his sharp, shiny, brown sharkskin suit. This coach's philosophy was simple: A fellow had to have two things to be both a man and a gentleman. One, intestinal fortitude. Two, bodily cleanliness. In regards to the latter, Coach had signs up all over the gym dressing room warning you to take your assigned shower after gym class and soap your ass real good or face the consequences.

—What's going on here anyhow? Coach inquired. —What the hell's bells is going on around here anyhow?

—He didn't take no shower, Charlie Wilkes said as he got up slowly from the floor, dabbing gingerly with his fingertips at the row of bloody toothmarks in his neck.

—Yeah, he never does, some other school chum offered.

—Yeah, he never does, he never does, he never does, other school chums began to chant.

—What's this here all about? Coach asked me.

I grabbed my pants from the floor and began trying again to pull them on. One of the legs had knotted. Coach stood directly over me.

—You hear me, mister? Coach asked me. —You got something wrong with your ears, mister?

—No.

—No? No *what*, mister? I am *sir* to you, mister, and don't forget that fact ever, mister.

—No, sir.

—No what, sir?

—My ears are all right. Sir.

—Well, mister, you answer me real quick from here on out when I ask you a direct question. Now what about this here shower business? You been duckin' the showers or something? You been trying to pull the wool over my eyes, mister?

—No. No, sir.

—No what, mister?

—I'm not pulling wool, or anything, sir.

—You been taking your showers like you should or what?

—Sort of, sir. Sometimes, sir.

—No he hadn't . . . no he hadn't . . . , all my boyhood chums corrected me.

—Woe to your ass, mister, Coach admonished me, —if you are prefabricating the facts. Now have you been taking your assigned showers or not, mister?

—No. No, sir, I mean.

—Do you have a legitimate reason for this breakage of the rules, mister?

—He ain't got no nuts, Charlie Wilkes offered. All the other boys standing in the circle around me nodded in agreement with this observation, which seemed to explain everything.

—Say what? Coach inquired. —Huh?

—Nuts, Charlie Wilkes said again. —He ain't got any.

—Do you possess a disability of some nature, mister? Coach was curious to know.

—Sort of. Sir.

—What does that mean, mister? Look, either you possess a disability or you don't, so which is it?

—It's a condition, sir. I mean, I'm not a cripple or gimp or anything like that.

—Sounds to me like an excuse of some kind to get out of taking your assigned showers, mister. Wool won't pull over my eyes.

—I have undescended testicles, sir. I mean, I have testicles, it's just that they're not all the way down in their assigned places.

—That's better, son. Don't you think that it's better to get something like that out in the open? Get something like that off your chest. A man can't go around keeping something like that inside. One thing you gotta learn in this man's world is that it's tough titty time, day in and day out. You gotta have the intestinal fortitude to stand up to the hard knocks. And you never see the sonofabitches coming. Life is no bed of roses. Life is a bed of Gawddam assholes you gotta hoe and kiss ever' day. You can't count on nobody but your own self. You'll learn that the hard way, ever' single one of you guys. Life is one hard row to hoe, and all any of you guys got is what kind of hardass you can turn out to be. Now, this just don't go for this fellow here. No-Nuts here is just doing the best he can for a guy with no nuts. This goes for all you fellows. Son, Coach said to me,—why don't you just hop up and go on in and take your assigned shower, okay?

—I don't want to, I told Coach. —Sir.

—What did you just say, mister? Coach inquired.

—I don't want to, sir. Please.

—Well, then, I guess you better get up off your tailbone, mister. Right now, mister. I don't want to have to ask you twice. Then you peel those shorts off. Right now, mister.

—Sir, what I really meant to say is I feel real barfy right now, sir, I tried to explain in more detail to my philosopher Coach.

—Go on and strip it down, son. Do it now, son.

When I had stripped down, meaning I peeled my soaking wet under-shorts off and for some dumb reason went through the pathetic motions of trying to fold them before I laid them on the bench, Coach told me to turn around and face all my boyhood school chums. What this meant was that all my boyhood school chums would have the opportunity to study the two long red scars that ran down my hairless abdomen to meet in a V at the base of what was surely the tiniest dick in the history of the world, and the more observant of my classmates perhaps might also note that for all outer appearances I really didn't have any noticeable nuts to speak of.

Coach requested that I walk out to the middle of the steamy dressing room. Coach told me that since I had been avoiding the assigned showers, I had to be taught a lesson, but it was a lesson for all the guys. I had broken the posted golden rules, Coach pointed out, tapping the end of his paddle lightly against his fingertips, and the reward for my breaking the posted golden rules was to be made a good example of for every other fellow in the room.

—Why don't you bend on over, son, Coach told me, tapping me gently on the shoulder with his paddle. —Touch your toes, son.

I bent over and touched my toes. I had five big ones coming, Coach informed me. As was the custom, everybody counted out loud with each stroke. One. Two. Three. Four. When I flinched upright with the last stroke, Coach informed me I had two more coming as a consequence.

I stood there for a few moments just shaking and shivering before I could get myself to bend back over. Coach did not seem to be that much in a hurry, though. I realized I was standing there covering my crotch with my hands and that my knees were knocked together like I was some sad girl trying to hide her pussy. Then I bent over again. I could actually see my tears plink plink in the puddles on the red-and-black (the school's colors) tile floor. My nose was a snot Niagara Falls, and for some reason it suddenly struck me as so funny that the tops of my toes looked as though they were covered with booger afterbirth. So like some sort of insane boy, I snickered. But then, although I blubbered like somebody being burned at the stake, I did not flinch upright again.

—Shit happens, son. Shit floats, were Coach's parting words of wisdom to me as he strolled from the dressing room and I went back to dressing as best I could, blubbering and shaking like, well, a leaf.

• • •

Charlie Wilkes was hanging in the hallway when I came out of the dressing room. He was standing by that wall water fountain I would always rush right out to at the end of gym class to drench my face and splash water over my head in order to look as though I had actually taken my assigned shower, another ruse in my life that clearly never worked. A bunch of other guys were leaning against the hallway walls, and as I passed each of them they stopped horsing around and they looked away from me and didn't say anything, and I accepted this as a sort of kindness.

As I skulked by the water fountain, I felt a tap on my shoulder. It was Charlie Wilkes. He looked down at me for a moment through his lidded, badass eyes. I could see the red bite-marks of my teeth on his neck.

—I know where that asshole parks his fucken car, Charlie Wilkes said and gave me a big brown gap-toothed grin.

Charlie Wilkes became my best friend from that point on, and we became famously dangerous together until he dropped out of high school some years later in order to attend prison for armed robbery. We were a famous outlaw gang unto ourselves, that badass school bus rural and a nutty nutless town boy. In truth, Charlie merely let me tag along with him as a sort of town boy sidekick as he toughguy-strutted the halls. I hardly ever saw Charlie outside of school. But when we did get together, after a ballgame, say, the singular purpose of our two-boy gang was to vandalize that coach's car. We did it a dozen times one year like going to church religiously. We regularly ripped off his radio antenna and windshield wipers and put sugar in his gas tank. We smashed his windshield twice and all the side windows, like satisfying a necessary bad habit. We pissed mightily through their shiny shards onto the fake leopard-skin seat covers until, under the cover of darkness one night, that philosophical Coach simply disappeared from our town, forsaking both his wretched red Ford convertible and his coaching career, as he floated out of our lives forever.

SCIENTIFIC BOY

B ut there was another side to that desperate outlaw testiclely-challenged boy. Back at about this same time in junior high school when I first began to evolve into a famously dangerous outlaw boy, and before I became too cool and evil, I was friends for a time with a nerdy, scientific boy named Johnny Meinser. He was a tall, strong, clear-eyed, blond boy who was intelligent and decent and interested in issues besides pussy and hot cars and getting drunk, issues such as the expanding universe and the nature of magic and all the mysterious arenas of the beyond. So I was lucky Johnny was my friend for a time, before he caught me cheating at cards in games that were designed to test our ESP in which nothing more important was at stake than statistics and shared wonder and trust. But for no good reason I can recall, I conned Johnny into believing I had the special powers that enabled me to listen to voices from the hereafter and to hold hands with invisible people from the next world and to always win at cards because of my special relationship with the future.

Johnny had a four-inch reflecting telescope he and his dad, this big-time successful electrical engineer, had constructed together as a touching father–son project, even preparing the mirror, taking turns polishing its curved surface for months, until it could reflect galaxies glowing from deep space.

There was a flat area at the top of the hill that rose behind my house on Crestmont Road, and Johnny and I would take our sleeping bags and his precious telescope up to this little plateau and camp out. We would dial in the seas of the moon with his telescope, the red moons of Mars, the rings of Saturn. We would spend hours dialing in starry circles of the night sky, as though they were celestial television channels.

Once during that brief, sweet, cherished period when I was a scientific boy, I put together an elaborate chemistry set whose gleaming flasks and delicate glass tubing looked like some strange, miniature, shining city of the future. I also had an old radio I had taken apart. I would often sit fondling the vacuum tubes and thinking strangely of alien eggs from outer space. What I dreamed most about as a scientific boy was becoming a bold intrepid spaceman, who would explore other worlds and claim them for America.

One night walking home through Huntington's Ritter Park from Jenny Black's house, while I rather absently sniffed the bittersweet, sticky middle finger of my right hand, I gazed up through the nearly bare autumn trees at a moon so full and magnificent and mysterious that I promised myself on the spot I would be the first human being to walk upon the virgin cheese of its pure white surface.

This is also during that time in my life when I learned how to cultivate strange dreams. In order to do this I constructed silver cones, magic transformers, which I had read about in *Fate* magazine, cones shaped from cardboard and coverered carefully with tinfoil, which according to the article I read was a surefire way to tune in to the fields and flows of ghost energies that haunt the universe as we know it. I then hung these silver cones from my bedroom ceiling on strings that had once supported model fighter planes I had constructed with my old man but which I had ripped down one night in a blind rage, and I focused the points of the transforming silver cones evenly upon my pillow, that sweet palm of sleep, and thus I had begun to dream the strange dreams that have essentially governed my life from that time forward.

Forbidden Planet was Johnny Meinser's and my favorite movie of all time. The *forbidden planet* of the movie was a speck in a galaxy at the very edge of the known universe upon which an amazingly advanced civilization had once flourished, and the zenith of their development had been the discovery of how they could project the pure energy of their minds into matter. Beneath the surface of their planet, they had constructed vast factories of engines and transformers, all geared toward converting the energy of their dreams and desires into the realm of the *Real*. The amazingly advanced civilization had vanished mysteriously, of course, as advanced civilizations are wont to do, eons before the bold intrepid space explorers from Earth arrived to discover that the only inhabitants of that forbidden planet now were a mad scientist, the only survivor from an earlier Earthling expedition, and his beautiful daughter, who promptly fell in love with one of the bold, young, handsome spaceman hunks. Their flirtation pissed off the mad scientist of a daddy to no end, and the next thing you knew the energy of that daddy's *"id"* was running amok (which was the first time I had ever even heard about this *id* business, as in the undifferentiated source of the human organism's energy from which both *ego* and *libido* are derived). So the beautiful daughter's mad scientist of a daddy's dark, dream-demon of an id had escaped from the maze of his mind to kick some bold spaceman butt, and what a magnificently frightening piece of business it was, that id, an invisible angel-cum-creature from the dark side of the soul caught up in the electrical forcefield the spacemen had surrounded their ship with for security, its half-beast, half-man Minotaur outline and huge, bat-like wings electrified and crackling like skin crisp with lightning and I had reflected, *holy shit!* Einstein always claimed that the *field* was the final reality (as opposed to matter), but one cannot expect to become pure electricity without being fried, too heavy a price for some.

Johnny Meinser and I had begun to suspect that the flat area at the top of the hill behind my house was actually a transport field for alien spacecraft, and if we could just make contact with the visitors from the cosmos and win their trust, the little plateau on top of that hill could turn out to be holy for us and our personal portal into another world. Johnny and I would lie there in our sleeping bags under that unfathomable abundance of stars and attempt to contact our alien brothers through mental telepathy. We projected thoughts into the night sky that basically begged our alien brothers to land and please pick us up please, please give us a lift in their flying saucer, please, oh please transport us to another world where even nerdy, scientific boys would be appreciated and get some nooky. We, Johnny and I, believed in Einstein and Edgar Cayce equally, and for us in significant ways aliens and angels were one and the same.

Then one chilly fall night we got lucky. After about an hour of big-time, intense, teeth-grinding mental telepathy, we finally saw bright lights flash through the cloudy night sky. We jolted up in our sleeping bags gasping and gaped at one another bug-eyed, passing by pure mental telepathy the shared sentiment—*holy shit*! And then I felt it for the first time, that sense of the woods shivering, that sense of something huge nearby breathing slowly, heavily, some invisible winged force or energy almost unimaginable in its terrible, dark beauty, something that became electrified in Johnny Meinser's and my imaginations as it moved toward us through the night. We tore-ass down the hill, for at that moment Johnny and I had concurred purely by mental telepathy that perhaps that night was not the opportune time to make contact with beings from another world.

In our hasty departure, we left behind our sleeping bags, all our camping gear, and even that precious telescope Johnny and his big-deal successful engineer daddy had so lovingly constructed together as father and son. Sometime before Johnny returned to retrieve it the next morning, some dark evil outlaw alien from another world had evidently taken up a big rock from that hilltop field and bashed the precious thing to smithereens. I never hung out with Johnny again, now that he no longer had that precious telescope he and his big-deal successful engineer daddy had built together.

SHADOW BOY

Back in 1994 I came to realize that my life was in a tailspin. I also realized that, serendipitously, I was due for a sabbatical leave from my university teaching position, which I could use as an excuse to blow town, so I took it. I didn't have any particular plan or project in mind, but I took a notion that there was a mysterious trajectory of personal identification as a true West Virginian-American I figured I had to come to terms with if I was to understand anything about that palpable alienation, that extraterrestrial feeling of often-chosen displacement that I had let direct my curious lengthening existence in regards to risk and closure and, on a couple of lucky occasions, new starts. I also took a notion to drive down into the hills of my West Virginia home state and look around for my lost sense of self.

My vehicle of choice back then was a bright red 1994 Honda Passport sport utility four-wheeler I purchased especially for my imagined new life of exploring the dark, haunted hills of my mysterious home state. I rather affectedly took to calling my vehicle the *Red Ride,* as though it was some redneck good-old-boy's pickup truck that had genuine business back on those twisty mountain roads, instead of what it basically was, a Yuppie-mobile driven by an old coot college professor wearing a baseball cap, a bespeckled meta-mountaineer on a sabbatical leave with no clear, purpose or project, except perhaps to presumptuously steal the stories of other people's *real* lives and then somehow twist their points to his own designs, locate the significant signs and symbols and sundry archetypes governing those stories, make metaphors out of them to suit his purposes. Plus, as I mentioned previously, I thought I might revisit the personal stories that more or less made up my own myth of self and get them straight. And, who knows, I might even discover the symmetry of yet another unfound secret self. And, who knows, I might just find a brand new story to inhabit myself. At least I was a professorial good-old-boy with a proto-plan.

When I moved to southern West Virginia that August in order to immerse myself in lives not my own and steal stories, I didn't rent some dented doublewide trailer down by a creek in a hollow near a friendly blue-neon-trimmed beerjoint after all. I moved to my sister's hometown, Billville, and rented a house from my brother-in-law's wild, wonderful sister Lovelene, after she had moved down to the bright lights of Charlotte, North Carolina, to live with her new boyfriend, Ron, in his own fancy doublewide. Now, Lovelene was a character. She was the kind of good-old-girl who could smoke a cigarette dangling in her lips to its nubbin dropping nary an ash, and who truckers had been known to ask to please watch her language. Lovelene was admired mightily for her ability to remove her bra from under her blouse with one hand while steering with the other at a high rate of speed to the nearest motel. Save for a slight beer-gut, Lovelene was a handsome woman with sharp brown eyes in a pretty round face, and the way she sang sad country songs could bring tears to a glass eye. Lovelene and I got on well enough. I had long ago figured out that being pissed at Lovelene was about as smart as being pissed at the weather.

Lovelene had moved back into her childhood home six years earlier, when Grandma Pearl, her mom, died. Lovelene had told Fuzzy, her husband of twenty-plus years, that she wanted a "fucken divorce" not ten minutes after we put Grandma Pearl in the ground on that sad steamy day up in Clarksburg. But the little gray-shingled house with the white shutters always still felt like Grandma Pearl's place to me, due mostly to Grandma Pearl's homey haunting of the old place. Down home, the old mountain ladies used to dab essence of vanilla extract behind their ears for perfume. And that's what Grandma's presence smelled like throughout the house, a sweet ghostified vapor of vanilla mist.

• • •

As I drifted around aimlessly in the West Virginia hills for days sometimes in my dubious quest for story, I passed through many little towns
I could imagine becoming my final hometown when I retired someday,
where I could hole up and grow ancient, reinventing myself as an engag-
ingly eccentric old coot character who could assuage his essential loneliness by becoming locally famous and beloved.

I loved the names of my possible final hometowns in the hills of West
Virginia. There are West Virginia towns with names like Big Isaac,
Crum, Cucumber, Droop, Left Hand, Letter Gap, Looneyville, Pickle
Street, Sam Black Church, Tariff, Uneeda, Wolf Pen. The town of Cinco
in the Kanawha Valley was named for the founder's favorite brand of
cigar. In the West Virginia hills you can find an Athens, a Berlin, a Cairo,
a Calcutta, a Geneva, a Glasgow, a Killarney, a Lima, a London, a
Moscow, a Palermo, a Palestine, a Rangoon, a Santiago, a Shanghai, a
Vienna. Like the gold-mining boomtowns out in the old west, coal-
towns often sprang up overnight for the singular purpose of mining
nearby coal-seams, and were named on the spot. Towns would appear
suddenly, be named by whim, or for a laugh, have people live in them,
love in them, be born, and die in them, and then those towns would
simply disappear like the shadows of clouds passing over the face of
the Earth.

Many coal-towns were named after their owner-operators. Eccles for
instance, or Page, or Thurmond over in the New River Gorge, or Welch,
or Elkins or Jenkinjones, named after a coal-baron named, well, Jenkin
Jones. Then there is the town of Itmann down on Route 16, named after
I.T. Mann, once president of the Bank of Bramwell and a big coal syn-
dicate member who ultimately owned over three hundred thousand
acres of Pocahontas County coal lands he acquired by hook or crook.
Some coal communities were named after owner-operators' mothers or
wives or whores, towns whose names were like tattoos on a truck driver's
arm, names such as Alice or Alma or Beatrice, Belle, Beverly, Chloe,
Dorothy, Ethel, Grace, Melissa, Myrtle, Rita, Sharon, Shirley, or Glen

Jean, where my sister taught school, named for T.G. McKell's wife Jean. McKell could do that; it was his wife and his town.

When I was driving around in the hills waxing philosophical, I would reflect upon what I would name a town if I owned one. Who would I name my town after? I decided that I would name my town *Cookie*. I loved Cookie. Cookie was my first pup. Or maybe I would name it something outrageous. I could do that if I wanted to if I owned a town. Fart Junction. Shitburg. Fuckville.

Seeking a sort of honkytonk healing of the soul, I would sit in dark lowdown mountain beerjoints late at night after I had checked into some cheap motel, and brood about life and love and my somewhat dented identity, and about whether or not it would be philosophically sound to order another order of blazing buffalo wings so close to bedtime. I would brood about such weighty matters as just how much of who you think you are is based upon the town from whence you hail. Based even upon simply the name of that town, even if the name was a joke, or the name of another man's paramour, how much does it finally mean about who you imagine you are? You arch your eyebrows, wrinkle your forehead, let your lower face collapse into seductive wily grins, which is your ancient James Dean cool moviemask, and proclaim to the fading beerjoint beauty with the brittle smile you are trying to impress in the dim bar that you hail from over at Looneyville, or Cucumber, or Urination Nob.

But because many of those places have disappeared off the face of the Earth, like Brigadoons *poof* into mountain mist, mirages of memory and imagination, shadow home towns full of shadow family members you never made final peace with and shadow lost love that eats at you yet, they are vanished shadow home towns where you could safely set any past life you could imagine, invent a shadow history for yourself, and employ that sad, brave, shadow tale to make the neon nurse at the bar come to love you for it, and maybe heal your broken heart.

One shadow I kept encountering as I drove around down in those haunted hills was the ghost of my own lost, handsome, heroic, youthful self.

On one road trip I found myself traveling east out of Welch on Route 52 along the dark polluted waters of Elkhorn Creek, passing through the depressed little towns of Kimball and Vivian before I came upon the notorious town of Keystone, which was even more of a grim, desperate, curled-up-cur ruin of a place. In its heyday, Keystone had been infamous as the "Sodom and Gomorrah" of the McDowell County coalfields. Most of the boarded-up storefronts I passed were now as vacant and faded as old photographs, their doorways cluttered with debris deep as family secrets. Now and then I'd spot some shabby old coot shuffling blankly along the crumbling sidewalk as hazy in the late afternoon light as a vague memory. I saw an old woman in a second-story window still and black as carved coal, like an artifact of royal bones, her elbows resting on a windowsill, her chin cradled on her clasped, storied hands. From the sunken eye-sockets of an elegant skull she stared fixedly at my slow vehicle like the expected arrival of a hearse as I passed down a street virtually deserted save for long threadbare afternoon shadows of folks no longer among us. In a rare unboarded storefront I observed a large winding-cloth of a banner draped inside the front window that offered up the advice: GIVE JESUS A CHANCE.

At the upper end of Keystone, I came upon the dirt-and-cinder road that led down to "Cinder Bottom," an area near the old coke ovens that once boasted as many as twenty-five thriving whorehouses. It had been the coal operators' contention that the entire economy of the county, and the value and permanency of their huge investments, were wholly dependent upon the brawn of the thousands of black and European immigrants lured into the area to work the mines, and that these workers, who were paid the highest wages of any coalfield in the country, would not remain long in that isolated, raw region without the gaiety, entertainment, and accommodations that were provided by wine, women, and gaming. Hence, the operators had demanded a wide-open county, and the purchased local authorities were willing. The whorehouse district had been celebrated for its "international" flavor. Indeed, it was a strange point of civic pride that in the dangerous dives around Keystone all barriers were down, and the district provided utterly democratic racial, social, and sexual congress.

I had passed that way before. I had been driven up that old cinder road in the dead of night once over thirty years earlier, in the company of a carload of drunken, whooping, hoody high school buddies, as they sought to initiate the new boy in town, who was that ghost of my own handsome, heroic, youthful self, with a local rutting ritual of romance.

I was expelled from Huntington High School after six suspensions my junior year for infractions such as smoking in the restrooms, engaging in fisticuffs in the hallways, and secreting a little pick-me-up half-pint of sloe gin in my locker. Worse, as the singular rebel-without-a-cause-on-the-road-beatnik-holy-outlaw-poet representative in the entire high school, I refused steadfastly in morning homeroom to ever uncoolly lead the Lord's Prayer or hypocritically salute the American flag of so-called liberty-for-all: high school hanging offenses. My old man used this expulsion as the excuse to transport his little nuclear family a hundred miles south to Bluefield (and for once not under the cover of darkness to avoid creditors or the sheriff due to any current business collapse and bad checks of his own), where he had finally found work again as a claims adjustor for State Farm Insurance, and where, for his hoodlum son's sake, our little family would launch still yet another new life.

As James Dean playing a character named Jim Stark discovered painfully in the movie *Rebel Without a Cause,* it is difficult to be a new boy in a new town. A new boy is a shadow boy. One must prove one's shadow self all over again. One must prove that one is cool. One must prove that one is not chicken. One must prove that one is tough and dangerous and wild and willing to live one's life like holy lightning. When one must prove one's shadow self, it is easy to be egged into roaring a stolen car through an incandescent tunnel of headlights crazily toward a cliff's deadly edge in a chickie-run for no better reasons than reputation and romance. When one must prove one's shadow self, it is easy to be egged into accompanying a carload of drunken high school boys over the twenty-six miles of twisty, late-night mountain roads from Bluefield to legendary Keystone's Cinder Bottom in that ancient search for forbidden love.

Much of my memory about what happened that night is dubious, I was so drunk, but the shards of those events that lifted me up into local legend shine in my imagination like the glitter in a summer sidewalk. Evidently, it was the Beaver High School boys' custom to basically roar up and down the dirt road of Cinder Bottom yahooing insanely and honking the horn and mooning the whores, who were surely peering out of the darkened windows of that row of ramshackle houses, both shocked and fascinated and quaking evenly with desire and alarm at the sight of high school boys' bare butts hanging out of car windows. This, evidently, was the ceremonial courtship the local boys considered to be the serious seeking of Cinder Bottom whore nooky. Until that night, however, when they egged on the new boy in town too far.

According to that old story, I had insisted that the driver, Butch Farley (who was the captain that year of a Bluefield Beaver High School football team, which went on to win the triple A state championship), pull the fuck over in front of the last whorehouse on the narrow road. It was said I flung myself from the car and lurched toward the dark front of the whorehouse alone. Alone until joined by my toady sidekick, Toby, a pimply, prematurely balding boy, who in some important psychological ways put me in mind of Plato (played by Sal Mineo), James Dean's own confused, sweet, sacrificial sidekick in *Rebel Without a Cause*. Toby had mistaken (not unlike Plato) a flicker of mildly kind attention on my part as genuine concern and an offer of real friendship from somebody generally perceived as possibly cool, and thereafter Toby had worshiped the ground such as that I evidently staggered toward the dark whorehouse upon.

I can recall pounding on the door of the dark whorehouse and pronouncing my keen interest in pussy until it was finally opened for me. I can recall a dimly lit smoky kitchen and an ancient, legless, toothless African-American called Spider who had terrible yellow eyes. I recall Spider was perched in a wheelchair at a kitchen table. I can recall a couple of other African-American gentlemen in the room. One enormous, impassive African-American fellow was standing with his arms folded in front of an old refrigerator which rattled and groaned like an

hole county that night, one that would leave all the other countless car-
ads of beer-drinking boys, who were also roaming around the moun-
in roads looking for a reputation and romance, in my legendary dust.

It was raining as we roared over the last mountain toward the lights
f Bluefield far below. I can recall the skip in my heart each time the car
un out on the oily corners of that twisting corkscrew of a road. But
utch Farley was driving, I had reminded myself. Butch Farley was the
aptain of the football team. If I flew off the road in the rain to die down
mountainside with the famous Butch Farley, I would be recalled like a
cal footnote, but recalled nevertheless, I consoled myself as I sensed
he next soft early spin of the tires just before the car would begin its
weet breathless slide sideways around the next deadman curve.

At some point I became aware of the peripheral sound of my toady
sidekick Toby's soft voice. And then it had dawned on me that the drone
of his soft voice had been buzzing vaguely in my ear ever since we had
peeled out for our lives back in Keystone, when my toady pal had begun
talking quietly but incessantly about what had apparently transpired
back there inside that fabled whorehouse. Toby was crunched back into
a corner of the back seat as usual (while I, on the other hand, was riding
in the center of the front seat between the two coolest guys in Bluefield,
Butch Farley and Zan Campbell, who was an all-state end for the Battling Beavers of Bluefield High and a blond, blue-eyed, movie-star-
handsome pussy hound). So my story-telling sidekick Toby was relating
the legendary events that had recently transpired within the kitchen of
that whorehouse in a sort of religiousy, recitation voice. One after
another of the Beaver High boys fell silent under the spell of Toby's
hushed, hypnotic voice. Butch Farley slowed the car down to maybe
eighty. You could hear the somehow sad sucking sound of the tires on
the wet road now instead of squealing rubber and the steady clicking of
the windshield wipers, and my heart slowed. The inside of the car was
warm with the heat of our bodies and beery breaths and the windows
were steaming over and my eyes grew heavy. His voice was so sure and
steady but soft, my pal Toby's, you had to lean toward him to catch his
exact words. And Toby was in no hurry. And at the most exciting,

appliance from a nightmare, and another was sitting
gnawing evilly upon a pickled pig's foot as though it w
What I recall most clearly was the thin beautiful mulatto
twelve in a fragment of red slip leaning collapsed in a d
smoldering flower. I can recall our eyes meeting in a
meaning, this lovely, lost girl's and mine, and I can reca
clearly love at first sight, or some other desperate hun
equally forgivable. I can recall from someplace in that caged
dim interior ticked like a time-bomb a radio lowly playing a
Muddy Waters tune about the sublime necessity of shooting
woman. I can recall buying a fifth of Thunderbird wine fr
bootlegger pimp in the wheelchair for a buck (. . . What's the
twice . . . !), and then whispering to him that I had arrived
baby. I can recall a sudden, general uproarishness of runnin
rying and shouts and some tremendous satisfaction of sho
doors banging and laughter booming and hoots and a car-h
above insanely squealing tires depositing rubber in the roc
dog of the old road.

Less clear in my memory, however, is the manner in which
dently French-kissed the beautiful mulatto girl, and she had
old, legless pimp to let her fuck me for free. Less clear to me
evidently slapped the pistol from the old, legless pimp's hand
turned him in his wheelchair onto the kitchen floor, where he
about like an amazingly wrinkled, bug-eyed, toothless turd,
evidently for good measure I punched out the large African-A
gentleman in front of the refrigerator when he pulled his slick ra
clear to me is how evidently the beautiful mulatto girl called o
as my pal Toby and I were effecting our escape that she would
me always.

All of these significant details were provided by my pal Toby
carload of Beaver High School boys roared back over narrow, m
roads toward Bluefield and the Beacon Drive-in, which stayed ope
2:00 A.M. on Saturdays, and would be a parked audience for the s
the biggest, wildest, most mythic adventure that had unfolded

unfathomable, mythic moments in his story of what I had evidently accomplished back in the dangerous whorehouse kitchen, you almost had to read my pal's nearly motionless lips in the dim dashboard light to catch his drift. After a time I closed my eyes, basking in a sort of faint incandescence I felt settling about me like the shimmering shadow of an aura, as I listened to my pal Toby sing of me softly in what was surely some ancient and holy tongue.

I can recall the rebel-poet that was my idea of my teenage punk self slouching surly and superior across the auditorium stage at my honor-less high school graduation after my hopeless senior year at Bluefield High. I can recall myself later that same night falling down drunk again and again as I tried to bop at graduation parties, and then stealing money from girls' purses after coming to on a bed of coats. Later I had bounced shirtless about the high school's parking lot barking battle challenges to all comers and winning two good tough fights before losing quickly to a freshman football star in the dazzling headlights of circled cars.

Mostly I can recall Peggy Tucker. I can recall that Peggy Tucker had hair as black as a crow's wing and skin white and smooth as fresh milk and wondrous breasts. Peggy Tucker was the homecoming queen and senior class vice-president and Miss Bluefield and eventually second runner-up to Miss West Virginia in 1960, and she was the girl who I would come to love and who loved me utterly too until I did her dirt. For the final senior class assembly Peggy Tucker had dressed up like a gypsy fortuneteller and sat at a table on the auditorium's stage gazing into what appeared to be a crystal ball, and amid laughter and hoots she intoned in her best idea of a gypsy accent the trajectory of the future for each senior.

And here comes Butch Farley twenty years from now, Peggy Tucker read from her Senior Prophecy script as she pretended to gaze earnestly into the crystal ball, and Butch has a big shiny whistle in his big smiley mouth because he is now Coach Butch Farley and he is happy because his 1980 Battling Beavers have just won another state championship, making that twenty in a row, Peggy Tucker intoned and the auditorium went wild with hoots and hollers and Rebel yells and a spontaneous eruption of the school fight song, which, if I recall correctly, had something to do about being Battling Beavers until the end of time. And here comes Zan Campbell pulling up in a snazzy red convertible, Peggy Tucker intoned like a gypsy Greta Garbo and I felt the first blink of a boner at the sound of her voice as she revealed the future to us. Zan has just wrapped up his tenth movie and his fifth divorce, Peggy Tucker intoned and everybody in that auditorium was absolutely cracked up by the future.

And who is this I see wearing a black suit and a high white clerical collar twenty years from now? Why, it is none other than Chuck Kinder, who is now the Bishop of Keystone, Peggy Tucker intoned and everybody hip to my mythic "Cinder Bottom" adventure turned to stare at that legendary outlaw shadow boy who would become the *Bishop of Keystone* in what I perceived to be awe. And I sat there back in the auditorium as my own best invention for the first time, cool and nonchalant, natural and accidental, shimmering with confidence, and entertaining an amazing boner from simply the way my famous name had sounded as it had issued forth from Peggy Tucker's sweet red lips, and the slow way her black eyes had lifted toward where I was sitting out in the dark prepared for anything the future had in store for me that perfect moment she had uttered my name.

I grinned and arched my eyebrows and gazed coolly out at the world at large through my fateful, lidded, dreamboat James Dean eyes. At that moment I knew exactly what the immediate future held in store for me in terms of true love. If you dared to live legendary and dangerous, it dawned on me at that perfect moment, anything was possible, including the true love of an impossibly beautiful girl with wondrous breasts, a homecoming queen with eyes of dark rainy lamplit Paris avenues whose red lips had caressed your name. Possible for a time anyway, for there was finally a heavy price to pay for being willing to risk it all, including your life, but in the heady air of that sweet ancient anarchy of youth we call the search for fame and love, what did it matter? I intuited another thing at that moment in which I felt as though I was at the end of everything and on the verge of it all. My inkling was that that stupendously hopeful moment I was immersed within was possibly the high point of my life.

OUTLAW BOY

In October of 1959 I was a freshman at West Virginia Institute of Technology and living with my paternal grandmother, Mimi, in Montgomery, when Captain Charlie called me one Thursday evening with the news that Morris Hackett, the man who I claimed I had merely worked for the previous summer when I had run away from home and disappeared for three months, had been arrested up in New Jersey for armed robbery, and that I was implicated in some of his earlier jobs. The New Jersey State Police had contacted the West Virginia State Police to pick me up, but one of the state cops was an old army buddy of Captain Charlie's, and he had called Charlie instead of arresting me straightaway.

Charlie made me swear I wouldn't run. He said he was leaving Bluefield right then for the two-hour drive to Montgomery to pick me up, and then we were going to head directly for New Jersey. Charlie had not yelled nor screamed nor raged at me during that phone call. Instead, his voice was unlike I had ever heard it. It was calm, quiet, matter-of-fact, and just sort of weary-sounding, as though he was resigned to his oldest son being a criminal at large.

Mimi, that tough old bird of a mountain woman, wept and clung to me and told me over and over how much she loved me and wailed that she would pray I didn't have to go to jail. But if I did she swore she would break me out. I loved Mimi.

Charlie picked me up and we drove all night and most of the next day, taking turns at the wheel. When Charlie asked me directly, I told him yeah, yeah I had been involved in some robberies. But that Morris

Hackett guy I had gotten tied up with had threatened to shoot me if I didn't go along on those jobs, I explained to Charlie in my best quivery sorry voice. And then after that first job, Morris Hackett had said there was no way out for me if I didn't go along with him except for prison, or to get shot down like a dog by the law. And Morris Hackett had gotten me drunk as a skunk every time we pulled a job, I swore, blubbering. And while I wasn't sure, I thought maybe he had sneaked some dope into my beer, because I had really felt creepy, as though I was in a daze, as though I was compelled to do exactly what Morris Hackett told me to do in terms of a criminal nature.

Charlie didn't say much during my tearful true confession. For hours and hours we drove along in dead silence. Out of the corner of my eye I watched the beams of headlights flow over Charlie's tight, John-Wayney face. I kept waiting for Charlie to finally simply pull over and pound me to a pulp. But Charlie didn't; he simply drove along in dead silence. Maybe Charlie figured he better not mess with me now that I was a hardened criminal, I reflected and arched my eyebrows in approaching highbeams.

The sun was just coming up when we pulled into the parking lot of a truckers' diner somewhere on Route 80 just west of Philadelphia. Charlie turned the engine off, and then we just sat there for a time, as though stunned by the mere absence of motion.

—We better grab a bite, Charlie finally mumbled. Just as he was opening his door, Charlie turned back and looked at me with an expression of utter bewilderment, as though he had no idea who his passenger was, as though I was some hitchhiker he had picked up someplace he couldn't recall. Whereupon, Charlie said: —Listen, soldierboy, we'll handle this. Everything will be okay, son. You'll see, soldierboy. Charlie said this and gave me a little punch on the shoulder, as though we were teammates, or old army buddies, or pals, instead of merely father and son.

The New Jersey State Police Barracks was on the Black Horse Pike outside of Atlantic City. Charlie and I rolled in there for me to surrender myself late on the second afternoon of our trip. That's where we met Detective Dick Umholst. Detective Dick looked like a prick with ears. He was an ex-Marine drill sergeant, with a blond crewcut and bulging neck and mean, ice-blue eyes. He directed us back into his shabby office and after passing a few rather insensitive comments concerning my criminal activities, commenced to take my confession, which he recorded by hand on a lined yellow legal tablet.

Detective Dick was a big disappointment to me. He was totally unlike that tough-but-understanding cop who I had always fantasized would be the one to take my true confession when the time came. When I was pulling those jobs with Morris Hackett, I had always carried copies of my poems, my dozen favorites anyway, of the seven or eight hundred I had written. In one of my favorite capture fantasies the tough-but-understanding cop, who would be very much like the Frank Framek cop character in *Rebel Without a Cause,* would read those poems. —Empty your pockets, son, the tough-but-understanding cop would tell me. A perplexed look would flicker over the rugged but kind features of his face when I placed the folded pages of my poems on his desk. —Sit down, son, the tough-but-understanding cop would say, nodding his head toward a chair beside the desk. Then he would unfold and slowly read each poem as though it might be the plan for a bank job. He would re-read each one of the poems twice, the perplexed look on his face deepening, a look of puzzled sadness really, of true adult confusion and guilt. At long last, he would look up at me. —You wrote these poems, son? —Yes, sir, I wrote them, I would confess to him. —Son, I don't know much about poetry, son, but these poems are beautiful, son. Son, how could such a sensitive, intelligent, talented boy like you get your butt into this mess, son? How could you pull those jobs, son? Son, you're clearly a poet, probably even a genius, not an outlaw. —I don't know, I would tell the tough-but-understanding cop. —I guess I'm just confused. I feel misunderstood, I guess, I would tell him and then suddenly I would begin to beat my fists bloody against his desk, mooing with pain, mooing and moaning that I was not born to survive, that I was never meant to grow old in America.

Detective Dick wrote my true confession down, and, with my voice quivering, I told him pretty much the same stuff I had tearfully trotted by Charlie, about threats and fear and drunken (perhaps even drugged) stupors and finally the pure hopelessness I had felt in the face of failed expectations and a lost future. To emphasize the fear that that career-criminal Morris Hackett had engendered in me, I related how Morris had once fired his .45 into the bathroom floor at Kluck's Cabins on the edge of Atlantic City where we had holed up for a while in order to impress upon me how prepared he was to use a pistola if necessary (actually Morris had fired those shots the last night I was with him, when he had gotten drunk and commenced to profess his undying love for me). Detective Dick was insensitive enough to roll his eyes a lot and snort with amusement as he wrote down my tearful true confession.

When we got to the part about Morris putting the moves on me at the end of the summer, when I had finally made good my escape, Detective Dick pressed me for dirty details. His oily ex-Marine eyeballs widened as he probed about whether Morris had wanted to have oral sex with me or anal or exactly what. And then he truly tried to corner me about whether any sick sexual activity had actually occurred or not. —No, I said earnestly to him, no, I had made good my escape from Morris's perverted clutches with my boyhood heterosexual cherry intact.

Detective Dick had me read my true confession back to myself before I signed it, and I was appalled. I couldn't believe his crappy grammar and spelling. I did not sound like a sensitive, misunderstood, on-the-wrong-track but talented and brilliant, young genius outlaw–poet in my true confession at all. I sounded like an illiterate, thuggy, ex-Marine State Police Detective Dickhead. I blame that traumatic session with that insensitive, doubting state police detective totally for the fact that even to this day I loathe law-dogs.

The bottom line was that for about seven weeks the during summer I was seventeen, I had been as bold as my old man had ever been when he won the Second World War pretty much single-handedly. I was involved in seven armed robberies in and about Atlantic City (four cabs and three bars). Morris Hackett, a forty-year-old ex-jailbird driving a stolen rental car, had picked me up just days after my high school graduation hitchhiking south to Miami in order to pursue a famous career as either a diver for sunken treasure or a gunrunner to Cuba or a pirate (*Miami*, god, how that famous name had burned in my teenage brain, visions of wild tropical nights in smugglers' beachfront-bar hangouts, glasses of dark rum poured by black-haired Cuban beauties with mystery in their laughs, how all that had burned, burned in my teenage brain).

How could I have explained why I returned north with Morris? How Morris had told me that when we got to New York he would introduce me to his famous old pal Jack Kerouac! who was my own personal all-time famous hero, who Morris had been *on the road* with himself; that, if the truth be told, many of the adventures recounted in my favorite novel of all time were really based on times Morris had been with Jack Kerouac and not that Neal Cassady character at all. How could I explain what it felt like to lie in the back seat smoking and sipping beer while Morris drove relentlessly north toward all of possibility and promise and surely fame? I watched the reflection of forests wash over the rear window like that green river of the future I was riding. At night, I watched approaching car lights streak across the curved glass like a swirling constellation named Chuck. On the radio, Nashville hillbilly stations played Hank Williams or Negro stations out of Memphis played Muddy Waters and advertised White Rose Petroleum Jelly, while Morris told endless stories about the risky back roads of his life and lost beautiful barmaid loves and lowdown honky-tonks he had held up in his own wild, outlaw, wilder-than-Neal Cassady youth. I would lie in the back seat listening to Morris's stories, and I would think about the fact that there I was: *Chuck Kinder*, snaking north along forsaken ridges on secret backcountry moonshine-runner roads through the eastern wilderness of America with a madman poet, a holy con-man character who could truly be right out of the famous Kerouac's stories themselves, mad to live, mad to talk, mad to be saved, desirous of everything at once, who wanted to burn, burn, burn like fabulous yellow roman candles exploding like spiders across the stars.

One thing led to another that summer of '59, and one night in early August found Morris leveling his .45 automatic at the face of an Irish bartender who had been a wiseguy. After I had cleaned out the cash register and collected the wallets of the three patrons at the bar in McGettahan's on the White Horse Pike just outside of Atlantic City, Morris had told me to go out and get the car started, and I hurried down the dark, tree-lined side street to the stolen Plymouth getaway-mobile. I started the engine and huddled down on the front floor of the passenger-side, just as Morris had instructed me so that we would not fit any two-robbers-making-their-getaway description. By the dim light of the dashboard I did a quick count of the take. Around three hundred lousy bucks, I figured and was real pissed. Morris had promised we would cop at least an easy thousand tonight on this our very last job, which he had promised I could take back with me to West Virginia to buy a car and big diamond ring for my girlfriend Ruthie and begin college and perhaps make a down payment on a little house.

When I heard the blast I jumped up, banging my head on the dash. Then I ducked back down on the floor. I must have been wrong. I had not heard a shot. I never once dreamed I would ever actually hear a shot. I had not heard a shot, I told myself again and again. Then Morris opened the driver's side door and slid in behind the wheel. He tossed a bottle of whiskey on the seat. He pulled the Plymouth out slowly. I grabbed the bottle from the seat and chugged from it until I almost choked. I shut my teary eyes and hunkered as far down on the floor as I could get. I listened to the rhythmic clicking of the windshield wipers and the sound of the tires on the wet pavement. Pungent, rainy-night air flowed in Morris's open window, filling the car's rushing interior with a smell as fresh and sweet and mysterious as my girlfriend Ruthie's skin. I was afraid to ask Morris about what had happened. I was afraid Morris would tell me that he had plugged that wiseass Irish bartender, and that besides being a robber and thief, I was now also an accomplice to murder, and would be on the run for the rest of my natural life. I crunched down on that front-seat floor and felt sick and excited at the same time as I reflected real hard on my life for perhaps the first time, and what I thought was this: that no matter what happened now, I was severed forever from my old ordinary world, and that in many important ways this was the beginning of a whole new story for me, which I envisioned as a lot of long and pretty lonesome traveling, a lot of hiding-out and laying low as I lived the rest of my life as an outlaw on the lam. It was at that moment I woke up to a sense of the self as story.

How could I have told them, either Charlie or Detective Dickhead, about that night after our last holdup when Morris had paced slowly back and forth at the foot of the motel-room bed, and had told me that I was a dead ringer for his dead son Nicky? I could have been this dead Nicky's twin brother, Morris told me for the first time that night.

I had sat with my back pressed painfully against the wall above the narrow bed. The only light in the room came from the small television set bolted on the dresser, whose sound was turned off. Now and then Morris would take a long hit from the bottle of whiskey he dangled at his side. Now and then Morris would pick up his .45 from the dresser and look it over in the cold snowy light of the soundless television.

As he walked up and back before the bed that night, Morris looked for all the world like his own personal hero, Humphrey Bogart. Morris had told me he and Bogie were distantly related. Cousins of some sort on his mother's side. And it was all there. The rugged, world-weary face, the tight, ironic grin, the heavy-lidded eyes that had seen it all. The story Morris told me that night was about how he had found out too late that the perverted bastard his bitch of an ex-wife had married had a habit of getting shit-faced and pounding the hell out of her, which she probably richly deserved, but then the pervert-bum would turn on Nick, and he would pound around on Nick and then screw Nick up the ass when he was in the mood. Morris had only found out too late that the cocksucker had put them both in the hospital more than once. —Nick had been exactly your age, Sonny, Morris told me and shook his head sadly. So one night Nick just blew the bum away. Then Nick had blown his whore mother away and then he blew himself away.

Morris stopped walking up and back at that point, and he took a long pull from the bottle. He set the bottle on the dresser. Morris picked up the small, gold-framed photograph of this Nick kid, who Morris claimed was his dead son, from the dresser and tilted it about in the television's light. Morris had pulled this photograph from his suitcase to show me for the first time that night. And it was true. I was a dead ringer for that dead kid. If any of this stuff were true. Morris stood there, weaving slightly, and he looked at the picture of his dead son for a long time. Finally, he placed it back carefully on the dresser. Morris looked at me then, and he asked me if I could even begin to imagine how he had felt when he had seen me hitchhiking by the road that first night. He had thought his eyes were playing tricks on him. He had thought he had gone crazy at last. There I had been, big as life. Like I was a ghost or something. Nick's ghost. It was like Nick had been reborn. It was like they had both been given a second chance, Morris and his dead son Nick. The reason why I couldn't leave him, Morris told me, wasn't because of that bartender he had blown away that night. Well, that was a part of it, sure. We had to stick together now, sure, Morris said. We were in this thing too deep together now to split up. But that was not the main reason I couldn't leave him. —Do you understand, Morris asked me, the main reason you can't leave me, Sonny?

—No, Dad, I said. I don't think so.

So that things wouldn't look *queer*, Morris had taken to signing us into motels as father and son. It had become a big joke, Morris calling me his sonny-boy and me calling him Pops or Dad. That's the way it started anyway, an innocent joke.

Morris picked up the bottle and took another long drink. He put the bottle back on the dresser, then picked up the .45. He held it in both his hands and looked it over. Morris began walking up and back again while holding the .45 loosely at his side.

—After I had picked you up, something else started to come over me, Morris told me. —Something that is going to be difficult for you to understand. You see, son, you started meaning a lot to me. And it wasn't just because you reminded me so much of Nick. To tell you the truth, it wasn't because of Nick at all. The truth of the matter is, you started meaning more to me than Nick ever did or ever could. That's hard for me to say. Hell, it's hard for me to believe. But that's the ballgame. You started meaning more to me than anybody ever has before. Anybody in my life ever, period. And I didn't know how to tell you. I was afraid of what you would think and do. You don't know the nights I've sat up watching you sleep, son. You don't know the nights I've put this rod against your head while you were sleeping, or against my own.

Morris raised the .45 and looked at it in the awful light of the television. Suddenly he stepped into the bathroom and fired the .45 twice into the floor. I jerked like I had been hit and slammed back against the wall. The air smelled burnt. Then Morris stepped back into the room and looked directly at me.

—Jesus Christ, Dad, I whimpered.

Morris smashed the barrel of the .45 through the television screen. It sounded louder than even the shots. I gagged back a rush of puke. In the sudden darkness, afterimages of the television screen floated before my eyes like tiny moons. Morris moved quickly to the window and with the .45's barrel parted the shades. In the faint slant of light, I could see that his trigger finger had blood on it. Morris stood there with his back pressed against the door and peered through the parted shades.

—They won't take us alive, son, Morris told me with a grin, and I think he winked. Then I squeezed my eyes shut and tried to pray.

THE REAL BEGINNING OF
MY FAMOUS LIFE

Captain Charlie checked us into a cheap motel out on the White Horse Pike after we left the State Police Barracks that night. Charlie was quiet and grim. I prepared myself for pain. The first thing Charlie did in the room was click on the television. To hide the screams of pain and pleas for mercy, I figured. But Charlie simply sat there on the end of the bed. He didn't even take his overcoat off. He simply sat there looking at the television, elbows on his knees, those huge hands flopped like dead fish between his legs. Popeye the Sailor cartoons were on the television. I sat down in a chair in the corner. I didn't take my coat off either, in case I had to make a run for it.

I was ashamed of myself and embarrassed for Charlie. Charlie had sucked up to that dickhead detective like he had no pride in the fact that he had won the Second World War pretty much single-handedly. Charlie had told Detective Dick how it was his own fault I had gone bad, for he had been a failure as a father. He hadn't given me the time and guidance I had needed, Charlie said, and his voice had started to break and I couldn't stand it. I had never heard my old man do something like that. I had never seen him start to crumble like that. I started to blubber out loud myself that it was nobody's fault but my own, that I had let everybody who loved me down, but that I was going to do better from here on out. I blubbered that I prayed every night for forgiveness and for another chance. I blubbered that I was going to turn my life over to Jesus. When I looked at him through my tears, I saw that Detective Dick was grinning.

At one point, Detective Dick led us out to his patrol car in order to drive us around to the various scenes of my crimes. He wanted to see if any of the bartenders or cabbies could identify me (and none of them could identify me as the outlaw boy, dressed up as I was like a clean-cut choir boy). As Detective Dick drove to McGettahan's Bar on the White Horse Pike, he informed us that when Morris Hackett had been arrested, he had tried to cover for me. Morris had told them that the boy who had pulled the holdups with him was not me at all, but a kid named Nick, whose current whereabouts Morris had no idea about. Morris told the cops that this boy named Nick was somebody he had first picked up in Atlantic City a couple of years earlier and paid to let Morris suck his cock, and that they had become partners in crime. Morris had told the police that I had had nothing to do with the holdups, that he had always left me back at the motel whenever he and Nick met to rob a place or have degenerate sex. Morris had informed the police I was innocent of everything, that I was not the kind of boy who would ever rob a place, or let a man suck his cock. I noticed that Detective Dick was watching my face in the rear-view mirror as he related this information.

I sat there in the cheap motel in my coat watching teevee that night not knowing what to expect. Maybe Charlie just wanted to talk. Maybe Charlie didn't plan to kick my butt after all. Television had become the final way we could ever talk. We would sit watching teevee, maybe cracking some jokes, making wisecracks about the shows, about the actors in them, about who they were banging in their teevee roles and in real life, about what their roles and their real lives added up to, which in our books was nothing much. What we were really trying to do was say things to one another in a kind of code. And that was it, the father and son business, being about the only time finally when we weren't yelling at each other or deadly silent. Charlie and I were like ghosts from different dimensions, different channels, and teevee was this strange medium we had to filter ourselves through to give each other the time of day.

After a time, the Popeye cartoons playing on teevee began to quiver and roll. But Charlie simply sat there with Popeye and Olive Oyl rolling and rolling right in front of him. It started to drive me nuts. I had had enough of that rolling teevee. I got up to adjust the thing. When I passed by him, Charlie grabbed me. He caught me by the collar of my coat. He pulled my face so close to his own I could smell his breath. It smelled like stale cigarette smoke and wintergreen mints. And I could smell sweat and Old Spice. Whereupon Charlie simply shook his head and shoved me half way across the room.

I flinched when I heard Morris finally put the .45 down on the bedside table that night after our last job. I still lay there with my eyes shut tight trying to pray. I felt his fingers touch my arm and squeeze gently. Morris's fingertips felt warm and faintly moist. I opened my eyes then, and blinked in the darkness. I could still see the afterimages of tiny teevee screens floating before my eyes. Morris was a dark form sitting there. I could smell the whiskey on his breath.

—Listen, old sport, Morris said quietly. —You know I wouldn't do anything to hurt you, don't you?

—I guess so, Dad, I said.

—Do you trust me?

—I guess so, I said.

—Listen to me then, son, listen closely. Try to understand this. I like to screw women, see. But I was in prison a long time. Nothing is ever just black or white. I care for you, Chuck. More than I ever did Nick. I care for you more than I ever have cared about anybody else. I care for you more than I could ever just love a son. I won't hurt you. I promise I won't hurt you, son.

—Can I think about this, Dad? I was curious to know.

—I can't wait any longer, son. I just can't put it off any more.

—Can't you wait until tomorrow, Dad? Just until tomorrow?

—No, Chuck, I can't wait any more. Try to understand, son, Morris said quietly and he began undoing my belt buckle.

—Please, Dad. Please.

—I'm not going to hurt you, son, Morris said and he unzipped my jeans.

—Don't take my pants off, please, Morris, I requested and I clutched my belt with both hands. —Please, please, Dad.

—Just relax, son, Morris said. He tugged gently. —I won't hurt you. You know that. Think of your girl if you want to.

I shut my eyes and tried to picture Ruthie but couldn't even remember what her pretty face looked like. Oh my God, I thought, how did I ever get in this mess? First I was an armed robber. Then I was a killer. A murderer. And now I was going to be a queer. A goddamn fag! The only thing I could picture was that old sock I used to jack off into. That old athletic sock with blue and green stripes around its top that I had kept under my bed at home. It was always stiff as a corpse, from constant use, and, as a sort of foreplay, I always had to whack the thing against the wall to soften it up. I was jacking off into that very sock one time when Charlie had roared into my room unannounced as usual to raise hell about some crime I had committed against nature and caught me red-handed, so to speak. Charlie had taken one look at my sex life and done a snappy about-face and force-marched from the room like he was leading a parade.

I could feel Morris's tongue licking in my bellybutton, which I hoped was full of crud. I could hear the faint sounds of traffic out on the Black Horse Pike. There was a sudden burst of laughter from some other cabin. I thought I could hear country music playing on some distant radio. I opened my eyes. I could barely make Morris out in the dark. But I could see him well enough. So then Dad went and did it. Dad sucked on my dick. I watched Dad suck my dick. And my dick got hard while Dad was doing it. Which meant that I probably really was a fag. If the truth be told, I didn't much mind being an armed robber, I even sort of liked it, but being a queer was the worst thing I could think of. I hated being a fag more than being a murderer.

After I had come in Dad's mouth, which proved once and for all I was a queer, he got up and hurried into the bathroom. I could hear Dad spit into the toilet. I heard him turn the water on in the sink, and then I heard him gargling. Morris must have gargled for ten minutes, spitting and gargling and spitting, and when he came back in the room and sat down on the edge of the bed he smelled more like Listerine than whiskey. Morris clicked on the small lamp on the bedside table. He lit a cigarette and sat there smoking and looking at me. He had wrapped a washcloth around the finger he had cut when he smashed the teevee screen. I lay there on the bed staring up at the glittery ceiling trying to recall what my girlfriend Ruthie's pretty face looked like, but I still couldn't. Everybody always told Ruthie she looked like Sandra Dee, blond and lovely, and she did. I tried to picture the blond and lovely Sandra Dee, but I couldn't remember her either. It occurred to me I might never be able to recall a girl's face again, now that I was a fag.

—I told you I wouldn't hurt you didn't I? Morris said after a time. —I didn't, did I, son?

—No, sir.

—I wouldn't hurt you, sport. I'm sorry it happened like it did, though. I got too drunk. I don't want you to feel bad about it. Do you feel bad about it, son?

—I guess not.

—I hope not. I don't want you to feel bad about it. It would bust me up if you felt bad about it, and wanted to go away or something. If I lost you like I did Nick, it would be tough, Chuck. I almost shot myself when that happened. I did, son.

Morris took me by the chin and made me look at him.

—You have a look on your face, Chuck, Morris said. —Are you feeling bad, son? Tell me the truth. Come on, now. Talk to me.

—A little, I guess.

—Listen, if it will make you feel better, I'll tell you something. I didn't plug that wiseass bartender tonight.

—Jesus Christ, Morris! I said. —Why did you tell me that in the first place?

—To keep you with me. It's that simple, son.

—What did you shoot, then?

—The goddamn television set, Morris said and laughed. —Just for the hell of it. You should have seen people hit the floor when I fired off that round. You should have seen it.

—Yeah.

—Listen, I'm going to take a long hot shower and sober up. I don't suppose you'd like to hop in with me, would you, kiddo?

—I'm tired out, Morris.

—Sure, kiddo. Been one hell of a long day. Why don't you just crawl into bed, then? Listen, sport, let me tell you something else. This won't happen again if you don't want it to, see? I promise you this. I won't come near you again unless you want me to, okay? I mean it. Do you believe me, son?

—Sure, Morris, I believe you.

—Good enough, old sport, Morris had said and patted my thigh. He got up and took off his trousers and tossed them onto the foot of the bed. At the bathroom door, Morris turned to look at me. —You're one tough customer all right, sport. Don't you ever worry about that. And your old buddy Jack Kerouac was a tough customer too, and he knew everything wasn't black and white. I'll tell you more about old Jack and the old days on the road when I get out of the shower. Christ, son, I gotta sober up!

You better believe I'm a tough customer, fag, I had reflected and arched my eyebrows. As soon as I heard the shower water I buckled my belt and sat up on the bed. I picked up the .45 from the bedside table. I tiptoed over to the open bathroom door. Morris was humming in the shower. I cocked the .45 and raised it. Gripping it with both hands like Morris had taught me to do, I aimed it at the dead center of the shower curtain. *Blam!* I fired that .45, its trigger giving, the smooth underbelly of the butt jogging my palm, in my mind. I pictured Morris clutching the shower curtain like a spastic as he tumbled out onto the bathroom floor, where he kicked and snapped and foamed.

I uncocked the .45 and stuck it in my belt. I moved quick as a cat. I took Morris's wallet from his trousers on the bed and stuck it in my own hip pocket. After peeling off a single dollar bill and tossing it on the dresser, I stuffed the roll of bills from that night's job in my front pocket. I slid the dead kid's picture from its gold frame. I stared into the dead kid's eyes for a moment. When they tried to fasten themselves, those dead eyes, onto my own eyes, I tore that picture into a million fucking pieces, which I scattered like confetti all over the bed. I picked up the car keys and the half-empty whiskey bottle from the dresser, and I backed toward the door. Morris was still happily humming his homo head off in the shower. I took the .45 from my belt and looked the thing over. I didn't want that thing. I didn't need to be armed and dangerous. I didn't want to be armed and dangerous ever again in my life. I tossed the .45 onto the bed. I picked up my unopened suitcase at the foot of the bed, and I quietly opened the door. Besides, I reflected, Morris might need his fucking .45.

As I backed out of the parking space in front of the motel, I hit the horn. I honked it wildly when I peeled out, burning rubber, fishtailing, as I made a perfect clean getaway into what I perceived to be the real beginning of my famous life.

THE HIGHEST TRADITIONS
OF THE AMERICAN SOLDIER

My favorite story about Captain Charlie's famous bold-boy antics in his younger days concerned the time he disrupted the town's Fourth of July celebration. It was supposed to have been the biggest, grandest Fourth of July celebration the town of Montgomery had ever witnessed. The mayor at that time, B. C. Hooper, a youngish, up-and-coming mortician and promising local politician way back in the '20s, had spent months planning the whole shebang, which included a big parade full of grand floats with patriotic themes, every high school band in the county, a crack Army Reserve drill team. The parade paraded all over town, didn't miss a street, went up and down Main Street maybe three or four times, and ended up finally on the old bridge late in the afternoon where later that evening they were scheduled to shoot off the grandest fireworks show of all time. But first the crack Army Reserve drill team was set to shoot off a patriotic twenty-one-gun salute from the center of the bridge, their spent shells bouncing brightly all over the bridge in the late afternoon sunlight, while kids scampered about swooping them up like exotic coins.

Another grand event was also planned at the bridge that day. Mayor B. C. Hooper had hired a certain Chief Soaring Eagle to perform a thrilling stunt to really give the townfolks something to remember the mayor by. Chief Soaring Eagle was a part-time wrestler and circus daredevil quite famous in that day. He claimed to be a bona fide Apache Indian war chief, although there were a few diehard rumors that the chief was actually a muscular, self-promoting, part-time Italian cop from Dayton, Ohio. At any rate, the great chief's explosive entrance into the dangerous current of the Kanawha River was to signal the first flares of the grand fireworks show. When with great solemnity Chief Soaring Eagle removed his beaded and brightly feathered ceremonial chieftain's cape to reveal his brown, mightily muscled body, there was no doubt in any local yokel's mind that he was truly an Apache war chief, maybe an Apache god. After removing his eagle-feathered ceremonial headdress, Chief Soaring Eagle balanced himself upon the narrow railing of the bridge, his head tilted back as though in worship, his long, black gleaming hair falling straight back almost to his waist, sunlight golden on his calm, brave face, as he prepared to ceremonially dive into the dangerous river far below. The county high school bands' drums rolled. The crack Army Reserve drill team was aiming at early evening stars poised to fire a final volley. Slowly, Chief Soaring Eagle raised his muscular arms above his head, rose up on his toes, hovered there in his magnificence.

Suddenly, bursting through the crowd, yelping and howling like a movie redskin devil savage, Charlie, my old man, my dad, captain of all the bad boys in town, jumped up on the railing beside Chief Soaring Eagle. Dad was bareback, and his body and face were streaked with bright red and yellow paint and he was wearing a handkerchief bandanna with several old bent chicken feathers stuck in it. Chief Soaring Eagle looked down at my painted, feathered, yelping dad with an expression of pure bug-eyed, open-mouthed, goofy astonishment. The crowd gasped. The drums stopped rolling. Mayor B. C. Hooper bellowed. My dad threw his head back, barking and hooting, and then he leaped feet-first into all of legend.

Chief Soaring Eagle climbed down from the railing virtually unnoticed as people surged forward to get a look at my dad hitting the water. The poor feathered Italian fellow from Dayton, Ohio, forlornly gathered up his Indian effulgence and moped off as a roar of approval went up when my dad surfaced and waved to show the throngs he had survived, and that for his next famous feat he would win the Second World War single-handedly.

The years of the Second World War when he was overseas, first in North Africa, and then in Sicily and Italy, were the happiest of Captain

Charlie's life and the high point. I have a photograph of my father having the Bronze Star pinned on his chest by Major General E. M. Almond for bravery in battle. In that picture my father looks like a young Gary Cooper playing Sergeant York as a reluctant, endearingly embarrassed American war hero.

Here is exactly what the citation says: "Charles A. Kinder, 01320466, Second Lieutenant, Infantry, 370 Infantry Regiment. For heroic achievement in action, on 26 December 1944, in Italy. Communications between a regimental GP and its 1st Battalion CP on the opposite side of a river were being repeatedly severed by intense enemy artillery barrages preceding a scheduled hostile attack on friendly positions. The enemy kept continuous artillery fire on the exposed road and bridge connecting the two CPs and the immediate area in which each CP was located. On four separate occasions during the day, Second Lieutenant KINDER left the regimental CP in a jeep, crossing and re-crossing the enemy-observed road and bridge, to transmit important messages between the battalion and the regiment, and to keep the Regimental Commander informed of the tactical situation on the other side of the river. Each of Second Lieutenant KINDER'S four trips was successfully accomplished in spite of the constant enemy artillery fire. His brave determination under extremely hazardous combat conditions exemplifies the highest traditions of the American Soldier."

Captain Charlie's own comments are included at the bottom of the press release of the citation: "I don't think it was as bad as they say. I was scared, but I did not think much of it until it was over, and then it must have sounded like a band coming down the road by the way my knees were knocking together."

After having smoked approximately four packs of Camels unfiltered for maybe fifty years, Charlie collapsed on the front lawn while mowing the grass one day. Dad had a respiratory arrest, and this led to a series of cardiac arrests, and he hovered at death's proverbial door for days, before beginning to pull out of it, to everybody's amazement.

What Mom noticed most when Dad returned home were the mental changes. Dad had become forgetful, and at times childish. And once that December on his way home from the post office after mailing Christmas packages, Dad got lost. His growing confusion frightened him, and he began to cry easily, and it made Mom sad and scared her. But Charlie had changed in other ways too. He was kinder than Mom had ever known him, and more thoughtful of her feelings, of everybody's feelings. All that new caring he showed made Dad like a stranger to Mom and made her come to love him in a way again. Dad would have Mom do most of the long-distance talking whenever my brother or I would call, listening in on the extension and mumbling occasionally, then blurting out the moment before we hung up *I love you.*

After a course at a local vocational school, Dad decided he wanted to be a master carpenter. This was a whole new side of him, loving wood and working with his hands. And his greatest joy was making gifts for the kids, decorative wooden geese and Early-American-style quilt racks and standing tilt mirrors that he made from kits, true, but you would think he hand-carved them he was so proud. Mom said she would not have wanted to miss those last eight years for anything. In some ways they helped make up for all the earlier years she considered wasted except for having the kids.

Mom and Dad had attended the fiftieth wedding anniversary celebration for their neighbors, the Lowreys, and as Dad and Mom were the next couple in the neighborhood with a fiftieth coming up, Dad began planning for it in a big way. He began making up guest lists and planning menus and music, all of this new to him, being goofy with nostalgia, sappy with sentimentality, all of it so out of character from the old Charlie, full of jokes again and even acting mushy on occasion. But what Mom knew was that all through their married life, Charlie had had big ideas and dreams and not a single one of them had ever come about. So as soon as he had started making the plans for their fiftieth anniversary party, big plans that included a fancy caterer and throngs of well-wishers and speeches and a band, Mom knew it was a bad sign, and she had tried not to pay much attention to Dad's bigger and bigger plans. Mom knew none of it would ever happen.

Dad died during one of my mother's family reunions two months before their fiftieth anniversary. All four of her living brothers and their families were coming in. Dad was in the basement game room he was so proud of having paneled himself, enjoying a glass of iced tea with a sprig of mint he had picked himself from his back yard herb garden, when he called to Mom, who was ironing cloth napkins in the utility room, that his left arm was feeling kind of funny, and he couldn't recall whether or not he had taken his heart pills that afternoon. Mom had gone upstairs to get his pills. A couple of kid cousins were playing a board game on the floor in front of the television. My mother's brother John, in from Arizona, was sitting on the couch with Dad, sipping a beer, while they watched a golf game. Some folks say that when he was young, Dad had been a good enough golfer to turn pro. Dad rubbed his left arm and he said to Uncle John, —You know, my doggone old arm does feel funny, kind of tingly like. And then Dad closed his eyes, rested his head back on the couch, and passed on to that great Second World War in the sky.

Back at my sister's house after Dad's funeral and interment at a little mountain cemetery outside of Ansted, the mourners set to grazing the mountains of covered dishes and cakes and pies and platters of fried chicken the Church-Ladies had groaned the tables down with, and then stood around sweltering while they gossiped and caught up, and I came upon one group of old coots out back passing a pint in a paper bag telling funny, outrageous Charlie stories. Unlike me, my dad had always been bold, and a leader of men long before he had become the Captain of the Second World War. Even as a boy, he would take any dare. Dad loved to fart in church like a baboon, or fake a fit and bounce down the aisle like a ball of foamy boy. He would water-balloon or snowball mean teachers who would surely recognize him, any preacher in town, the passing patrol car of that trigger-happy, nihilist deputy sheriff they called, well, Deputy Death. Long before his Second World War derring-do, heroics in honor of which the whole town turned out at the train station for his homecoming with a band and speeches and a parade, my dad had been famous for stuffing three fingers down his throat and, off the balcony of the only movie theater in town, puking like a dog.

When I snuck out to the side porch for a breath of fresh air and a serious belt of my personal pint of George Dickel, I found my sister and mother sitting in the swing bawling their eyes out. I tried to duck back into the house, but they had spotted me. At some point, my mother apparently had slipped the wedding ring off Dad's finger, and now she wanted me to have it, she said. Then my mother told me again that old story about how she and Dad had driven for hours in the rain that night they eloped to Kentucky where she was old enough to marry without her volatile daddy's approval (the age of majority in Kentucky being about eight), and how Dad had been so nervous he lied about her age anyway, making her on their marriage license two whole years older than even the twenty-two he nervously claimed to be himself (one of my abiding fears is that I was conceived that night in *Kentucky,* for God's sake, that crazy country across the Tug River famous mostly for its ritual pig-fucking). I reminded Mom that I would never have any kids to pass something that meaningful on to, so maybe she should give it to my brother, who wanted kids, or why not my sister, who already had two kids, but Mom had folded the ring into my hand anyway and insisted that as the oldest son I take it with me, and, being a basically good boy when it came to Mom, I did as I was told.

BELT OF ORION

That night in the cheap motel room in Atlantic City, after Charlie had shoved me halfway across the cruddy room, I skulked back over to the chair and sulked with dignity. Let Popeye the Fucken Sailor cartoons roll until the end of fucken time, was my basic tough-guy aloof attitude. Charlie and I didn't say another word that whole night. I didn't even brush my teeth, my way of showing Charlie who was the real boss. Charlie and I had to sleep in the same crummy bed together that night. The television was still rolling merrily along. Charlie didn't turn the thing off. Neither did I.

I lay there on the utter edge of my side. I stared at the ceiling glittering in the teevee's cold polar light, until my eyes burned. I stared at ancient constellations twinkling in the Milky Way of that sparkly ceiling, constellations whose myths of famous heroic figures I knew by heart from my cherished scientific-boy days before I turned bad. East of Taurus on the glittering ceiling was Orion the Hunter. As a scientific boy, I had read that the ancient Egyptians had aligned their three greatest pyramids and their inner sepulchral chambers with the three stars in the belt of Orion. This was to mirror heaven with their world and provide their pharaohs with an easy landing in the afterlife. My own myth was mirrored on that heavenly ceiling that night. My own destiny was to dwell in those stars. I gritted my teeth and longed to land safely in some afterlife. I tried not to blink my eyes. Not once. I let my eyes fill with water until tears ran down the sides of my cheeks like a faucet had broken in the middle of my face.

I was afraid that if I closed my eyes, I might fall asleep. If I fell asleep, I might roll over onto Dad's side of the bed, and our starry skins might touch in the dark.

book two

FAMOUS
LITTLE
SISTER

THE SWEET SAFETY OF
THE REST OF OUR LIVES

There's only about a three-year difference between my little sister and me, and when we were kids we offered one another absolutely no quarter in a basically kill-or-be-killed sibling rivalry. But I had this bad dream once, in which my little sister fell out of the car, which forced me to cherish her in a new and odd way.

In the dream, which had seemed so real, as they say, Charlie was driving the little nuclear family along somewhere late at night. My sister and I were routinely tormenting one other silently in the back seat with sneaky punches and pokes and pinches, when suddenly my sister opened her door. I could feel the night air flowing into the car and see my sister's long auburn hair blowing in it. She looked back at me once, with a strange sort of got-you little grin on her face. Then she simply leaned out the door and disappeared into the rushing dark.

For years after that dream, I wouldn't ride in the back seat with my sister unless I was permitted to bind us together with a length of clothesline I had cut just for that purpose. I would tie one end of this cord around her wrist and the other around my own. My little sister let me do this only because she took pleasure in jerking the cord violently whenever I dozed off. Once when I fell asleep, she looped the thing around my neck. I woke up choking and spluttering. She strangled me until my face turned blue and I slipped onto the back seat floor, muttering mommommommom. . . .

I figured out early that my little sister was smarter than me. After I taught her the basic moves, it took my sister three games before she began beating me easily at chess, an imbecilic game I renounced on the spot. And she was more intuitive than me. Whenever we played that dumb game *Clue,* I didn't stand a chance. She usually divined which of those characters named after basic colors were guilty, and what their weapon of choice had been, before I had rolled my dice twice.

My sister had read every single one of those royal-blue-bound Nancy Drew mystery books, knew them almost by heart. She had intuited each of their intricately plotted endings long before the girl-sleuth heroine herself solved the case. When it came to collecting and interpreting clues, when it came to the search for sinister criminals and concealed treasures in hidden compartments or passageways or in secret attics, my sister was purely prescient. For a long time, my little sister had wanted to be a detective when she grew up.

For a time in college, my sister entertained the notion of becoming a writer herself. I read a few of the handful of stories she wrote. They were so good they scared me. She was a true story-catcher. My sister could tell stories like the old country great-aunts could, like our grandmother Mimi could, making the utterly mundane mysterious, and funny, and so full of life in the retelling that, no matter what the outrageously far-fetched so-called facts were, those stories rendered their own fantastic truth. When I think of the mystery-arc of my sister's life, of the disappearance of that youthful, daredevil detective and would-be famous writer, I think in terms of the secrets that remain unsnooped, the cases unsolved, the stories she could have conjured purely out of whole cloth that would have put my own fictional efforts to shame.

My sister recalls our shared childhood in the framing context of that classic American novel by Harper Lee, *To Kill a Mockingbird.* In my sister's memory, I am much like the older brother in that book, Jem, and our cousin Bill is Dill, that delightful, delicate character based on Harper Lee's childhood friend, Truman Capote. In that reimagined past my sister is, of course, the dauntless daredevil Scout.

Montgomery, a little town on the Kanawha River thirty miles east of Charleston, the state capital, was essentially my home town. My paternal grandparents, Mimi and Papaw Kinder, lived there, Charlie had grown up as a boy there, and it's where I was born. Over the years, as Charlie had moved our little family from town to town in southern West Virginia as regular as clockwork, and routinely under the cover of darkness, Montgomery was where we most often ended up. That tiny town, begrimed by the pollution of the Alloy Plant downriver and by clouds of coal dust settling from the surrounding hills, became something like our family's wound-licking hideout home base, although we never actually lingered there long. My sister and I always spent holidays with Mimi and Papaw, and summers too, when, in our capacities as detectives, we would roam the downtown streets daily in our endless crusade to stamp out crime and bring crooks to justice.

On Saturday mornings in Montgomery, the streets were packed with miners and their families come in from the hollows. To my sister's trained girl-sleuth eye, these streets were loaded with cutthroats and thugs and thieves. You could tell by their piercing, dark, disrespectful eyes and wicked facial expressions and swarthy skins and crude, vulgar manners, not to mention their bad grammar. They were clearly gangster Gypsies, schemer Gypsies, notorious in the Nancy Drew books as exotic, evil mystery violinists and robbers, who were only disguised as poor miners pouring into town for a brief boozy respite from their downtrodden lives.

My sister and cousin Bill and I would tear down to the post office after breakfast, where I would sketch a reasonable likeness of one of the hardened criminals pictured on the "wanted" posters. We then set out in search of the culprit in places like the hardware store on Front Street, which had an old deep-well water smell like oil and nails, where surely outlaws would go to shop for rope and knives. Murphy's Five & Dime was another potential hotbed for hoods, and we would snoop the narrow aisles of board floors, the air thick with the smells of peppermint candy and popcorn and the vague mossy smell of mountain people. Hillbilly music seemed to press palpably against my skin as I drifted along, perusing counters of treasures that clearly criminals would long to shoplift. Sometimes we would case the benches in front of the train station for our fugitive, a place hard men congregated to sit, chewing tobacco and whittling and jawboning. We always identified our culprit.

One crook we spotted, with his "dark, mottled complexion and piercing black eyes," could have stepped from the pages of *The Clue in the Old Album,* according to my sister. We shadowed him relentlessly for an entire day as he wandered from beerjoint to beerjoint, clearly attempting to organize a gang of jewel thieves. The crook ended up at the Top Hat on Third Avenue, a depraved place, where we loitered about the front door and hopped up and down to investigate him through the high front windows for hours. Finally the ill-tempered villain suddenly charged through the door after us, yelling and waving a beer bottle by its neck like a little bat. Our cover compromised, we discontinued our surveillance and ran off wildly down the street.

Nights, we would pull the twin beds in Mimi's front bedroom together and construct a tent of the sheets to hide under. While making scary shadows on our faces with flashlights, we rehashed the legends of local mayhem and murder until we could hear Mimi and Papaw snoring like bears in their back bedroom, whereupon my sister and I would crawl out the window onto the front porch. Bill always bravely volunteered to stay behind to serve as our "watchout." My sister and I would then go skulking down the dark streets for clues amidst the eerie adult night.

Every small town has its version of Boo Radley, that essentially sweet, secretive, mysteriously wounded bird of a human being who the kids transform into a bogeyman in *To Kill A Mockingbird*. Back then Montgomery's resident bogeyman was Slim Bolt, a middle-aged, supposedly retarded, only scion of a once-prominent family who lived in a large, ramshackle, shuttered house. Slim Bolt was known to *walk by night*.

Clearly Slim Bolt was the source of all evil in our little home town. We followed Slim Bolt at every opportunity in order to gather evidence against him. It was our duty to see Slim Bolt behind bars. Late one night, my sleuth sister had gasped when we spotted Slim Bolt coming out of the Checkered Cab stand in the heart of town carrying a brown paper bag. To my sister's trained eye, that brown paper bag was clearly stuffed with the clues to a major mystery. We immediately put him under surveillance, this suspicious Slim Bolt character, a great, goofy, bald ostrich of a fellow who carried an enormous cane, who must have been about seven feet tall and thin as a, well, bolt, and often he would disappear in between the sharp edges of shadow and streetlight as we skulked along behind him down the dark street. Ducking and scurrying, we trailed him across the tracks into Colored Town and then up that dirt road toward the old cemetery at the edge of town. In the melodramatic moonlight, Slim Bolt vanished and reappeared like vapor as he rose toward the impenetrable darkness atop those stone steps that twisted up the hillside into the overgrown graveyard. My own inclination had been for us to crack the Case of the Cab-Stand Brown Paper Bag the next morning by the light of day, but my headstrong sleuth sister was sidling up that forbidding staircase before I could even whine and blubber effectively in protest.

My sister and I skulked about three-quarters of the way up the steep narrow stairs undetected, and huddled there with our arms around each other's shoulders, gasping and letting our eyes adjust to the darkness of the old overgrown graveyard, which hadn't seen a fresh burial in maybe thirty years. It was full of toppled tombstones and sunken graves that stretched on up the hillside under gnarled, twisted, tortured trees and bushes thick with briars like little razors and what appeared to be the shadowy eye sockets of the dead. Wind blew up into the screaming trees and, above us, rain clouds shaped like skulls skudded across the face of the full moon. An evil owl hooted. I shivered like a cowardly leaf. I couldn't help it. But my sister appeared to me to be incomprehensibly rock-hard and unafraid. She patted my shivery back.

When Slim Bolt reached the large Montgomery family monument just past the top of the steps, he stopped. We could see Slim Bolt fiddle with the clue in his mysterious brown paper bag. He then lifted the clue to his mouth. He tilted his head back and gulped the contents of that clue down. We heard Slim Bolt cough, and then he seemed to speak, but so softly that we couldn't be sure. Not unlike a corpse rising from the grave, a Shadowy Figure that suggested a short, skinny bogeyman came staggering from behind the monumental Montgomery family tombstone. The short skinny Shadowy Figure wobbled up to Slim Bolt, who appeared to hand the Shadowy Figure the clue in the brown paper bag. The Shadowy Figure put the clue in the brown paper bag to his own mouth and threw his head back. When the Shadowy Figure was finished, he wiped the back of his hand across his mouth. Whereupon the Shadowy Figure, who came up to about Slim Bolt's waist, put his arms around Slim Bolt's knees. Slim Bolt leaned way down and hugged the Shadowy Figure back. They then just stood there for a time, weaving back and forth like that, two bogeymen hugging in the dark.

Then Slim Bolt stepped back and drained the clue in the brown paper bag. He tossed the paper bag back over his shoulder. It exploded a few steps above us, which was no excuse for a brave detective boy to scream, but I did, loudly. Slim Bolt whirled around. The short Shadowy Figure scurried back around the Montgomery family tombstone. Slim Bolt peered down the dark steps. When he spotted us, Slim Bolt came charging over the hill, grunting and swinging his huge knobby cane in the air like an Indian war club.

As we tore down the steep stairs, my sister tripped and fell. She lost a shoe, which she searched about for frantically on the dark steps. But she did not once whimper or call for me to come save her, her big brother, who had already stumbled, tumbled, and rolled to the bottom of the stone staircase. I was set to tear off across the train tracks when I glanced back over my shoulder, and about barfed when I saw my sister's peril.

What ensued had nothing to do with bravery or boldness. I don't know what it had to do with. Maybe I just couldn't face the thought of Mimi's irritation when I tried to explain why my baby sister had been beaten to a bloody pulp on the steps of the old cemetery. But in a heartbeat, I transformed into that insane shadow bogeyboy who lives just beneath my skin. I raced back up those steps screaming like a banshee. My sister had found her shoe, and she had rolled down a few steps more, where I clamored around her and crouched there growling and spitting and snapping like a feral werewolf child. Which stopped old

Slim Bolt in his tracks. Do not doubt that that bogeyboy would have flown for that bogeyman's throat, had he but moved another inch toward my sister. But he didn't, lucky for him, lucky for me.

I felt my sister clutching the back of my shirt as she tugged me back down to the bottom of the steps, where we turned and ran like bats out of hell into the sweet safety of the rest of our lives.

THAT PLACE LUCK GOES WHEN IT IS FINISHED WITH US

Just a few days after I had moved down to Billville late that summer of '94, where I hoped to become a slave to solitude while with any luck at all I reinvented my life, I rather reluctantly accompanied my sister to a birthday party one Saturday for old Billy Ray Daniels, a short, stocky, bald, affable fellow who used to own Billy Ray's Restaurant and Roadhouse out off the four-lane on Laurel Creek Road. My brother-in-law was playing a gig at the bash with his current band, *The Mountain Palm String Ensemble*. The music the group played was a wondrous blend of country and traditional and acoustic bluegrass, and my brother-in-law did the vocals.

When my sister and I arrived in the early evening, my brother-in-law and his bluegrass group were already at the party, playing in a gazebo a bit over the hill from Billy Ray's back yard pool, around which the guests, mostly retired regional gangsters and their blue-haired molls, were milling. Billy Ray, that old outlaw, was throwing the birthday party for himself, about his one-hundred-and-fifth, I think, and he greeted me warmly as always, with a bear hug and several celebratory blasts in the air with his heavy, old, long-barreled .38. Billy Ray, that old devil, gave my sister a series of hugs and kisses about her pretty face. My sister really is a good-looking lady, who folks have always declared looks like a dead ringer for the lovely, albeit late, Natalie Wood. Billy Ray then commenced to usher me about for a series of torrid introductions. Presently my sister and I managed to disengage ourselves. We meandered on over to a picnic table near the gazebo where we sat and sipped icy longneck bottles of Budweiser and listened to my brother-in-law's little band cook. But even over that twangy, hypnotic music, which always quickened my willing hillbilly heart, I could hear the melancholy hum of the four-lane traffic from Route 19 right over the hill, which somehow made me feel restless and forlorn, regretful and exhilarated, not an unusual state of mind for me at that time.

About then, my sister and I heard this odd popping sound, or a sound like a small explosion actually, something like a gunshot or truck back-fire or a big tire exploding down on the four-lane over the hill. We walked down the hill to the fence from where we could see the highway to take a gander, but there was nothing unusual to see, simply traffic barreling relentlessly by.

The following day I read in the *Billville Tribune* that authorities had recovered the body of a fifteen-year-old boy who had apparently committed suicide by leaping from the New River Gorge Bridge the previous evening. Two fishermen had spotted the boy's body floating in the New River at Teays Landing about a mile downstream from the bridge. Sheriff Bill Laird was quoted as saying that the victim had been tentatively identified, but the sheriff was not releasing the boy's name until his momma had been notified. The boy had been listed as missing and endangered since about 5:00 P.M. Saturday, when he was reported to have flung himself heartbroken from a vehicle driven by his thirty-six-year-old ex-wife in Beckley, a town twenty miles away. Witnesses said they had observed a desperately distraught boy hitchhiking on the four-lane toward Billville. Other witnesses saw the weeping boy leap from the bridge about 6:25 P.M.

When my sister and I compared notes, we realized that the peculiar exploding sound we had heard while we were at Billy Ray's back yard bash occurred at about the same time as the boy had jumped. But, although the Gorge Bridge was just down the four-lane from Billy Ray's place, we decided that it was surely too far and the gorge much too deep for us to have heard that poor boy burst like a balloon when he hit the water, or, as my tenderhearted sister and I suddenly wondered with a sorrowful uncertainty, was it?

• • •

This New River Gorge Bridge is maybe the biggest tourist attraction for Billville, a little two-stoplight courthouse town in southern West Virginia, where the mysterious, American small-town life of my sister and her family unfolds. The Billville turnoff is only a couple of miles past the bridge going south on the Route 19 four-lane. The steel arch span of the Gorge Bridge, which measures 1700 feet, is the longest in the world. The bridge is also the highest of its type east of the Mississippi River, and, at 876 feet, it is the third-highest bridge in the country. It took sixteen 1250-ton-capacity hydraulic jacks to lower and lock together the two 850-foot arch sections on October 18, 1976, while astonished onlookers held their collective breaths at the sight of this engineering marvel of mating, a dangerous, steely embrace of high-beams that made the air crackle with a sort of sexual tension and vague arousal at the odd intimacy of this act.

At the opening of the arch span bridge, an ancient hillbilly custom of asking for the blessing of the river spirits was observed. A rock shaped not unlike a football-sized egg, and about as white and smooth and with an odd crack along its surface that suggested either an enormous omelet or imminent alien birth, which had been discovered beneath the lambent swiftness of the New River, was ceremonially embedded in concrete at the center of the bridge.

On the third Saturday of every October since then, the good townfolk have reenacted this blessing ceremony on what is called "Bridge Day," during which the northbound lane of the bridge is closed off to traffic, and pedestrians are permitted to walk the length of the span. This has evolved into an annual Fall Festival, which has become a sort of combination country fair, flea market, and immense revival meeting, and as many as 100,000 souls have arrived from all over the South to stroll that world-class span on a lovely West Virginia autumn day, the sky so clear and blue it burns your eyes, the high mountain air crisp and pure save for a pungent hint of wood smoke, the autumn colors of the Appalachian hills in their fullness, brilliant golds and reds and oranges and shimmering coppers, just a typical heartbreakingly beautiful fall day in southern West Virginia, impossibly poignant with the technicolor intensity of a postcard from

Almost Heaven, as we inhabitants of that small, odd, outer planet, that window to other worlds, are wont to say.

The visiting hordes also have had the unique opportunity to witness the hundred or more evangelical men and women who each year ritualistically leap, not utterly unlike virgins into a volcano, from the bridge during the course of the day. From about ten o'clock in the morning until around six P.M., one pilgrim after another climbs up on the low railing, and sacrificially sails into the abyss of the New River Gorge.

Unlike sacrificial virgins, however, these fearless aerialists employ parachutes, fast-opening parachutes in fact, specially designed for low-altitude descents. They are what are called "BASE" jumpers, BASE being an acronym for Building, Antenna, Span, and Earth, and they come from all around the world on this one day out of the year to legally daredevil dive off that bridge 876 feet into the chasm of the New River. Three of these BASE jumpers have perished leaping off the New River Gorge Bridge. Two of the unlucky leapers drowned after landing in the wild rapids of the New River, where the Charybdisian current tangled them in their parachutes and seized them there beneath the white, frothy torrent before they could be fetched by the rescue motorboats.

One death was due to equipment failure. This unlucky aerialist was with a group of six jumpers who did an unauthorized leap off the bridge in the dead of the night. The "bandit" jumper's main parachute apparently failed to open and he hesitated a heartbeat too long before activating his reserve chute. One would presume he died instantly upon hitting that rock-hard surface of raging water at an estimated one hundred miles per hour.

When asked to comment on the fifteen-year-old boy's suicide leap off the New River Gorge Bridge, Beckley, West Virginia, psychiatrist Dr. Ahmed Faheem was quoted in the local paper as saying that parents can never be too up-to-date on their teenagers' thinking and problems. Parents needed to be constantly wary. Though those around the young people might not realize it, hopeless, dopey, self-destructive teenagers often expressed their intentions before snuffing out their brief lives, according to Dr. Faheem, whose specialty was actually suicidal rubes.

Watch out for changes in behavior, Dr. Faheem suggested, and pay attention to comments such as: "Well, catch you later, alligator, after a while, crocodile, in case we never see each other again in this life." For such enigmatic comments reflected that those troubled young people had lost their faith in luck, that they believed all the luck they would have in their young lives had come and gone, that the luck that made their lives worth living had gone back to that place luck goes to when it is finished with us.

And just where is that place luck goes when it is finished with us? a reporter inquired of Dr. Faheem. Dr. Faheem said he didn't really know. He sure wished he knew. But he didn't. He had been told once, though, by an old mountain woman who had been his patient before her own suicide by induced pet copperhead bite at age one hundred and seven, that her own personal luck, that old polecat, had gone off to hide in a cave in Kentucky.

BLIND DOG

Trying to settle into my new, quiet, reflective life in Billville, I sofa-sailed for a solid week. I dozed day and night, dreaming fitfully, sunk deep in an intrigue of total exhaustion and solitude while hatching plots of personal deliverance, with wakeful interludes only for whiskey or melancholic masturbation, the silent television's sad polar light my threadbare accompaniment, every night of my life to kill. Before one Saturday night, after a long-distance phone-fornication with my girlfriend back in Pittsburgh, Holly, that had left me in orgasmic chaos, I finally admonished myself to forsake this whiny shit, and I set out in search of old timey havoc. Thereafter, I began closing Billy Ray's down like every night of my life was Saturday, and after one of those ceremonial Saturday night roadhouse sojourns, for no good reason I can recollect, instead of making the turn into town, I cruised on out to the Gorge Bridge at about two o'clock in the A.M.

There was no traffic that time of morning, not even a solitary semi hauling ass, so I stopped in the middle of the bridge and put my flashers on. I climbed out of my vehicle and walked around to the railing to take a peek into that fabled abyss. Unlike other great bridges, such as the Golden Gate in San Francisco (a town where for a dozen years I had once lived in an illusory dopey state I recall as something akin to expectant), there are no sleek arches or high, elegant beams soaring over the New River Gorge Bridge, and at night you might not even be aware you are crossing over a wondrous, blessed bridge, save for road signs you can't really read as you hurl insanely by them in the dark and then this sudden sense of vastness spreading out about and beneath you, this sudden, startling sense of suspension in essential emptiness.

I leaned on the low metal railing and gazed down at billowing banks of fog luminous in moonlight, fog that lifted from the New River hundreds of feet below to fill the immense gorge. Ironically, this so-called New River is actually the second oldest river on the face of the Earth. Only the Nile River over in Egypt is older. This so-called New River, once a part of the ancient Teays River system, flows anciently north out of the Carolina hills in the same bed it had followed sixty-five million years ago when it ran into a vanished inland ocean which once covered that flat endless geography we now call Ohio and all those other states in the vast yawn of the midwest. The vertically walled chasm that the New River has cut, over the countless ages, through hard rock descends dramatically as deep as a mile, nay, two miles, three or four even, bottomless maybe, it is speculated, in certain places so remote as to remain unmapped to this day. And on the soaring heights above the river, where huge, silvery hawks unique to West Virginia nest, tree-topped shelves of sheer rock cliffs run along the rim of the canyon like a volcanic vulva. The gorge averages a mile wide, or two even, it is said, in unreachable stretches far downriver. It is a far-out (as we aging hippies are wont to say) old river and groovy gorge, and I was real reverent when I reached deep within myself and then expectorated mightily down through the fog into the unfathomable depths of that abyss, an ebullient activity that always tends to put me in a philosophical frame of mind.

As I tarried there on that great bridge brooding and expectorating, I reflected about whether or not a leaper waxed real philosophical himself in those final moments before doing the big belly-buster, maybe cultivated a final aerial, allegorical view of life 876 feet up. I wondered if a leaper forsakes longing and regret in those moments of final flight. And responsibility. And becomes disdainful of gravity, sure, that too. What I reflected upon as I stood there gawking and more or less drooling into the great abyss was this: Where does feeling gravity finally get a fellow, anyway, but down?

Albert Einstein, back in 1907, while he was still yet nothing but a lowly clerk in a Swiss patent office, had had a beautiful, elegant, and deceptively simple insight about the nature of gravity that would ten years later blossom into his revolutionary Theory of General Relativity. The beautiful, elegant, deceptively simple insight was this: If a person could fall freely, they would not feel their own weight. Not feeling your own weight; now fancy that, I reflected, whereupon I leaned far out over that low metal railing and stared down into that ancient abyss and entertained the whirlies.

And then I heard the faint drone of a plane as it approached the bridge through the fog from downriver. A couple of moments later I saw the lazily blinking blue lights of Five Dollar Bill's tiny Piper Cub as it lifted from the fog, and then the plane disappeared beneath the bridge as old Five Dollar flew under it. I turned around and sat up on the railing and watched as Bill emerged on the other side and banked south following the four-lane toward Billville and his little blacktop landing strip at the far end of town. Old Bill did that sometimes late at night when he was restless and lonely, when he was feeling the tug of the past. He would go out and climb aboard one of his three little aircraft and go sailing up through the night sky toward places where he could no longer arrive, pondering irretrievable things.

His actual name was Bill Thomas, and he was this white-haired banty-rooster of a local character who was famous as Fayette County's *Mister Aviator*. Bill had been flying the skies above the New River Gorge for nearly fifty years, beginning in 1945 when he earned his first dollar from a sightseeing trip, and he had been offering rides for a mere five bucks ever since. For that mere five bucks, Bill took his passengers on a trip that lasted twenty minutes or more up over the Gorge, and then either six or seven miles up the river to Keeney's Falls or downriver to Hawks Nest—the passenger decided the direction. As old Bill flew you above the Gorge, he would recite poems he had composed over the years about the old, spooky pyramidal mountains of West Virginia far below. (Bill was also the author of two books that I can recommend highly: *It Is This Way with Men Who Fly*, and *State of Confusion—West Virginia, The Good and the Bad*.) So, basically, Five Dollar Bill lived to fly and write about it poetically, as he painstakingly sought that pure state of unembodied emotion, and even for all his essential loneliness, I couldn't imagine a much better life than Five Dollar Bill's.

Even though Bill had been flying the Gorge area for over half a century, one Thursday afternoon not three weeks after my arrival in Billville, when, during one of my dubious flying lessons, we were up soaring over the sweet curved surface of our home planet waxing philosophical about writing and love and life and the elegant nature of gravity, Bill spotted something he had never seen before. It was an odd tubular rock formation way downriver that was maybe fifteen feet tall and slender and of a sort of reddish hue, and it was just standing there like a stone totem pole, a singular sentinel gazing out over the river below deep in the gorge. And the more we looked at it, as we banked and buzzed about, the more we thought that it did, indeed, resemble a statue of some kind, with a stoney, bug-eyed, gapey-mouthed Aztec expression that suggested inscrutability, and with protrusions like big dumbo ears. Bill couldn't believe he had never spotted the odd thing before, and he poetically opined that the formation was some sort of prehistoric giant Injun that had been caught and frozen there somehow during the Ice Age and over time turned to stone.

Bill named the unique formation *Old Redskin Rock* on the spot, and exclaimed that he couldn't wait to share his newest discovery with tourists for not a nickel more than he had been charging them the past fifty years. But I opined that it looked to me more like a huge, amazing stone prick with ears, and I suggested we name it *Boner Boulder,* and then I went on to suggest, in that essentially false, shamefaced jocularity that older men often embarrassingly employ when they cannot help but brag about much younger, beautiful women with whom they have been intimate, that we keep it our little secret until my girlfriend Holly came down to visit, when we would show it to her first of all, that tower of love, for a little gal couldn't help but be all over a fellow after observing a thing like that.

When we swooped down to buzz under the Gorge Bridge on our way back, Five Dollar Bill had reminded me gravely of what I had related to him about my determination to launch a new life down in Billville. Bill had patiently parroted my whiny manifesto of remorse and resolve about turning over a new leaf or two, about laying off the booze and controlled substances, about writing my heart out morning, noon, and night, about keeping Trigger in the barn, about coming clean at last with my good wife of nearly twenty years concerning my life of elaborate, desperate, sorry lies. Hollering to be heard over the whine and rattle of the old engine, Five Dollar dutifully reminded me about how I had proclaimed that I planned to do the right thing finally by that wonderful young woman I had fallen head-over-heels in love with, by scaring her off, if it came to that. At least I had convinced Bill, for one, of my fervent redemptive desire for a path of renewal and righteousness. More than I had myself, anyway. Old Five Dollar, God love him, who gave such great cloud himself.

By the time Bill's plane had disappeared into the dark that first night I had stopped to brood on the New River Gorge Bridge, I could see some traffic halted at the bank of stoplights back at the highway turnoff into town: a couple of eighteen-wheelers, judging by their high-beams. I hawked again into the dark chasm of the gorge.

Some years back, my brother-in-law's depressed, drunken dentist had jumped off of this same bridge to his death hundreds of feet below. He had only been in his early fifties, but he had been an unhappily married and fretful man who had let himself fall foolishly in love with his young, beautiful, bleached-blond receptionist, and then he lost her, as he should have known he would. He drove out onto the New River Gorge Bridge early one foggy morning after the beerjoints closed and parked in the middle. He left his flashers on because of the fog. He had brought along his faithful dog, a seventeen-year-old blind collie named Buddy, whom he feared nobody would look after properly when he was gone. The depressed dentist cradled his old, blind friend, Buddy, in his arms, and over the rail they went together. There was a strange twist to the demise of that dejected dentist, however. When they performed the autopsy on his broken body, they discovered surprisingly that it wasn't the fall that killed him. That sad dentist had died of dog bite.

I returned to my vehicle then, where I shut my eyes and leaned my head back on the seat, listening to a heartbroken Hank Williams tune on the tape deck. Presently a couple of giant eighteen-wheelers roared past me on the bridge, blaring their horns at my precariously parked vehicle, which rocked slightly in the mighty wake of their passage. I opened my eyes to watch the red lights of the long-haul rigs diminishing up the four-lane until they disappeared into the dark of long-distance.

UGLY BABY

The late Richard Hugo was one of my favorite poets. During a time when he was on the wagon, Dick had mixed my wife Lindsay and me drink after drink one New Year's Eve up at his house in Missoula, Montana. Dick had sat there across a kitchen table from us with glittering thirsty eyes, while he stuffed huge spoonfuls of vanilla ice cream he dug directly from a carton into his mouth each time either of us took a drink. I entertained long slow drinks, and sort of noisily gargled that infinitely sweet stuff around in my mouth before swallowing hard and grinning at Dick.

Hugo once said that *towns* were what often "triggered" poems in him. Hugo lived in Missoula, Montana (the *garden city of the Northwest*), for twenty-some years before he died. Hugo was a habitual wanderer, but he always returned to Missoula, both in his real life and his poetry, and re-imagined everything anew. Hugo had grown up in Seattle, but was Seattle his home town? Or was *the garden city of the Northwest* his home town? Or was the real home town of his poems a model in his imagination from which all possible towns could be conjured? Hugo said this about poems and home towns, the poem is always in your home town, but you have a better chance of finding it in another town. However, not just any other town will do. Though you've never seen it before, that town must be a town you've lived in imaginatively all of your life.

The first thing I had learned about my new home town of Billville was that, not unlike many other old mountain towns loaded with vivid local history, it entertained a sort of poetic sense of itself, *mythical* even, not to mention a profound *mystical* sense of another world of mystery in its midst, namely that invisible parallel world of the past, which to many local current citizens was more magically alive and rewarding than the bump-and-grind business of everydayness. Daily life in Billville was full of little respectful rituals of recognition and acknowledgement for long-departed souls you might come upon shopping in Ben Franklin's Five & Dime or sunning on a courthouse bench or buying a drink out at Billy Ray's. More than once while driving through town with my brother-in-law, he had politely nodded toward somebody passing by on the street and announced he hadn't seen that old son-of-a-bitch since his open casket service, and by golly he didn't look half bad for being dead as Hank Williams. The little mountain town prided itself equally upon being haunted and "historic."

Nothing of real national "historic" consequence had ever occurred in my relentlessly "historic" new home town of Billville, and apparently things became "historic" simply by gathering moss. It was a rare building or tree or bench that didn't sport a brass plaque denoting its local historical significance. Don't leave your vehicle parked overnight downtown, is my best advice about my home town, if you don't want to risk it slipping into local historical significance and find a plaque screwed onto your car door for proof. Don't fall asleep on a courthouse bench.

The "historic" buildings of my home town really were lovely, how-ever, mostly two- and three-story buildings constructed of brick and stone by local Italian stonemasons, part-time Mafiosi generations back, including the stately brick- and stone-columned "historic" courthouse on Court Street. The spiteful Yankees had burned the first courthouse down when they were driven out of town in 1863, and the next version burned down in 1895 under mysterious, spooky, agitated circumstances (Yankee ghosts was the main suspicion), with fires blazing up suddenly in a dozen different places throughout the building during a mighty thunderstorm that rained sheets of water onto the flames with no effect, after which the current structure was erected and at some point ritually became "historic."

Every year, the Fourth of July parade in my home town passes around this "historic" courthouse approximately eight times. The marching band from the high school is always in the big parade, and the fire truck, and a few floats decorated to reflect patriotic themes, and any number of vehicles festooned with banners ferrying around local politicians and celebrities, such as the local teevee weathergirl, and one year I rode in it. My brother-in-law had waxed and polished that old, battered, yellow Caddy convertible that he had traded a shotgun and motorboat for, and on the waxed dented doors he had fashioned banners proclaiming FAMOUS ORTHUR. We had cruised around and around the "historic" courthouse block of spreading old shade trees and cheering small-town Americans approximately eight times directly behind the marching band, enjoying that magic twinkle on the backs of majorettes' man-tanned thighs, me waving and smiling and just generally shedding beneficent, magnanimous grace like a movie star or some queen mother.

Say you are standing near the corner of Maple Avenue and Court Street in the heart of my home town, say you gaze across Maple Avenue and south down the street, what you will find is a "historic" flower shoppe and a "historic" bank and a "historic" old-timey five-and-dime named Ben Franklin's. Right around the corner east on Court Street in my home town, you will find the restored "historic" Fayette Theatre, and a "historic" Gino's House of Pizza, and Billy Bob's "historic" Gulf gas station and garage.

You will also find the "historic" offices of Billy Bob Bodine, on whose front window is printed in bold, gold letters: CONSULTANT, OPINIONS EXPRESSED, INC. Which the old, white-haired, craggy-faced Squire, who back in the '50s was the only Republican ever elected mayor of Billville, lived to do. He would sit on the white bench in front of his office on sunny afternoons, or on cold days cozy back inside on ratty overstuffed couches sharing a taste of bourbon and branch along with his opinions, below walls cluttered with framed photographs of the Squire shaking the hands of prominent Republican political crooks, from former President Richard M. Nixon to former West Virginia Governor Arch Moore, who in 1990 was sentenced to five years in prison for extorting money for his so-called "underground political campaigns" to set up scholarships for coal company whores.

The redoubtable old Squire was about the only Republican and Methodist left in town, outside of my own old Momma, and he was also the nemesis of the formidable Fayette County Historical Society, ever since for a chuckle he had had one of those old-timey, country-road, black-and-yellow CHEW MAILPOUCH TOBACCO signs painted on the street side of his garage beside his own old "historic" family home up on Maple. When the Fayette County Historical Society matrons had marched on the Squire's home, armed to the teeth with their ritual plaque-removal screwdrivers, he had been waiting for them with a hose.

Do not think that I mean to make light of the historic proclivities of the decent, friendly folk of my home town, who can be justifiably proud of those hardy pioneering forebears who braved the wilderness to settle those rugged hills. But none of that "historic" trailblazing business interested me much, of course. And I wasn't much interested in the accomplishments of prominent politicians or distinguished judges or local lawyers of any stripe, or eloquent windbag preachers, especially Southern Baptists, past or present.

The tall tales about the days when Fayette County was infamous as a very wicked place were what interested me. What interested me were the darkly funny anecdotes and stories my brother-in-law could banter about out at the beerjoints endlessly concerning the misdeeds of the local loafers and louts and misfits and winos and oddball characters of my home town.

What happened was that at the turn of the century, Fayette County had changed almost overnight from a small farming region into an area overflowing with booming mine towns, each one with its share of saloons buzzing with early mountain bands and painted barroom babes and gamblers and con men eager to relieve the miners of their hard-earned pay, and the atmosphere was rich with the scent of raw sex and danger and drunken bloodlust. Violence was such that the *Cincinnati*

Enquirer published an article on May 14, 1904, that proclaimed that Fayette County was the "county where they shoot a man every day," and, further, that "Fayette County can lay dubious claim to being the wickedest county in America."

One payday Saturday night in 1904 had become particularly infamous when fourteen men were shot around the county, four fatally, the most interesting of which was the demise of Wake Murell, better known as "Blue Steel." The shooting occurred in the saloon of Stanley McNorton in Glen Jean, wherein Blue Steel met his end from the ball of a .44 caliber pistol fired by a jealous woman, which ball had pierced his "historic" penis (the source of his nickname), and he died from shock and loss of esteem, not to mention blood.

Peanuts Kemper was the sort of "historic" character who interested me. Peanuts secured his place in Billville history as the ugliest man to ever live within the city limits. And his wife was just as ugly, and they had sixteen of the ugliest children ever born. So one day Peanuts was loafing as usual with his drinking buddies Billy Johnson and Billy Clark and my brother-in-law (who was about twelve at the time) out in front of the old Rosie's Place on Court Street. They were all helping hold up Rosie's front wall and sipping wine from bottles in paper-pokes and philosophizing, when Peanuts's ugly wife (she was reputedly so ugly she couldn't cry, for tears refused to run down the front of her face), who was carrying their one-month-old ugly newborn, came loping up the street, along with all of their other ugly children, their knuckles scraping the pavement in their passage. Peanuts couldn't have been more proud.

The proud papa made each of his drunken-lout buddies hold the ugly baby in turn, except for my brother-in-law, who was too proud to hold something that ugly in public. He pleaded a cold he didn't want to pass on, and stepped briskly back away from all that ugliness. Whereupon Peanuts, that proud papa, rocked the ugly baby in his own skinny arms and cooed at it through his blue, toothless gums, and then he lifted the amazingly hairy infant into the air and wiggled it around like a baby baboon. Then Peanuts tossed the ugly creature into the air and caught it by the scruff of its neck coming down. Peanuts was making those grunts and barks that passed as laughter, and the baby's beard was wet with happy, blue slobber. Then Peanuts sent the child sailing aloft again. At which point one of the Billys let wind like a clap of thunder, and Peanuts, whose favorite jokes centered around gas expelled in public, became amused, and he began yipping and barking and thrust a hand under an armpit to make some funny fart sounds of his own.

Even if he had had the reflexes, my brother-in-law, if the truth be told, could not swear he would have tried to catch that ugly baby before it hit the pavement, where both its little hairy legs were broken and the features of its little, hairy face, such as they were, shifted considerably about. This historic anecdote has a happy ending, however, for many locals attest to this day that the baby's looks, after the swelling had gone down, were vastly improved upon.

BODY PARTS

My perfect poem of a home town has only two stoplights, both of which I invariably hit red the entire time I lived there. I never found this disconcerting, for I often solicited slowness at that time in my life, and sometimes even celebrated caution. The fact that the stoplight on the corner of Court and Maple was by all local accounts haunted and, not unlike some sort of medium, blinked its seemingly random series of greens and yellows and reds prophetically, I found engaging. I often stopped even on a rare green at that spooky light, to linger in the deep downtown night, and attempt to interpret the meaning of the traffic signal's message concerning the future. The languidly blinking traffic lights, and the pale yellow light from the old-timey streetlamps, cast a lovely sheen over the old, shadowy, haunted downtown buildings, and over the stately brick- and stone-columned haunted courthouse on the corner, in whose dark windows you might often observe reflections that could easily have been faces illuminated by candle flames flickering from another time.

Often the famous ex-sheriff of Fayette County, William Landcaster, decked out in the full regalia of his old uniform, including the epaulets, bandoliers, and white Texas Ranger ten-gallon cowboy hat, would be positioned beneath the haunted stoplight directing the erratic late-night traffic from the beerjoints, some of which was visible only to the famous ex-sheriff, ghost carloads of good-old-boys who had wiped out around some tree a generation ago.

Ex-Sheriff Landcaster was famous in the county because sixty years earlier, he had become the youngest West Virginia high sheriff, at sixteen, to ever win that job by ritual redneck combat, a custom they practiced back in those pre-election days. Sheriff Landcaster was famous also for having fought and lost a four-round decision to Cassius Clay (a.k.a. Muhammad Ali) in Clay's very first professional fight at eighteen. In his final professional fight, Landcaster (whose ring name had been "the Shit-Kicking Sheriff") had been knocked out by one Shotgun Shelton from Cincinnati, Ohio. Landcaster had lingered in a coma near death for close to a year, before awakening miraculously during a bedside visit by his old nemesis, by then named Muhammad Ali (Ali also graciously attended the grand festivities years later when Sheriff Landcaster retired from office).

Ex-Sheriff William Landcaster was directing the mostly invisible traffic under the haunted stoplight one night when I was returning home from a broody visit to the early morning New River Gorge Bridge, another night that I had once again seen old Five Dollar Bill rise up out of the fog to fly beneath that world-class span. Even in his dotage, Sheriff Landcaster was an impressive figure, tall, erect, rugged-looking, with the confident cowboy carriage of a, well, Marlboro Man. The primary problem with Sheriff Landcaster, and what precipitated his early retirement, was his ever more frequent attempts to arrest outlaws only he could see, which had resulted in a couple of ghost gunfights conducive to neither public confidence nor safety.

I admired ex-Sheriff Landcaster mightily, and often I would pull over at the curb and climb out to chew the fat. I had sought him out early upon my arrival in Billville, to pump him for stories of the good old outlaw days, to talk with a man whose face had tasted the sweet fists of the greatest fighter of all time. It was not unlike a dance Landcaster did there under the haunted stoplight, a ritual tango, part old fighter shadowboxing, part old sheriff shadow-directing the invisible traffic of spooks, a shadowy choreography full of mystery and grace. That particular night when I was returning home from the bridge, however, the sheriff didn't seem to recognize me when he raised his hand for me to stop at a rare green light, and I didn't wave or honk at him, but simply waited patiently to be signaled on. I was still feeling broody from the bridge; mostly, though, I wasn't in any mood to be mistaken for some spirit miscreant from the old days and shot at.

When the sheriff directed me to proceed, I threw a left on Maple Avenue at its intersection with Court Street, and drove up the little hill past the "historic," haunted courthouse and jail jammed with ghost outlaws. A little piece on up the road I passed the "historic" Baptist Church on the right (reputedly haunted by three ghost members of the choir killed years ago in a beerjoint fire), where my sister and her family worshipped in their fashion, talking in tongues and tossing copperheads into the air for all I knew.

About an eighth of a mile up the road, past maybe a half-dozen other "historic," haunted houses, where the road leveled at the top of the slope, Grandma Pearl's little gray-shingled house with the white shutters sat on the left at the back of a long yard, and I swung into the narrow gravel drive. I just sat there for a spell listening to Waylon Jennings on the tape deck sing about how women love outlaws like children love stray dogs, while I watched the shadows of clouds running before the moon as they moved over the little hideout house I had come to love. When I saw the curtains in the front bedroom window move slightly, and an old, pruney, albeit very sweet and pale face peeked out, I gave the ghost of Grandma Pearl, who always waited up for me, a little wave.

The decor of my hideout's front room, I would characterize as Early Ohio Chic. There was an old out-of-tune upright piano and a couple of overstuffed chairs and a threadbare couch with a quilt thrown over it pushed against the fireplace at the far end, antiques Lovelene had collected from one yard sale or another. Against the front window, whose curtains Lovelene had always kept drawn, stood a sort of rickety Sears-issue entertainment center, metal poles and laminated wood shelves with clear plastic doors for a touch of class, wherein I put my television and books after I had moved Lovelene's framed pictures of herself and her collections of seashells and salt and pepper shakers. The faded wallpaper of pale roses in the living room, my sister had pasted up when she had lived there over twenty-five years earlier as a bride. The lowered ceiling and cheap motley imitation-pine paneling on the wall behind the fireplace and in the dining room, my brother-in-law had put up when he was about thirteen, the first handyman work he had ever done, back when his dad was newly dead and somebody, namely the boy of the house, had to do it.

The dining room was mostly bare, no table or anything obvious like that, simply a couple of heavy oak china cabinets against the walls, about the only items of Grandma Pearl's beautiful old furniture Lovelene and her crew didn't grind down to dust. Their tops were stacked high with treasures Lovelene had left behind, mostly boxes of family photos, old beach trip souvenirs, and unpaid bills.

Standing back at the kitchen sink, letting cool water run over my hands, I looked out the window all the way across the moonlit valley to the shadow of ghostly Gauley Mountain, famous as the most haunted hill in West Virginia, not to mention the most dangerous. People have gone missing on Gauley Mountain. Body parts have been discovered on its steep mountainsides. Mike Rogers's body was found in thirteen pieces scattered over the hill along Route 60. His internal organs and left rump were found in a Navy-issue duffel bag. His head was found at the bottom of the hill tightly sealed in a clear plastic bag, its eyes wide open. At the autopsy, they determined that his liver and left kidney had tooth marks on them, plus the peculiar stains of a substance finally identified as Worcestershire sauce. The phone began to ring about that time, but I didn't answer it.

I went through the closed-in side porch off the kitchen, where the washer and drier were hooked up, to the back porch and stood out there where I could barely hear the phone. I pressed lightly against a railing while I studied the back field and little dark houses scattered on yonder down over the hill in the valley. Old Ike came out of his dog-house to study me. Ike was a big, old white pit bull infamous in that town due to his taste for and success in catching cats, other dogs, mailmen, and preachers, preferably Baptist, for whom he had acquired a particular liking. Ike was chained to a clothesline that stretched the length of the back yard, and as it turned out Ike was mine for the dura-tion of my time down in Billville. Lovelene claimed that she had tried desperately to find Ike a good home before she skipped town. Her new boyfriend, Ron, wouldn't let her keep Ike down in Charlotte in his fancy doublewide, not after a trial visit there when Ike had eaten three of Ron's pet rabbits, two neighborhood cats, and a parrot named Bob. Nobody in Billville would touch old Ike with a ten-foot pole.

—Hey, Ike, I said, —good boy. Ike seemed to sort of cock his old furrowed brow and give me some dubious, killer-doggie consideration. —Meow, I said to Ike, and he began to growl and drool in the moonlight. —Praise God and Amen, I said, and old Ike began to bark and howl.

The phone was still ringing when I went back inside. I sat down at the kitchen table, turned on my laptop, and listened to its accusing haughty hum. I put my fingertips on the keys, closed my eyes. Starting tomorrow, I vowed to myself yet again, I would chain myself to this table before this malevolent machine. Tomorrow I would seriously begin becoming somebody bright and shiny and new. Startled as always, I popped my eyes open when the refrigerator, which could have been a hundred years old, clicked on, gurgling and grunting like a corpse rising from the grave. The appliance was clearly haunted. But it was a steadfast, dependable old refrigerator, I had been assured by Pete, Lovelene's abandoned local boyfriend, who I had also more or less inherited along with Ike out back, and I had come to trust anything that old, steadfast, dependable Pete told me. I can't tell you how much I had come to love that little, airy, clean, and well-lit kitchen with its haunted refrigerator and blue curtains and that view of old Ike and spooky Gauley Mountain.

The phone, which had stopped for a minute, began to ring and ring again, and I got up and walked around the house smoking a fat joint. The house smelled a little like essence of wet killer pit bull and stale beer and cigarette smoke. Old Pete had been holding down the fort up there in the house before I moved in (and then often after I moved in), letting Ike in to curl up on the end of the couch in the evenings, while Pete hung out and smoked and drank beer and watched television and brooded about Lovelene and the nature of forbearance. Poor old Pete lingered in that limbo-land of lost love. What Pete had become, it was clear to me, was the ghost of love past.

I went back out to the kitchen and fixed a George Dickel ditch, then flopped down in the old overstuffed chair in the dim little hallway area between the two bedrooms and bath. I looked up the dark stairs that led to what my brother-in-law called *Peanut Heaven,* his boyhood attic bedroom. He and my sister had launched their married life up there, when they had moved in with Grandma Pearl directly after their honeymoon. That was where their son, the Boy Red, was conceived during one of the two times my baby sister and bizarre bald ugly brother-in-law have had sexual intercourse over the duration of their long marriage (they have two children). Sometimes I heard Grandma Pearl's soft footsteps pacing around up in Peanut Heaven all night when she was restless and lonely and confused about why she was a housebound spook instead of being up in some Promised Land with Jesus. The phone, which was on a rickety red stand by the old chair, rang and rang and rang.

I must have dozed off. But suddenly I woke with a start. For a moment I didn't know where I was. I was sitting in that old chair inexplicably clutching a certain stiff body part. The air was thick with the scent of vanilla. I was sure somebody had nudged me on the shoulder, and I looked wildly all around the dark little hallway. I was also sure I had heard somebody yell in my ear to please answer the damn phone before it drove somebody nuts.

PULLING UP ACES

Permit me to hesitate for a moment in this narrative, gentle reader, to say a word or two concerning Grandma Pearl. Grandma Pearl had been the quintessential Christian church-lady, and I say this without smugness or irony. She was a genuinely good person with great generosity of spirit. But on top of all that truly Christian business, Pearl was a card. And although she could be tight with a day-to-day dollar, over the years Grandma had sent off thousands of dollars in donations to those television preacher frauds. As a reward for her generosity, whatever pompous, posturing, preening God those people pray to turned Grandma Pearl to stone. It was as though the muscles in her body began to quit moving one by one and simply seize, and she was as smart and alert as ever as her body turned to rock.

My brother-in-law and sister carried Grandma here and they carried her there, trying to find out what was going terribly wrong. At last, down in Charlotte, the doctors diagnosed the rare, incurable disease that was making Grandma Pearl freeze up like Laurel Creek in winter. The doctors spelled it all out to my brother-in-law and sister first, telling them what to expect, how Grandma was lost to them, and how they would have to watch while, wide awake, sharp as a tack, Grandma turned into a living stiff, unless blessedly her lungs or heart would arrest. After he had stopped bawling, my brother-in-law told the docs to deliver every bit of the bad news to Grandma straight, what she had and the worst she could expect out of the rest of her natural life. Grandma had focused her eyes on my brother-in-law's face as she listened to the docs' hopeless news. When the doctors were done, Grandma had wiggled her fingers for her notepad. Sweat was shining on Grandma Pearl's old, pruney face by the time she had managed to scratch out her shaky message on the notepad. What Grandma Pearl had scribbled on the notepad was simply *shit*.

Back at my hideout, I had answered the phone and entertained approximately two hours of ritual, erotic abuse. I then went into the tiny bathroom to attend to the new blister on the big toe of my right foot. This meant that I balanced myself on my left foot—a little drunk, true, but deftly, like some sort of strange stork—while I stuck my right foot under the water in the bathroom basin to wash it (when I had almost lost my right foot four years earlier due to a diabetic infection, I had resolved to pay more attention to things such as my diabetic dogs). Now, I really wasn't very drunk. I had had a big meal earlier, so there was something on my stomach, having eaten that evening over at my sister's, where my brother-in-law had cooked up a Chinese dish, one of his specialties, which he called *Chop Sewage*. Nonetheless, I *was* a little drunk, and stoned, and I was distracted by thoughts of what Holly had just told me over the phone about her new resolve not to continue our relationship as long as I would not leave my wife to launch a new life with her immediately if not sooner, and then for no good reason I was suddenly amused at the image of myself, a fat old bird in his underwear, balanced there like that, washing his diabetic dog in a bathroom basin where other, more normal, folks had been known to brush their teeth, when I lost my balance.

I didn't really have a case of the whirlies; I really wasn't *that* drunk. I simply lost it, and I tipped slowly over backwards, one strange stork going down, and it truly did seem as though I was falling in slow motion, moving as they say you do in tragic moments, for I had ample time to reflect upon the folly of my life as I fell backward toward what easily could have been my demise, if not for luck.

• • •

So it was a chilly Tuesday in late September '94, 6:05 in the A.M., and I was wide awake, although up until God knows when, and in pain so amazing I felt as though I was starring in a *film noir* death scene. When I had fallen the night before, the lower right side of my back had bounced against the rim of the bathtub. I mean literally *bounced*, like a basketball, once, hard, and I had been able to both feel and hear, literally, whatever crunched inside. And I had seen them, stars, exploding like skyrockets behind my eyes as they say you do in moments of amazing physical misadventure. And I had slid down on the floor, breathless with the pain, on fire with it, blind with it, and then I had barfed Chop Sewage like a fountain.

But I wasn't exactly dead, I had realized, after a few minutes of crossing back and forth over that frontier borderline of consciousness due to the pain, self-pity, and the extremely unpleasant aftertaste of regurgitated Chop Sewage. What occurred to me, however, when I started to come around was that I could have awakened dead, as they say, as a doornail, easily, if I had hit the back of my head; or, if I had landed on my neck, I could have been simply paralyzed for the rest of my natural life, I reflected. And then I had reflected upon which woman in my life would mourn me the most, or which one would just simply love to wipe a cripple's butt for the rest of his sorry days. But there I was again, it had dawned on me, a broken, old, fat fart flat on my back on a bathroom floor in amazing agony and still pulling up aces.

Time and again that sorry morning I Frankenstein-staggered back to the bathroom to regurgitate strings of vomit as thin and elegant as DNA. Then I lay back down in my dark bedroom masticating fistfuls of Tums into mush, until, at 6:31 A.M., the phone began ringing, and I pulled myself painfully up. Holly always called after walking her sweet dumb dog Fergus, but before waking her kids for school. After I finally answered, we continued the previous night's two-hour fight and intermittent phone-fuck. I didn't tell Holly about my injury, or the acute agony I was enduring like a movie star. Not because I was being a brave boy, however. But because I was afraid of Holly finally reaching the right conclusions about me. About 7:00 A.M., Holly hurriedly got off the horn to wake her kids, just as old Pete rolled in the front door.

In Billville, folks don't lock their doors. In Billville, visitors don't even feel compelled to knock as they come and go with their own motives through one another's unlocked doors (and sometimes right through walls). Pete, this wiry little fellow with a billygoat beard of white hair, was on his way to work looking quite dapper in his green Park Service uniform. Pete dropped by every morning on his way to work, and every evening when he got off, to feed Ike and provide him with fresh water. Lovelene had set up this awkward arrangement, so that Ike wouldn't bother me one little bit. I would have much rather dealt with the dog myself than have old Pete rolling in and out like a cannonball, but old Pete still needed to drop by the house he and Lovelene had shared off and on during the happiest five years of his life, before she had dumped him for Doublewide Ron and the lights of Charlotte, and I understood this.

Pete shuffled back through the house, jingling the change in his pockets and whistling with a forced merriment. He waved mightily as he passed where I was collapsed in the old overstuffed chair beside the rickety red phone table in the side hallway, bare-ass naked and hiding my fading boner with a frilly souvenir pillow from Virginia Beach. I could hear Pete discussing the coming day with Ike on the back porch, where I had been letting him sleep on cool nights. In fact, I had often been permitting lonely, sad old Ike to curl up indoors on his smelly end of the couch and watch teevee with me until the crack of dawn sometimes. I had discovered that Ike and I had similar tastes, in terms of television. Not unlike myself, Ike preferred programs such as *Melrose Place, Beavis & Butt-Head, Hard Copy, Bounty Hunters, Unsolved Mysteries, ET, Dukes of Hazzard,* any wild kingdom programs that featured successful predators, the TOON and country music (TNN) channels, movies such as, say, *Swamp Thing* (1982), and television evangelists, especially Jimmy Swaggart (who made Ike drool). Old Ike was not a fussy or mean dog, really, if you were not a cat or dog or bird or Baptist preacher, and if you spoke to him as though you were genuinely interested in his opinions.

Ike responded favorably to good conversation. Old Ike was simply a seemingly beloved dog who unluckily got suddenly parked. The greatest confusion of Ike's life was simply: Where in the world did everybody he loved disappear to, and what in the world had he done wrong? I could hear Pete fasten the thick chain to Ike's studded collar out on the porch, and then I heard it rattle like the thunder of tiny storms down the back stairs.

I boiled my busted back red as a lobster in the shower. Then I gazed in the mirror at my scraggly beard. Holly had encouraged me to grow a beard. Holly said she had never had the opportunity to make love with a bearded man before. Plus I might look just like Papa Hemingway, Holly had speculated (not a few discerning folks have mentioned my resemblance to that famous, albeit late, author). But after permitting my beard to sprout for a couple of weeks, I realized that the Hemingwayesque throes of passion Holly contemplated would be more like a tryst with Santa Claus. I had broken down and borrowed my brother-in-law's *Just For Men* brush-in color gel, natural medium brown, and I had attempted to paint my old, grizzly, gray stubble with that stuff, but instead of looking outlaw cool and badass like Waylon Jennings, or the Boss, say, I looked like Gabby Hayes after getting drunk and shaky on shoe polish. On that sorry, sick morning, I almost cut my throat in my fervor to be clean-shaven. Holly would simply have to fornicate with some other old billygoat with a beard, I reflected with fury and resolve.

Right then all I wanted was for Holly never to call me again in order to tell me how I was living my life like some sort of movie I was making up in my mind as I went along. How she could compete with a real woman any day, but that I had reinvented my wife as this tenderhearted, warm, wonderful, perfect woman I couldn't bear to wound. So then just who was she, *Holly,* anyhow, Holly had demanded to know, and just how did she fit into my stupid script? How, Holly had been furiously curious to know, did I really view her? Did I have to make her up too? Did I have to reimagine her somehow too in order to love her? Did I ever see her for who she actually was, even when I fucked her? Was she just playing that pathetic *part* of the *other woman?* The thought of which made her friggin sick to her stomach! That friggin role went against everything she had ever thought good about herself. That trashy role not only undermined her self-respect, but reinforced the realization about how far down our relationship was on my bullshit list of priorities, and that really hurt her feelings a lot, not to speak of her pride, and how could I continue to do this to her, not to mention my saintly wife, for that matter? How could I continue to exploit them both like that?

—Butbutbutbutbut, sweetie-pie, sweetie-pie . . . , I kept attempting to interject, to no avail.

I put coffee on in the kitchen and clicked on my laptop. I gazed out the kitchen window as the ghosts rose disguised as morning mists on spooky Gauley Mountain. I reflected upon the nature of Mike Rogers's rising ghost. Would it rise up in pieces? His internal organs mere wisps of mist? His head floating up like a balloon of ghost? What about Shirley Gene Arthur, the hitchhiking sailor who disappeared on November 22, 1963? Shirley Gene Arthur was assumed to be another of the seven known victims of the famous Mad Butcher of Fayette County. That sad sailor's torso was found on December 6, 1963, by three teenagers looking for firewood. It was discovered at the autopsy that nineteen puncture wounds had been made around the heart in the shape of a circle. What sort of ghost would a torso make? Could a ghost-torso see its way around, or hear the wind, or enjoy a single thing about being a ghost? And what about the ghost of Grandma Pearl? Why did that Southern Baptist butthole of a so-called Heavenly Being make Grandma Pearl linger in this wretched dimension of the living dead anyway?

When the coffee had perked, I filled a mug and flipped my laptop the bird, and I limped into the front room moping. I turned on the teevee and collapsed carefully in stages onto the couch, whereupon I began watching the *Today Show* with that cute little Katie Couric and rather half-heartedly jerking off.

At 7:48 Holly called back, just before she headed out the door to take her kids to school and then go on to work. Holly apologized for what she had said earlier. She told me she knew I thought I was trying to do the right thing by everybody as usual, but that sometimes I was too kind and thoughtful for my own good, and I let people take advantage of my generosity of spirit, and so forth and so on. And then Holly said she couldn't wait for our impending planned train trip down to Matewan, couldn't wait for me to hold her in my big arms. —God, hon, Holly suddenly chirped, —I've got to get those kids to school, bye, hon, God, hon, she added hurriedly, gaspily, —I can't wait to run my tongue through your thick chest hair and give your nipples little nips until you groan, then lick slowly down your body. Whereupon Holly whispered sweet suggestions concerning erotic manipulations of sensitive albeit hoary body parts. —Oh, God, hon, Holly suddenly chirped again, —my kids are gonna be late. Gotta run, hon, bye. —I just shaved off that stupid fucken beard, I blurted out, but Holly was long gone.

I moped in pain and despair and general self-loathing (albeit entertaining an amazing boner) out to the kitchen to pour another cup of java, into which I dribbled a dollop of Dickel. I dialed my radio to the local country music station, and lowered myself like a swimmer entering arctic water in front of the mocking machine on the kitchen table. I stared blankly at my latest stoned, brilliant late-night epiphanies for a full fifteen minutes before thinking to myself: *huh?*

Suddenly the refrigerator rose from the dead, which as always about gave me a heart attack. Whereupon I called it a morning's work, and returned to sofa-sail and surf the storied channels of television for a higher truth.

CRIPPLED FLASHER

At 9:30 on that sorry drizzly Tuesday morning, I headed out to pick up my morning papers and have a little ritual belt with the Squire downtown, and then make the ritual reluctant drive on out to the Skyline Drive-In for breakfast as usual, where I would attempt to make amends to Mary X.

That sorry morning, as I had paused downtown at machines in front of the "historic" post office to pick up my papers, the *Charleston Gazette* and *Beckley Register-Herald* and *Billville Tribune,* as I did every morning at about that same time, I gazed about my home town like a tourist. I *was* a tourist, I reckon, although I had lived in my new home town in my imagination most of my life. I stood there that morning in the heart of my home town feeling the curious gaze of strangers the first names of whose grandparents I knew as well as I knew the color of their mothers' eyes. We changed each other as we looked, those townspeople and myself. Who was I in their eyes? Who did they imagine I was? The tall, dark, handsome stranger who had moved into their midst with unfathomable motives, dangerous and evil motives maybe, but maybe not? Maybe I had come to save them. We were all shape-shifters to one another in the vast voyeurism of our imaginations. With that sweet kiss of imaginative empathy, my emotions oceanic, I could embrace them and make them all my own. That old prune of a granny yonder, pushing her shopping cart out of the Daniels grocery store, bent and stooped, she was once a great beauty and queen bee of this town, married to the mayor maybe, although it was well known that she was Sheriff William Landcaster's secret limpid blue-eyed lover for over thirty years, and her name is Rose. There, Rose, just like that, you are mine, and you are saved, Rose. You are preserved for posterity in prose like a bug in amber, Rose, amen.

As I stood there that day, I could feel myself slipping inexorably into local historical significance, and it was not unlike slipping into a warm bath. I kept a wary eye out, nonetheless, for any approaching gaggle of august old ladies armed with screwdrivers and plaques. Presently I limped around the corner to have my ritual morning eye-opener with the aforementioned redoubtable Billy Bob Bodine, the wily old Squire.

What the Squire and I usually discussed when we shared a bourbon and branch eye-opener each morning was the dubious and often criminal nature of politics in West Virginia, especially as reflected in those frequently elected outlaws called governors. Generally I rested my corruption and stupidity case against the Republicans by relating ad nauseam that episode in 1984 when then-Governor Arch Moore, the Squire's one-time crony and my old man's political hero, had taken possession of a $573,721 bribe from a big-time coal operator at halftime of a state championship high school football game in the form of cash stuffed in a pillowcase in the presence of state troopers. The old philosophical Squire had loved Arch anyway (as had my old man), the first Republican governor in decades and the only politician to beat that Yankee carpetbagger rich-boy Jay Rockefeller, and they had exchanged letters all the years Arch was down in that Texas federal pen.

I never told the Squire my two-fisted Jay Rockefeller story, but here it is for whatever it's worth. For a time after he had lost his first bid for governor to that old outlaw Arch Moore, Jay Rockefeller had laid low to lick his political wounds while disguised as the president of a small Methodist college in the north-central part of the state. He was demonstrating to the hardheaded people of West Virginia their essential wrongness, by proving to them he was a destined man of patience, immune to impertinence, and, although privy to lavish worlds beyond their ignorant imagining, that contrary to all predictions he would not pick up his marbles and sulk back to his native New York State simply because they had spitefully not elected him their new governor.

I met Jay Rockefeller back then when I spent a couple of days around Buckannon, West Virginia, while interviewing him for *Esquire* magazine. Jay had waxed truly poetic about the bountiful small-town life he and his wife Sharon (the late former Illinois Senator Charles Percy's daughter) had come to embrace, about how anonymous neighbors often left baskets of garden-fresh vegetables and fruit on their back porch for them to find, about how he and Sharon had never felt so accepted nor at home as among these patriotic, plain-living, honest, hardworking, homespun, surprisingly well read, church-going, generous, gardeners-extraordinaire, decent, albeit deeply wary people. When I asked Jay if he felt impeded by West Virginians' perverse, not to mention mealy, inability to forgive that he would always finally be an outsider to us, Jay had expounded at length about how he was one hundred percent behind progress in the beautiful mountain state, plus he was for jobs and improved education and for a better life and greater opportunities for all West Virginian-Americans. The article I wrote was dead in the water.

Perhaps I should have included an account of those events that had transpired after greasy burgers and a few beers out in the parking lot behind the Lula-Bell Inn that Saturday night long ago, but I didn't. Perhaps I didn't disclose any of that old business because I felt I was to blame after all, for I was the bird, not Jay, who had passed those untoward remarks to the beautiful barmaid (whose coal-black eyes I can see flashing to this day, and her grin of gold). And it was not at all Jay's fault that the comely barmaid's boyfriend was a biker whose nickname was Tree. I will say only this about that old matter: In spite of being such a seemingly feckless four-eyed sort of prep-school rich-boy Yankee from the North, out under the pale yellow lights in the parking lot that night Jay, who was about as tall as Tree anyway, purely reinvented himself as a genuine West Virginian-American, and in the process made purchase of my vote forever.

Colorful criminal or two-fisted governors notwithstanding, my favorite former West Virginia governor was William Casey Marland, who ended up not a crook but a human-interest story. Marland was elected in 1952 at age thirty-four, and his political future appeared bright until he took on the coal companies by proposing a severance tax upon the robber-baron industries of the state. Marland never recovered, and after losing a couple of political races, he secured a position as a shyster with a coal company in ironic desperation, and, rumored to have become a hopeless drunk, faded into obscurity.

Years later, he was discovered driving a cab in Chicago. He made an appearance on the old Jack Paar show as a, well, human-interest story. Ex-Governor Marland commented that he believed he had been a pretty good governor of West Virginia. He sure had tried his best, anyway. He went on to comment that the fall from being governor of West Virginia to being governor of a Chicago cab wasn't as long as it might look. Not long afterwards, Marland died of cancer, and his ashes were scattered from a plane over those hills of West Virginia he had once governed with so much hope and pride and courage.

I knew immediately that the Squire and I would not be leisurely sipping bourbon and branch while we discussed politics that particular sorry morning when I discovered him handcuffed to the bench in front of his office and in a highly agitated state of mind. The Squire's old boiled cabbage of a face was redder with outrage than even usual, his hair looked like an Andy Warhol fright wig, and he was fairly frothing with fury. Without subjecting gentle readers to the absolutely profane albeit eloquent venomousness of the Squire's caustic tongue, suffice it to say that the focus of his sustained and bitter condemnations were the local Southern Baptist preachers.

Deciphering the Squire's ranting and railing with some difficulty, I deduced that some of the local God-fearing, teetotaling Southern Baptist preachers had objected to authorities about the Squire's long-accustomed daily habit of tippling a taste of bourbon and branch and providing opinions to the passing world at large from his perch on that bench in front of his office as he got boiled. The Squire had responded to this complaint by handcuffing himself to said bench, where he sat with a bottle of Old Crow between his feet and clutching his club of a cane, while he censured and berated Southern Baptist preachers severely, and solicited signatures on a petition to ban all said Baptist preachers from the downtown area into perpetuity.

While I did not tarry there for long with the Squire, for who knows when the sheriff would arrive, and I was, after all, reality-challenged and carried upon my person a supply of controlled substances, namely two joints, I readily signed the Squire's petition, being in total agreement with its sentiments concerning Southern Baptists, not the regular folks but the preachers, those mealy-mouthed, moral midgets, hypocrites and right-wing gay-bashing butt-cracks. In enormous letters beneath his own name (the only name, I had to notice, as yet on that document), I boldly wrote JAY ROCKEFELLER.

As I turned to go, the Squire clutched my elbow, and looked up at me with his boiled brussels-sprout eyes. —Your daddy should have been governor of West "by gawd" Virginia, is what the Squire told me. — Your daddy would have been a great governor, I'm here to tell you. I always tried to get your daddy to toss his hat in the political ring around here. Your daddy was famous statewide. And your daddy wasn't a drunk or a crook or, worst of all, a goddamn Southern Baptist preacher. Your daddy would have kicked those Southern Baptist preacher butts for them just like he done the Germans.

—Old Charlie would have given good governor, I conceded.

At which point, I wished the Squire good luck in his just and good cause and hastily bid my adieus. Whereupon, I had flung myself from that scene like a crippled flasher.

A MULTITUDE OF BILLS

I drove through the cool foggy morning four or five miles south on the four-lane, then threw a left onto Route 16 for the couple of miles to the wide-spot-in-the-road community of Hilltop, where I pulled right into the gravel lot of Barb's Skyline Drive-In to grab breakfast, and hopefully explain things and make peace with Mary X.

The Skyline was a little, low-slung, whitewashed cinderblock building where you could blink your lights any time of day or night for curb service. Out front was a big red historic Coca-Cola sign peppered with bullet holes. The wide front windows were steamed, and when I got out of my vehicle I could hear the jukebox playing the old Hank Williams tune "I've Seen The Light," sounds as holy and wondrous as hearing church chimes on this chilly, repentant Tuesday morning. This Skyline Drive-In was historic and famous for the fact that it was the location where, on January 1, 1953, the late, great country-singing star Hank Williams (who had been, by the way, as I had convinced the local folks, my great-uncle) had come to the end of the line.

As I limped toward my usual booth in the back of the rather shabby but nonetheless immaculately clean breakfast-and-luncheon beerjoint, I nodded and spoke to Biggest Bill, a five-hundred-pound whale of a jolly human being plopped precariously on one of the low stools at a counter evidently made for midgets. Biggest Bill beamed and greeted me back: — Hey, there, Little Hank. And I then spoke to Oldest Bill, an ancient white-haired gent the weight of whose 113 years had contorted him into the approximate shape of a 7, who was bent over one of the half-dozen video poker machines. I acknowledged Smartest Bill, who was sitting in his usual booth by the front window working crossword puzzles, and who, like me, read all the local papers and, unlike me, entertained opinions. There were at least a dozen good-old-boys named Bill who frequented the Skyline daily, and sometimes above the breakfast and beerjoint din the room rang with the oddly oriental and affecting birdsong sound of that beloved name, *Bill, Bill, Bill.*

I stopped to slip some silver into the historic tombstone of a jukebox and punch out a few of my late great-uncle Hank's historic tunes: "I'm So Lonesome I Could Cry, Holly"; "I Can't Help It If I'm Still in Love with You, Holly"; "Baby, We're Really in Love, Holly"; "Take These Chains from My Heart, Holly." There was nothing on that old historic jukebox but tunes by my great-uncle Hank, save for a few by Hank Williams Junior, and a couple by West Virginia's own Little Jimmy Dickens, plus a Lefty Grizzel tune or two, and "Honky Tonk Angel" by Kitty Wells.

Mary X, this pretty, twice-divorced, twenty-eight-year-old mother of six with a hornets' nest of a blond beehive, whose slightly sagging but still yet lovely breasts moved like little wild animals when we fast-danced, brought me my first mug of steaming java. She seemed a little distant today as I expected she would, on account of the little fracas I had almost found myself immersed in on those very premises the previous Friday night with Baddest Bill, and the lies I told that scary man, but neither of which were totally my fault to begin with, as Mary well should know, if she would just give me the benefit of the doubt. After all, I had my side of the story, and I planned to stick to it like white on rice.

—The usual, Little Hank? Mary X asked me in a voice as cold as a witch's tit, with her penciled, witch-hat eyebrows arched haughtily to her hairline. Mary X slouched there by the table popping her gum in extravagant disdain and superiority and ritual disapproval. —Shore, I said, cool as a cucumber myself, smiling like a copperhead, as Mary turned abruptly and stalked away like Joan Crawford in black & white. I sipped my java and unfolded my first newspaper careful as a napkin, to the editorial page, and began to peruse my editor-buddy Neile Clarke's informed, bemused mutterings. Two could play that little game.

Mary X returned presently with a breakfast platter piled with my usual grub du jour, a pyramid of perfectly scrambled eggs, a half dozen strips of extra-crispy bacon, a heap of hash browns with ramps, a couple of thick scratch biscuits, with a side bowl of possum gravy, all for $2.85. By the manner in which she had high-hipped toward me, there was no doubt to my trained eye that Mary truly did have a little bug embedded firmly up her sweet butt.

—Mary, my dear, I inquired, —are you okay today? Are the kids okay? Do you feel ill or anything? Can I do anything to help you? Whereupon Mary X slammed my breakfast platter onto the table, sending a fistful of those tasty fried potatoes flying all over the funny-page. —You didn't have to go and tell him we didn't mean nothing real important to each other, Little Hank, Mary snarled with great dignity and turned on her heel. —But, but, but . . . , I tried to explain as Mary marched off.

What I sought to explain to Mary was that I was sorry if I ever gave her the wrong impression about my intentions. I had truly enjoyed the dozen or so times I had dropped by her doublewide with family-packs of sirloins I had fried up for her brood, and I had enjoying horsing around with her six kids, and I had enjoyed the long, intelligent, intense talks we had had about literature, especially about our mutual all-time fave novel, *The Bridges of Madison County,* and, shore, the loving had been sweet; but when her ardent suitor, Baddest Bill, who was the lifetime Grand Dragon of the West Virginia chapter of the Pagan Angels motorcycle gang and famous for the creative forms of pain he enjoyed inflicting upon folks who he thought had shortchanged him in life, and famous also for that tattoo of a python that began at the toe of his right foot to twine about his leg and torso to end at his thick, red neck: well, when Baddest Bill had inquired as to my motherfucken motives in regards to his private pussy, namely that cunt Mary, admittedly I had more or less attempted to impress upon Baddest Bill that my intentions were zip in the long-range romance department; that, after all, I was a married man, for one thing; that, if anything, I had come to look upon dear young Mary as a sort of niece or daughter, granddaughter even; that, at my age, I was, believe me, post-passion; that, indeed, I wasn't certain if love and passion even went together successfully, for I had come to believe that love is constant, not consuming, not jealous, not destructive; that, if the truth be told, what I most wanted to avoid in the few remaining years, nay, months of my life (for I was not well) was the fiercely theatrical light of passion; that, while I enjoyed talking with him, I really had to run, for my wheelchair-bound, blind old mother could not sleep unless we had prayed together before she rested her dear old silver head upon her pillow for what any night could be her last in this vale of tears.

DELIVERING THE BODY
OF THE DEAD STAR

Like many successful country music stars, my great-uncle Hank
Williams owned a special magnetism which won him the hearts of
his fans. Uncle Hank's singing voice was not smooth and refined, but
plain and unstudied. The quality that made his voice touch the hearts
and souls of thousands of country music fans was not its beauty, but its
truthfulness. Hank Williams sang of loneliness and heartbreak in a way
that made fans feel that he, like them, had been there and done that.
Uncle Hank made them feel as though he was expressing their own
heartfelt emotions. Uncle Hank sang as if he knew firsthand just what
loneliness and heartbreak were all about. This understanding of loneliness and disappointment was much more than a performing style. Uncle
Hank led a life marked by great successes followed by great failures and
disappointments. In the end, Hank Williams spent his final hours and
moments on Earth alone, in the back seat of a blue Cadillac traveling
through Fayette County, West Virginia, on his way to still yet another
performance. Like with so many *stars,* the love of thousands of fans
was not enough to ease the essential solitude and loneliness within his
own heart.

Ironically, it was his unhappy personal life that gave Uncle Hank the
inspiration to write his most successful songs; but this same unhappiness
eventually led to problems with whiskey and women, problems that
began to seriously threaten his career. After four years on *The Grand Ole'
Opry,* Uncle Hank's drinking led to his being dropped from the show.
At age 28, when many young performers were still struggling for recognition, Uncle Hank was making a comeback. Claiming to have his love

for whiskey under control, Uncle Hank had scheduled a series of personal appearances in an attempt to win back the love of his fans.

On December 31, 1952, Uncle Hank was scheduled to appear in Charleston, West Virginia, but bad weather at the airport forced him to return to Knoxville, Tennessee. Determined to make his scheduled New Year's performance in Canton, Ohio, Uncle Hank decided to make an effort to get there by automobile. Uncle Hank had not, however, overcome his love for whiskey. Before Uncle Hank left Knoxville, a Dr. P. H. Caldwell was summoned to the Andrew Johnson Hotel to treat him. The doctor gave Uncle Hank two injections of morphine and B-12. After the doctor's call, porters at the hotel helped to dress Uncle Hank and carry him to his car. While virtually unconscious, Uncle Hank was placed in the back seat of his blue Cadillac convertible to sleep it off while his driver, Charles Carr, departed for Canton, Ohio.

Who knows at what point Charles Carr began driving through the night with a dead *star* in the back seat of the blue Cadillac. Those hours and moments before anybody in the world knew yet that Hank Williams was dead and free from history, Charles Carr continued on his way to Canton, Ohio, believing Uncle Hank to be peacefully asleep in the back seat of the blue Cadillac. About 6:30 on New Year's morning, the young driver stopped at the Skyline Drive-In on Route 16 at Hilltop, West Virginia, right outside of Oak Hill, to grab some java and breakfast. When Charles Carr attempted to rouse Uncle Hank to see if he would like some scrambled eggs and extra-crispy bacon and hash browns with onions and scratch biscuits with a side of possum gravy, Uncle Hank's favorite breakfast when he wasn't barfing his morning away, Charles Carr was unable to get any response. To his horror, Charles Carr discovered that his famous passenger had fallen into a deep sleep from which he would never awake. Hank Williams was only 29 years old when his luck ran out on January 1, 1953, and returned to that place luck, either good or bad, goes to when it is through with us, which to my mind is the cold comfort of history.

Charles Carr and an alternate driver, who had accompanied him on the trip, took Uncle Hank to the Oak Hill hospital where he was pronounced dead on arrival by Dr. Diego Nunnari. At that particular point in time, only the drivers of the car were aware of just how famous the deceased man really was. But the word spread. The blue Cadillac convertible was parked at the former Pure Oil Station on Main Street of Oak Hill, and soon crowds of curious townspeople gathered at the gas station to stare at the historic vehicle with the cursive golden initials on its doors: HW.

The body of the dead star was sent to the Tyree's Funeral Home and an autopsy was performed by Dr. Ivan Milanin, a pathologist from Beckley Hospital. The autopsy revealed that Uncle Hank had suffered hemorrhages in the neck and in his heart. The cause of death listed on the death certificate was acute ventricular dilation. Uncle Hank's mother traveled to Oak Hill and chose a white cowboy suit, from the wardrobe her son kept in the car, to bury him in. She asked that the body be transported to Montgomery, Alabama, for funeral services and the burial.

Joe Tyree, the operator of Tyree's Funeral Home, although he preferred classical music and opera to country music, insisted upon personally driving the hearse carrying the body of Hank Williams to the Greenwood Cemetery in Montgomery, Alabama. When he arrived, Joe Tyree found the town thronged with an estimated 20,000 mourners. For fifty miles around, hotels were packed.

After delivering the body of the dead star, Joe Tyree turned right around and headed back home to West Virginia. He dialed in country stations all the way back, listening to endless Uncle Hank songs. He would never listen to classical music or opera again. Joe Tyree knew how lucky he was to be driving the most historic hearse the county would ever know, and what that vehicle would mean to his burying business. Joe Tyree drove slowly, stopping often to park by the roadside and reflect on the ironies of destiny and fame. It took Joe Tyree almost a week to get home from his historic mission. Whereupon Joe Tyree returned rather sadly to his regular, everyday real life, delivered now from history forever.

STALKING THE STORY

B ack at the house on that sorry September day, I wrote from 10:42 to 5:37 straight through, forgot even to eat, and then the phone rang and it was Holly. We talked real whispery, for her kids were scampering about, and only briefly because I was expected at my sister's for dinner and for our usual Tuesday night date out at the Naked Spur, where my sister went for her line-dancing lessons. Holly and I made our own date for an 11:00 bedtime phone-fornication, and I made her promise not to fight with me about the far-off future please please. I made her promise that we would only talk about our impending train trip down to Matewan together and the dirty-deed stuff we planned to do at every opportunity. We were crazy in love, I recall that clearly. Holly was so angry at me, though. For not being with her. For not telling her when I would be with her definitely. We were crazy in love, but I was begging the question. We were crazy in love, but I believed I had built up enough courage to finally do the right thing and break things off with her once and for all when she came down, after we had had one last wild sweet fling together as best friends and lovers. Whereupon out of the blue I had blurted to Holly that I loved her like I had never loved another woman. I told her I was crazy in love with her. I told her that somehow things would work out. I told Holly everything I thought she wanted to hear about the future before we hung up and I limped pathetically out the door.

Why had I done that? Why had I told Holly those things about the future that as soon as I was out the front door, I didn't believe in really? Why had I told those good folks over there at the Skyline Drive-In, all those good old Bills (Baddest Bill notwithstanding), and dear Mary X, that I was the grand-nephew of the late, great Hank Williams? Actually, the answer to that one is pretty clear, I guess. An easy entree, an easy identity and alias, a history to hide in, borrowed fame, for the pure sake of story, seduction.

(So many fans visited Uncle Hank's grave over the years that we family members were finally forced to move his remains to another gravesite that provided the public easier access, I had told my new best friends out at the Skyline, all the Bills and Mary X, and at one point I had drunkenly promised to lead a caravan of those pilgrims to that sacred place down in Alabama, plus pick up everybody's traveling tab, gas, food, lodging, you name it, everything would be on me, good old diamond Little Hank.)

God, but Holly deserved better. My wife deserved better. Everybody deserved better from me. As I drove toward my sister's house that sorry day, I found that I couldn't picture Holly's pretty face clearly, and I couldn't conjure the sound of her voice. Her words wouldn't come to me, the things she said, and how she said them, her expressions and gestures, they were all lost to me right then. Thank fucken God, one side of me said, the sappy, sentimental side that would suffer when I gave her up. But the other side, the lowdown Redneck Writer side, said doggone, and whispered evilly in my ear that I needed that stuff for juicy material.

Much later, after I had returned to my good wife in Pittsburgh and Holly had finally broken off with me, saying she absolutely refused to be the *other woman* any longer, I would start calling her number when I knew she was at work simply to hear her voice on her answering machine. It would be then that I realized I was capable of becoming a *stalker* for the sake of the story. This was soon after I had returned to Pittsburgh and had moved home with my wife where I really belonged instead of in with Holly as she had begged me to do, and she had started seeing her anal architect boyfriend.

One morning I called Holly at work, asked the receptionist to let me speak with her, just to make sure she was there, and then hung up before she answered. I still had a key to her front door. It was a cold, clear January morning, and although my vehicle's heater worked fine, I was shivering as I drove across town to the North Side.

I don't know what I planned on doing or looking for. Some sort of evidence of our enduring love story, I suppose. To get to the heart of her current love story, I guess. To see if my toothbrush was still in the second-floor bathroom medicine cabinet. To see if a new toothbrush was there. To see if there were any recently burned scented candles around the bathroom. To see how I would react if there were. To see where the story would take me. To go up to her third-floor bedroom and count the condoms she kept in her top dresser drawer. The night I had brought Holly that box of condoms as a demonstration of my belief she should experience life as a single but *safe* sexually liberated woman before we committed finally, we had used one, which she had unrolled on old mister monkey herself, something she had never done before on any-body and was tickled to try. So she should have eleven left, except for the ones she had more recently unrolled. And what if she had? What would I do? Would I wreck her bedroom in a jealous rage? Would I fling myself onto her antique canopied bed in a titillated tizzy and jerk off until I fainted? All of these possibilities lay ahead of me that day in the fan-shaped future of the moment-to-moment fiction that I call my life. I didn't know how the story would work out. The movie version of my life was going a mile a minute in my mind. I was scared and thrilled and felt like a sweaty shooting star.

I parked on the street around from Holly's ramshackle townhouse on busy Cedar Avenue. I had brought along a painting she had done for me of an old cemetery in Florida when she was down there the previous summer with her folks for a family wedding. The painting was a ruse, a prop, in case I encountered anybody and had to explain why I was over at Holly's house when she wasn't home. I don't know who I thought I might encounter. My hand actually shook when I put the key in the lock. I opened the front door and stepped into the tiny entry.

Holly's mail was scattered on the floor beneath the slot. Her big, brown dumb dog, old Fergus, came bounding down the stairs, and, clearly excited to see me, his old patient pal who used to take him out for his protracted morning poops, he hopped about like crazy on the other side of the inner door. I looked through the glass panel at Holly's front hallway and into the living room on the right, and back through the dining room into the kitchen at the far end of the house. Everything looked exactly the same. How could that be? It was all too real for me. It was all utterly ordinary. Suddenly I failed the fiction of my life. Or that fiction failed me.

I spun around like a top and flung myself from that place, all trips and stumbles and teary. When I got back to my house, I stood in the back door and threw Holly's key as hard as I could, hoping to heave it over my garage into the next yard, the next planet. The key landed on the garage roof, and there it lay, all shiny and plain as day. One more thing to explain. But before I fetched the ladder and risked breaking my neck retrieving that telltale key, I needed a little something to settle my nerves.

The sky clouded up meanwhile, and before long it was snowing, and it snowed and snowed. Weeks later, when the record snowfall began to melt away during a rare Pittsburgh-winter warm spell, the key was gone. At weak moments over the next months, I would search around in the layers of sodden leaves on the ground beside the garage, where I figured the key had slid off the roof and buried itself. I would kick and scratch around in the dirt under the fallen leaves like an old dog after a fabled lost bone. I wanted another crack at that story of some poor pathetic character stalking lost love. I wanted to watch that pathetic character count those condoms and drive himself deliciously nuts imagining Holly naked and writhing in the arms of other men. That sad character dug in that cold, hard, winter dirt like a grave-robber until his fingers hurt and bled, but to no avail. End of story.

MY BAD SIDE

For several years during the middle '80s I had invited some of my writer-buddies down to Billville to run the best whitewater in the East, a gathering that my brother-in-law took to calling the "Writers' Raftin' Ruckus." He even silk-screened T-shirts for us with that logo. Everybody would roll into Billville one way or another on a Thursday night, flying into Pittsburgh or Charleston and being picked up or renting cars, and arriving over the course of the evening at my sister's, where a huge vat of simmering chili would be waiting. We'd put everybody up at my sister's, some folks even camping out in her yard, or at friends' and relatives' places around town.

The next day we would run either the New River or the Gauley, a serious six- or seven-hour whitewater rafting trip, depending upon the height and speed of the water. Whereupon it was back to my sister's for a major blowout party of roast pig and mountains of covered dishes and moonshine martinis and country and bluegrass band music, until the last drunken clog-dancing cow came home to collapse in the misty wee hours of Saturday morning.

Everybody pretty much came through this experience unscathed, except for the time one fictioneer almost drowned in the bottom of a boat hung up on rocks in the Lower Gauley, and the time this poet, after sampling much moonshine, fell down my sister's second-floor steps and broke a multitude of ribs.

The raft my sister was riding in one year flipped at "Surprise" (or "Bouncin' Shoals," as old-timers call it), the first rapids you hit in the trip after a long and leisurely early morning float down the New River.

The raft I was in had already run "Surprise," and we were pulled up in an eddy to cover their run. Their raft plunged out of sight into the foamy trough of the rapid, and then as it shot up out of the deep hole it began to flip. I saw my baby sister floating through the air as though it were molasses. I saw my sister disappear in the raging river.

The other six or seven rafters began popping to the surface downstream, but not my sister. We rowed out into the current and began pulling people into our raft, and grabbed the lunch coolers as they swept by. I don't know how he knew, but when the overturned raft raced by us, our guide, "Captain" Keith Spangler, dove into the churning water, only to disappear himself. When he surfaced from under the raft, he had my gasping, choking sister in tow. My sister had been trapped beneath the overturned raft, and she had resigned herself to a death by drowning.

After my sister was flipped into the river that day, I began having a bad dream about her again. In the recurring dream, my sister never surfaces after her raft flips. In the dream, folks in dozens of boats search for her frantically. Folks line the rocky banks looking for her. Then in the dream somehow it is much later, days maybe, weeks, before they find her body, as drowned as Natalie Wood. I have to go identify her body. Only when I look at the body they show me, I can't identify it. Its face is gone, eaten away by fish and turtles. The dream makes me bolt up in bed, wide awake but still somehow deep in the bad dream, my heart pounding wildly.

A mile or so from the center of Billville going south, Maple Avenue becomes the Nickelville Road at the city limits, and on the right maybe a mile further is the old Hess family homestead, a white frame house with a pillared front porch, which is set back off the road by a broad yard of hickory and oak and maple trees, and that is where the mysterious American small-town life of my baby sister and her family unfolds. My sister and brother-in-law had designed and constructed a barn-sized back addition to their rambling old farmhouse, which they used as a family and music room. It is a swell room, with twenty-foot-high ceilings with skylights and hanging plants and long comfortable couches spread about and two antique grand pianos against a far wall. Another wall is covered with my brother-in-law's collection of musical instruments, old-timey guitars and fiddles and ancient banjos. To cement my credentials as a redneck, I had always told my friends back up North my sister lived in a doublewide. Some doublewide.

This is the room you entered from the side driveway, and when I did just that thing that sorry September Tuesday, I observed that my niece, who was stretched out on one of the couches in front of the teevee, seemed a little more sullen than even usual, which probably meant she and her mom had been at it again about cigarette and gas and clothes money my niece felt her mother owed her for being born and bored with life. Actually my niece was a sweet, pretty, brown-haired girl, with a generous heart. It wasn't her fault that pimply teenage life basically sucked.

Judging from the frown I saw on my sister's pretty face when I limped back to the kitchen, they had clearly gone a round or two. My sister was chatty and cheerful as usual, as she scrambled about getting hot food on the table in time for her kids to stuff their faces before they roared out into the night in search of worry and pain to cause their mom. My sister made her living as a kindergarten teacher, and she taught at two different local schools on different days of the week. My sister was one of five teachers nominated by the Board of Education for Fayette County's Teacher of the Year the fall I lived there, an unheard-of honor for a mere kindergarten teacher, as opposed to the usual hotshot high school science teachers or physical education teacher–coaches with winning teams. My sister worked her behind off, and then she rushed home to prepare dinner nightly. My eighteen-year-old niece, who had graduated from high school the previous year, would have spent the day chain-smoking while she talked on the phone and watched her soaps, her way of finding herself. My twenty-two-year-old nephew, the Boy Red, would have probably spent the day in bed, only to get up around dinnertime and gobble his food and rush off to one of his evening classes, and then head on out to the honky-tonks and one of those cradle-robbing thirty-five-year-old hussies who were always landing in his lap, as opposed to mine.

That night, I could really tell something was on my sister's mind. But, I told myself, if it was something really major, like Mom having dropped dead earlier in the day, I was sure she'd get around to mentioning it eventually.

The Boy Red was on the phone pacing up and down in the next room, which had once been a porch but was now a sort of sun room. He had stretched the cord from the phone, which was on the kitchen counter by the door, and he was clearly pissed about something himself, talking low but urgent and agitatedly pumping a fist in the air. Probably a drug deal gone wrong, it occurred to me. It occurred to me to swing back by Grandma Pearl's house, before my sister and I went over to the Naked Spur in Oak Hill, and stash my dope better.

I headed on back to the bathroom, where I found the Boy Red's wet towels and jeans and sweaty shirt and dirty, shit-stained jockey shorts in heaps around the wet, slippery tile floor. The medicine cabinet door was hanging open and water was still running from a faucet in the sink. The commode seat was down and wet with piss. I tore off some toilet paper and wiped it off and then lifted it to take a leak. I started to put the seat back down, as I have been trained to do by the various women in my life, but didn't see the point. But I did turn off the faucet and close the medicine cabinet door and pick up the kid's wet, shitty clothes and towels and put them in the hamper.

Back in the kitchen, I fixed a stiff one and flopped into an old oak chair Charlie once had in his office, which constituted my sister's inheritance, and I tilted it back against a wall. My sister was busy at the kitchen sink across the room, distracted and tense. My brother-in-law had to work late Tuesday nights, so I figured my sister and I would get a chance to talk later out at the Naked Spur, and maybe she would tell me what was wrong. But probably not, especially if it concerned one of her kids. Although I really didn't know either of them very well, I had become a real red-ass when it came to my sister's kids.

As for my nephew, I had never spent any real time around him outside of routine family functions. Basically, the Boy Red was a flesh-and-blood stranger to me. He was tall and wide-receiver rangy and wiry with muscle, and had a flag of flaming red hair that fell to his butt. Basically, my nephew's problem was that he was twenty-two and a cool dude. He had his old man's musical gene, and if something had a string stretched on it he could coax its buried blues or make things rock, and he played a mean mandolin for a hard-driving rock bluegrass group called the Rock Garden Bluegrass Band. The previous year, the kid and a buddy had spent the summer bumming around Europe. They took trains on a Europass and hitchhiked and let pretty girls they met drive them around. They had run the bulls in Pamplona, and my nephew made the nightly national news by being slammed into a wall by a passing pissed bull, which broke his wrist. The boy was fearless and wild, I'll say that for him. When he was younger, he had attempted to skateboard down Fayette Station Road, nearly a vertical downhill run on rough pavement around hairpin turns, an impossible feat, and he had about killed himself, crushing his collarbone and suffering a concussion that put him into a week-long coma. After successfully outrunning the law more than once on a motor-scooter, he tried it driving drunk in his first vehicle at six- teen, and had had his brand-new driver's license suspended for years. He once wrote a school paper about the person who he most admired in the world, and, for God's sake, it was me. My sister had read it to me over the phone, and I swear I choked up. At the end of that summer the Boy Red had bummed around Europe, I gave him the money for school that fall term. I knew he was broke, and, besides, for all the hell he raised, the boy was a good student. The Boy Red was smart and determined and disciplined and I figured he would go places, if he outlived his youth.

Where the Boy Red got on my bad side was when, earlier that summer, he had taken my Red Ride without permission. Not only that, but while my brother-in-law and sister and I were gone, he had skulked into the front downstairs bedroom I always used when I stayed at my sister's house, and he must have searched it high and low before he found my extra set of keys in my Dopp kit. My sister and brother-in-law and I were supposed to be on a road trip in their Chevy van, and it was just a fluke we happened to swing back by their place after we had gassed up and stopped to see Mom, so I could get some tapes from my vehicle.

Only my vehicle wasn't there. When the Boy Red had finally come roaring back in, he was full of more whiny, bullshit excuses than apologies. As far as I was concerned, the kid had to worm his way back into my affections.

So I sat there in my sister's kitchen working myself up into a mood, as I watched the Boy Red storm around in the next room, pumping a fist in the air and jerking the phone this way and that. Then the agitated Boy Red had stretched the cord too far at one point and pulled the phone-machine off the kitchen counter. It crashed to the floor and my sister about came out of her skin. She spun around from the kitchen sink and gasped: —What in the world was that? The Boy Red picked the phone-machine up off the floor and slammed it on the counter, and then he hammered the receiver down on that. —It's the fucken phone, so big fucken deal! Don't make a fucken federal case out of it, all right? the Boy Red suggested to his mother. My sister put her hand to her throat and said: —You don't have to talk to me like that. The Boy Red stepped over beside his mother and leaned down into her face. —I'll talk any fucken way I want, the Boy Red informed his mother, my sister.

I tipped the oak chair back onto the floor and stood up. I reached over to fetch an old iron skillet off a hook on the wall where my sister hung her collection of antique kitchenwares. I walked toward my nephew entertaining the notion of bashing in the side of his skull. Then I saw the stricken look on my sister's face, and I stopped cold. The Boy Red skulked hurriedly out of the kitchen. I hung the skillet back on its hook. I told my sister I would wait for her out at the Naked Spur.

BEERJOINT BALLERINAS

The Naked Spur was the closest thing to a gay bar I came across in Fayette County. It was in a transformed storefront in one of those shabby mini-malls off East Main Street over in lower Oak Hill. The owner had tried several businesses at that location, including a flower shoppe, a bridal boutique, and a dog-grooming salon. He seemed to have hit pay dirt in the gay bar business.

Wagon wheels lined with lanterns hung on chains from the Naked Spur's high ceiling, and the walls were covered with murals depicting old Western-town street scenes in which the sultry cowboys had real cute bubble butts. This was where my sister and some of her girlfriends went to take their line-dancing lessons on Tuesday nights. I would usually tag along and hang out at the bar, shooting the breeze with the homosexuals. Now, these were homosexuals you wouldn't want to fuck with (unless it was their idea), real redneck homos, who were funny and friendly and didn't act so superior and stuck-up to somebody straight like a lot of citified homosexuals do. They were just good-old-boy fairies who liked to share the joys of oral sex, maybe dabble in a little blissful buggering out in the beds of pickups in the parking lot. They were my best drinking buddies in the entire county.

That Tuesday night the Boy Red almost died for breaking bad on his mom, I sat at a table alone, broody and dark while I watched my little sister spin and kick and hop in a herd of mostly beefy but to my eyes beautiful babes bulging in tight, fringed, colorful Western wear, who were as light and graceful on their feet as beerjoint ballerinas. Their dance instructor was a dandy dude who wore a chartreuse cowboy hat sporting a pink feather and a cowboy shirt that looked as though it had been cut from a chartreuse Confederate flag, with silver sequins on its fringed, stars-and-bars shoulders. He was famously light-footed in his pink lambskin cowboy boots and, buddy, could he dance. Outside of him, my sister was the best dancer out there, though, as they all spun and scooted and boogied to that Billy Ray Cyrus idiot tune "Achy Breaky Heart." When the dance instructor called for a break and my sister returned to the table, she downed my nearly full bottle of beer in a gulp. I got up to get another beer for me and a tall glass of ice-water for her. We sat there for a while, quietly watching a few of the cowboy couples dancing cheek-to-cheek with one another like Marlboro Boys In Love to some suggestive k. d. lang tunes.

My sister hadn't had much to say when she first arrived at the Naked Spur for her line-dancing class. We'd just made the usual chitchat about Mom's travails, and by her very avoidance of the subject I could tell my sister was truly embarrassed by the Boy Red's behavior. But I knew my sister forgave him anything; he was her Baby Boy Red, after all. I hate that afternoon talk-show Oprah jargon, but basically my sister's excuses for him *enabled* the Boy Red to be a piece of shit, too slick and cool to pick his own crappy pants up off the bathroom floor. The fact that he had a wild-boy rap sheet didn't bother or impress me much. In that respect, I had been a real role model for him. In that respect, I had delivered up a lot more criminal activity than the Boy Red ever dreamed of being forgiven for. I was real curious, though, to see what sort of excuses my sister would make for her son, that he was on the rag maybe, or he had been sleep-cursing his Mom, or that he stole my vehicle that time because he had to transport a dying friend to the hospital. Finally my sister simply rolled her eyes with annoyance, and launched lamely into how the Boy Red had stayed up all last night studying for a test (right, I thought, studying for a biology test out at the Pines with that thirty-six-year-old black-haired harlot named Susie who had caught my own eye), and how he hadn't eaten all day and how he had a blood sugar problem like his dad, and when he didn't get his proper rest and didn't eat he had mood swings he couldn't control, and how terrible he felt that he had showed his ass like he had in front of his uncle (right, I thought, because his uncle had been prepared to dispatch his brains with an iron skillet up beside his head, which is absolutely the only way his uncle, being so deep in his dotage, could have whipped that big rangy redneck). At that point, my sister reminded me of the time the Boy Red had written that essay about admiring his big uncle Chuck more than anybody else in the world. I got to thinking, well, the Boy Red couldn't be all bad if he had my baby sister for a mom and admired his big uncle Chuck.

When my sister finally wound down with her lame loving litany of excuses for the Boy Red's butt-hole behavior, I announced to her out of the blue that my friend Holly would be driving down from Pittsburgh to visit me at some point and that I wanted my sister to meet her. My sister didn't say a word. She looked off toward the cowboys in lust at the bar.

My sister fanned herself with napkins, and when her line-dancing professor fluttered his hands like little flapping rebel flags to signal for everybody to get back out on the floor pleasepleaseplease, she gulped down her mug of ice-water and got up groaning. My sister turned back to me suddenly and hissed that she didn't want to meet this Holly person, that she didn't even want to set eyes on this Holly person, and I understood this.

I moseyed on up to the bar and got a George Dickel Ditch. Somebody tugged lightly on my ponytail and I looked around. A big, burly, unshaven, badass-looking guy with a clearly oft-broken nose and fierce black eyes and evil scars on his battered face, who was wearing a patched plaid shirt and baseball cap, loomed there before me. This fellow was another frequent patron of the Skyline Drive-In, and he was known as Sweetest Bill. You would never in a million years guess Sweetest Bill's sexual orientation if it weren't for his bright red lipstick and heavily massacred Tammy Faye Bakker big blues. We high-fived and punched each other in the shoulder, and I bought Sweetest a Grasshopper. Yep, I told Sweetest when he mentioned it, yep, I knew Baddest Bill had a boner about me. Apparently old Baddest had been out at Charlie's Pub Saturday night looking for that asshole Little Hank, namely *moi,* on account of Mary X. But Sweetest had taken my side of things, he told me, by informing Baddest that if he fucked with me, the nephew of the late great Hank Williams, he just might end up one maligned sorry son-of-a-bitch in somebody's country song. I thanked Sweetest from the bottom of my heart. Then I bought him another Grasshopper. Sweetest soon became involved in a mild dispute with a couple of fairies at the bar about the relative merits of the butts of George Straight, Billy Ray Cyrus, and Garth Brooks. George has the best butt, I opined, and after a heartbeat of reflection we all high-fived on that, and then I turned away to sip my Ditch and big-time brood.

Frankly, the thought of Baddest Bill after my butt gave me the serious willies. Maybe I should have Holly postpone her visit, maybe forever, I reflected. Maybe I should simply get out of town. Maybe I should simply call Holly that very night and tell her once and for all that I was too old for her, and then just get the hell out of the country. What manner of fifty-something, so-called college professor would find himself in such circumstances? I was supposed to be on a university sabbatical, doing research, reflecting, having insights, epiphanies, coming to conclusions, for God's sake, and writing about it all sagely for the sake of posterity and to belatedly justify my tenure. I was supposed to be an *author,* for God's sake! A published *novelist*! I took a sip of my George Dickel Ditch and looked at my reflection in a blue-tinted mirror behind the bar. I arched my eyebrows and wrinkled my forehead and etcetcetc. . . , for all the good that old false-face got me.

According to *The West Virginia Book of Lists,* compiled by Gerald Tomlinson and Richard C. Weigen, there are ten "well-known" novelists who were born in West Virginia. Mary Lee Settle, who was born in Charleston in 1918, won the National Book Award in 1978 for her novel *Blood Tie.* David Grubb, 1919–1980 (Moundsville), wrote *The Night of the Hunter,* which was made into a movie in 1955, starring Robert Mitchum. Then there was William Hoffman, *The Trumpet Unblown* (1955), and Clyde Ware, author of *The Innocents* (1969) and *The Eden Tree* (1971). John Knowles, author of the wonderful *A*

Separate Peace, was born in Fairmont in 1926. Then there was Keith Maillard and Richard Currey. Then there was Meredith Sue Willis, born in Clarksburg in 1946, who spent ten years writing the Blair Morgan trilogy, and Denise Giardina, 1951, of Bluefield, author of *Storming Heaven.* And then there was Jayne Anne Phillips, 1952– (Buckannon): "One of the most gifted writers of her generation, Jayne Anne Phillips won many awards for her short stories before the appearance in 1984 of her novel *Machine Dreams,* praised by Nadine Gordimer as 'an elegiac work that reaches one's deepest emotions.' "

Was it too late for me to write an elegiac work that could reach a reader's deepest emotions? This hillbilly book about southern West Virginia I was supposedly writing, say? Was it too late for me, at fifty-something, to become a "well-known" West Virginia writer? Could I finally secure that fame which had so far eluded my grasp? Or would Baddest Bill kill me dead as Hank Williams, end of story?

BOGEYMEN IN LOVE

Sure, my little sister was smarter and more intuitive than me. But I'm the detective who finally solved the ancient Case of the Cab-Stand Brown Paper Bag. I solved that case years after we had witnessed those bogeymen hugging on the old cemetery steps, when I had discovered by pure serendipity that late at night at the downtown cab-stand, a fellow could purchase mason jars filled with tasty full-tilt bootleg liquor served up for toting in brown paper bags. That's where by pure serendipity I met Boomer Bill, another regular customer at the cab-stand.

Boomer Bill was the town drunk back in those bygone days of my sister's and my youth, a position he held for decades. Boomer Bill was this kindly little stick of a fellow whose ex-miner lungs were so coal-dust black, he had to shout to get any air behind his words. His shout sounded like the croak of a frog. Boomer would cough and croak, croak and cough, to get his point across. Then he would take a drink of tasty full-tilt bootleg cab-stand booze in a brown paper bag as he collapsed back, wheezing and blue-faced, into the frail, failing fish-lungs of himself from his effort to tell. His wormy lips always had a greasy dark line of expelled coal-grime around them. His tongue wiggled like a black worm. His breath looked like a shadow passing before his blanched mushroomy underground face.

Boomer lived in an old Second World War-era canvas tent pitched behind the monumental Montgomery family tombstone in the old cemetery at the edge of town. For a time in my late teens and early twenties, Boomer Bill had become my steadfast friend, chief drinking companion, and mentor. Then one night Boomer saved my life.

125

A light rain was falling that night. Boomer and I were sitting in his tent, our backs pressed against the monumental Montgomery family tombstone, facing uphill into the overgrown graveyard, passing a brown paper bag of tasty full-tilt, watching the shadows of our feet swell and fall like scary television puppets in the lantern light. We listened to the soft puckpuckpuck of the rain on canvas, while jawboning about life and love and the essential nature of loss. I was in a heartbroken mode of mind that night. My blond and beautiful high school honey Ruthie (a dead ringer for Sandra Dee) had returned all my 471 love letters and 502 sad gothic poems concerning the nature of teenage true love. Ruthie had found a new true love. A handsome Marshall College star halfback whose butt I would kick in exactly three weeks, as it turned out, for all the good that got me. So why should I go on living at all now, was my current urgent question for Boomer Bill that rainy night. It seemed to me my life had been basically reduced to two options: one, lay down on the railroad tracks that cut through town and let a freight train run over me, or two, jump off the bridge into the cold swift dark waters of the Kanawha River to drown like a doomed rat of romance.

I passed Boomer the package of 471 love letters and 502 sad gothic poems that I had re-taped and marked "return to sender." I asked Boomer to drop that package in the mail for me tomorrow, for this rainy night was my last on the face of this Earth. Boomer pushed his old battered gray fedora back on his head with a thumb, and he took a drink of tasty full-tilt. Boomer coughed for a spell before croaking out that I was a dumb-ass squirt what didn't know what love was. I was a dumb-ass idiot squirt what didn't have no idea what loss meant. Boomer began blubbering then, which wasn't all that unusual really, for he was a sweet sentimental soul, who could cry at the mere sight of pretty flowers fading or hobbling old folks or fresh road-kill. Boomer was the only person I ever met who would mourn road-kill. Boomer started telling me a story he had never shared with me before that night.

Boomer had been in love only once in his life, he coughed and croaked and blubbered to me, his mustache shiny with black snot. The love of Boomer's life had been this really tall person people considered strange and scary. This really tall different person had been as misunderstood and maligned as Boomer had been over the course of his own miserable life. What Boomer and the only love of his life had basically shared besides love was an understanding of the nature of real isolation and loneliness. They were both of them really different oddballs, Boomer and the love of his life, which set them apart from the rest of the folks in this world. They were all each other ever had or needed, this really tall oddball and Boomer. Their time together had been wonderful. Boomer's only love had loved things like poetry, and music, good music, classical stuff, high-toned guys like Liberace. Boomer's only love had been gentle and kind and had a generosity of spirit that was almost religious in nature. But finally it had got to be too much for the very tall oddball Boomer loved. That tall oddball Boomer loved could not stand life as a freak that even little kids followed around town and chased and tormented to no end. So that sweet, gentle, strange, tall person had done exactly what I was bragging I was about to do, namely lay down on the town tracks and wait for the next train to heaven or hell. Well, the very tall oddball Boomer had loved with all his heart had caught the express to heaven, that much was sure to Boomer. What I claimed I wanted to die for was mere pussy, pure and simple, Boomer blubbered to me, plus loss of esteem. Pussy ain't love. Pridefulness ain't no kind of love, Boomer coughed and croaked and blubbered.

Boomer coughed and croaked and blubbered on and on that night, the rain falling soft and sentimental on the canvas as though from clouds in a black-and-white movie about Ireland. Deep in the embrace of sentimentality, I put my arm about that old blubbering bogeyman with snot rolling out of his nostrils like midnight worms. His beard was shining with it. Old Boomer clearly had not bathed in maybe ten years. But I held that little smelly bogeyman in my arms for a while. It was like hugging a turd. But I was a kid and kindhearted in those days. I hugged that old drunk snotty bogeyman who smelled like a fart, patted him like a puppy. I heard a train whistle. I heard a train rumbling down over the hill as it passed through town. The very train I had hoped to hitch a ride on into either the hereafter or beginning of the next chapter of my unfolding famous life.

I watched my little sister twirl and spin across the board floor that night at the Naked Spur, her joyful pretty face radiant. All the friendly fellows at the bar watched her too, tapping their pointy pink boots in time with the country rock-a-billy boogie my little sister danced her heart out to. In the enormity of that small-town now, my little sister was as famous as you would ever need to be. My little sister's small-town fame utterly filled the mysterious immensity of that local moment. My little sister was famous in that county for just who she was, a woman married to a bald ugly—albeit funny beloved—man who could pick and grin and carry a tune, a mother of two children who were not currently incarcerated, a loving and beloved teacher of ignorant wood-hicks infested with head-lice. My little sister was regal in all her ordinariness. Now, that was what fame was all about, I reflected. A lot of immediate ordinary local folks who knew your basic best story by heart and mostly believed in it. I felt my heart swell with love and pure pride for my little sister and the famous dance she did.

Nevertheless, I entertained a tossed salad of mixed emotions that night concerning my little sister and what her life meant in comparison to my own. When my sister finished her famous dance, she walked back toward our table, waving her hands before her glowing face like little fans, only to be intercepted by a bevy of bouncy cowboys from the bar, who were dying to embrace my little sister, blowing kisses by her cheeks and twittering about the essential grace of her boogying-on-down dance. Loads of famous people are stuck-up snots. A few famous folks are full of gracious magnanimity. My sister was full of that. If I ever got famous, I'd be a stuck-up snot. But my little sister was uppity about meeting my girlfriend. Okay, so I was pissed, not to mention jealous. So my little sister was smarter and more intuitive than me, and famous to boot. And magnanimous too. How dare my little sister judge me?

If bogeymen can be in love, why not old coots and beautiful women young enough to be their daughters? As my smart, intuitive, magnanimous, famous, glad-hearted sister sashayed through the hugging crowd of admiring homos, I made a decision. I had never told my sister that I had solved the Case of the Cab-Stand Brown Paper Bag all by myself, plus the Secret of the Cemetery Steps Hugging-Bogeymen. Basically I hadn't told her this because I wasn't excited about my sister discovering that my best friend and boon companion, not to mention mentor, during my formative years had been the falling-down town drunk. But now I wanted to clear the air. I wanted to come clean. I wanted to tell my smart, intuitive, magnanimous, famous, glad-hearted sister Scout how I had solved the Case of the Murdered Sweet Innocent Bogeyman, how in our shared storied youth we, who had stalked after the love of Boomer's life, were the real Evil-Doers who walked by night.

book three

FAMOUS FEUDISTS

SWEET SUICIDE

Cultivating what I considered to be a courageous and admirable melancholy, I spent much of my time while I was living in southern West Virginia driving for days on end around the twisty mountain roads of Fayette and Wyoming and Wayne and Logan and Mercer and McDowell and Bloody Mingo Counties, heartland of the southern West Virginia coalfields. This was the country where the infamous Hatfield and McCoy feud occurred, whose bloody battles raged for years back and forth across the Tug Fork River after the Civil War. The bloody, shootist saga of Two-Gun Sid Hatfield also unfolded down in those parts, including the famous *Battle of Matewan,* or *Matewan Massacre,* depending upon your politics. I had no real clear notion of what those histories of spastic mayhem and bloodshed had to do with my own mock-heroic, essentially comedic ceremonial old-coot rite of passage, but I transversed that sacrificial landscape seeking linkage to the violent, albeit vital, stories of another time, attempting, I guess, to invoke the fervor of that other day, a dangerous, turbulent, adolescent era, when folks imagined that they harbored hopes worth living and dying for, and had a few laughs amid the general bloodletting to boot.

On a road trip I made down to Matewan, I picked up a tourist brochure advertising a special Powhatan Arrow steam train excursion. The old steam train was to travel down through the picturesque Ohio and Tug River Valleys from Ironton, Ohio, to Matewan, that infamous shootout site, where the townfolks would host a shindig. How rewarding, I reflected, it might be for my girlfriend Holly and me to travel together by old-timey steam train down into that dark disaster-haunted country.

How romantic it might be, I reflected, to wander the streets of Matewan where nobody knew us, hand in hand openly, casting each other extravagant looks of longing, unconcerned with glares of Christian admonition at the sordid sight of an old coot kissing a girl young enough to be his daughter in public, clearly no outing with an aging uncle, while I pointed out places of historical interest to Holly, such as the exact spot where the brains of Albert Felts had splattered like sudden fierce rain upon being bushwhacked by Sid Hatfield, that sanctified miners' hero of the great coalfield wars.

I drove to Pittsburgh to fetch Holly, and before we headed south again to make our trip to Matewan, we took her kids north to a halfway point between Pittsburgh and Oil City, Holly's home town, where we met up with her parents at a KFC in some little wide spot in the road. Holly's mom, a woman a year younger than myself, was chatty and tolerant like the couple of other times I had encountered her. Holly's daddy, who was eight months my senior, could barely stand to look in my direction on this, our second meeting. Every year without fail Holly's daddy, the quintessential, well, Marlboro man, employing simply a bow and arrow, bagged at least one deer deep in rugged woods he knew like the back of his hand. He was a lineman for the phone company who still shimmied up poles daily for a living. He was wiry and muscular and he was a fifty-something-year old man who could still walk on his hands. A few years back, his once-jet-black beard and hair had turned snow-white almost overnight upon being informed by Holly's mom that his beautiful darling daughter, his own shining girl, was knocked up. All during that hurry-up wedding ceremony when the apple of his eye *had* to get hitched to a boy Holly's daddy considered a total jerk (correctly, as it turned out), he had bawled like a baby. Averting our eyes and mumbling hellos, Dad and I shook hands briskly, and then everybody turned their undivided attention to the antics of the kids as they pretended to sword-fight with KFC extra-crispy chicken legs.

The boy who got Holly pregnant was from her home town. They had ridden bikes together as kids. Holly was a high school majorette, and he was the captain of the football team. She had never much liked that beer-loud, loutish boy back then. Only years later in college when their paths crossed, and Holly was on the rebound from losing her first true love, a beautiful, 6'5" muscular boy with a waist-length mane of blond hair who played drums in a Buffalo band, did she give her future husband a second look. Holly dropped out of college when she gave birth to a darling baby daughter. Three years later a darling baby boy had been born. Holly settled into life as a stay-at-home mom baking bread or cookies daily. She planned perfect meals and labored relentlessly to transform the old, ramshackle, Victorian townhouse they had purchased into a showcase home you might someday find in a magazine. Only late at night alone in her tiny attic studio would Holly work on her oils of old graveyards she painted from memory and misty seashores she only imagined, while she listened to an obscure campus radio station which played '80s retro-rock that stirred her memories. Holly would yearn with all her heart for that boy who had smelled like Copenhagen Cologne and played drums for a traveling Buffalo band.

Time passed, and after many pitched battles with her husband about her wish to return to school and payoff blow jobs that made her gag, Holly finally signed up for classes at Pitt in 1992 to complete her degree in fine arts. She was required to take a certain number of English courses. Holly had always enjoyed writing, even suspected she had a talent for it, although most of her recent reading had been trashy, juicy, romantic paperback novels with Fabio in a clawed shirt on their covers. On something of a lark, Holly signed up for an Introduction to Creative Writing evening course. She had had to miss the first class because her husband didn't show up in time to baby-sit. He had stopped to watch sports and drink beer with work buddies, claiming he forgot it was Holly's first class night. One of my pet peeves is students blowing off the first class. Holly claims I gave her some serious grief about it when she showed up for the second class, and she seriously considered dropping that suck course from an obvious asshole of an aging, so-called college professor with an aging-hippie ponytail and tattoo, but then Holly didn't.

• • •

After leaving the kids with her parents, Holly and I headed directly for Billville. I had told Holly that Lovelene was up from Charlotte for the weekend and staying at Grandma's Pearl's little house, which explained why, for the first night of Holly's and my trip down to Matewan to ride that old train, I made reservations at a bed & breakfast in Billville called The White Horse Inn. It was a twenty-two-room mansion, built in 1906 by a Fayette County coal operator, that had been known as the old Ballard Place. It was a great old white-frame house of unusual architecture, a sort of huge Cape Cod bungalow with Southern-plantation pillared porches wrapped around it and steep, green gable roofs, and it was surrounded by vast yards. The old house had stood vacant and crumbling for decades due to feuding siblings, and at one point I had even considered attempting to buy the ruin myself, but when the old house finally had come on the market, a wealthy Yankee couple had snapped it up.

After dinner that night, Holly and I wandered all around the old beautifully restored house hand in hand, Holly daydreaming whispery about what all she planned to do with it after we had murdered our gracious, albeit obviously healthy-as-horses hosts, and got our bloody hands on the place.

Later, Holly ran a bubble bath and lit scented candles she had placed around the bathroom. She tried to float these little green candles shaped like seahorses in the tub, but they toppled over as soon as we slipped into the steaming water. I shampooed her hair and shaved her legs and under her arms while we talked whispery about our day, and every time our water would begin to cool Holly would unplug the tub and let it drain while running more hot steaming water. When we finally got out, we dried each other off with big fluffy white towels and then, as she slowly turned around in front of me, I rubbed almond oil over every inch of her warm skin, which glistened in the candle flame. Holly was a lovely girl, slim and petite, with long, thick, coppery hair that she often suddenly swung loose and wild for effect back over her soft sweet-smelling shoulders.

We made love in the big brass bed, and then, after Holly had banged on my chest and further revived me with mouth-to-mouth resuscitation, we lay there listening to rain on the slate roof and wind that blew against the old leaded windows. We held one other and fantasized about the future. After we buried our hosts out back in the woods, and I secured my divorce (Holly's divorce had become final that March), we would buy this place and move down here and raise the kids in this timeless small town. And we'd do anything necessary to have a little baby of our own, artificial insemination even, if it came to that. What Holly said she wanted more than anything was to go through a pregnancy with a man she loved. Holly's ex-husband Bert had been such a butthead about it. Ex-Bert hadn't wanted to touch Holly when she was pregnant, and after both her kids were born he made her wear a nursing bra whenever they had sex so that icky milk from her breasts wouldn't leak on him.

We snuggled while Holly chattered on and on about how she would change things in the great old house. Our doomed hosts had good taste, and the restoration was admirable, but Holly had her own ideas. She would turn the barn out back into a huge studio–gallery, where she could paint and hang her artwork, and I could use the cottage out back for my office. And maybe we could put in a pool for the kids in one of the enormous side yards, and a tennis court, and with all this land the kids could have ponies, and we could have all the dogs we wanted and cats (Holly already had four goddamn cats and counting). And chickens, I suggested, and pigs and goats and cows. Holly said over her dead body. Unless they were pets. Pets, Holly? Pigs for pets? Chickens for pets? I thought you were a real redneck girl! I flabbergasted. Well, the only chicken that will ever get choked around here is this one, Holly said and reached down under the damp sheet and gathered my hoary old member in her dear little hand. Whereupon she gave that old buzzard a squeeze that brought tears to my eyes. When Holly shivered at a flash of lightning, I pulled her tighter against me, and the fragrance of her hair and face made my old heart skip a beat. What occurred to me at that illuminated moment was that I could have died right then about as lucky as I figured I would ever get in the love department.

That sweet night wore on as Holly wet my neck with further

admonishments of love and whispered urgently in my old echoing cave of a hairy ear that she would take care of me. She would feed me right and, to make sure I got my exercise, she would fuck me morning, noon, and night. The obvious irony of which was that it would surely kill me, stop my old heart cold some morning, noon, or night, but oh what a sweet suicide. She would love and care for me, Holly whispered. With her taking care of me, Holly argued, I might not finish falling apart for another five years, or ten or twenty years for that matter. I cannot deny that when Holly talked like that, my old heart would soar for those moments I let myself dream along with her.

Most often when Holly talked like that, we would be clutching one another after making love, me struggling for breath, blue in the face, collapsed there sweaty and exhausted, clearly on the cusp of a heart attack. When my coughing and wheezing had abated, and I could focus my sight, we would gaze deeply, nakedly into one another's startled eyes, those amazed, googoo orbs, and sure, I let myself believe in tomorrow, assuming that I didn't croak in those ensuing critical moments. But I was fooling myself, and I was fooling little Holly.

Much later, I lay there in the dark holding Holly in my arms as she slept, feeling her warm breath on my bare shoulder, my nose buried in damp hair that smelled like apples, and I thought about what lay ahead. Had I imposed upon myself a future as irrevocable as the past? I felt myself scattered among a hundred places in parallel worlds. I had come to feel as though I woke up every day in a different world. Was Holly simply dream material? When I was with her, I wasn't stuck with being myself. But what I could not let myself imagine yet was leaving that sureness with my wife (that pathetic old story I know), and that bossy little cat we called our baby, and that big yellow brick barn of a house on a hill we called home. I called it the Norman Bates Boarding House, and it looked so spooky and haunted that neighborhood kids trembled deliciously when they skulked up the twisty, broken-concrete steps to trick-or-treat us on Halloween. It occurred to me at that point that a big boohoo might hit the spot, but I had company, so I swallowed hard and squeezed my eyes shut.

What I also could not imagine was continuing on in a perfectly comfortable way of life that would kill me with contentedness. But whose fault was that? I could not imagine life without my wife of nearly twenty years. I could not imagine life, what I had left of it anyway, without Holly. But what life was possible for a damaged old coot like me and a wonderful young woman, finally? How long would it be before she rolled over one morning, her young fresh skin knowing first, and took a real hard look at that old fart beside her in bed? There was absolutely no private mythology left behind what passed for my personality. Not unlike other foolish, floundering middle-aged men, I didn't believe in a thing that seemed to matter. My life had broken down like an old heap on the highway.

I wanted to talk with my wife of nearly twenty years. I wanted to call her and tell her the truth I owed her. I just wanted to hear her dear voice. I just plain old missed her. But I knew that if I did call her I would simply lie some more. I would lie my head off about what was really going on in my life, and at some point I would ask my wife to put the receiver against our kitty's little ear, who would be cuddled up on my wife's lap, and let me whisper her dumb little name over and over, Lulu Lulu Lulu, tease her until her little black ears twitched and she pulled back from the phone to give it a look of utter kitty astonishment, which would crack my wife up. And I would crack up.

Yeats wondered if art could exhaust life. I know I mine the substance of my own life for material whether I mean to or not. I sure wish I had more imagination. I've always admired writers of real imagination. I didn't know whose story I wanted to tell finally, or how many stories I wanted to tell, of all the curious stories to choose from in that window to other worlds called West Virginia. I only knew I would finally find those stories among the maze of dark hollows and hills of an interior landscape, stories that I felt would echo the stories of my own interior landscape. And the exploration would be vertical, like a deep-shaft mine. Maybe I was simply writing to escape, after all, to make a workable fiction of my own life, the caricature-in-chief. And if I couldn't be trusted with the story of my own life, how could I be trusted with the stories of other people's lives?

Feeling old and tired out and afraid of the dark, feeling as shadowy and lost as the sad, renegade ghost of Elvis, I pulled little Holly tightly against me and held on for dear life. So I lay there feeling sorry for myself that night. I try without success not to remember, reflecting again upon how rewarding a big blubber might be, if only I had been alone, and I had sort of metaphorically hung down my head instead and sniffled, while I imagined myself tragic and handsome in the dark.

HILLBILLY HISTORY

My middle name is Alfonso. Laugh at that at your own peril. As a secretly poetical, testiclely-challeged boy trying to grow up tough in southern West Virginia, this middle name occasioned more than a few fisticuffs. I got this pathetic moniker from my paternal grandfather's older brother. My Great-Uncle Alfonso had been a mild-mannered bookkeeper by nature and trade and had been considered peculiar because he was rumored to read books he didn't have to and even, for God's sake, pen poems. A story about my Uncle Alfonso has come down in the family concerning one night when he was traveling by train from his current coal company bookkeeping job in Williamson to his home with his folks in Charleston. An hour into the trip, Uncle Alfonso decided to stretch his legs a bit and repair to the club car for a cigar. Uncle Alfonso was alone for a spell as he smoked in that late-night car, until a slim, well-dressed young man walked in and took the seat opposite him. They nodded and presently took to passing the time talking about the weather and what-not. They got to talking about the troubles in the Tug River Valley coal-fields, and at some point, it dawned upon Uncle Alfonso that he was conversing with the notorious Sid Hatfield. After a time, Sid pulled a flask from his coat pocket and suggested they have them a little nip. My Uncle Alfonso, who was not a drinking man, said thank you anyway, sir, but I don't believe I care for any spirits at present. Sid Hatfield grinned and nonchalantly reached back under his coat, and this time he pulled out a long revolver, which he placed on the seat beside him. Then Sid offered Uncle Alfonso the flask again, while smiling that famous golden smile of his, and he quietly commented: —There ain't nothing lonelier than a

feller drinking all by hisself on a train at night. In relating this experience, my Uncle Alfonso was reputed to have always wound up the story
with the remark: —That was the first and last time I ever got drunk in
my life.

I had heard stories about Sid Hatfield since childhood, but I first
became truly interested in him when I watched John Sayles's critically
acclaimed 1987 movie *Matewan*, which basically deals with the people
and events that led up to—and including—the bloody shootout on May
19, 1920, down in the streets of Matewan when ten men were shot and
killed. In the movie, the character of Sid Hatfield (played by a young
actor named David Strathairn) emerges rather slowly, appearing suddenly at key points in the narrative, and then fading back into the
shadows of the story like the *Lone Enigma*. Dapper but unprepossessing
in a dark suit, vest, starched high white collar and tie, wearing a bowler
hat and a big shiny badge on his coat and two huge revolvers in holsters
on his belt, Sid is an armed and clearly dangerous presence on the edges
of the action, but mostly an onlooker, until the final bloody showdown
with the Baldwin-Felts gun thugs in the streets of Matewan, in which
Sid was a principal participating shootist. Sid is a sympathetic character
in Sayles's movie version of the Matewan battle, a hero even, certainly
to the miners. But finally I found Sid's characterization too one-dimen-
sional, too righteous and taciturn and grave, to capture the laughing
wily trickster Sid Hatfield of mountain legend.

In so-called real life, Sid Hatfield was a little bastard-boy who went
into the coal mines at thirteen. He grew up to be a tough hardnosed
little banty-rooster of a character who had a way with his fists. He was
also considered to be a rather good-looking boy, with soft light brown
hair, high dramatic cheekbones and cleft chin, and a big engaging grin
that sported teeth of gold (picture the actor Matt Dillon with a real sunburst of a smile). One of Sid's various nicknames was "Smiling Sid." Sid
also sported dumbo-size jug ears, which apparently the gals found fun to
fondle. And Sid did have a reputation as a ladies' man, not to mention a

reputation as a fun-loving hell-raiser who could be found almost nightly at the Blue Goose Saloon drinking and playing pool and poker and hooting and hollering it up with his wild buddies.

Another of Sid's nicknames was "Two-Gun Sid Hatfield." Sid and his pals, including the wild, dangerous Ed Chambers, who looked like a choirboy, liked to hang out on the banks of the Tug Fork River, sipping moonshine and target-practicing. Somebody would toss a few potatoes high in the air, and Sid would quick-draw his gun and blast them to smithereens in the blink of an eye. The Wild West pulp fiction and the shoot-'em-up cowboy movies, the very mythos of the old Wild West, had found their way back even into the isolated mountains of West Virginia by then, and it was as though the Wild West sense of frontier had folded back on itself there, layered itself like a seam of coal running through the West Virginia hills. And that Wild West movie-mythos had found itself resurrected there in that ongoing frontier called Appalachia. Sid was respected and feared far and wide as a first-rate Two-Gun Shootist.

Which was one quality that caught the eye of C. C. Testerman, the popular mayor of Matewan. Mayor Testerman was a respectable thirty-seven-year-old married businessman with a young son, so his fast friendship with the redoubtable Sid Hatfield was surprising to many townfolk. Mayor Testerman was a pudgy, balding man, but he was a natty dresser like Sid, and he favored the miners in their disputes with the coal companies, as did Sid. Mayor Testerman made Sid the town's first chief of police, which was a widespread popular choice. The miners considered Sid to be one of them. He didn't put on airs and he was fair-minded. He wore his badge and guns, but no uniform. Rarely would Sid arrest a miner. When they became wild and woolly, Sid either cooled them off or joined in the fun himself. When they got in fights, Sid either broke them up or joyfully jumped into the scrap himself, and he got them home safely when they got drunk. To the amusement of the miners, Sid had his own brushes with the county law that winter of 1919–20, once for possessing illegal moonshine and once for soundly kicking a mine guard's butt. Both times, Mayor Testerman posted bond and kept Sid in his job. Sid took to taking his suppers at his new best friend's house and whiling away most evenings sitting out on Mayor Testerman's front porch, along with Mayor Testerman's twenty-six-year-old wife Jessie, a brown-haired local beauty famous for her dewy skin and dimples.

Both Sid and the mayor backed the miners' unionizing efforts in the Tug River Valley. Sid stood guard when, night after night that spring, the miners packed Matewan's tiny Baptist Church to join up. Three hundred miners joined the union in one night alone. Those were brave, heady days. It was as though, in their imaginations, those mountaineer miners moved fearlessly within a fiction of the old frontier, wherein, dead-tired at kitchen tables after shifts in the deep mines, and maybe having farmed rocky hillsides long into the dark after their shifts, they could be free-spirited Wild West cowboys or famous gunfighters in their dangerous daydreams as they ate their cold suppers late and alone. They could become frontiersmen, holy outsiders, magical West Virginia warriors, who would join up with the union no matter what the risks, and fight tooth and nail for their rights as men and miners and shoot down fucken scabs and Baldwin-Felts gun-thugs and strike for as long as it took, passing that mason jar of moonshine around the blazing campfire night after night, until hell froze over if it came to that.

As the union drive heated up, Al Felts, field manager of the hated Baldwin-Felts detective agency, bragged that he would crush the union organizing effort "if it puts one hundred men in jail and costs a million dollars." Felts offered a secret five hundred dollars apiece bribe to Mayor Testerman and Sid Hatfield if they would let his boys place machine guns in Matewan in order to mow down striking commie miners. Sid told Felts to kiss his ass and stay the hell out of town. By May 15, Sid's twenty-seventh birthday, three thousand miners along the Tug belonged to the United Mine Workers. And hundreds of them, who had been fired and evicted from their company homes the moment they joined the union, lived in tent colonies, where women and children circulated hungrily about the swampy cities of patched canvas on bent boards for sidewalks, and raggy clothes flapped like the sad flags of some defeated army on lines along the dark Tug Fork. The miners were angry and seething for atonement, for mountain revenge, for frontier justice. Guns bristled everywhere.

• • •

Wednesday, May 19, 1920, was a dark, drizzly day in Matewan. A posse of thirteen Baldwin-Felts detectives, led by Albert and Lee Felts, had come into town on the noon train from Bluefield that day to evict more miners and their families from their company-owned homes. Word spread that the thugs had forced families with children out into the rain at gunpoint. Word was that the gun-thugs had thrown a pregnant woman out on the street, and a sick child and a little baby in its crib. Union miners hurried home to get their guns.

Back in town after their day's dirty work, the Baldwin-Felts gun-thugs were waiting around for the 5:00 train back to Bluefield. Al Felts was standing on the sidewalk in front of Chambers Hardware talking to one of his men, when Sid Hatfield approached him from behind and jerked a pistol from under his coat and fired directly at the back of Felts's head at very close range. The front of Felts's face exploded, bloody brains flying all over the street, and he collapsed dead as a doornail on the spot. Instantly the firing became general from every direction. That was one story. Sid's story was that near the railroad tracks in the center of Matewan, he and Mayor Testerman had confronted the force of thirteen heavily armed Baldwin-Felts gun-thugs over the day's illegal evictions and contested arrest warrants. Sid said that after heated words, Al Felts suddenly drew his pistol and, without warning, shot a hole in the middle of Mayor Testerman's belly the size of a fist. Instantly Sid whipped out his own pistol and commenced shooting that dirty vicious dog Al Felts to pieces. Other witnesses said miners in the hardware store shot first, killing Mayor Testerman by accident. Others claimed they were certain a bullet from Sid's own gun was the one that killed Mayor Testerman, making a widow of the woman Sid was known to admire. But whoever fired first, on the rainy streets of Matewan that day the scene suddenly erupted into an orgasmic explosion of gun-blasts and splurting blood and blasted men tumbling into all of death, and in a heartbeat Albert Felts and Mayor Testerman lay on the ground dead and dying, and before it was all over, seven Baldwin-Felts gun-thugs, two miners, and Mayor Testerman were hillbilly history.

Sid Hatfield had become an instant folk-hero to the unionized miners in the coalfields. After ten days of intense mourning, Jessie, the lovely young widow of Mayor Testerman, eloped with Sid to Huntington. Before they could be married, Sid and Jessie were arrested in their room at the Florentine Hotel and charged with "improper relations." Carted off to jail, the couple was unrepentant. When Tom Felts, the last of the Felts brothers, called a press conference to trumpet the sordid news, the set-up was clear. Reporters found Jessie in the women's section of the jail, reading a magazine, modestly dressed in a blue suit. She handled the press with grace and charm. The next day a mob of reporters and onlookers followed Sid and Jessie, who had been bailed out by relatives, to a nearby church, where, with a nephew and niece of the late Mayor Testerman looking on approvingly, Sid and Jessie were married.

Sid and twenty-two other defendants were acquitted of charges arising from the shootout after a lengthy trial in Williamson that autumn. At Sid's trial for murdering Albert Felts, a scumbag spy named Charles E. Lively had testified against Sid. With secret coal-company funds, Lively had opened a restaurant in Matewan a few months before the shootout, and had befriended Sid and many union miners. One of the things Lively claimed was that Sid had told him that he would like to get Mayor Testerman out of the way. All of Sid's supporters had figured that was simply scumbag spy bullshit. But what if it was true? What if late one night, while Lively and Sid were up drinking whiskey together and talking nooky, the way politically incorrect men will, Sid did say what Lively claims he said about being in love with another man's brown-haired wife, and being willing to go through hell to have her? It is, after all, only the scumbag company spy's word against that of the famous folk-hero of the minefield's sacred hills and hollows. What if Sid, the miners' two-gunned, mythic hero did, in fact, plug poor old Mayor Testerman, his best friend and benefactor, when the opportunity presented itself in the chaotic midst of general firing and thick gun-smoke in order to have the Mayor's dark-eyed, creamy-skinned wife with

wondrous breasts? Was Sid Hatfield capable of such a monstrous decep-
tion and betrayal purely for the sake of nooky, if not love?

Imagine Mayor Testerman burying his sad fat face in his hands and
weeping while he tells his lovely young wife Jessie that if anything ever
happens to him, she should go ahead and marry Sid Hatfield if that's
what she wants to do. Sid would take care of her and be kind and good
to her and get up in the middle of the night to hold her when she wakes
up screaming as though she is being murdered in those crazy nightmares
she has, and make her cocoa. Imagine Mayor Testerman sitting there
sobbing and hoping with all his heart his wife would say no, no, dear,
honey, baby, darling, that's not what I want to do ever. But Jessie doesn't
say anything of the kind. Jessie simply sits there quietly at the kitchen
table looking so heartbreakingly beautiful in the soft lamplight. The
same kitchen table where not twenty minutes earlier maybe Sid had sat,
his chiseled features rugged and handsome and dramatically shadowy in
the same lamplight as he talked about the danger he would face when
the Baldwin-Felts came back to town. How dangerous and daring Sid
seemed, how tough, yet somehow tender and vulnerable, and boyish and
brave at once, and vital and intense and sincere and so in love with Jessie
that he couldn't keep his dark hungry eyes off her.

Imagine Mayor Testerman burying his sad fat face in his hands and
blubbering his heart out in front of both his best friend Sid and perfect
wife Jessie while he asks Sid to please treat her good. While he asks Sid
to love his little Jessie lamb with all his heart and treat her good like he,
Mayor Testerman, had always tried to do himself. Maybe it was the night
before the big battle when Jessie and Sid confirmed the Mayor's worst
suspicions and those rumors rampant around town that Sid and Jessie
had been seen walking hand in hand down by the Tug Fork. Maybe Sid
didn't have to plug the mayor at all to win his Jessie lamb. What if the
mayor, a fat, ugly, smart, philosophical man who was just thankful to
have had it all even for a little while, to have held heaven in his fat arms
a few times, he was just thankful for that, went down into harm's way
the next day unarmed and gentle and soft-hearted and unendurably sad
and sacrificial. Imagine such a romantic, sentimental, fat, hopeless,

heroic husband offering himself up for the sake of his beautiful, beloved wife's future happiness, and maybe even stepping in front of that beneficent bullet meant for his best friend who had gone and betrayed him like that.

Only a little over a year after the famous battle, Sid and his friend Ed Chambers, along with their wives, Jessie and Sally, after being promised protection by the local sheriff, but against the better advice of their friends and supporters, rode the train south from Matewan to Welch, the McDowell County seat and a coal barons' stronghold, to stand trial on some trumped-up charges stemming from still yet another shootout between miners and company gun-thugs.

The streets on August 1, 1921, in Welch were packed. Folks flooded up from the train depot toward the courthouse on the hill, everybody in town for the forthcoming trial, many as witnesses or co-defendants. Sid's name was on everybody's lips. The massive stone, ivy-covered, Victorian McDowell County Courthouse, with its high clock tower, loomed like a fortress on the hillside. An eight-foot-high, heavy stone wall bordered the sidewalk, and above the wall the lawn sloped upward toward the courthouse. A double set of stone steps, running parallel to the street, intersected at a common landing at the top of the wall. A single wider set of steps then turned perpendicular to the street and led up another flight to the front entrance of the building. Charles Lively and a half-dozen other heavily armed Baldwin-Felts detectives waited at the top of those steps. The gun-thugs watched steely-eyed as the Matewan group strolled along on the far side of the narrow street, and then crossed at the corner.

Sid, Jessie, Ed Chambers, and his wife, Sally, started up the steps amid the slow-moving throngs of people. The sunny, bright day was dazzling. Sally carried a parasol. Ed, blond and boyish in appearance, despite his reputation for explosive violence, led the party, one hand on the stone balustrade, the other holding his wife's arm. They reached the first landing and started up the next flight toward the courthouse. Behind them, Sid put an arm around his lovely young bride, Jessie, as they mounted to the first landing. Sid looked up the stone steps to where his old friend and enemy Charles Lively stood waiting, and their eyes met and seemed to lock for a moment, and some say they both grinned. Just then a group of Sid's supporters reached the landing from the opposite direction, and Sid Hatfield took his arm from around Jessie to raise his hand in friendly greeting. He grinned his famous, golden sunburst grin, and spoke the last words he would utter on this Earth:—Hello, boys.

The story swept across West Virginia like wildfire from mining camp to camp that Sid Hatfield and Ed Chambers had been shot down like dogs in front of their wives on the courthouse steps at Welch, and the killers were free on bond, paid by the coal barons who ruled southern West Virginia with a fist of iron. And while the murderers went free, hundreds of Mingo County miners, the miners Sid had defended all his life, remained thrown under the jailhouse, without formal charge or bond. Newspapers screamed the news in headlines all over the country, and the United Mine Workers of America closed its district office in Charleston, posting a placard on the door which read thusly: CLOSED IN MEMORY OF SID HATFIELD AND ED CHAMBERS, MURDERED BY BALDWIN-FELTS DETECTIVES WHILE SUBMITTING THEMSELVES TO A COURT OF LAW. In Charleston, miners held a mass meeting on the capitol lawn, whereupon they passed a resolution of outrage and grief. Soon thereafter, miners along Little Coal River, halfway across the wild mountains between Charleston and Matewan, began arming themselves, and multitudes of men with guns began to come down out of the dark hills, calling out for their rights and vengeance for Sid Hatfield. These drastic actions touched off a series of tragic events that culminated in August 1921 with the Battle of Blair Mountain, a basically unplanned, leaderless rebellion in which 10,000 miners fought coal company gun-thugs and lackey state police for three bloody days before federal troops finally intervened, in what was the largest insurrection in the United States since the Civil War.

For many of the combatants on both sides, who were World War I veterans, the Battle of Blair Mountain was as fierce as any they had fought in France. Although no accurate count was ever made, there were many casualties on both sides, including, according to family legend, my Uncle Alfonso. Uncle Alfonso had been a rather reluctant draftee during the First World War, and then later had returned home suffering from a chronic nervous condition due to shellshock. So it had been unfathomable to family members when Uncle Alfonso, that mild-mannered bookkeeper, who was nearly spastic with that nervousness, had for some reason donned his old uniform, including his "tin derby" trench helmet, and loaded his rifle for the first time since he had returned from the Big One, and he had marched off with several of his miner uncles and cousins to join Sid Hatfield's avenger army.

Somehow Uncle Alfonso became lost on Blair Mountain during the battle, and he wandered about for a whole night essentially in solitude, while men on both sides who couldn't see one another took pleasure in simply shooting into the darkness all night purely to see the flames spit out from their gun barrels. The next morning Uncle Alfonso emerged onto Crooked Creek Pass, where he stumbled into a miners' campsite certain that he was the ghost of a doughboy who had been killed by a single bullet in a French forest far from anybody who had ever loved him. He was wrong about that, however, both the ghost business and the love part; for while Uncle Alfonso was put away for his own good for the rest of his natural life, he remained beloved and unforgotten. My middle name, gentle reader, is Alfonso.

GODDAMNED RHODODENDRON

Holly and I planned to catch the Powhatan Arrow for our train trip down to Matewan at a little whistle-stop south of Huntington called Fort Gay, and I flew there from Billville, whipping around those mountain roads like a maniac, until Holly reached over and jerked on my ear, with the admonition to slow the fuck down, dearest. We arrived way too early of course, and while we waited for the train we sat in the Red Ride sipping coffee we had bought back up the road at a truck stop. We watched as other vehicles began to arrive, pickups and old cars packed with train-excursion pilgrims like ourselves, extended families of the most amazingly friendly, down-home but often, frankly, enormously fat and homely folks you could ever expect to meet. Because it might become her own home state someday soon, Holly told me she had been reading up on old West Virginia. We got into a little tiff about the state flower of West Virginia, Holly claiming it was the Mountain Laurel, and me informing her smugly that it was the Rhododendron. We made a bet. If she was right, I would finally tell her exactly how old I was. If I was right, she would tease and torture me with sexy stories from her past, packed with dirty details, while tickling old mister monkey into a titillated tizzy.

When we heard the one long whistle blast that announced the train was arriving, we pressed forward toward the tracks with the crowd to watch it come around the bend. *Hot dog*! I reflected when I laid eyes on that wondrous machine. I was as excited as a kid to be riding the finest steam locomotive ever built, the Class J Number 611. It had first rolled out of the Norfolk & Western's Roanoke Shops and into service May 29,

1950, at a cost of $251,544. The old Number 611 was one of fourteen gracefully streamlined "Northern" (4-8-4 wheel arrangement) locomotives built by the railway between 1941 and 1950. All the Js wore the distinctive black, Tuscan red, and gold livery that characterized NW equipment of the time. The Js were so well built that a handful of men could pull one along level track with a rope. After pulling the last steam passenger train from Bluefield to Roanoke in October 1959, old Number 611 had been retired from service and eventually donated to the Virginia Museum of Transportation in Roanoke for display, the only J to escape the cutting torch and scrap heap. Old Number 611 was removed from the museum in October 1981, and restored to working condition for use in excursion service. It was a beautiful old machine and, buddy, I was going to get to ride on it.

We found a seat all to ourselves in the very back of one of the cars, and Holly pressed her little nose against the window like a kid, making breath angels on the glass as we pulled out. Holly looked lovely that day. She wore a short black skirt over a sort of paisley-print thong bodysuit, and she had a black cloth choker around her neck. I ran a finger along one of her smooth, bare thighs and told her she looked like a postcard picture of a French hooker, and I would pay her anything. —Your life, Holly said, and looked at me with the limpid eyes of a silent movie star, and I put the check in the mail.

An older couple with a big-eared kid sat across the aisle from us, and, eavesdropping on them, it became clear the kid was the older woman's grandson, and the old coot was granny's new boyfriend. The oldest boyfriend on the train (thank God!) passed the kid a few bucks, and the little fellow scampered up the aisle in the direction of the club car, and then in a flash the old coot was all over granny. The old rooster ruled, as the kids say, and Holly was mightily impressed. She jabbed me in the side and said —See there, baby, you old hillbilly boys never get enough.

When the big-eared boy came screaming insanely back down the aisle, he was wearing a new baseball cap that was balanced on the tops of those dumbo ears, and he was carrying a half-eaten hot dog in each hand. The old Romeo and granny disentangled themselves in a heartbeat, and sat up panting. Granny looked over and gave us a gap-tooth grin and rolled her eyes and winked. She must have weighed three hundred pounds. Her boyfriend was skinny as a rail. What I speculated was that she was this mountainous West Virginia widow-woman waiting to be mined again. He was this old, skinny, disabled, coal-mining coot who could use some deep-seam work. He had been a deep miner in his youth, before his back bent and his lungs turned black, and he had to make his way on the surface now, is what I figured. —Ma'am, I said to her, after she swiped the mustard off the boy's mouth and forced him to sit down before the window with the admonition to watch it like it was goddamned television, —Ma'am, I said, —could I ask you a little question, please? —Why, *shore*, honey, what is it? —Well, I said, —it's kinda dumb, but we were wondering what the state flower of West Virginia is. —Why, sugar, the old woman said, —the state flower of West Virginia is the goddamned rhododendron.

I thanked her from the bottom of my heart and wiggled my eyebrows suggestively at Holly. Holly jabbed me in the side and whispered —Oh, what does she know? Somebody with no teeth. How old are you really? Why don't you just tell me? I said: —It is you who is going to be revealing succulent secrets. —You might just get more succulent secrets than you can swallow, Holly said and gave me that sort of holding-back-a-smile, out-of-the-corner-of-her-eye, sassy, enigmatic look that always won. When she looked at me like that, what did it mean? Did she truly love me? How could she, for God's sake? Was she nuts? I was old enough to be her daddy, for God's sake. I tried to conquer her back with my steely-eyed, frowny gunfighter stare, but to no avail.

As we passed through the little towns along the Tug Fork, Glenhayes, Kermit, Naugatuck, Nolon, Crum, folks came out onto their sagging porches or to the ends of their steep, fenced yards to wave at the train from the past passing through their lives, and we waved back. I told Holly that a fellow West Virginia rednecky writer named Lee Maynard had written a real good, sad, funny, albeit outrageous, hillbilly book, a novel, about a boy's life in the town of Crum. The novel's title was, well, *Crum,* and one of my favorite lines in it was a description of Kentucky as being that "mysterious land across the Tug Fork full of pigfuckers."

I tried to impress Holly with my knowledge of the Tug Fork Valley and its turbulent history. I related its legends and lore and tall tales, some of which, of course, I made up on the spot. Holly couldn't get over how lovely the river was whenever we could glimpse it through the trees, and how lushly wild and intensely green the rugged hillsides were. I tried to impress her with my knowledge of West Virginia's unique flora and fauna, and told her of winged cats, of giant hairy humanoids, of spectral hogs roaming deep in the woods, and of snakes that bit the ends of their own tails when they rolled down hillsides like hoops, but Holly didn't bite.

Whenever the train rolled into a long, dark tunnel, Holly and I, following the example of the old Casanova coot and granny (whenever the big-eared boy was out running up and down screaming like a banshee in the aisles), necked like teenagers. —Are you really and truly having a good time? Holly had asked me once when we came up for air at the end of a long tunnel. —I'm having about the best goddamned time I've had in my life, I told Holly and I meant it.

—*Goddamned rhododendron,* I leaned over and whispered into Holly's cute little pearly shell of an ear. —*Goddamned rhododendron* is any of a genus of the heath family of widely cultivated carnivorous shrubs and trees with alternate leaves and showy flowers that suck and swallow, I whispered.

THAT SWEET ANARCHY
WE CALL YOUTH

During my days and days of rambling through the hills while I lived down in southern West Virginia, I would often dip down to Welch, the site of Sid Hatfield's bloody demise. I'd park in front of the old courthouse on the hill, and for a few reflective moments settle my butt on that third stone step up from the landing, the one where the head of Sid Hatfield had come to rest seventy-plus years earlier. Then I'd leisurely walk around that tired, gritty-brick town with its frequent empty storefronts and lonesome streets for a time, looking for old landmarks from the shootout days.

Right around the corner from the courthouse on McDowell Street, I had found the entrance to the building that once housed the old Carlton Hotel, where Sid and Jessie and their party had rested up before walking over to the courthouse for Sid and Ed's trial that fateful day. Big gold letters above the Romanesque corner entrance, which still retained a certain old-hotel elegance with large carriage lanterns attached to its white, stone pillars, announced that the three-story brick building was now named TYSON TOWERS. Now the spacious old lobby was home to Taylor Optical, which advertised quality eyeglass service. Right down the street under a small, green-striped awning, I found another entrance that had the old Carlton Hotel crest above the door. This entrance now opened into the Pizza Plus dining room. There was a sign in the window that advertised that Robert Tyson Realty had an apartment for rent, and for no good reason I wrote down the number, 436-4358, in my notebook. You could never tell. Anything was possible at that point in my life.

As best I could figure, the old railroad depot down over the hill toward the river where Sid and his party had disembarked that day was now a nearly empty concrete parking garage building. But across the street from the old Carlton Hotel corner entrance was Ray's Barbershop. I recalled that Sid had gone out alone to get a haircut that morning before the trial. When I peeked through the window of the shop one day, the barber, Ray himself as it turned out, who was sitting in his barber's chair reading a newspaper all alone in the place, waved for me to come on in as though I were a long-lost son. So I ducked into that old barbershop, whose high walls were lined with shelves filled with what could have been literally thousands of beer cans, which was what caught my attention in the first place.

The friendly barber looked like still yet another hillbilly version of a local aging Elvis, with black shoe-polished, piled pompadour hair and thick pork-chop sideburns down to his sagging jawline. He began babbling as soon as I walked in the door that his name was Ray *the third* and that this here personal beer-can collection of his was the biggest in the known world and how he had personally emptied every dead soldier son-of-a-bitch on those shelves over the past ten years, two months, and five days. So what appeared to be a regular old everyday barbershop I had stumbled innocently into was in reality a world-class beer-can museum, and I had never felt so quickly at home. Suddenly I felt something akin to that old tingly, expectant, hopeful feeling I recall as a sense of arrival. I love museums. To be a barber named Ray *the third* disguised as Elvis in a cozy, corner barbershop that smelled like hair tonics from a bygone time and housed a world-class beer-can collection struck me as a wonderful way of life. What was each of those empty beer cans, anyway, but a goodtime trophy?

But then the friendly barber found it necessary to inform me that every one of them empty son-of-a-bitches up on them shelves was like a tombstone over some good time wasted loving a bad woman. The barber's voice turned sad and theatrical and holy at that point, religious with loss and pure Elvis, as he launched into a clearly old lament about the woman who had done him dirt ten years, two months, and five days ago. I, for one, didn't need that boohoo business. I interrupted that whiny barber. I asked that barber a historical question. I asked him if this could have been the barbershop where Sid Hatfield got his last haircut that day he was shot down like a dog seventy-plus years ago. —Yes, buddy, it was, the barber said, his voice still resonant and churchy. —It was my own old granddad, Ray *the first,* what gave Sid Hatfield his last haircut in this world. And a shave too, as a matter of fact. And my old granddad, Ray *the first,* always told as how Sid Hatfield was the friend-liest feller you'd ever want to meet. Sid Hatfield sat in this here very chair and popped jokes and wisecracks while he got his last shave and a haircut and not an hour later that feller was laying dead as a doornail on the courthouse steps.

I asked the whiny albeit friendly barber if I could sit in that chair, and, eyeballing my aging-hippie ponytail, he said yes, indeedy. I stepped up and settled down slowly into that barber's chair, whereupon I tried to put myself in Sid's shoes. I tried to imagine being Sid Hatfield as he sat in that very barber's chair seventy-plus years earlier not an hour before he would meet Mister Death. I imagined the barber, old Elvis *the first,* turning Sid in the chair to face the mirror. The old barber, old early Elvis, who was surely beloved in those bygone days for the stories he told and his jokes and his generosity of spirit, put a hand on either side of Sid Hatfield's head. The old barber positioned Sid a last time, and then he brought his head down next to Sid's. They looked into the mirror together, the old barber's hands still framing Sid's head. Sid was looking hard at himself, and the old barber was looking at Sid too. Maybe Sid cracked that famous grin of his, or tried out some dangerous expressions in the mirror for a laugh, but maybe not. Maybe Sid and the old barber simply looked into Sid's eyes together, as though some hidden inkling of the future might be reflected there. But if the old barber saw something, he didn't offer comment. The old barber ran his fingers through Sid's hair. He did it slowly, as if thinking about something else. The old barber ran his fingers through Sid's hair tenderly, as Jessie might have done it, like a lover.

• • •

What we cannot forget is that those were fierce, feudal times, bloody, barbaric Dark Ages down in the hills and hollows, a period of pure rebellion, which is romantic and adolescent in nature anyway; in other words, a perfect time and place in which to clutch that sweet anarchy we call youth, and Sid had a big decision to make. Sid had spent a year trying on for size his new life with Jessie in an apartment over Mayor Testerman's old store back in Matewan, and he had to make up his mind about how much this new life meant to him in terms of what to risk. It was so different from his old, wild, free shootist life, this new married life living over a store, feeling hapless and stuck in time to grow old just like everybody else through the long years. What if Sid went back to the hotel after his haircut and fetched Jessie and simply left town on the next train? Sid could do that. Nobody would blame him. Folks would think Sid was smart, not afraid. Surely that thought must have passed through Sid's mind: to go back down to Mingo County and dare the Baldwin-Felts to come and try to get him there if they thought they could. Or he could just go around to the courthouse in less than an hour and face the music like the legendary two-gun shootist he had always imagined himself to be.

Everything that day had seemed so dreamlike to Sid, from the moment he had first awakened in his old friend Mayor C. C. Testerman's big brass bed and for a full minute could not remember where he was, much less why, and who the beautiful, young, sweet-smelling woman asleep beside him was. All day long, Sid had felt strangely unstuck in time, like he did sometimes when he was drunk, as though everything had already happened five minutes ago. All day long, Sid had felt a sort of weird elation, a sort of weightlessness. Maybe Sid looked at his reflection in the barbershop mirror, and his eyes looked unbearably old to him, and maybe even a little bit frightened, as did my own eyes that day I tried on that barber's chair for size, but not necessarily frightened of death. Maybe Sid was thinking that in less than an hour, he really might say hello to old Mister Death. That the Baldwin-Felts would surely try to shoot him down. He sure would do it if he was them. Maybe during the time he looked at his reflection in the barber's mirror, Sid tried to apportion what could turn out to be his last moments on Earth in terms of what to remember and reflect upon. So many moments from his life to reimagine. To see anew in the fiercely lucid light cast by these, his last moments. And, Lordy, so many lives left to live, even now. A whole hour of lives left, an endless stretch of time, no need to imagine the last moment.

A part of Sid couldn't imagine growing old, couldn't even bear it. So what if he was dying today, truly, 28 years old, healthy as a horse, strong as an ox, and this hour ahead of him was his old age. And maybe another part of Sid thought oh, how I want to live some more, how precious life can be in the arms of that sweet-smelling woman! Was it really possible that in less than an hour he might no longer be around? That he wouldn't breathe this sweet old mountain air again, he wouldn't see the old sun rise higher in the old sky, casting its sweet light on this old world? Could it be that he would never lick up the front of Jessie's smooth, white legs again? Dimple her soft, creamy skin with his tongue. Flop her over and drop his bait in that sweet swampy favorite fishing hole too. All this could still be his, this old world, and Jessie, Jessie, the taste of her sweet mouth, her warm, sweet breath on his face and neck and going on down warm on his body real slow, if only he didn't have to be who he had always figured he was, and maybe have to quit his life now for it.

So long, old-timer, Sid had said to the old barber named Ray *the first*, and flashed that famous grin as he strolled out the door toward death. Lately, Sid had felt as though he was somehow sailing backward into his life, as though somehow the future was a distant, receding shoreline. Sid walked out of that barbershop young and strong and handsome and in love and famous, with a fresh shave and a haircut and smelling of that ruby-colored hair tonic and talcum powder, toward all of death. Sid had practiced for death all his life. Everybody knew the future was all smoke and mirrors anyhow. Freedom was knowing that a choice made today, in the right here and now, throws itself backwards through our lives and changes the nature of everything we have ever done, making us all live finally backward to be free. Old Sid was a philosopher in his final moments. It's pretty to think that Sid had made up his mind about what he was going to do and why he was going to do it while sitting in the old barber's chair. Sid's choice had had something to do with that sense of calm he had felt when he closed his eyes and let Ray *the first's* tender old barber fingers move through his hair, the sweetness of those fingers, his hair already starting to grow again.

What if Sid Hatfield, that wisecracking, wiry, killer nihilist magical West Virginia warrior, walked unarmed into the trap that day in Welch because he had come to understand that death was the final myth of freedom. Say Sid went to his date with doom, went to his ceremonial sacrificial slaughter, with a sort of sad relish. What if Sid realized that the central, legendary story of his life had already unfolded that bloody day in the Matewan Battle, and to emerge finally into myth as a holy magical warrior hero meant dying now like a martyr in a movie.

In tense situations in West Virginia, what we say is that things are about to get "real West Virginian," which is a lot like things getting "real Western," and then some. Showdown shootouts in West Virginia do tend to turn pure cinema and mythic at once. In an act of obsessive, pathologically frightening behavior, Charles Lively suddenly broke real West Virginian the moment Sid Hatfield said "hello, boys" and gave that friendly, fateful wave to his pals on the courthouse steps, when, as if by signal, Charles Lively and the other Baldwin-Felts detectives pulled their pistols and began firing. It was all over in ten seconds.

In her testimony before a select committee formed to investigate the shootings on the Welch courthouse steps, Ed Chamber's widow Sally, who was a pretty, brown-haired young woman of twenty-four, described the murders in minute detail thusly: "Well, as we went up the first flight of steps, just as we landed on the first landing, the other defendants and their witnesses were coming up the other flight of steps on the other side of the landing, and Sid kind of hesitated just a little bit when the boys were speaking to him and kind of waved his hand at them, and at that time the first shot was fired about three steps up the second flight of steps that led into the courthouse. I don't know how many of them were there shooting. It looked like there might have been a hundred or two hundred of them there shooting that day. But I reckon there was about six or eight of them right there on the steps firing down. Mr. Charles Lively put his arm across in front of me and shot my husband Ed in his neck. Right there was the first shot. I don't mean that that was the first shot that was fired, but that was the first time my husband was shot. Sid was shot first. Sid Hatfield. My husband was shot about eleven or twelve times. Some say Sid was shot nine times, and some say eleven, so I am unable to say how many. My husband, he rolled back down the steps and I looked down and I seen him rolling down and blood gushing from a hole in his neck, and I just went back down the steps after him, you see, and they kept on shooting him, and when he kind of fell on his side leaving his back up, you know, toward the steps and they were shooting him in the back all the time after he fell. And then Charles Lively shot my husband Ed right behind the ear. My husband was lying down kind of on his side at the time that Charles Lively shot him the last time. Mr. Lively just reached down and put his gun just about a inch from my husband Ed's ear, but before he did that, though, I seen him coming down the steps toward us, and I said, 'Oh, please, Mr. Lively, don't you shoot at him any more, you have killed him now.' But I didn't know if Ed's life was gone then, but you know I just said that because I knew in my heart Ed would die, so Charles Lively just run down and stuck the gun behind my husband's ear and fired it. And then I struck Mr. Lively with my umbrella, and he turned around to me and said, 'Oh, don't you hit me with that umbrella again, you dirty devil, or I will shoot you too,' and he stuck his gun out, but he didn't shoot me, and then he went back up the steps. I went down on my knees beside my husband and had hold of his hands, and I just begged for someone to come to me and no one did come, but there was some men started to run up to me, you know, and those detectives told them 'Go back, stay back, we will take care of this,' so those men had to stop, you see. I was rubbing my husband's face and had hold of his hand, and Mr. Salter, the man that had been shooting at Sid, and Buster Prince, of course I didn't know the men's names at that time, but I recognized their faces, and I said to Mr. Salter, I said, 'Oh, Mr. Salter, oh, what did you all do this for? We did not come up here for this.' And then he said to me, 'Well, that is all right, we didn't come down to Matewan last year for that either.' Then they took me by the arms and pulled me away from my husband and I told them, 'Oh, no, I am going to stay with my husband.' But they pulled me up the steps toward the courthouse and as we got up at the top Charles Lively was standing there and he looked at me like he was so glad he had done what he had done that I could not resist the temptation and I just had to hit him again with my umbrella."

Two thousand people walked in the procession that carried Sid Hatfield and Ed Chambers to their final rest in a Kentucky hillside graveyard directly across the Tug Fork. The rain poured down in buckets that day, and Jessie and Sally were near collapse. At one point, Sally had to be helped to a chair when she grew faint, while Jessie sobbed nearby. As her husband's casket was lowered into its grave, Jessie Hatfield cried out: —I'll never forget you, sweetheart. Not for the rest of my life.

The Baldwin-Felts gun-thugs were tried in the same courthouse where they had gunned Sid and Ed down, and were promptly acquitted by reason of self-defense. Charles Lively worked in the coal mines around Mt. Hope, West Virginia, for several years afterward, and later as a railroad detective and hotel operator in Roanoke, Virginia. He died in Huntington, West Virginia, in 1962 at the age of 75.

Sally Chambers married Harold Houston, the UMW attorney who had defended Sid and Ed in the Matewan Battle trial, and eventually retired to Lake Worth, Florida.

Jessie Hatfield married a state policeman and moved to Huntington. She later divorced her third husband and married a fourth. Jessie lived with the son she had by Mayor C. C. Testerman in the last months of her life in Huntington, and she died in 1976 at age 82.

MOUNTAIN LAW

Ruling-class, outsider sons-of-bitches took the coal out of the West Virginia mountains, and they took the timber; the Yankee thieves and corrupt local officials stole about everything of value they could get their hands on, and natural resources that should have made West Virginia prosper did not. One thing West Virginia has left is its wild, turbulent, bloody history that is the vivid, startling, legendary stuff of books and movies.

The passengers all climbed down off the Powhatan Arrow in Matewan that day, tourists in time and potential big-spender shoppers. And history sure was on sale that bright, high-blue, warm windy day. There were historical bargains to be had. The town had a full-blown *First Annual Feudist Festival* going strong, with a good bluegrass band blasting from a little stage by the old bank. Locals were dressed up as feudists carrying long rifles, and two-gun sheriffs in frock coats, and ladies in long, old-timey dresses who sat at tables selling lumps of coal carved into the likenesses of Devil Anse and Sid Hatfield, and Devil Anse and Sid Hatfield T-shirts were for sale, and Johnse "Romeo" Hatfield loving-cups, and jars of pawpaw preserves homemade from fruit picked off those same pawpaw thickets the McCoy boys had been tied to and blasted to smithereens.

Serious shoppers could also find souvenir bargains among more modern items, such as bumper stickers that said things like: HONK IF YOU'RE A HATFIELD, HONK IF YOU EVER SHOT A HATFIELD, HONK IF HATFIELDS MAKE YOU HORNY. I bought a bumper sticker for my brother-in-law that said EAT MORE POSSUM. I bought several little potted-meat tins of sun-dried West Virginia possum for my brother-in-law, which he considered a delicacy. The label on the side of the cans guaranteed pick-of-the-possum-parts, guaranteed the possom was freshly killed by a coal truck on Route 39 and picked up within an hour by alert road-kill crews. Hatfield Hot Dogs were for sale, slathered with an old Hatfield family recipe for feudist sauce that was blazing hot and red as blood. Holly and I gobbled a couple apiece, smoky feudist sauce dripping down our fingers and off our chins as we wandered about, goofing off. We didn't care. We were tourists. Nobody knew our names. Screw locals and any of their homegrown opinions about old men holding hands and making googoo eyes with beautiful young women, was our main motto. A sign beside an old beat-up station wagon parked down Mate Street advertised tours to The Tomb of the Unknown Feudist. Around in McCoy Alley, we came upon a couple of enterprising old boys who had set up an ice-cold lemonade and moonshine stand. Nothing hits the spot like ice-cold moonshine laced with lemonade, so I had me a couple of cups at two bucks a pop.

Postcards made from old photographs of feudists posing armed to the teeth, or of "Two-Gun" Sid Hatfield with his own pistols drawn, or of famous feudist bloodbath sites were for sale. All you had to do was put a stamp on a picture from the wild, bloody West Virginia past and drop it in the mail, a postcard for posterity imprinted with the faces of dead feudists you could mail to anybody currently alive with any fateful message. The locals were transforming history into tourism dollars galore! There were buckets of old bullets for sale, bullets advertised as having been found amid old feudist bones buried deep in the woods. There were ritual hog relics, polished bones and teeth said to be from some of old Devil Anse's own beloved backwoods consorts, and in one huge glass jar were pricey barbequed pork rinds advertised as being carved from a descendant of Johnse Hatfield's own favorite fiancée.

Perhaps I should pause once again in this narrative and relate the tragic story as I gathered it about those famous old feudists and their mountain paramours. If you are not particularly interested in hearing even more bloody Hillbilly History, gentle reader, or, as I have suggested earlier, are of a sensitive nature, my best advice is to forego the following few pages, and simply skip ahead to where the narrative concerning cheating hearts and skulking around after cheap romance heats up.

Some folks say that the roots of the famous Hatfield and McCoy feud spread all the way back to the War Between the States, when Hatfields were generally Confederates and McCoys Yankees. But clearly there had been years of bad blood before two disputes essentially concerning *romance* brought things to a head, so to speak.

Devil Anse's oldest boy was a good-looking dandy named Johnse, who had been described by one newspaper of the time as "a small-boned rounder who was ruddy faced and sandy haired, with a pair of insinuating blue eyes that set the mountain belles' hearts all a flutter." When Johnse Hatfield showed up at the Pike County precinct polls for the spring election of 1882, he was a mountain Romeo looking for love and laughs. He knew there would be tables of homemade food spread out beneath the fine shade trees around his uncle Jerry Hatfield's house, the Blackberry Creek precinct polling place, and all the whiskey a voter could possibly drink, and dancing and laughing and good-natured bullshitting, and maybe in that heady, dangerous mix of politics and booze some recreational bloodshed, and most likely every mountain beauty in the area. Already famous at eighteen for really putting on the dog, Johnse showed up for that occasion dressed fit to kill in a new mail-order blue suit and high celluloid collar and yellow shoes. When twenty-year-old Rose Anne McCoy, a dark-haired, dark-eyed girl famous herself as one of the most fetching of the Pike County mountain beauties, showed up riding behind her older brother Tolbert on his horse, and her flashing dark eyes met those insinuating blue ones of Johnse Hatfield, and she took in those yellow shoes, neither one of them stood a chance. When they staggered out of the woods in disarray hours later at dusk, Johnse and Rose Anne were desperately in love and big trouble.

Now, fans of feud lore have long had a field day promoting this star-crossed romance and resultant illegitimate pregnancy as being the dramatic, immediate cause of the open hostilities between the Hatfields and McCoys, but another incident apparently was of much greater import in explaining the intensified ill feelings between the families that led directly to the initial serious bloodshed, and that incident involved the disputed ownership of a beloved hog.

It was a razorback hog of the type backwoodsmen still ran loose frontier-style in the forest, and with whom the mountain men were known to sometimes form deep, abiding, and even passionate attachments. Randolph McCoy claimed the hog, whose name he said was Hilda, was his, and Floyd Hatfield said that that wasn't true, that the disputed hog was named Lilly and she was his alone. A Kentucky jury had awarded ownership of the contested hog to the claimant, Floyd Hatfield, and Randolph McCoy was heartbroken. Randolph McCoy accused one of the key witnesses, Bill Staton, a Hatfield relative, of lying and hurled a rock at him. The trial was followed by growing bitterness on both sides, and dangerous talk continued to pit clan against clan, with frequent flare-ups and a few pot-shots fired across the Tug Fork.

Hence the scene was set for tragedy when the polls opened again at the Blackberry Creek precinct on Monday, August 7, 1888, in the little hollow near the home of Jerry Hatfield. The West Virginia Hatfields appeared, armed to the teeth, as was their custom. Early in the day it was clear that men with grudges were ready for trouble. The whiskey flowed, and quarrels broke out over politics and the relative beauty of various hogs, but only fists were thrown. In the early afternoon, Ellison Hatfield, a large and powerful man of forty who was a brother of Devil Anse's, wobbled out of a nearby orchard toward the election officials' table under a big beech tree to get another free drink and vote again, where a crowd of men was standing around passing the jug and arguing politics and hogs and just basically jawboning the hot, summer day away. Ellison had just awakened from his third drunken nap of the day, and he stretched and yawned and scratched his balls down his britches as he took a swig from a passing jug. Some of the bystanders ribbed Ellison about the new large straw hat he was wearing, which had a much wider brim than customarily seen in those parts. Ellison laughed and waved the

straw hat over his head and said —Boys, I just brought this here rough-
ness for to steal your dearest hog.

Everybody was laughing along with Ellison when suddenly Tolbert
McCoy, the thirty-one-year-old son of Randolph, stepped out from the
small group in which he stood with his brothers and cousins and
advanced toward Ellison. Tolbert walked to within a few feet of Ellison
and stopped, staring belligerently, his face distorted by fury and booze.
Tolbert pointed his finger at Ellison and hollered: —I'm hell on earth!

Ellison, much the bigger man, looked at Tolbert quizzically and said:
—Huh?

—I'm hell on earth! Tolbert hollered again.

—You're a damn shit hog, Ellison remarked.

Tolbert sprang forward and slashed Ellison across his belly with a
knife. Blood splurted from the wound and Ellison's shirt was red in a
blink. Ellison grabbed Tolbert and held him, trying desperately to take
the knife. Two of Tolbert's younger brothers, Phamer, age twenty-one,
and Randolph, fifteen, jumped into the fracas with their own drawn
knives and began stabbing at Ellison repeatedly. When Preacher Anse, a
respected religionist and peacemaker, and cousin of Devil Anse, rushed
over to separate the fighters, the wounded Ellison grabbed up a rock to
bash Tolbert, but before he could strike, Phamer shot him in the back
with a revolver, and Ellison fell face downward in the dirt, gasping, his
quick breath shaking the leaves and grass where they had been scuffed
up near his mouth. Angry Hatfield clansmen pushed in toward the circle
forming around the mortally wounded Ellison with their guns drawn.
The McCoy boys struggled through the throng in an attempt to escape
into the woods.

On Wednesday, August 9, 1882, Ellison, who had been stabbed
twenty-six times before being shot in the back, died across the Tug Fork
in West Virginia at the Warm Hollow home of Anderson Ferrel, where
he had been carried on a crude stretcher. Devil Anse, who had visited his
mortally wounded brother and heard from the dying man's own lips an
account of the election-day fracas, had already made up his mind about
what to do. All along, Devil Anse had said if Ellison lived, he would let

the town law take its course. If Ellison died, then the Hatfields would handle things according to mountain law. By the threat of force of arms, the Hatfields had already taken charge of the McCoy boys from out-gunned Kentucky officials, and had carried them across the Tug Fork into West Virginia, where they had kept the bound boys prisoners in an old, abandoned schoolhouse up Mate Creek.

It had rained all the night before Ellison died, and at some point two drenched women appeared from out of the heavy downpour into the little clearing in front of the one-room schoolhouse. They were Sarah McCoy, the mother of the boys, and Mary Butcher, Tolbert's wife. They stood in the rain pleading with Devil Anse for over an hour to let them see the boys, before he finally relented and stepped aside from the door so that they could enter. For a time, the only noise around the tiny cabin had been the rain, still beating down hard, and the low mur-muring among the women and the prisoners. By ten o'clock, Sarah McCoy had lost all control of herself, however, and was becoming hys-terical. Her sobs grew louder and louder as she knelt on the floor in the frail light of the lantern, praying and weeping, and now and then above her supplications could be heard the soft, soothing words of Mary, standing over her. The bound boys had remained quietly grim. Finally, Devil Anse had ordered the women to begone, and they had staggered out into the rain, both sobbing now, and had disappeared clutching one another into the dark.

The next night, Jim McCoy, the older brother of the three captured boys, was sitting on the porch of Asa McCoy's cabin, at the mouth of Sulphur Creek. He had been attempting to intervene all day on his brothers' behalf, to no avail, and he had heard the rumor that Ellison Hatfield had died earlier in the day. Jim, a man even his enemies respected, was bone-tired and heartsick, and upon hearing a roar of gun-fire down the river on the Kentucky side of the Tug, he suspicioned the worst. What he heard was an outburst of shots, continuous but short, followed by a single blast, which sounded like a cannon. Jim jumped up and hurried to the edge of the porch, where he managed to get a glimpse of the flashes from the final shots that he feared had just killed his three brothers. Then, after a period of deep silence, what he heard faintly from downstream, in the same direction of the shots, were the hoots of an owl, a little too loud, it seemed to him, a little too strained to be natural.

Years later, when a Hatfield partisan named Ellison Mounts, who was said to be feebleminded and who ended up being the only feudist ever hanged for his crimes, was captured and kidnapped to Kentucky for trial, he testified about what had happened that night on the banks of the Tug Fork thusly:

"I was present and participated in the murder of the three McCoy brothers, namely, Tolbert McCoy, Phamer McCoy, and Randolph McCoy. It was on the night of the 9th of August, 1882, at the mouth of Blackberry Creek, Pike County, Kentucky. The three brothers were taken from a log school house in Logan County, West Virginia, where they had been guarded for a day and night, and brought over the Tug River, which separates West Virginia from Kentucky. They were tied arm in arm with a plow line and led by one Charles Carpenter to the river and placed in a boat, accompanied by Anse Hatfield and myself and others. We brought them to the Kentucky side and led them by the rope up the bank fifty feet from the river. Carpenter tied them to a pawpaw bush and hung a lantern over their heads. Some of the men squatted down to smoke and everybody started to cock their guns and pistols and somebody, I don't know who though, said this was going to be too easy of a shooting match to be much fun. After a short time, Anse Hatfield said to the McCoys: 'Boys, if you have any peace to make with your Yankee Maker, you had best do it now.'

"Tolbert and Randolph took to praying, but Phamer, who we all called Dick, did not. Dick hollered out that Devil Anse Hatfield could just kiss his ass. Dick hollered that Kentucky hogs put West Virginia hogs to shame, and then Johnse Hatfield shot Dick between the eyes. Then before the other McCoy boys finished up their prayers, Uncle Anse gave the order to fire, and shot as he gave the word, killing Tolbert and then emptying the contents of his revolver into the dead body. As soon as the first shots were fired, the others had followed suit, and soon the bodies of Tolbert and Phamer were riddled with bullets, and were swinging about in the pawpaw bushes like a wind was ablowing them. But nobody shot the boy, Little Rand'l, at first, and he was on his knees still praying and crying when the firing died down. Then Uncle Anse said, 'I'm sorry, son, but you was a stabber like your brothers and you have to pay on the account too. That's the code, boy.' And then Uncle Anse put his big bear gun against the little boy's head and fired it. After the boys was killed, we crossed the river back into Mingo County, where we found Wall Hatfield and some others waiting for us. Wall then ordered us into a line and administered an oath to all of us binding us to take the life of the first one to tell the name or names of any who were along that night, and swore us all to solemn secrecy, and wound up the oath by asking us if our feelings were not gratified. And we all said yes they were."

Later on that fateful night, Jim McCoy had rounded up some of the men living in the area, and they had rowed down the river in the direction of the gun flashes. Holding their lanterns high, they had climbed the steep bank, and then walked slowly toward a sinkhole in the terrain sloping toward the stream. As they topped the rise, a nauseating stench came to their nostrils, and they recognized it as the odor from sheep-killing dogs shot there a few days earlier and tossed into the sinkhole. Only a moment later in the flickering lantern-light, they glimpsed the bullet-riddled bodies of Tolbert and Phamer, swinging from pawpaw bushes. Tolbert's hand was still clasped over his forehead, as if he had smacked himself aside the head for forgetting something important, or tried to ward off bullets like they were bees, one of which had passed through his hand and into his head, gluing his hand there with blood like a salute to death. Phamer sagged like a sack of grain, slumped forward, swinging from the armpits, a smirk on his face. Fifteen-year-old Randolph was in a kneeling position, the top of his head blown clean off. Jim McCoy and his companions stared at the gaping hole in the boy's skull and recalled the single final blast, louder than the others. And such was the scene of that foul murder, only the first of many over the ensuing years of bloodshed.

Jim McCoy stumbled back down the bank to the river through darkness thick as that that covers water in a deep well. The summer night was in full bloom, and the air by the river smelled freshly of flowing water and flowering bushes. Again Jim McCoy heard the unnatural hoot of that owl. Overhead was a cat-grin moon and vast multitude of stars. Never before or since, some old-timers say, have the folks along the Tug Fork who noticed them that night seen such an abundance of stars at one time in a summer sky.

BLIND TOURIST

As Holly and I wandered the crowded streets of Matewan that warm day, we came upon a sign hanging above a narrow door that had a bright red heart on it, with ALIBIS painted in white on a black banner across the heart. Cracks that looked like twisty rivers on a map were also painted on the red heart, which suggested that it was a broken or at least seriously cracked heart. Holly and I stepped through the open door from a sun-bright sidewalk into a black cave of a beerjoint. It was as though we had entered into another dark dimension.

We stumbled across a Great Plains of a dance floor by a wall of mirrors into a vast area of tables beyond which were pool tables and then a long bar. My brother-in-law and I had spotted this beerjoint one time we were down this way before, but it had been closed due, as I later found out, to a knife-fight between barmaids over tips and a handsome devil the previous night. Holly and I sat at a tiny round table beside the dance floor, and when my old eyes became more accustomed to the dark I stumbled on back through the place to hunt for heads. The joint was packed with clearly armed-and-dangerous, fierce, long-bearded feudists. A dead ringer for old Devil Anse himself, with his own long, savage, black beard and high boots, was standing at the bar, drinking a Bud Light. And, playing pool, big irons sticking out of holsters under his coat, was a fellow who could have been the movie double for Sid Hatfield. In the head I read some graffiti that said: Fuck Feudists, and Hatfields Give Grate Head.

Back at the table I fell into a dark brood, which I hoped would be brisk. I felt unstuck in time. And I was full of foreboding, about the future, about the past, about right then and there. When Holly went back to take a leak, the Sid Hatfield look-alike stopped a shot in mid-stroke and stood back away from the pool table to watch her walk past. Then he turned to check me out. He grinned that famous grin when he saw me, and I gave him the finger under the table. I felt ready for any-thing, and that mood always scared me about myself. When Holly walked past him on her way back from the head, Sid Hatfield passed a remark to her and she laughed. Holly had a way of tossing her long hair back when she laughed that made it look all snakey and wild and elec-tric. I had told Holly that I had never considered myself to be a jealous-natured man, but that wasn't true. I don't know why I was suddenly in the mood for trouble. In West Virginia it is legal to carry a pistol as long as it is not concealed. Just before we got off the train, I had clipped on my horsehide holster that Holly had carried for me in her suitcase of a purse. I was packing a blue snub-nose .38 Detective Special. I guess I just wanted to fit in down in Matewan, West Virginia. Maybe I just wanted to show Holly another side of me.

When Holly got back to the table, I asked her what old Sid Hat-field had had to say. —Old? she said and laughed. —He's a kid. I'll bet he's no more than twenty-two or -three. He's even got pimples. —So you didn't think Sid Hatfield was cute? I inquired. —Not par-ticularly, why, do you? Holly said. I said: —Nope. But what did the asshole say? Holly said: —He asked me if I'd like to win some money at eight-ball, but I told him maybe some other time. I said: —Too bad he's not cute. —Too bad, Holly said, and then she said: —Please don't start on that single woman business. I don't want to hear that stuff today, okay, hon? —Well, I said, —it's true. You should experience some life as a single woman. —Look, Holly said, —if it's dirty details you want, I'll give you plenty tonight, okay? —That is not what I'm talking about here, I said to Holly, but she wasn't biting. She just rolled her eyes, and reached across the table and took my hand. I noticed the Sid Hatfield punk and some of his bearded, feudist, lout buddies who were hanging around the pool table caught that, and, for some reason, I felt immensely pleased.

• • •

Whenever I told Holly she should experience life as a single woman before she ever considered being tied down with a damaged old coot, I meant it. I was pushing her to do it, and she really didn't want to. The thought of it, though, of her being with some other man, terrified me, but it titillated me too. What I was afraid of was using the immense pain and jealousy I knew it would cause me to help me break things off. A boundary I would force her to cross, which would enable me to tell her that my doubts and fears were justified after all, and she really did need to be with a younger, more appropriate man. When I fantasied about sexual scenarios between Holly and other men, what bothered me most was not merely the sexual acts, the old bump-and-grind business, but the way she would behave with those men, the funny flirting, the silly winking and blinking, her sweet sexiness, the cute naughty sassiness she was so good at. It was that wonderful part of her personality she would share with somebody else that would not be mine, not those particular intimate moments anyway, which would be the province of another man's memory, for him to call up in his imagination at will from that time forth and employ in any manner he so desired.

Holly and I sat in that dark cool cavern of a bar and drank ice-cold beer from bottles and people-gawked as the place began to fill up with other tourists, many of whom we recalled from the train. Including this blind guy who appeared to be traveling alone. He was a big, blustery, bearded blind guy who looked more like one of the local feudists than a tourist. His white cane looked like a pole some wild prophet might carry, as though it had been roughly hand-carved from a huge tree-branch, and he swung it in front of him like a sort of fender. He had banged into Alibis alone, clobbering the sides of the front door as he flailed with his pole, and he had pounded his way across the dance floor leaving dents. Not far from us was a table of local gals, a couple of whom were wearing the long old-timey dresses, but the others halter-tops and short shorts, which was not a pretty sight, for every potential consort was huge as a backwoods hog. Those big babes were over at their table throwing beers back and wobbling over to push silver into the jukebox and just generally whooping it up. When one of them passed a remark to the big, blind guy as he banged by, he threw back his head and roared out a laugh and then plopped down into a chair one of the gals pulled out for him.

—If it's tourist season down here today, Holly said, —then do we have to worry about any of those country clowns at the bar shooting anybody? I mean, if tourists are in season.

—I reckon so, I said. —But don't you worry none, honey, I said and patted my blue snub-nose .38 Detective Special for effect.

Holly rolled her eyes.

I sat there listening to the big blind tourist joke and laugh and hoot, and I envied him bitterly. I envied him for his spirit and boldness and for the way he had clearly embraced the Black Hole in which he had fallen. Clearly not seeking any sense of anonymity, any loss of self, the blind tourist began pouring bottles of beer into that blind universe of himself, and I closed my eyes tightly, and I tried to imagine myself entering into all that vast darkness which is not myself. Not twenty minutes later, the blind tourist and one of the bovine babes, a tattooed, bleached blonde whose name apparently was Shirley, and who had the sweet giggle of a schoolgirl, got up and arm-in-arm strode across the dance floor and out the door into the dazzling sunlight. Holly cracked up. Tipping back in her chair and laughing, Holly said: —I don't think I've ever seen a seeing-eye whore before.

About that time Willie Nelson's song "You Were Always on My Mind" began playing on the jukebox. —Professor Honey, Holly said and smiled sweetly at me, —let's dance. We've never danced together. Why the fuck not? I reflected, and then I said: —Why the fuck not? We stood up and I pulled Holly gently against me, and we started slow-dancing a two-step around and around across the floor toward the light of the distant door. Maybe Black Holes, be they collapsed stars spinning crazily deep in space or coal mines or hillside graves or dark beerjoints in the middle of the afternoon, are merely wormholes through which one may pass with any luck from one reality into another, transformed and new.

As we danced slowly around, I watched Holly and me in the mirrored wall. I had never so purely desired a woman before as I did Holly. And I knew that I probably never would again, not like that. And I knew that somewhere in the fan-shaped destiny that spread into the future from that moment, I would lose Holly. Or, rather, that I would let her go, let her slip through my fingers, and that my desire for her then would be greater than ever. I was dead right about that, brother, as it turned out.

It was a bittersweet slow-dance we did that day before those mirrors. What I saw that day in Matewan in the blue-tinted, mirrored wall of the Alibis bar was little Holly and myself dancing in imaginary time. In the mirror what I saw clearly was a fifty-something-year-old, damaged man slow-dancing with a beautiful woman of twenty-nine with two precious babies at home to raise.

And then Holly had to go back to hit the head again. I had had to go too, bad, but had held it, not wanting to go back by the pool tables again out of pure bashfulness. The dead ringer for Sid Hatfield pulled his bug-eyed business again as Holly swung by. With her perfect little ass, it would have been unnatural for Holly not to swing it nor that idiot not to oggle its orbit.

So there I was, an old coot, unsteady already in my gait, with a splitting headache, feeling really pukey, in the company of a beautiful young woman in the midst of a badass beerjoint full of contemporary armed-and-dangerous feudists who could have easily just stepped out of one of the old photographs in that little storefront museum down the street Holly and I had paid a couple bucks each to whiz through earlier. And to top it all off, there was that leering nihilistic young gun-thug with the sweaty, horny eyeballs with nothing to lose and clearly looking for a reputation and nooky.

When Holly came out of the head that time, the Sid Hatfield wanna-be passed some remarks to her, which I, of course, naturally assumed were lewd and suggestive. But as I came to find out too late later, Sid had simply asked Holly to stand there beside him for luck while he tried to pocket the eight ball for a two-buck bet. Holly had dared him to let her sink that eight ball for him. Ever since her husband had left, Holly had been going out with her friend Sharon on those Saturday nights she could get her ex-husband to take the kids, and since Sharon, a cow who was about my own age and who disapproved of me mightily, was in lust with a married old cop, they would go drinking in Pittsburgh's North Side bars where Sharon's boyfriend and his copper pals hung out and got drunk and chased pussy and played pool, something that had driven me crazy with jealousy. Sometimes Holly wouldn't return home until four or five in the morning, drunk and giddy, which I knew only because I'd sit up all night calling her every hour, every half-hour, every fifteen minutes, every thirty seconds sometimes until the sun rose. Holly had become quite a little pool shark.

Sid laughed at her dare, but he didn't back down. Holly threw her wild, shaky hair back and smoked that eight ball amid cheers and friendly feudist hoots and toasts tossed back in honor of her shot and perfect ass and firm, lovely breasts and dazzling smile and shimmering eyes and skin that glowed in the dark. Grinning like the Miss America of Fallen Honky-Tonk Angels, Holly sashayed back to the table to find her old coot lover-boy sunk deep in doubt and growing despair and more ready than ever for trouble.

Through tight tough-guy Robert Mitchum movie-gangster lips, I told Holly I had to go tinkle. I put my shades on and pushed back my chair, and stood up slowly. Sid was chalking his cue as I walked up to him. He really was just a kid, twenty-something with pimples on his chin, but then the real Sid himself had been just a kid when he had entered legend. The first thing Sid checked out about me was my blue snub-nose .38 Detective Special in my holster. Because I had my shades on, Sid couldn't see my eyes, which were all bugged-out with embarrassment and scaredy-cat.

—I hear you're interested in a little game of eight-ball, I mumbled in my best Marlon Brando to Sid, who was a rather slack-jawed young man, and I wondered if Sid himself had looked that simple.

Now sometimes I can shoot a decent game of pool and sometimes

I can't. But I asked Sid if he would like to shoot one quick game for, say, twenty bucks, and he grinned and said shore. Holly came sashaying over from our table and stood at the edge of the crowd with her arms folded across her perfect breasts and a look of concern on her pretty face. She did look a bit like a cute little French hooker that day. Everybody always told Holly she looked a lot like that rising young movie star Sarah Jessica Parker, and it was true, except Holly was cuter.

What can I say? Everything went my way. I broke, took solids, and shot maybe the best game of pool under so much pressure in my life. When the eight ball fell, I picked up the ten and fiver and five ones Sid had placed over my twenty. Then I noticed something in Sid's dull, moss-green eyes, a sort of flash of fierce light in the morass of those primeval swamps, some sudden alligator gleam of anger and hate and a hunger for violent amusement at my expense, and suddenly, as if by magic, my blue snub-nose .38 Detective Special appeared in my hand.

My God, I don't even recall quick-drawing the thing, perhaps because I had practiced that magic move maybe a million times in front of mirrors since I was a kid with a cap-gun. But there it was, my piece, my heater, my roscoe, my rod in my shaking hand, and that dirty sneak-shot Sid Hatfield's idiot eyes were about bulged out of his frog-face. Talk about a deadly silence descending upon a scene, except for Holly, who gasped, and the jukebox blaring from the far front reaches of the bar. So now what? I had reflected. There I was in probably the baddest beerjoint on the face of the Earth full of grim fierce feudists with a gun in my hand. Now what? I reflected. Rob them? So I simply stood there dazed by my utter stupidity and concentrated upon not shaking too visibly. Finally Sid, who had regained his composure, said quietly: —You need to chill, Dad, man. And that was oh so true, I reflected. And then Holly said, —Hon, don't forget we have a train to catch, and I said, —Oh, that's right, I'd almost forgotten, dear, thanks, and then I simply started backing away from that bad scene, sort of nodding good-bye to all and grinning like a sap to show that basically I meant well, with Sid and his fierce pals all frozen in place, toward Holly, until I felt her hands spread themselves on my shoulder blades like little, sweet, warm wings.

Without a word, we both edged backward across that endless Texas of a beerjoint until we passed through that bright portal of delicious light into what felt to me like pure legend.

A Dead-End Town Named Romance

Holly and I stayed in a Ramada Inn in Huntington that night, and the next day I drove her around town. Huntington, whose population according to the 1990 U.S. Census was 54,844, is the second largest city in West Virginia, right behind Charleston, the state capital. I had lived in Huntington in one neighborhood or another from the time I was in the third grade until my junior year in high school, when I had been expelled about the same time my old man had lost another job and he had moved our family south to Bluefield for a new start. I showed Holly some of the various houses we had lived in, including three different ones on Crestmont Road. I drove her by my rich high school sweetheart Ruthie's big house over on Staunton Road on a bluff above the Ohio River. Holly pumped me for details about Ruthie, sexy stuff, and she had me show her places Ruthie and I had parked up on Snake Road in old Ritter Park. It was her turn today, Holly said, to hear dirty details.

We got on Interstate 64 outside of Huntington, and followed it east to Charleston, where we picked up Interstate 77 North. It was raining cats-and-dogs by then. We drove along in silence while Holly studied the map. The plan was to turn east again on Route 33 and try to find that old turn-of-the-century octagonal-shaped church over in Calhoun County where my great-grandfather, Jim Kinder, had been its first preacher. One thing I had told Holly I wanted to do during my travels down in southern West Virginia was to visit towns at the dead ends of roads. I wanted to visit these little dead-end towns, and take pictures, and talk to people who lived there about what it felt like to live at the very dead end of a road, with only one way in and one way out. Holly had spotted a town not many miles off Interstate 77 North that was, according to the map, at the dead end of a road. The town's name was *Romance*.

Because of the stormy weather, I told Holly that I thought it might be a good idea to drive back into the hills in search of Romance on another trip, but Holly insisted we do it then. A few miles past Sissonville on 77, we turned east and headed into the hills in the driving rain on a road that seemed to be crumbling before our eyes and so narrow my right tires repeatedly dropped over the berm. It was like driving through soup, and the wipers were helpless in the sheets of rain that swept over the windshield and the windows began steaming over in spite of the defrost going full blast. —Come on, honey, I said, —let's find it another time, sweetie-pie. —I want to find Romance today, Holly insisted, affecting that cute little-girl pout featuring a lot of lower lip that always gave me a chubby and made her point. Holly said: —I have a feeling that if we don't find Romance today, we never will, sweetie-pie. —Sure we will, I told her, —but on a day when I can see to drive faster than five fucken miles an hour. By that point it had started to hail ice objects the approximate size of golf balls, and I was absolutely driving blind, so I pulled over off the road to wait for the hurricane to blow over. We had been on that road for miles past where, according to the map, we should have hit the turnoff to Romance, and I hadn't seen any signs of side roads that would lead us to that place. Holly sat there quietly watching the water pour down her side window, deep in thought. I smoked a joint and listened to the radio and looked out my own window, deep in my own thoughts.

After a while Holly said, —I thought you were supposed to be this big-time, fearless good-old-country boy with a brand new four-wheeling *Red Ride* that could take you anywhere. I thought you were going to look for adventure and excitement back in the dark, dangerous hills. My old boyfriends and I used to go up and down hills a lot more rugged than these in old, beat-up pickup trucks. My old boyfriend Johney would have taken me to find Romance in a minute, Holly said and grinned crookedly, giving me that sassy, dare-you, expectant look. —I know, I told Holly. I had heard all about old Johney last night, I reminded her. I had heard all about how she and old Johney had slipped into a shower at the campgrounds of a state park one foggy morning before dawn. I had heard about how they had soaped each other up, and then did it standing up all hot and slippery in that steaming shower. How they had kept on doing it even after they heard other people come into adjoining stalls. And then old Johney had turned Holly around and started plunging it into her from behind, and when she had cried out for him to please stop or she would go crazy, you could hear everybody else in the place drop their soap. But good, old, dependable Johney had kept plunging it in and out until Holly had thought she would die and go to heaven. And she had bit the back of her hand to keep from crying out again. But she couldn't help it. And when Holly had come she had screamed out at the top of her lungs *Rhododrendron* for God's sake *Rhododrendron!*

Holly laughed quietly and tugged lightly on my ear, and then we had just sat there listening to the vehicle tick and the low radio and the buckets of rain beat on the roof. I knew there was no town named Romance at the dead end of an old mountain road in our immediate future. Not that day for sure. Finally, as it continued to rain relentlessly, and streaming water was turning the narrow road into a river, I had simply put the vehicle in gear, and, without comment, turned the Red Ride around and started back toward the four-lane. After a while I said to Holly that we would come back some other day to find the town of Romance at the end of that road, to which she had offered no comment. But little Holly had been right as rain about that too, like she turned out to be right about so many things, for we never did return.

There is a strange little one-room church in Calhoun County that sits next to W.Va. Route 33 just outside of Sand Ridge. According to an old article about it my mother had clipped out of the *Charleston Gazette*, it is called Albert's Chapel, and it is on the National Register of Historic

Places and is also listed in *Ripley's Believe It or Not* as one of the world's most oddly shaped churches, for it is octagonal. It is called Albert's Chapel after Albert Poling, who, along with the help of relatives who were carpenters and lumberjacks, built it in 1899. Matilda Belle Poling got the inspiration to build a church in the shape of a circle from a dream in which a heavenly voice coming from a burning bush quoted a line from Isaiah that said: "It is he that sitteth upon the circle of the Earth."

Eight whitewashed wooden panels make up the circular, eight-sided exterior, and old-fashioned oystershell glass fills the windows. The pews, pulpit, and door frames are handcrafted maple, and were cut, carved, and polished by Albert's brother, Nicholas Poling, and his cousin Charlie Poling. Copies of *Heavenly Highway Hymns* fill the upright shelves that line the back of each pew. Hanging on one of the walls is an old electric clock with Roman numerals that looks like a giant pocket watch. To the left of the pulpit is an upright piano. A wooden "Register of Attendance and Collections" keeps track of the chapel's business. Spare black and white letters for the register are kept in a tattered silver box on a stand underneath. A small framed copy of the Ten Commandments hangs on one side of the register. On the other side of the register hangs a small photo taken in the early 1900s of the chapel's first preacher, The Reverend Jim Kinder, or "Big Red," as my great-grandfather was known far and wide in his day.

According to family legend, Big Red mined coal during the week, and on the weekends, as an itinerant preacher, he traveled a circuit of mountain Methodist churches. He also made about the best moonshine in Calhoun County. From what I've been told, Big Red was sipping a little of his quality product while he was soaking in a hot bath late one Sunday night after he had come in off his grueling horseback holy trek through the hills doing the Lord's work, *amen,* and he had fallen asleep and sort of slipped beneath the water to his reward.

That rainy day Holly and I located the church, I walked all around taking photographs of that mountaintop white-frame building with the little cupola on its top, from every angle. I shot pictures of the graveyard that spread about it, including one unusual tombstone that looked like a granite tree-stump. Holly and I walked around peeking in the nearly opaque windows and then we stood on the front stoop to peer through the clear glass of its narrow double doors. I could barely make out the small, framed photograph of my great-grandfather, old Big Red, up by the pulpit. It had been raining off and on all day, and now, in the late afternoon, mist rose from the mountaintop graveyard around the church and the air was close and muggy, and then it began to sprinkle again as we stood there on the stoop under a narrow awning. The only house I could see nearby was maybe a hundred yards down the road back in some trees on our side. In the time we had been looking around, only one vehicle had passed, a beat-up old truck that had not even slowed for a second look.

I went out to the Red Ride and got my little pack of picks and jimmys my cousin R.J., a locksmith and successful sometimes burglar, had given me and taught me to use. Holly was grinning that I'm-ready-for-any-thing-in-the-world-you-can-possibly-think-up sexy grin when I came back up on the porch, and while I fiddled with the lock, she placed her fingertips in the small of my back and sort of bounced lightly up and down on her toes like an excited kid in line to ride a roller coaster.

Holly and I wandered around the little chapel, checking it out on that muggy, drizzly Sunday afternoon, and then we stood in front of that old photograph of my great-grandfather, old Big Red himself, while holding hands, and then Holly told me when we got married she hoped it would be right in this little oddly shaped church and then we took to kissing.

The next thing I knew I was sitting on the front pew with Holly strad-dled across my lap, and we were kissing deep and long. The rain had picked up, and I could hear it on the shingles of the roof, and I thought I could hear the faint, lazy drone of a bee up toward the ceiling. The air was hot and close, and soon the ends of Holly's long hair were wet and the back of her summer dress was damp under my hands. When I lifted her hair and cupped the back of her neck it was slick with perspiration, and my shirt front and the front of her dress were wringing wet and sticking together as we rubbed, and then we began licking the sweat from each other's faces and necks, and so then we had just gone and done it right there, made love like that, her going up and down on me, slowly, her short summer dress high on her bare, smooth, slippery legs, her hands gripping the top of the pew, her head thrown back, both of us dripping wet, and before long we were fucking like we were fighting, like we were feudists going at it tooth-and-nail, as though somebody could win.

At some point I gazed over at the photograph of my great-grandfather, old Big Red, at his stern, fierce, piercing black eyes and bushy eyebrows and thick mustache, at his wavy hair and big hairy ears and small chin, a man who I didn't look like at all, thank you, Jesus, and what I thought about as I tried not to come was Big Red slipping to his reward beneath his bathwater bone-tired and pleasantly drunk and pleased with himself for doing such a good job preaching the word of the Lord Jesus Christ Amen in the backcountry churches that weekend, and I sort of knew how he felt. I could identify with my great-grandfather Big Red as he had sunk down to his reward.

BIG IRON

I hear you're a lowdown, yellow Yankee dog, Shane says, his eyes cold and calm.

—Prove it, the gun-fighter dressed all in black says, his face spread with an evil grin, his gloved hands hovering near his guns.

—Why is it I have to run into a punk kid with a big mouth in every town I hit? Ringo says, standing calmly at the bar with a whiskey in his hand.

The punk kid is plugged before his gun clears the holster. Ringo just stands there at the bar calmly, smoke swirling about his drawn gun, the drink still steady in his hand.

My hobby when I was a kid was gunfights. I collected them from the Western movies. My best boyhood buddy, Jim Handloser, and I would spend hours re-enacting our favorite gunfights time and again in exact detail. We could spend a whole Saturday afternoon going over and over just the shootouts in *Shane* or *High Noon* or *The Gunfighter*. And on the final showdown between Gary Cooper and Burt Lancaster in *Vera Cruz*, we could spend a weekend.

My best pal Jim and I draw and fire in the same instant with blinding speed. Playing Burt Lancaster, I stand there grinning his famous Burt Lancaster grin. With a fancy twirl, I holster my big iron. I still just stand there grinning. After a couple of moments, still grinning, I topple forward dead as a doornail into the dust of the Western Movie.

* * *

Quite simply, I have always longed to star in a gunfighter story wherein I pull the Big Iron first. But I am compelled to tell the utter truth here. I have to stick with the pure facts here. I have to come clean here before I can advance honestly in this narrative.

I did not exactly quick-draw a blue snub-nose .38 Detective Special on that Sid Hatfield wanna-be pimply slacker back in Matewan. But why did I tell you, my gentle reader, that I had drawn a gun, something so contrary to my essential poetic nature? I could not help myself at the time, gentle reader. Maybe I wanted to show you another side of me. Maybe it simply seemed necessary for the sake of the narrative at that point. The story just took over, that's the basic reason.

I admire Flannery O'Connor and her fluid, organic sense of the essential flow of story; I admire her perfect sense of the nature of narrative. In one of her letters, O'Connor talks about how in "Good Country People" she didn't have any idea that that evil Bible salesman would steal that poor woman's wooden leg up in that hay loft until maybe two sentences before he did it. And she was not only surprised but appalled that one of her characters was capable of doing such a horrible, bizarre thing. And she tried to undo it. She tried to rewrite that scene. But she found she couldn't. The story had taken over and come into a life of its own. That Bible salesman character she had created from the whole cloth of her own imagination had broken free from her control and did exactly what the story demanded he do. That's a magic moment in fiction, I tell my students. Trust the accidents, I tell them. A story is a story is a story. Only the story counts, I tell my students.

But at its heart this book is not fiction; it is not some novel, gentle reader. I simply forgot for a few lines that I wasn't writing fiction. I slipped into old fictioneer habits. It was a relapse. It was an accident. I wasn't in control enough not to let a character named Chuck Kinder take over the narrative and do exactly what he thought the story demanded he do, no matter what the true facts, or consequences, for that matter. I must remember that reality is not governed nor ordered by such artificial fictional considerations as rising action, crisis actions, denouements.

But everything else is true. I swear it! That bold blind tourist and his seeing-eye whore were real. I did win that game of eight ball and the twenty bucks. I danced that bittersweet slow-dance with Holly before that wall of blue-tinted mirrors reflecting us in imaginary time. I swear it, gentle reader.

book four

FAMOUS
ANCIENT
INDIANS &
MOTHMEN &
MOMMA

LAND OF THE SKY PEOPLE

Thousands of years before the first Europeans showed up on the scene in the seventeenth century, a mysterious race of giant ancient Indians wandered into what is now West Virginia out of the misty twilight of the Paleolithic Great Hunt following mammals long since extinct, such as the giant ground sloth, the great bison, woolly mammoths. These Adena Culture people, more commonly called the Moundbuilders, due to the tumuli in which they buried their ochre-painted dead, constructed such impressive burial mounds and earthworks that many West Virginia archaeologists have entertained theories that they were not built by ancestors of the "lowly Injuns" at all, but rather by a lost race of superior beings, such as the lost tribes of Israel or relic peoples from the sunken continent of Atlantis.

Hundreds of earthen mounds remain in West Virginia, the most mysterious legacy of the Moundbuilders, whose tribes once settled throughout the Mississippi drainage basin and southeastern states. The Adenas were unusually tall—enormous, in fact. Bones of women over six feet in height and men approaching seven feet have been found. They had large flat skulls, huge foreheads, heavy brow ridges, jutting chins, and massive bones. This band of really big Indians battled its way into the Ohio Valley before 10,000 B.C., and then kicked indigenous native butt all the way up the Kanawha River, where remnants of their culture lasted until about 200 A.D. Where these huge ancient Indians came from remains a mystery. Some archaeologists have suggested Mexico as the migrators' distant matrix, and have presented long lists of parallels between the Adena peoples and those of early Mexico. Take for example the use of trophy skulls in burials, or the common custom of head-binding to flatten the skull.

Only in very ancient sites in the Valley of Mexico, Tlatilco, El Arbollo, and Ticoman, can you find comparable evidence of people who so deformed their heads as did the Adenas, beginning with circular bindings in infancy. The adult skulls found in mounds exhibit foreheads that are among the widest known in the history of the world. The distinctive, almost artfully misshapen skulls of the most select individuals buried in the Adena mounds suggest a fascination with deformity that approaches deification. Deformed holy subjects were not uncommon in Middle and South American art. The large ear-spools and the bent knees of an Adena Pipe figurine found in a burial mound in Ross County, Ohio, definitely suggest Olmec influences. Somebody noticed that this little figurine was a dead ringer for a achondroplastic dwarf with a goiter and rachitic joints. The actual skeleton of one such achondroplastic dwarf has been found in an Adena mound near Waverly, Ohio, surrounded by wondrous grave riches.

What this boils down to is that the Adenas had a highly developed cult of the deformed and dead, and at their ceremonial sites built impressive mounds over the remains of their contorted kings, misshapen shamen, gnarled priests, and others of their honored gimps. They buried their royal monsters in barbaric splendor, sealing their grotesque giants and twisted dwarves in the dark with grave goods that must have been tribal treasures. There were pounds of freshwater pearls and crystals of quartz found, necklaces of exotic gems and shells and nuggets of mete-oric iron, beautiful stone and terra-cotta rings, sheets of hammered silver and gold, ornaments made from the shells of sea-going turtles, ceremonial copper axes and breastplates, mica ornaments of such delicacy as to suggest transparency, bones carved like birds, human bones beautifully engraved with crested-bird swastikas, the effigies of animals long extinct carved upon the teeth of bears and panthers, headdresses of copper deer antlers with a hundred points, all sorts of copper effigy figures suggesting shamanic transformation, copper shamanic figures that could depict either men wearing masks made from the skin of the dead or the dead masked in the skin of the living, suggesting that dominant theme of evolving planter cultures: that life and death are one, that life comes out of death and death comes out of life, that out of the plant king's death comes the life of the tribe.

The Adena constructed their mounds over many generations, layering their dead in new burials as they needed to for their select few. Apparently those select few were accompanied into eternity with various of their servants or slaves or assorted family members or really good friends. The Adenas lived near and used their ceremonial cemetery mounds over periods that may have lasted for centuries, but the burials in these mounds were relatively rare.

To be sealed ceremonially in consecrated earth was clearly an honor, perhaps one in which the selected ancient Indian holy cripples, with the ritual songs of the shamanic visionaries in their ears, would limp toward willingly, and undertake the perilous dream journey into the invisible world for the people.

When the Great Smith Mound, which was located in the town of Dunbar on the Kanawha River (a mound leveled in the 1940s in order to build a tennis court for the local high school), was first excavated in 1883, they found skeletons at different levels from different Adena eras, including one skeleton that measured seven and one-half feet in length. This gigantic skeleton was surrounded by ten other skeletons arranged so that their bony toes pointed toward it. The surrounding skeletons were in such contorted positions as to suggest unhappy live burials.

When archaeologists excavated the Grave Creek Mound at Moundsville, which is perhaps the most striking prehistoric earthwork in West Virginia at 69 feet in height and 295 feet in diameter at its base, they discovered the skeletons of a man and a woman. Their bones were entangled, as though they had been embracing when death approached to claim them, as though that ancient couple was making love in the moments before their ritual assassination. Clearly that couple was having sacrificial sex, dream-screwing for their tribe to demonstrate that death meant nothing. Their ritual fornication was clearly a ceremony in honor of the eternal loss and restoration of innocence. Clearly their Wedding

Ordeal in their Honeymoon Tomb was a pilgrimage to and back from that sacred land of timelessness, where, untouched by the transformative force of *becoming,* there were no lasting pangs of loss and desire.

Earthworks on the crests of the mountains along the Kanawha River stymie archaeologists. Along the hilltops above Montgomery, that little river town where I was born, there are these remnants of a stone wall that once ran along the mountaintops for many miles. Most archaeologists say they have no idea what these hilltop earthworks were for. Old Timey Red Injun Devil Worship, a few West Virginia archaeologists have opined. When I was a boy I climbed up into those pyramidal mountains every day. I spent hours up there, sitting on that old stone wall alone.

Years later, when I was a student at West Virginia Institute of Technology in Montgomery, for maybe the second or third time, one lovely autumn afternoon I took a girl I loved but couldn't get to first base with up to see that old wall. We made a picnic of it, taking along a bag of apples and some cheese and bread, and a bottle of red wine, plus several joints I had rolled the night before. As an experiment, I had soaked these joints with Pernod and let them dry overnight. I really wanted to get to first and second and third base with that girl. I longed to engage in ritual fornication with that girl. I longed for us to entangle our bones.

The girl I loved with all my heart wasn't much of a hiker, though (she fancied herself a hip, arty type, a poetess who cultivated paleness). We had to stop often to rest as we wove our way up the steep mountainside among the trees and rock outcroppings. When we finally reached the top ridge, I showed her a section of the old wall where I had hung out a lot as a kid, which was just barely recognizable as a man-made construction now, and looked more like an oddly shaped mound. But it still excited me, and I babbled to the girl I loved about how I had spent hours simply pressing my hands against the earth-matted stones while trying to imagine the touch of the hands that ages before had positioned those stones. Why, I had wondered out loud to her, did those ancient Indians build a wall along the tops of the mountains? What were they building it against? And, more curious than that, which side of the mountain were they afraid of? Were they afraid, maybe, that some monster might awake from the river far below and stalk into the hills to eat them raw?

I told the girl I loved that a lot of Indian names, many of them of great beauty, had been preserved in the names of rivers in Appalachia. There was *Ohio*, which meant "river of whitecaps" or "the white foaming waters." There was *Shenandoah*, "daughter of stars." And *Monongahela*, "river of falling banks." And then there was that river winding in the valley far below us, the ancient *Kanawha*, which meant "place of the white stone" or, in the language of the Shawnee, *Keninsheka*, "river of evil spirits," which clearly might be a clue as to which side of the mountain the ancient Indians believed their concept of King Kong would come clomping up to get them.

I told the girl I loved that by the time the white man came into this rugged area, not many Indians were left, and the explorers found only a vast wilderness broken here and there by old "ghost fields" that Indians had once cultivated, and by the remnants of Indian "ghost villages" long abandoned. There was still plenty of game in the hills and the soil of the bottomlands was rich, but, for whatever reason, disease, intertribal warfare, the Indians had mostly vanished. But it was curious, I told her, that many of the Indians' origin legends and creation myths were set in the mountains of West Virginia. Maybe the old pyramidal mountains of West Virginia had simply become too mythological, too sacred, too full of the ghosts of ancient ancestors for the profanity of everyday Indian life. Finally they had visited that religious landscape, that cult arena, that they had come to call the *Land of the Sky People*, only for ceremonial rites of passage or to pray.

—How do you know all this neat Indian stuff? the hip, poetic, pale girl who I loved wanted to know. —Indian stuff has always just blown my mind, man, she added.

—Because of all the Indian blood that flows in my veins, I informed her. We had piled dry leaves at the base of a large rock to sit upon while we leisurely nibbled our apples and cheese and bread and sipped our jug red wine and passed the Pernod-soaked joints, which really hit the spot, by the way. As the afternoon slowly lengthened into evening, we watched down the slope through the limbs of the bare trees as the lights began to come on in the valley below, which from such a height as ours looked so frail, those valley lights, the bleached halo about each one seeming so small yet resilient in the falling darkness. I had whispered to that hip, poetic, pale girl I loved how there was Indian blood flowing in my veins from both sides of my family, blood I could trace back through my mother's lineage to the great Shawnee warrior-chief Cornstalk, and on my father's side to the great Delaware shaman, priest, and poet–prophet, Chief Bull, who Bulltown on the Little Kanawha River was named after. Which accounted for my own Indian middle-name, *Alfonsohontas,* which translated roughly as "he who can carry his tale."

What I can remember to this day is how the dry leaves gently scratched my bare back and crackled sweetly, and how the clean smell of the fall air rose from the cool, smooth skin of the girl I loved. But then suddenly she screamed, that girl I loved, and jumped up off of me, and covered her perfect, pale breasts with her arms, then pointed toward the darkness under an old oak and screamed again.

—Whatwhatwhatwhatwhat? I was curious to know.

—I saw him, man! the hip, poetic girl screamed and pointed under the tree.

—Saw who saw who saw who? I inquired. I jumped up and looked about wildly.

—Something! Fucking somebody! A fucking Indian, man! the girl I loved wailed and began to frantically pull her clothes on, as she slid and slipped down the steep mountainside.

—What fucken Indian? I inquired, as I put up my dukes and spun around and around. —What fucken Indian? I don't see any fucken Indian!

And I didn't. But that girl I loved sure had seen something. And I could hear that hip, poetic girl whimper *shitshitshit* as she scrambled down the mountain, her lovely pale back soon lost to my sight in the encroachment of night.

GHOST OF THE INDIAN
UNDER THE TREE

In November of 1777, the great Shawnee Chieftain Cornstalk was murdered in cold blood, along with his son Elinipsico and a couple of other warriors, by militiamen at Fort Randolph. Chief Cornstalk, a man of honor, had repaired to Fort Randolph in an attempt to maintain peace with the colonialists. Legend has it that Chief Cornstalk, before he died, placed a curse upon the militiamen and all their generations, and upon the point where the fort stood, a wide, lovely, and peaceful expanse of land lined by tall trees where the Ohio and Kanawha Rivers converged that was known by the Ayamdotte Indian phrase "tu-endie-wei," translated as "the point between two waters," or "the mingling of waters."

Many years later this area would be named Point Pleasant, but that did not lift the curse. Now, legend has it that Cornstalk's curse was not to avenge his own death, which he accepted with calmness and nobility, but for the murder of his son and other young companions. True or not, over the two hundred years since the murder of Chief Cornstalk, many calamities have befallen that otherwise pleasant part of the world, such as great recurring floods and fires and the frequent visitations of strange, unearthly beings, call them aliens or angels, that as often as not have proven to be portents of disaster.

The curse of Chief Cornstalk was once visited upon my mother in the form of a great wild bird when she was a little girl in Point Pleasant. It happened during the course of one of the monotonous floods when she was nine or ten. Her father, who had not yet lost his garage and car lot

197

in town, where he repaired and bought and sold automobiles, had moved all the vehicles, either by driving or towing, to the high ground of the field above their house, where looking out over them one foggy morning, Mom let herself imagine they were a herd of some wondrous, giant, dreaming turtles.

The floodwaters had driven the wild chickens and roosters from their roosts in the willow trees in the mudflats by the river up into the hillside woods and meadows, and many had nested among the cars and trucks parked above the house. One sultry, buggy afternoon, Mom's mother sent her to the little country store over the hill to buy a bottle of vanilla extract for a big batch of macaroons she had to bake for her church circle. This was a trek Mom dreaded, for it meant that unless she wanted to follow the blacktop road around over the hill, a good mile walk roundtrip, she would have to go down that shortcut path through the woods, where at the path's sharp right turn, Mom had seen the naked body of a dead man back under the bramble bushes. Because none of her little brothers were around to go with her, Mom took the long way, and upon her return she had cut down through the field of great dreaming turtles.

Mom was weary and hot but mostly just bored from the walk and she drug her bare feet through the high grass as she drifted along. Her head was in the clouds as usual. Her own mother always accused Mom of being a dreamy girl with no sense of direction, like a little cloud. Mom trudged along that day only half-hearing the sweet drone of bees back in the apple trees at the edge of the field and dreaming of faraway places and love. As a child, Mom had always imagined that she was somehow a very special person. She never mentioned this to anybody else, but she knew she took special pleasure and comfort from things other children did not, like walking luxuriously barefoot through the rain, or hiding in the top of the old apple tree by the house, where its gnarled branches held a secret lap only for her. She would sit curled up in the bay window of her bedroom over a beloved book for hours. She took so much private pleasure it hurt sometimes, in the beauty of storm clouds moving across the sky or a crow's call or tiny blue wildflowers struggling up through slowly melting snow. Mom's dreams of love and solitude were her best friends. Not romantic boy–girl love, kissy stuff, necessarily, just love, love, tender, gentle love that would make you not always want to be alone.

Mom's head was in the clouds as she hummed and strolled down over the hillside meadow among the dreaming turtles. The sky was clouding over again for even more rain, which meant more flooding, but Mom didn't care. Mom prayed for rain. What Mom thought at first was that something had exploded, a can of gas or something, in a blazing ball of red flame out of the back of the pickup truck she was passing. But then she realized that she was being engulfed by feathers, not flames. Blazing red feathers surrounded her like fire she could burn up in!

The wild rooster was red as an Indian and big as a turkey. It was a great warpath headdress of a killer rooster. Its claws were as blue as a wound and its popped-out, lidless, yellow eyes insane. It was a pure malevolent commotion of flapping, snapping comb and racket of red rattling feathers. Mom began to scream as it raged about her pecking and clawing and flying at her face with its fierce spurs. The field was a hysteria of cackling and clatter and Mom screamed and ran for her life as that devil bird flew through the air after her for revenge. It was as she ran terrified down through the field with that bird at her back that Mom caught a glimpse out of the corner of her eye of the Indian standing under the apple tree. Then even as that devil bird landed on her head, Mom slowed to look. The Indian under the tree was wearing a bright war-bonnet with red feathers and buckskins and the right side of his face was painted blue.

Mawmaw, my grandmother, Mom's mother, saw the ghost of the Indian under the apple tree too. Mawmaw was accustomed to seeing ghosts, but she had never seen the ghost of an Indian before, so when she spotted him through the kitchen window standing out under the apple tree, she had gone onto the back porch to get a better look. It was then that she saw her daughter tearing down the path from the upper field screaming and flailing her arms frantically at a giant red bird that rode her head like her own Indian war-bonnet.

That wild rooster was real enough, Mawmaw could see, it was no ghost chicken. She picked up a hoe at the edge of the porch and hurried out into the back yard to greet that bird blazing atop her only daughter's head. Mawmaw was a short, stout woman with veiny forearms as thick as a man's. She swung that hoe like a baseball bat when she bashed that wild rooster, which sailed like a fly-ball of a bird backward across the yard to land at the feet of the Indian ghost. Clubbed silly, the huge bird flopped about in crazy, dizzy circles as Mawmaw descended upon it with the gleaming blade of the hoe raised high. In the flushed, shifting light under the apple-trees at the edge of the yard, the ghost of the Indian dissolved like fluttering specks of tinsel. Mawmaw clobbered the bird again, and then she thrust a hand amid the spastic flurry of feathers and grabbed the rooster up by its blue claws, and she carried it head-down across the yard to the chopping stump. The bird flapped its giant, red wings awkwardly, upside-down, as though trying to escape into a strange, dizzy, dirt sky.

Mawmaw swung the rooster solidly across the bloodstained block, stunning it still. For maybe a heartbeat her axe hovered above the thick, feathered neck, then it thudded down. The rooster ran headless back in the general direction of the field where the giant turtles were dreaming, as though now that its hunger for vengeance was sated at long last, it wanted to return to the chicken nations and have things be just like they had been before the evil, wily white man came. After several yards the headless rooster folded into the long grass, a pile of trembling feathers and spastic little kicks and twitches. Finally, only its bloody red feathers quivered, as though stirred gently by unseen breath.

From up in the field, the ancient racket of fear and alarm was soon gone, and the wild chickens went back to pecking about in the tall grass among the dreaming turtles, the great rooster ancient history. Mawmaw hung the rooster by its legs from a fencepost, to let its blood drain. There did not seem to be all that much blood, though. At least not as much as Mom might have expected from such a great bird. What there was, though, was bright red. It dripped soaking into the dirt, absorbed in dark swirling patterns that drew Mom's eye, as she stood there on the back porch shivering, crying soundlessly, as she had taught herself to do, wishing her mother would hold her, would caress her and rock her and kiss those scratches instead of burning them with iodine and slapping band-aids over them abruptly, as though Mom had done something personally wrong to incur the wrath of Chief Cornstalk's curse.

PICTURES OF THE DEAD

Mom hated change. The greatest sea-change Mom made in her life after Dad died, besides learning to drive, a very dubious undertaking, was to sell their brick house in Beckley with its big back yard, which was way too much for her to handle. With the proceeds she bought a little house in Billville, twenty miles away, near my sister's home, on a tree-shaded dead-end street inhabited by other little old widow-women. It was a fairy cottage of a white frame house, with a working fireplace, which Mom had always wanted. Mom immediately had champagne-colored carpets installed, which she had wanted all her life. She hung pictures of her side of the family on walls she had painted off-white champagne. Mom then commenced to transform herself into a Baptist church-lady.

Mom had actually been baptized as a Baptist, something I never knew, because all of her married life she had been a nominal Methodist, the religious flavor of Dad's side of the family. In Billville, Mom joined my sister's church, which was Baptist and the religious flavor of my brother-in-law's side of the family. Mom blossomed as a small-town Baptist church-lady. She dressed to the church-lady nines, and, trusting utterly in the Lord, drove herself to church twice on Sundays and on several weekday evenings, times when my brother-in-law had to be almost forced at gunpoint to get on the road.

My brother-in-law had taught Mom to drive, more or less. He considered that endeavor to have been one of most dangerous things he had done in his turbulent life. Fortunately, when Mom had barreled through that red light and plowed into that pickup truck, nobody was killed nor seriously injured, although all involved, including my blathering brother-in-law, were afforded free ambulance rides to the hospital for various cuts and bruises and observation.

Mom became the Love Gift chairlady for the Leota Campbell Circle. Her monthly Bible program presentations were much admired by the other little church-ladies for their insight into Scriptures that dealt with the elderly and their special loneliness and hopelessness and loss of self-worth. Mom, the new widow-woman on the block, became universally admired for being well read and articulate and refined and for her generosity of Christian spirit. Mom was known for never ever spreading back-fence gossip as the other old busybody church-ladies did like farmers layering a field with ripe manure. Mom was also still quite a looker for an oldster. Folks still told Mom she reminded them of that beautiful movie star Loretta Young.

At 70-plus years old, Mom began to sing. Neither my sister nor I had ever heard Mom sing since our days of childhood lullabies. On all those car trips as kids when Dad would drive along singing the old World War Two standards at the top of his lungs, flapping his tongue out the window like a flag, Mom would sit there quietly, her arms folded across her breasts, looking at the blur of passed life out her side window. My sister usually sat in church with Mom amid the rows upon rows of little blue-haired widows (my brother-in-law sang in the choir). My sister told me Mom had a high, clear, watery, beautiful soprano voice, which she lifted unabashedly to the Lord in old gory Baptist favorites, such as "Washed in the Blood," or "Power in the Blood," or "Singing in the Blood." Mom had transformed herself into a warbling widow.

After I moved down to Billville, I was able to spend more time with Mom than I had since I was a kid. A couple or three times a week, I would take her out to lunch at Shoney's, where she adored their spaghetti and garlic toast. Sometimes I would take Mom to Billy Ray's, a respectable enough restaurant if you avoided the bar area, which we did so Mom wouldn't worry about being compromised in the reputation department. Billy Ray's was also adequate in the spaghetti department, and I could get a drink there. I often took Mom grocery shopping at Kroger's out at the mall or over to Beckley on errands or to see one of her dozen or so doctors. Three or four evenings a week, I drove Mom over for dinner at my sister's. I was a good boy.

I called every morning to check in on my old momma. I called to listen to her lament about how she had no appetite, how she had gotten dizzy earlier going down the basement stairs in order to hunt for old pictures and letters and any other bones she could dig up about the family to help me write my book. Mom lamented about how she couldn't sleep on account of her ancient dreams of that dead naked body in the woods.

Each morning when I called, I ritually drug Mom's daily needs from her. Sometimes she said she needed skim milk and lite bread. Sometimes she needed cottage cheese and some nice skinless chicken breasts. Or maybe a pound box of no. 2 spaghetti noodles, plus a jar of Paul Newman's Own chunky mushroom & black olive spaghetti sauce. Plus cherry popsicles, sugar-free, and maybe a nice can of beets. Or a can of sardines in spring water, say, and maybe a little bottle of church-lady elixir. She would be home all day all alone as usual, Mom informed me, working on her crossword puzzles and watching television and crocheting until the pain in her fingers became like fire, so I could just drop the stuff off any old time at all. For she sure wasn't hard to find. She sure wasn't going anywhere. It had become clear to me that what Mom needed most in life was a cute, clean, little old man. And rich would be nice. Mom had too much time on her hands, clearly. And the crocheting madness was only the most recent manifestation of that sorry fact.

Mom had only taken up crocheting in the months before my arrival in town, and in no time had crocheted several really lovely comforters, most of which she had given away for presents. Then Mom heard about a crafts store up off Route 19 at Birch River, which apparently specialized in local church-lady handmade items. She cajoled my niece into driving her up to Birch River, and sure enough, the proprietor took a half dozen of her comforters on consignment. He claimed he would sell them at fifty bucks apiece and give Mom half. Mom was elated and hope-simple. Mom began counting her comforters before they hatched, and she spent her 300 bucks in about a dozen different imagined ways. Then weeks passed, and no sales. The crafts store proprietor grew a little testy at Mom's twice-daily calls. Presently my old momma became quiet and distant. At one point Mom said to me: —Chuckie, I feel about as low as whale bowels on the bottom of the ocean.

It grieves me to see my Mom mope. One afternoon when I was buzzing by that crafts store up on Route 19, which was in an old barny-affair of a building, I dropped in. The place was stuffed to the rafters with handmade old-coot carved goods, wooden toys and whistles and duck decoys and coal figurines, plus piles of church-lady brooms and corncob dolls and patch-quilts and maybe a million comforters. I found Mom's comforters on a table along a back wall.

Up front I told the proprietor, this artsy-fartsy artiste type with a goatee and wire-rim glasses, that I had heard some Eileen Kinder cro-cheted comforters were there on consignment. I told him I had driven all the way down from Pittsburgh looking for some Eileen Kinder com-forters, that Eileen Kinder comforters were becoming all the rage and real collectors' items for craft-goods connoisseurs in the city.

Hastily wire-rims big-hipped it back to that table, and returned with all six of the comforters. Grinning not unlike a cat that had just eaten an extremely tasty canary, wire-rims told me Mom's comforters were selling for two hundred bucks apiece. I smiled evilly and informed that fellow he was full of crap. I told him I would take all six at sixty apiece if he would assure me Eileen Kinder would get half of that, and when he said, well, all right then, I pulled my plastic out like a pistol.

The fellow looked up at me quizzically when he read the *Kinder* on my plastic. I arched my eyebrows and wrinkled my forehead and informed him in my best, tight, tough-guy Robert Mitchum voice that if my old momma didn't get her fair share, or ever got wind of this here transaction, I would come back and pay him a real serious visit of a crim-inal nature.

Mom went nuts, of course. Mom burned up the phone-wires to all the relatives, such as my kid brother in Houston, about God's blessing, amen, and how she planned upon sharing her bounty with her children. She planned to buy out the Sears catalogue for Christmas presents that year. Mom informed us that she planned to become, in effect, a church-lady cottage industry. Mom planned to quit doing her beloved yard-work or attending church morning, noon, and night in order to stay home and crochet comforters for the sake of her children, amen. Mom figured that if she worked day and night, stopping only for a little nourishment now and then, she could finish maybe two comforters a week, meaning she could make 104 of those babies a year, which would bring her in an annual bonanza of $3,640 to shower on her loved ones, amen.

I consulted with my sister. I told my sister it was up to her to do something, to put a stop to that madness. I told her to catch the old woman's fingers in a car door if it came to that. But it hadn't quite come to that. Mom only completed maybe another three or four comforters at her day-and-night pace, before she could barely bend her dear old swollen fingers. At sixty bucks apiece, I figured I could afford that.

Sometimes after experiencing uncanny seizures of the general guilts about my various failures in life, in particular as a husband, twice, and as a son too, when all was said and done, I assuaged my shame by buzzing out to Kroger's and loading up on Mom's adored fatty favorites, those guilty treats that would probably someday stop her heart. Shopping in a sentimental frame of mind or half drunk is a dangerous enterprise for me, but with every can of salty Campbell's cream-of-shit soup I tossed into my cart for Mom, I felt better about myself.

As Mom and I packed her shelves one day with the six bags of epicurean delights I had paid an arm and a leg for, I pointed out how each item, each can of oyster stew or cream of mushroom soup, proved how much more I loved her than my sister ever could. Sure my sister had for years driven Mom to and from places maybe two dozen times a week, to church or the bank or to K-Mart or Kroger's or to the doc's or the dentist or out to decorate graves like clockwork. Sure my sister dropped by Mom's at least twice daily and called a dozen times and cooked Mom supper several times a week. Sure my sister forced my brother-in-law to fix Mom's furnace or pipes or roof. So what if my sister made the kids mow Mom's grass and rake her leaves and clear out brush in the back yard. So big deal, Momma!

So when was the last time my sister ever bought Mom a big bag of red licorice, Mom's and my fave candy of all time? was my basic question. And as evidence of my superior love, I held aloft a big plastic bag of what looked like long red worms, which Mom and I tore open together. Whereupon we commenced to chew and chomp piece after piece after piece extravagantly. Or, Momma, I mumbled, with my choppers nearly stuck together with red goo, but as smug as Perry Mason clinching a case, what about OVALTINE, baby?! I mumbled as I whipped out one of the three bottles of magical Church-Lady Elixir, which I had swung by the liquor store in Oak Hill especially to purchase.

Only in the matter of her bedtime beverage of choice did Mom backslide from her new church-lady incarnation. I called it Church-Lady Elixir, and Mom called it her Special Ovaltine. The liquor store called it Kahlua, licor de café, a product of Mexico (hecho en Mexico). Kahlua is great with coffee, or cream, or both. Mix a little Kahlua, an ounce say, with 1 and 1/2 ounces of vodka over ice in an old-fashion glass and you've got yourself a pretty decent Black Russian.

Because of her neighbor lady, an old bat who watched her window like it was television and told all, Mom cautioned me to make Ovaltine deliveries in Kroger's grocery bags. Every time I pulled up in front of Mom's house, that nosy neighbor looked like a spastic sheep with her woolly white head bobbing in her front window. I always had an amazing impulse to flick my dick and give the old bat a heart attack. Instead, I always settled for simply flipping her a subtle bird, and she always smiled and waved back.

Mom was confused by the passage of time and change, but she understood that all she could do was accept it with dignity and fortitude and maybe a nightly belt or two of her Special Ovaltine. Mom would face the amazingly long lonely nights sipping that magical elixir and worrying, for Mom a form of prayer. Mom watched late-night CNN news of floods and fires and hurricanes and worried about Billville being blown off the face of the Earth or about her basement flooding. Mom worried about having a stroke like Mawmaw did and not dying quickly with dignity, but being left paralyzed, left mute maybe, and blind, being left to live out her days with tubes up her nose in an old folks' home drooling and soiling herself helplessly. Mom worried that her granddaughter would get pregnant, or that her wild grandson would be killed in a car wreck. Mom worried about her old rattletrap breaking down while she was driving alone on the four-lane. Mom worried about getting cancer. Mom worried that her life had amounted to nothing. Mom worried about the secret lives of her children, especially mine. Mom worried she would never really forgive Dad for her life of lost opportunities and for leaving her in the poorhouse. Mom worried that because of her abiding anger she would never be the good Christian church-lady she longed to be. Mom worried that she would die bitter.

Mom worried about not being able to get that Ovaltine stain out of her champagne-colored carpet. Mom worried about being cursed and invisible and forgotten. Mom worried she wouldn't go to heaven. Mom worried that that O. J. Simpson killer would somehow get off scott-free and come to Billville and cut her throat. Indeed, Mom entertained that seemingly not uncommon old white widow-woman fear of having a gentleman caller of the African-American persuasion, who would look not unlike that Mike Tyson person, appear at her door in the dead of night crazied with the sudden burning uncontrollable desire for some ninety-year-old white church-lady nooky.

That particular afternoon Mom and I had loaded her larder with forbidden goodies, I saw that her living-room couch was stacked with her old family photo albums, which meant she had risked breaking her neck by carting them up the steep basement stairs. Clearly Mom had been waxing nostalgic and brooding, not a good sign. It meant Mom had been looking back through those musty tomes again, page by page, to linger among that great community of the lost.

I picked up the album on top and we repaired to the kitchen, where we sat at the tiny table, Mom sipping her Church-Lady Elixir and me doing shots of Dickel neat, as we pored over the pictures of the dead for hours. Mom told me anecdote after anecdote about those departed family members, bringing them briefly back to life for herself, and for me. The residue of whole lives, long eventful lives, emerged distilled in snippet-moments that flickered up in Mom's memory like little movies. As the day lengthened into evening, and the light became oblique and rosy in the kitchen, I wrote those little stories down in my spiral notebook. Those little silent movies, I should say, whose mute stars jerked and twitched in my imagination as I wrote as fast as I could. I captured what I could of Mom's living memory in those pages before it was too late, transforming her dead loved ones into word ghosts, shadowy rhetorical beings, whose only remaining existence was an exchange across that borderland between memory and imagination at a tiny kitchen table as night fell.

—Momma, I said at one point, —why don't you write down these memories yourself? I'll get you a book, you know, a journal. And you write down memories you don't mind sharing with me. Maybe I can use them in my book.

—What's your book about, Chuckie? Mom asked me. —You have never told me exactly.

—It is, I told my old momma and did a stiff shot of Dickel straight, —a do-not-go-gently, grumpy, grouchy, corny coming-of-old-age story, on one level anyway. It is also a forlorn, tear-jerky, but essentially true and finally foot-stomping country-song-of-myself. I want it to be a big jukebox of a book, sans any fancy, Yankee, outsider sentiments such as irony or understatement.

—Well, that certainly should be a best-seller, Mom said, and laughed. I loved Mom's laugh, high and lilting. But her old brow wrinkled with perplexity and doubt. —Who in the world would want to read a book about some old jukebox? she said.

—The book is also about the past, Momma, that land you love. It's about how the past lives on in the present, and the present lives in the unspeakable future, and the future lives in the escapable past.

—You always did talk in riddles, Chuckie, when you didn't want people to know you didn't know what you were talking about.

—Well, that's just what your old Bible does, Momma! Holy Moly! Talk about riddles! Talk about babble!

—Don't you dare compare your old book about jukeboxes or whatever to the Holy Bible! Shame on you, Chuckie! You can be such a turkey, son.

—Turkey! Where did you come up with that? You've clearly been spending way too much time with your hoodlum granddaughter. How can you call your handsome son a turkey, Momma?

—If the gobble fits, Chuckie.

—Mom, the book is partly about you. It's about your own story.

—You better not put me in some old jukebox book, Chuckie, Mom admonished me. —Don't you dare go around telling stories on me. Putting words in my mouth I never uttered in my life. Making me into somebody I'm not. I know you better than anybody in the world, Chuckie, and I know you lie like a rug. I won't allow you to do it, Chuckie.

—Okay, Momma, I said, but I knew I wouldn't do as I was told. I knew I was really a bad boy at heart.

—I don't need any journal to write my memories down in, Mom said. She took a sip of Ovaltine and stood up slowly. Her old knees were clearly killing her. She hobbled out of the kitchen.

I took a hit of Dickel and fired up one of my little cigars. Mom loved the smell of cigars. They made her think of her dad, who had always smoked cigars. I looked at a picture of Papaw Parsons when he was a young man. He was big and brawny and had thick strong wrists. I personally recalled Papaw as this big blustery man who seemed to suck the oxygen out of a room by his very presence. Papaw raised the roof beams high with his hearty laugh and he was known to take a drink. Mom had loved him more than about anybody. She had been the proverbial apple of his eye too. He personally took her to buy her prom dress, and when Mom purposefully picked the least expensive dress, Papaw insisted she take the elegant green one she truly loved instead. It didn't matter to Papaw that fine green dress cost fifty dollars, a fortune in those days.

Presently Mom came back into the kitchen. She was wearing her nightgown and robe. She placed a small blue-bound book on the table and then sat down with a sigh. Neither of us said anything for a few minutes. I looked at Mom, that essential stranger to me I loved, in that fading light of day, and what I wondered about suddenly was the nature of my own mother's secret life. What was Mom's secret story? What was the secret story of my mother's life?

—I used to write things down in this from time to time, Mom said, nodding at the small blue bound book. —You can have it if you want, Chuckie. I don't write in it any longer.

—What if I use it for material, Mom? You know I'll put it in the MOM MATERIAL file. I'll do it, you know.

—I just don't want you to put words in my mouth, Mom said. Mom didn't say much more that night before I left after a nightcap. She simply looked at me and sipped her Ovaltine while I puffed on my little cigar.

Mom had beautiful brown eyes that shone. Her hair shone in the bright overhead kitchen light too. Mom's hair was still long and brown and lovely like the late movie star Loretta Young's hair had once been when she was young and beautiful too. Mom was prettier than Loretta Young had ever dreamed of being, even when Loretta Young starred in movies such as *The Farmer's Daughter* or *The Bishop's Wife* with David Niven as her distracted husband and Cary Grant as the handsome, charming angel. I loved my Mom's dyed brown hair and her beautiful brown eyes. You could look a mile into those ageless brown eyes. You could get lost in their oceans of sadness and wisdom.

The Story of My Mother's Life in Her Own Words

As a child of around eleven, I really felt a special person. This I never mentioned, but to walk barefoot in a heavy rain, sit in the top of an old apple tree where its aged branches made a place just for me, or to curl up in the bay window over a loved book for hours, these things were special to me alone. The beauty of the rain, a crow's call, small wildflowers struggling through the quiet of melting snow, these were special things I cherished as nobody else could. And I had special dreams of love. During those years, dreams of love and solitude were my best friends.

Many people in my family have had the sixth sense. Mother had it. She first knew she had it when as a child of about eight or nine she and her cousin Muriel discovered they had a spirit for a playmate. She was about their age and always dressed in a blue party dress. She had very fair skin and dark hair and dark eyes. She would play with them but they could not play with her. They could see her plainly but could also see through her and Mother said the little ghost girl sort of flitted about in and out of their play place, always with a slight smile on her pretty pale face. They saw her so often they accepted her as their "fairy playmate." There was never any fear and Mother said they talked openly about it and their grandparents seemed also to believe them. I don't how long this lasted but I remember being told for years. I believe I have the sixth sense also, and that is behind me seeing the dead body in the woods that nobody else ever saw.

Who I loved most as a little girl was my Grandma Parsons. I spent most summers with her and how I loved those times. A part of each day was spent in the front-porch swing learning needle-work. Grandma's house was always immaculate and perfectly arranged, every pot with its own lid put in a certain place. She could cook or bake anything. I loved her cottage cheese and fresh-made butter and her lemon dressing was the best ever. In her younger days, Grandma taught school and rode horseback to get there, usually with a little one in both the front (she was always pregnant) and back of the saddle. Come evening and the apron came off and she would brush up and coil her long dark hair with its streaks of white high on her head with huge pearl-like hairpins and beautiful combs. She would put on a collar and fasten it with a brooch. On Sundays or on special occasions Grandma would wear earrings and use lipstick, which some people frowned on in those days. Grandma was truly a beautiful lady and had the smallest waist in the world. She must have worn a corset but one would never know for certain. I can still see those twinkling eyes and compressed lips when she had something on her mind that needed to stay there. Grandma was so adept at saying nothing loudly. I wanted to be just like her. I loved her so and she loved me too.

I suppose my parents loved me. I cannot be sure. Surely Dad did. I loved him so. My brothers, except little Sonny, must surely dislike me because I am always reprimanding them about their manners. Sonny is so dependent on me. I hold him at night. Why does he cry so? Why doesn't my mother know why? Sonny loves for me to rock and sing to him. Those are happy moments. My childhood was a salad of tossed feelings. The only really happy times were when I was alone thinking undisturbed thoughts or taking care of Sonny. I swore that when I grew up I would love my husband and my children in a way they would have no doubt about it.

They tell me I am very pretty, which makes me rather vain. I didn't really think much about being pretty until I started to high school, and at first I was shocked that people called me pretty, and really embarrassed also. Now I like it and want it to make me loved and cherished. I am. I cannot talk to Jimmy, but he seems to understand. In fact, it's like a mental and touch communication. I see Jimmy every Friday night, and there is a soft rain every Friday night. I am so happy.

I was so positive I would marry Jimmy. The months went on their way as if they were in such a hurry, so I locked a few very special memories away where I have always put my pieces of happiness. Some days (bad days) I take those happy pieces out to fondle and think about them. They are like fragile glass pieces of great value to be placed in any pattern I momentarily wish but to be put neatly back in place and locked up until needed again. They have become my strength (escape!).

I had decided to become a nurse, then a doctor. Those three years of nurse's training were so busy my life's happy pieces were rarely brought out. So little time to be alone. It was so strange being away from home. I became homesick and realized I loved my brothers so much more than I had ever shown them. And my parents, such sad people. If only I could have the chance to be good to them in some special way.

I am torn by this life I lead. I do not enjoy any part of this, but I cannot let anyone know except Jimmy. We do write. If it were not for his letters I would not want to live. Sometime I believe I am sick. My grades were good. I am told I am a good nurse.

I have met and fallen in love with Charles or in love with love. Jimmy was not there when I learned this new kind of love. Sometimes I write in the present tense as if these things are just happening. Can one love two people at once? No longer am I free to know. I will marry Charles. Now I feel guilty about the "happy beautiful pieces" I kept locked away. A few times I have taken them out, but before I can really touch them all I quickly replace them. They will not be tarnished in there and I might need them again. Not during this time though.

I have (had) a beautiful baby boy, Chuckie (Charles Alfonso Kinder II). He was a precious, long (21 inches), rather thin baby, with large dark eyes and a lot of black hair, the most anyone has seen on a newborn baby. Charles came into the hospital room before 6 A.M. to tell us "goodbye." The nurses let me keep the baby with me most of that day. I heard the train whistle as it left Montgomery. I thought how frightened and alone we were, how would we ever get through this? In those days you stayed in the hospital a good week at least. From there we went to Charles's parents, for there was nothing else to do. Chuckie became the town baby as Papaw and Mimi were well liked and between the three of us had him all over town in his stroller. Chuckie started talking earlier than any baby anybody ever knew. He soon was taught to say "Vote for Dewey." I believe everybody in town knew him and would stop us on the street and teach him something to say. After six months we packed up our few belongings and went down to Macon, Georgia, where Charles would be stationed for at least a year. I found a little place for us to live, renting a bedroom with a tiny kitchen and bathroom privileges. The house had a huge wrap-around porch where we spent a lot of time on those hot summer nights. As I had no car, I carried Chuckie 2 ½ blocks to get a bus to go to the grocery store. In a way those were happy times. Charles got home every few days but could never stay long. Eventually we found a little cottage in the country and here it was really pleasant.

Of course in time Charles was sent overseas. We returned to Montgomery and lived in an apartment. I was pregnant with Beth and actually those times were not too terrible.

Charles was in active combat and we were always on edge wondering where he was and if he was in danger, but it seemed everyone was going through the same thing so we were a comfort to one another. When Beth was a few months old we rented a little brown-shingled house in the lower end of town. During those years after the war ended Charles and his brother, Noyes, had a restaurant and we lived a typical all-American life. Chuckie began playing every day with "Jeto," an imaginary playmate. I used to listen to Chuckie through the window talking for hours with his little imaginary friend. It was unbelievable, Chuckie's imagination. Or maybe he has the sixth sense too, I thought one day. Anyway, Chuckie will become great because I can tell he is special. My Beth will love deeply, so she will be special. My Dave! What a joy he was when he came along, and in a way he meant more to me than should be told.

It's a long time since I have unlocked my life's happy pieces, for I know when I replaced them a few sad ones would slip in. I have not been a wise person. The children told me I was a good mother, but I disagree. I have not been the kind of wife my husband needed, at least in some ways.

Sonny is dead. So young, such a waste. He had left a very child-like young wife and a little boy, Ernie. Dad is dead and so is Mother.

Chuckie has married a fine person. I am sure they will be happy and have a good life. I have tried to teach my children how very important it is to find and hold happiness. Seek out what you do well—work at it. Hold onto good values. Set high standards for your life. Material things are not so important.

Beth has married and given us Jon Clay. Oh the joy he brings in.

These past few years I have again begun to take out my "life pieces." They are no longer all happy, but they are such an important part of me.

Today I am 50. A very unhappy day filled with misunderstanding. Sometimes I am tempted to start walking and never look back or turn around again. And the sooner I come to a cliff or ocean the better. When I think of death it does seem that I will walk into it. Why walk to it? Most people think of walking away from it. I have been depressed for so long, it's tiring to pretend all the time. I dislike pretense in any form but this must surely be the worst. There is no exact one reason for this state of mind. I remember years ago when the depression nearly possessed me. I actually wanted to die then, but at that time I was needed by the children. I am not needed now by anyone, so I must keep this depression under control. Surely everyone should live for something. I'm too tired to think about it.

There are many books in our formal old-fashioned living room, and countless times I have read them all, choosing a special chapter as the occasion arises. Romantic, sorrowful, happy, it's good to have such friends to match your moods with merely a flick of the finger. Do I want go back? No, just in thoughts.

Even at a tender age I expected so much of myself and too much of others. No one could ever meet my standards, or at least what I felt was the way they should be. Not even myself.

One half a century of my life is over. I have this compelling urge to put down on paper something of me. Why?? My life for so long has been lived from one event to another of the children or Charles, and suddenly the events have become fewer and further apart. Am I becoming autistic? Why am I thinking more of my own justification? I have all my life held back from being myself to some extent. No longer! At 50 I will say and do what I want, and live my life for me. No more cowardice. I cannot be so nil of personality, not with these deep convictions I have.

I am going to make a resolution. The most difficult one to make, more so as time goes by. To abandon a dream. A dream from real life and as much a part of me as life itself. The time has come when I must face the reality; it just wasn't meant to be. Too much time wasted wishing for the impossible. This will take time. One doesn't shed a piece of one's life that has been such a joy and inspiration. Already I feel partially dead. What does it matter that I have lived at times only because I felt some day a part of my dream would come true. Such strange things happened that it was as though they were telling me not to give up, but now it's been too long a time since I have had any encouragement to keep hoping. I will have to reshape my life. The glow is gone. At this time, I am in limbo. Not really caring. Perhaps later. I must not let my family notice the change. It seems I am forever having to make true that "all the world's a stage." How I would like to go away, be alone, sulk, cry, scream, whatever it takes to feel alive again.

Much has been written about facing your true inner self. Not with me. I have always been as one with mine, it is only now I must part with it and become another person. My true self can never survive in my world, and it's too difficult to explain, even on paper. Let's hope my dreams and thoughts die a dignified death even if my body has to wither away.

GIRL ON THE RED BIKE

My sister and Mom and I put off the day trip to Point Pleasant a couple of times because of Mom's bum knees, but we were off on a sunny autumn Sunday. I turned west onto Route 60 (the old Midland Trail) a little north of Billville and followed it over the winding mountain road through Ansted and Hawks Nest, where Mad Anne Bailey, the fearless Indian scout, purportedly rode her horse Liverpool off the Hawks Nest cliff into the New River far below in a fierce successful effort to escape a war-party of whooping, brightly painted Native Americans.

When we had twisted down off Gauley Mountain into the Kanawha Valley just east of Gauley Bridge, that little town where the New River joins the Gauley River to form the Kanawha, my sister's and my hearts had quickened as always, and we felt something akin to religiousy, for we had entered into the valley of the shadows of our own history there where the shining river runs wide and fast between the high sandstone cliffs.

Out there on one of the rock islands far across the river we could see a set of three crosses, a gold cross in between two blue ones, which was one of the approximately two thousand sets of crosses old Bernard Coffindaffer, another weird albeit wealthy West Virginian, had constructed up and down the Eastern Seaboard and throughout the South. The crosses on the rock island had been Bernard's own personal favorite set, as a matter of fact. My sister recalled coming down to stand on the river bank when those crosses were being erected to drink beer and scoff along with some college friends. The crosses had looked so lovely on that rock in the shining river, however, she had come away entertaining a strange sense of awe and vague longing.

Even in these latter days West Virginia is still yet a uniquely religious landscape. As we passed through Gauley Bridge that Sunday, I recalled the occasion a couple of my old aunts had taken me out nearby Scrabble Creek to a snake-handling church the summer I was eight, where I had watched a lovely, blond, teenage girl wearing a sundress lift a huge timber rattler above her head. I had studied the damp haze of hair under her round, tan arms. While I had ogled her, collecting a congregation of flies in my dumbfounded gapey mouth, that blond girl had draped that enchanted lucky serpent around her slender neck, as summer light falling through the bubbled, wavy old glass of the cinderblock building's windows washed soft prismatic colors over her shining, upturned face. Her eyes were closed in that holy moment. Her moist mouth was open enough so that I could see the edges of her white teeth and the tip of her damp tongue, whereupon I had enjoyed my very first religiousy semblance of a boner praise Jesus amen.

My sister and I both recalled the times the old aunts took us to tent revivals in the valley, and how once Great-Aunt Fanny, who was maybe one hundred and two at the time, had gotten so full of the spirit of the Lord Savior Jesus Christ Amen that she had turned cartwheels and somersaults down the aisle between the folding chairs, sawdust shedding from her old bony back like a bright skin of sparks.

My sister's and my own religious upbringing was less colorful. I can recall a couple of brief periods during my childhood when we attended church regularly as a family. But mostly what I recall about my religious background was Dad dumping my sister and me at the church door, so that he could tell Mimi and Papaw Kinder truthfully that he made sure his kids never ever missed a day of Sunday school and church. Dad would then retire to the golf course or to his office on the living room couch, for a nap. Mom would be home in bed dead to the world after pulling another long nightshift. I can recall vividly that particular part of my religious upbringing when my sister and I would piddle and play or simply sulk on the church steps waiting for Dad to complete his eighteen holes or wake up from a marathon snooze and finally pick us up late in the afternoon. I can recall waving to little Christian friends, who we had sat with in church hours earlier, as they drove by in the back seats of their parents' cars, probably on their way to an extended-family fried-chicken Sunday supper somewhere. I can recall how they looked at us, at the little, sappy-looking, waiting waifs, with genuine Christian concern, as though we were pathetic scumbag orphans selling matches in the snow.

We drove around and around the streets of old turn-of-the-century houses at the edge of Point Pleasant's nearly deserted downtown, looking for Mom's early childhood home. We would slow as we passed the houses on corner after corner, but the big frame house was nowhere to be found, and Mom was working herself up into a tizzy. Mom fretted about her memory. Mom fretted about losing her mind. Mom cracked jokes about it, about her failing memory and those crazy ideas that kept her up nights, but it worried her nonetheless.

But Mom had never had much of a memory to begin with, save for dreams. Directions were lost on Mom. Mom would get lost driving to church in downtown Billville, that metropolis of two stoplights. Mom would get lost in Kroger's. When it came to maneuvering around in the real world at large, Mom was basically at a loss. In an emergency room situation, Mom's blood turned into ice water, and she had been a highly respected nurse whose calmness in the face of knife or gunshot wounds or mangled car-crash victims or miners with body parts crushed flat as pancakes was legendary. But outside of the intense focus of a life-and-death situation, where every move and moment counted for everything, Mom was for all intents and purposes daffy as a duck.

Mom's family lost that house we couldn't locate back during the Depression. She had had no idea as a child what the Depression was all about, but it was something terrible, she knew, something that was turning their world upside-down, and she had come to imagine it like some dreaded disease the adults talked about behind closed doors in hushed voices, as though America had had a heart attack, as though the country was dying of colon cancer. Mom could remember riding her little red bike into the center of town carrying her dad's meals to him in a paper bag. He was standing in a long line outside the bank building and he needed a shave. He could not leave his place in line though, or he might lose everything. He had to wait in line like everybody else in town to withdraw what he could of his life savings. He waited in that line for three days and two nights to get next to nothing of what he had worked for all of his life.

Papaw was cracking jokes to the other people in line, making them all laugh in spite of everything, when Mom pulled up on her red bike. Papaw had bought Mom that bike for her birthday, when even she knew he couldn't afford it. Papaw had Mom get off her bike and meet some of the folks in line. Papaw introduced Mom around as his own little princess. He called her his own little lucky charm. Mom would be a big movie star someday, Papaw told everybody, and they would be standing in another long line to see her up on the silver screen.

Before everything was said and done, Papaw Parsons lost his garage and used-car lot, and they had to sell the house she had loved so as a little girl and move into the empty old family homestead that her great-grandfather Furguson had built up on the hill ten miles down the road in Leon.

Now Mom couldn't even find that house, as we drove around the quiet, nearly empty, tree-shaded streets, trying one turn that looked vaguely familiar to her after another, and in some strange way it was as if she had lost it again, that wonderful, old, childhood house. Finally Mom decided that a corner Gulf gas station was sitting on the spot where her childhood home had once been, and this made her sad, but she also found it reassuring, for it meant that she wasn't losing her mind after all, at least not before lunch.

After expressing differences of opinion with Mom about where to eat lunch that Sunday in Point Pleasant, Mom voting for one of the Wendy's or Shoney's or even a Dairy Queen we had seen driving around rather than the ramshackle, truckers' pit-stop we had passed at the edge of town with blinking neon beer signs, we compromised on about the only place open downtown, a sort of semi-low-rent-looking diner called something like Granny's Greasy Spoon, where, sitting at a rickety Formica-topped table featuring place mats with puzzles, Mom ordered what she always ordered when we ate out anywhere, spaghetti, and my sister got a BLT, and I got a mystery meatloaf sandwich with mashed potatoes awash with Granny's tasty albeit somewhat green gravy.

When Granny (who must have weighed four hundred pounds and sported the highest blue beehive I have seen in my life) served up our lunch, I bowed my head and said —Now let us pray. Pray the phone don't ring and the food don't get cold. Come, Lord Jaysus, be our guest.

—Mind your manners now, Chuckie, Mom said. —Don't gobble your food.

—I blame everything on my religious upbringing, I said.

—Gobble, gobble, Mom said.

Mom ate in her slow, dignified, dainty way while I gobbled my lunch down, eating with my mouth open and making snorty sounds to drive Mom nuts, which she studiously ignored. Then I sat there digging at my choppers with a toothpick, being as redneck as I could be but to no avail. My sister simply rolled her eyes, and Mom smiled benignly with Christian forbearance, while they talked between themselves somewhat solemnly about my sister's daughter's trashy friends from out at an area of Billville called Gatewood, where way too many young, unwed mothers survived on welfare in bent trailers, but I knew that what was probably foremost on both their minds were their vague, unvoiced fears about my own destructive, trashy, secret life. My sister and I had not spoken again about Holly's impending trip to Billville, and I was simply waiting for that particular unpleasantness to hit the fan.

I studied my mother's soft crepey skin in the shadowy light that filtered through the greasy smudged glass of the front windows of the diner. I tried to imagine her as a sweet, dreamy, little girl. I tried to imagine Mom riding on her red bike through these small-town shady streets on summer days, as carefree as a constant worrier like Mom could have ever been even when disguised as a child, not suspecting for a moment that someday she would come to feel that her life was almost over before she lived it.

If Mom could step outside this diner somehow back in time, and if she would encounter her girlhood self as that child pedaled her red bike by, what would Mom tell her girlhood self if she waved that girl down? What advice would that lovely, lonely old lady who felt that she had somehow missed out on her life have for that little girl still on the verge of things?

Where is she now, that little girl, riding her red bike through the lost soft summer shadows of the past? Where did she go? Where did she ride off to? Could Mom's life have turned out to be another story, if only she had made one different turn on those streets of the past? Maybe it would have been the story that she was meant to live instead of the ungraspable one that had unfolded before her as strangely as fiction? What could have prepared Mom for the story she had lived? How could Mom have known that every single thing that had happened in the history that was herself was for keeps? And now, suddenly, without warning, the end was in sight.

I resolved on the spot to purchase my Mom a red bike for her birthday, if not sooner.

I bowed my head and closed my eyes. I prayed hard and meant it. Jesus, I prayed fiercely, please don't let anything else bad happen to Mom, that beautiful, brave, sad old lady, please don't you do it, please, before that day you decide to kill her.

MYSTERY MIDGETS
AND OTHER BIZARRE BEINGS

Visitations from the dead and mysterious beings from other worlds are not that uncommon at all in any part of West Virginia. Virtually the whole state of West Virginia has been classified by investigators of paranormal events and bizarre beings as a *window,* meaning an area in which incomprehensible creatures and events tend to visit and recur time after time, year to year, even century to century.

There are many *window* areas throughout the world, both large and small, famous and not, such as the Bermuda Triangle or Stonehenge or the Valley of the Kings, where due to some anomaly of nature, energies, both spiritual and natural, focus and flow, and make that vortex of the inexplicable both holy and demonic and tear that curtain between our own and other worlds.

In the haunted hills of West Virginia there are demons and dark angels, fallen and horny, and freakish forces and dream denizens of unseen worlds or realms or unfathomed dimensions that surround us. They shape the very lives of West Virginians, perhaps even controlling West Virginians by molding their beliefs and manipulating their emotions until more than a few lift up serpents to pray for salvation and relief and deliverance into a new spiritual geography.

The big debate that rages in West Virginia is whether the frequent visitors from the beyond are, indeed, actually angels or aliens, and if angels, are they holy or fallen, and if aliens, where are they from and what do they want, besides rustling livestock for ritual mutilation and abducting countless West Virginians in order to examine them head to toe and frequently have other-worldly sex, especially if they are young, juicy majorettes and or homecoming queens.

My great-uncle George R. Rairden (1891–1972) served thirteen terms as a Republican member of the State House of Delegates from Mason County, one of the longest legislative service records in the history of the state, being elected in the years 1926, 1928, 1930, 1932, 1934, 1938, 1940, 1942, 1944, 1948, 1950, 1952, and 1958. As a legislator he was a crusader for morality in government and temperance. He introduced legislation and zealously fought for laws to curb gambling, liquor, and fornication that was merely for the sake of fun. Always advocating law enforcement, he introduced legislation to create the office of state prosecuting attorney. He also took pride in his successful effort in obtaining a property tax exemption for elderly persons receiving welfare assistance. While always for economy in government, he faithfully lent his full efforts toward adequate appropriations for education and schools.

In 1927, my uncle sponsored a bill that made June 20 West Virginia Day and a legal holiday. In 1958, he sponsored a bill that proclaimed that the frequent unearthly and uninvited visitors to the Mountain State were fallen angels doing the demonic business of Baal, and each one was to be considered by law enforcement officials as *persona non grata* and arrested upon sight on felony charges of incitement to sin and confusion. The bill failed by six votes.

Point Pleasant, West Virginia, is considered to be a *window* within a *window*, due to the abundance of weird occurrences and strange visitations within its general area, which has included continuous UFO activity over long periods of time, plus a multitude of bizarre monster sightings. The mysterious comings and goings of unusual persons is commonplace, such as oriental midgets and dwarfs dressed in black with long black painted fingernails. And then there are the famous so-called "Mothmen," those huge feathered, bird-like beings with red glowing eyes and the powdery faces of moths, that were spotted so frequently around the old TNT Dump area.

The old TNT Dump site is on the edge of town and consists of several hundred acres of woods and open fields filled with large concrete domes called "igloos." These structures were used to store high explosives man-ufactured at nearby plants during the Second World War. The igloo shapes of these domes puts one in mind of the pyramidal shapes of the West Virginia mountains themselves, and everybody is aware of how pyr-amids can focus an array of natural forces, including gravity, and natural magnetism, not to mention other powerful spiritual energies, which may help explain the strange phenomena.

It is probably erroneous to blame the collapse of the rickety old Silver Bridge on the sudden appearance of a mystery midget in town on the day of the disaster, or the frequent traffic of flying saucers or those Mothmen who infested the area at the time, but the intense paranormal, psychic activity around Point Pleasant, especially in the old TNT Dump, on the night of the collapse does suggest some tangible relationship between the calamity and strange invisible forces that would seem to go far beyond the curse of an ancient Indian, the other favorite explanation for the catastrophe.

Beginning in the fall of 1967, the color teevee sets and telephones and late model cars in the Point Pleasant vicinity began to act up, as queer blobs of crystalline white and blue pulsating lights appeared regu-larly in the night skies. Many of these lights moved at treetop level, sometimes hovering, sometimes speeding about making crazy impossible turns. There were also many daylight sightings of strange circular objects, or objects that were described by locals as looking like giant, slowly blinking penises, particularly in the skies above the old TNT Dump. By early December, over one thousand UFO sightings by respon-sible witnesses had been recorded throughout the valley. Cars passing along Camp Conley Road, south of the old TNT Dump, stalled inexpli-cably. Television sets and radios, some brand-new, burned out suddenly without cause. By mid-December, the UFO sightings hit an incredible peak with the blinking penises appearing nightly at low level over the old TNT Dump as if they were following a regular flight schedule. Thousands of people invaded the area again to view this new wonder. Sheriff

Johnson and most of his deputies were among the witnesses but soberly refused to comment on the extraordinary phenomenon to the hordes of media.

The afternoon of December 15, 1967, was winding down in the town of Point Pleasant. Christmas shopping was at its peak, and the streets and bridges were packed bumper to bumper with rush-hour traffic. At 5:05 P.M., the aptly named Silver Bridge, which connected West Virginia and Ohio, suddenly collapsed, carrying dozens of vehicles into the dark icy waters of the Ohio River.

That night the Lilly family on Camp Conley Road divided their stunned attention between their teevee set with its shocking, tragic news about the collapsed bridge and the eerie lights that were racing at treetop level over the woods behind their home toward the old TNT Dump and deserted power plant. They counted twelve unidentified flying penises altogether, more than they had ever seen on a single evening before.

People in Point Pleasant had been truly proud of the Silver Bridge. An old picture postcard describes the bridge thusly: "A shining example of man's engineering ingenuity is this magnificent bridge in historic Point Pleasant, W. Va." The Silver Bridge was opened Wednesday, May 30, 1928, in a gala ceremony attended by 25,000 Ohioans and West Virginians. The bridge was the first of its particular design in America (only three of its kind were ever constructed), pioneering the use of heat-treated I-bar chain suspension. It was made almost entirely of steel, had three piers, and two lanes. It was the first bridge in the world coated with aluminum paint, which made it shine like silver in the sun, hence its name.

The worrisome wobbling notwithstanding, the bridge stood for nearly four decades as a marvel of strength and beauty. It had been called the most beautiful bridge on the Ohio. The unique suspension—30-foot I-bars resembling elongated dog-bones pinned together in a chain—was never discredited from an engineering standpoint. Later, state road officials did not deny that the Silver Bridge had wobbled and vibrated the last years. But, they said, that did not necessarily indicate weakness. Suspension bridges were designed flexible.

According to eyewitnesses, the packed Silver Bridge suddenly just disintegrated on that cold early December evening. Garry Roach of Henderson, who had been shopping at Tiny's Foodland at the base of the bridge and was an eyewitness, said the vehicles were lined up with two big trucks on the Ohio side and a couple coming from the West Virginia side, and when a fifth big truck pulled onto the bridge, it simply went down. One of the truck drivers, a man named "Red," who had been driving a truck with a 32,000-pound load of gravel, miraculously survived. Red later said that he was at the center of the bridge when it started to really sway. "It went to the right, then back to the left, and then to the right again, but this time it didn't come back, and that was it. Next thing I knew I was down in the cold water along with four or five other people holding onto stuff. I still don't know how I got out of there."

Several downtown residents and businessmen said later they had seen a giant blinking penis shoot across the night sky and heard a boom that sounded like a jet breaking the sound barrier. Other reliable witnesses claimed they had observed an oriental-looking dwarf dressed all in black scampering away from the disaster site as fast as his tiny legs could carry him, whereupon he had scrambled into the back seat of a long black limousine with tinted windows which sped off into the night, never to be seen again. A multitude of Mothmen were seen circling in the sky above the old TNT Dump, and then flying off together in a huge V like geese going south.

When the recovery operation was discontinued some four months later, it was determined that forty-six people had lost their lives when the Silver Bridge collapsed. Of this number, forty-four bodies were recovered, while two were never found. A small memorial park was established at the location of the Silver Bridge approach.

• • •

As we walked slowly back to the Red Ride that Sunday in Point Pleasant after lunch, Mom holding onto my arm, for her old knees were killing her, I asked her if she could direct us to the little memorial park at the old approach of the Silver Bridge. Mom said she didn't know. She said that it might be too sad of a place to go. She didn't think she could find it after all these years. Mom said she could remember playing on that bridge when she was a little girl, though.

In the evenings during the summer of 1928, when the bridge was being built, Mawmaw would take Mom and her brothers on walks down to it. She would let them play around the construction site. As the bridge progressed, they would go out on it, and drop rocks and sticks into the river. Mawmaw would even let the boys spit in the river, but not Mom, for that wasn't lady-like.

One evening Mom found a little yellow-and-black butterfly flopping about in the grass at the base of the bridge. One of its lovely wings seemed bent. It kept fluttering up trying to fly, and falling back. My mother picked the butterfly up very gently, and she carried it onto the Silver Bridge. She placed the butterfly ever so carefully onto the railing. Mom thought that up high it might get a good enough takeoff to sail away. But when Mom gently nudged it off of the railing, the little butterfly simply fluttered around and around downward like a frail leaf falling, until she lost sight of it over the river, an event, Mom said—and she took hold of my arm and looked up into my eyes with a scared, knowing look—that she had always feared set in motion a vast series of subsequent events that culminated in 1967 with forty-six people plunging with the Silver Bridge into the Ohio River to drown like the little yellow-and-black butterfly she had murdered.

Body in the Woods

We backtracked on Route 32 toward Leon ten miles down the road, and I could have sworn I saw a road-sign warning that said: *Mothman Crossing*. But Mom wouldn't let me swing back around to check it out. At Leon, which consisted of several houses back off the road and a country store, we swung left up a narrow blacktop road that circled up around a hill maybe a quarter mile, and then turned right onto an even narrower, crumbling road, which we followed past the small, white-frame Methodist church and old cemetery on the hill's high point overlooking the Kanawha River.

Mom's Grandfather Furguson had been known all over Mason County for his beautiful roses. On Memorial Day, everybody knew they could gather all the roses they could carry from his gardens for the graves in the old cemetery right around the road. But my Great-Grandfather Furguson, who had been the postmaster in Leon and a farmer and carpenter, was famous mostly for his singing. He would sit in the swing on the front porch of that enormous frame house he had built with his own hands and sing so loudly on Saturday nights that folks could hear him all the way over the hill in the little town. They loved hearing Grandfather Furguson sing. Over time, townfolks began dressing up as though they were going someplace special, and then simply sat out on their porch swings every summer Saturday night, the whole town, to listen to my great-grandfather sing. And that was how folks remembered Grandfather Furguson over in Mason County, that was his legacy, to be recalled fondly as a man with a hillside of beautiful roses who loved to sing loud on Saturday nights.

The night Grandfather Furguson died, the big old frame house was packed with family members attending his deathwatch. When he dozed off, all the relatives slipped quietly from the back bedroom where he was lying. They moved out to crowd into the roomy, formal front parlor, where they got to talking about how much he had always loved his roses and who would tend to those roses now. At some point, one of his six sons happened to look out of the window, and there stood Grandfather Furguson, dressed in his nightshirt, outside in the yard gazing over his hillside of rose bushes in the moonlight.

Everybody clamored out the front door to fetch Grandfather, thinking that he must be wandering about out of his head. But then right before their very eyes, Grandfather disappeared into thin air. The family members ran back inside to his bedroom, where they found his dead body. More than once over the years since his death, Grandfather Furguson had been spied out under the moonlight in his nightshirt moving among his famous roses.

The old homestead house that Great-Grandfather Furguson built by hand was not a quarter mile down the road from the old church and cemetery, and as we bumped down the crumbling road there, Mom described it again, that house where she had lived during the Depression and which she had loved so dearly, that beautiful, big, white-frame house, with its many large windows, bay windows even, one in Mom's own bedroom, and stone fireplaces in every room, and surrounded by broad porches, and a well of cold, sweet water in the kitchen that never ran dry, and a cool cellar where apple cider was kept chilled, and smoke houses and barns over the hill, and shade trees all around, including those six maples Grandfather Furguson had each of his six sons plant, each son going into the woods in turn when they were twelve and finding maple saplings to dig up and replant with a family ceremony in the yard, trees that kept the rambling house cool and rippling with shadowy light like flowing water even during the worst dog days of August, and a hillside of roses of every name and color on countless trellises.

• • •

It was still a great house, to my mind, no matter how old and funky. I was worried about how Mom would take it, though, what with those ugly chickens pecking around in the yard and those old appliances along the back wall, a couple of stoves and a refrigerator with its door removed. The old house's windows were covered with torn pieces of plastic, and that wide screened-in back porch where Mom said the family used to eat on sweet, warm summer evenings had been covered over with strips of plywood. There was only one visible concrete-block chimney left standing.

I helped Mom out of the vehicle, and while my sister and she were rubbing on Mom's stiff knees, I snapped a couple of pictures of the old homestead, which occasioned an enormous old coot about my own age with a fantail of white hair to stick his head out the porch door and eye-ball me evilly.

I proceeded up the crumbling sidewalk toward him, dangling my camera from its cord to show him it wasn't some exotic, urban hand-uzi. I grinned and waved the other hand to demonstrate its emptiness. His yellowy shock of white hair stood on end like a cat's as I approached him, and his watery eyes hissed. Employing my most obsequious, head-bobbling, foot-shuffling, friendly, unthreatening mode, I explained to the huge old coot about how my great-grandfather had built this very house by hand generations ago, and how it was my dear little old church-lady mom's old homestead, and how much it would mean to her if he gave his kind permission for her to totter about the place for a bit for old times' sake.

The mountainman of old coot squinted his phlegmy evil eyes at me and spluttered: —I ain't got no time fer that dumb shit. Whereupon I smiled and leaned toward him and quietly said, sir, my dear, old, nearly crippled, church-lady mom is going to totter about her old homestead for a bit this day, and if he gave me any crap about it I'd punch his fucken lights out, or maybe I'd just snuff his old mothman motherfucker ass. I've been looking for one of you alien pigfucker life forms all day to blow away, I informed him quietly, smiling. I mean I'll stuff and mount you. I'll call you a stuffed Abominable Mothfuck. What I'm saying is, don't let this faggotty professor corduroy coat fool you, sir, I'm redder than your asshole and armed to the teeth, you old butt-hole, but, hey, instead of all this hostility maybe he might be willing to consider accepting the fin I had in my hand as a sort of donation for the privilege of walking around for maybe ten fucken minutes, if that long, considering the fact my mother was an old almost crippled woman who grew up in this fucken old barn.

The miserable old coot caught my drift. He put his hairy old paw of a hand out palm up, and I greased it, whereupon he turned to lumber back toward my mom's dear old homestead. —Hey, mister, I said to him, and he gave me a malicious, edgy, edentulous look back over his shoulder. I said: —Let me ask you something, mister. You ain't from around here, are you, mister? I mean, you weren't born and raised in the hospitable hills of southern West Virginia, were you? —Shitfire no, the old rude coot spittled, —I was born and raised way over in Kentucky. —I can always tell, I told him and backed away with my steely eyes leveled on him all the way up the sidewalk.

Only one maple tree remained. The front porch where Grandfather Furguson would swing and sing on Saturday nights had caved in. Mom's bedroom bay window was there, but covered with blankets. Mom had not expected any of the rose trellises to be left, and they weren't. Grandfather Furguson would hear or read about a new hybrid of rose and he had to have it, Mom told us, had to try to make it grow in his hillside rose garden. Growing roses wasn't a thing a man usually did back in those days, but Grandfather Furguson had been such a big, burly, strong fellow and famous for his temper, who was going to pass a comment? The yellow roses had been Mom's favorites. Trellises of roses had once grown all along the length of the side yard, and down over the hill above that evil path, which was still there.

Below that evil path had been a deep, overgrown hollow, a chasm, filled with tangled briery bramble bushes that had looked like those rolls of barbed wire, Mom said, you see on battlefields in war movies. Mom had seen the naked body lying not ten feet from the path amidst those brambly bushes, facedown with brown hair, and a man, she was sure.

There were no scratches or bruises on the body that she could see, and that body had always looked the same. Mom always had the thought that she either knew who it was and had forgotten, or at least she knew why it was there, that dead naked brown-haired man. She never told anyone about seeing that dead naked body, and no one else ever saw it that she knew, but of course she didn't want them to. Mom had wanted that dreadful but somehow sacred sight of a dead naked body of a man with brown hair to be hers alone. It made her feel special somehow. Mom had dreamed of that evil path many times, and she always saw the dead naked body of a man with brown hair facedown in the dreams, and upon awakening she always had the same feelings of fear and guilt and a terrible wonder like awe. That dream had cursed her for seventy years, Mom told us, if it was a dream; for could it be simply a nightmare, to have endured in her memory over all this time?

—Momma, I said, and took her hand, which was trembling. We were standing at the south corner of the house, looking down over the overgrown hillside. I could see where the old path entered the briery brambles just past the stained stump of an old maple tree.

—Momma, I said, —would you like for your dauntless daughter to go over there and take a peek for old times' sake?

—No way, Jose! my sister informed me (a phrase we had all picked up from her own daughter, our eighteen-year-old transport into the future who we all feared was going straight to hell in a hand-bucket).

—Momma, I said, —how's about I take a little peek for you since your once dauntless daughter is too chicken-shit?

—You turkey, my sister opined.

—You both just think I'm crazy, don't you? Mom said, and pursed her mouth. —Well, maybe I am then. And maybe I just don't care. If that's the way I am, then that's the way I am and I can't help it.

—Hey, Momma, I said, —I need to take a leak anyway.

—Chuckie, don't you dare! Mom requested of me, looking with old-timey sternness and pleading into my eyes.

—Momma, I said, —if that crazy old coot comes out and tries anything, tell him I have an uzi aimed at his heart.

—Chuckie, now don't you dare go down over in there! Mom ordered me.

—But, Momma, I said and sort of pranced about in place, —I really have to do number one!

And then, following the strange trajectory of my life, I strolled without permission across the yard toward the overgrown tunnel of an evil path into the nightmare woods of my mother's childhood. I had an inkling of who that dead, naked, brown-haired man was who had been lying face-down in my mother's nightmares for all those years. I had solved the case of The Naked, Brown-Haired Dead Man who was in the woods of my mom's memory and imagination. It was me.

GIRL BY THE ROAD IN THE RAIN

INDIAN CAMP proclaims the historical marker in a pretty little flat area beside the road on the east side of Drawdy Mountain. I pull over, as is my custom, to read the marker. Pull over to read markers, is my best advice, especially when you are doing a little drinking and driving and discover you are drifting into that old mythology called lonesome traveling and lost highways and all that other worn-out drifter syncopation stuff big in the heart-broke country music business. Pull over and read the markers and mull over the ironies of destiny when you drive on. Be interesting to yourself and learn to like your own company.

UNDER ROCK OVERHANG ACROSS HIGHWAY WAS AN INDIAN CAMP SITE. HERE WERE FOUND SEVERAL BURIALS. ONE OCCUPATION, FORT ANCIENT, DATES FROM A.D. 1400; ANOTHER, BUCK GARDEN, FROM A.D. 1000. POTTERY AND OTHER ARTIFACTS WERE FOUND.

I sit sipping my morning breakfast beverage of choice and entertain a brisk brood. It sure is a pretty little spot. I can hear the Big Coal River and catch glimpses of it through the dripping trees. Mist rises from the steep wooded sides of the rainy mountains. I can almost imagine ancient Indians huddled around a warm fire under that overhang across the road on a morning much like this a thousand years ago, as they lingered over their breakfast of scrambled squirrel, or whatever ancient Indians ate. They gnawed on the rodent and talked about the dreams that had visited them during the long scary night, and what those dreams might portend. Then they went out to their dangerous jobs as ancient Indians. Ancient life, Indian and otherwise, first fired my imagination when as a kid I found an arrowhead in a dry riverbed among smooth, white rocks shaped like skulls, whereupon ancient life had gripped my abiding interest by the short hairs.

There beside the Big Coal River, I polish off my second-to-last luke-cool breakfast beverage. On a whim, I stroll across the rainy road to cast my own trained eye upon the remnants of that old human shelter. Due to time and erosion, not much of an overhang is left now. Unless ancient Indians had been about the size of elves, that shelter couldn't keep many out of the rain. But the secret of any place is only in the hearts of the people who have passed through it. People buried other people, tiny people true, but people who loved one another, under that shallow rock overhang, sharing in the poignancy of the transient, and the charm and peacefulness of mortality, and the calm parallel life of the dead, which makes it holy moly enough in my book. *Boo!* I hoot into the shallow rock shelter, but it is not even cave enough to carry back an echo.

With my trained eye I peruse the petroglyphs on the rocks of the crumbling inner wall of the ancient Indian cave. The only "old Injun cave turkey-tracks" (as West Virginia archaeologists call them) I can truly decipher say things like: Billy Bob loves Brenda, or Bubba Gives Blowjobs. Those somehow overlooked ancient Indian toe bones that I uncover when I scratch about in the cave's dirt floor only fool my trained eye for a fleeting moment, before I realize they are merely the butts of menthol filters. The only artifacts I can decode with any confidence are some of the crunched Budweiser beer cans, and maybe a dozen used condoms. I collect all this material into a paper bag I fetch from my vehicle for no good politically correct reason except perhaps that my sister would be proud of me. I toss all that cave-crap into my back seat. As I drive away from that place, I reflect upon the ironies of destiny.

I also reflect upon the sacred nature of burial sites and the ghosts that haunt those places. Some folks say there are places and moments where eternity breaks into time, and that is where we find the places that are sacred to us and the myths we can abide by. Mythology, and its sacred primordial dreamtime, can be a vehicle of religious experience, some folks say. Some folks say that the mythic past and the mystic present are equally timeless.

There is a linguistic connection between the three words "myth," "mysticism," and "mystery." All are derived from the Greek verb *musteion,* which means to close the eyes or the mouth. All three words are rooted in an experience of darkness and silence. Some say ghosts are only wishful manifestations of that sad sweet grasping for something we know we can't have. The Ainu of Japan believe that the dead think of themselves as living and see the living as ghosts. The ancient Egyptians painted eyes on the faces of their mummies so that they could look back from the land of the dead.

I pop my last luke-cool breakfast beverage as I cruise on through the misty morning beside the Big Coal River listening to a Hank Williams tape and feeling sort of sappy and sentimental and in the presence somehow of a vague old memory that won't quite come to me. "I've Seen the Light," Uncle Hank sings, "I've Seen the Light." I pull my cap-bill down a bit to shadow my teary eyes and swallow hard. What I feel like suddenly is a real genuine West Virginian at long last. I feel like a real genuine West Virginian riding down a lonesome two-lane rainy morning road listening to an Uncle Hank's song of long-overdue enlightenment and sipping a breakfast Bud and knowing more or less where and what I should be for the rest of my natural life.

Then it hits me. Holy moly! As a real genuine West Virginian, I'm allowed to believe in things like ghosts. It's almost my duty to believe in things like ghosts. I can't say I believe in Jesus, or any God that I've heard of lately, especially any God those idiot Southern Baptists throw snakes into the air to worship, but I can believe in ghosts, at the very least. Plus it is part of that inherited sixth sense cross I must bear like my kind. And the first chance I get, I'll toss a mess of my own copperheads high up in the shining air to celebrate that tortured fact.

I'm here to tell the world that I have seen ghosts with my own ancient eyes, amen! Unsealed from their dark, rising up disguised as mist on rainy mornings like the mist of this morning, or as clouds before the moon, or smoke in the sweet autumn hills of West Virginia, or on cold wintry days the vapors of my own breath. I've seen ghosts all over this haunted landscape of the Sky People.

Or take the girl by the road in the rain up yonder. I've seen her before. She looks like a bride in her long white dress. But I know her story. It's her prom dress. This morning I can barely see her in all the river mist. I know her hair is long and brown and I've heard her eyes are green. I've never seen them myself. I've never gotten close enough. Her name is Rose Anne, or Alice Anne, or maybe Brenda Lee, depending on who is telling her story. She was killed on her prom night in a terrible car accident. Her boyfriend Billy Bob, or Boover, or Bubba, was driving drunk. That old story. I told Mom about seeing the ghost girl beside the country roads down in Boone County. I described as best I could the ghost girl's lovely long white prom dress. I told Mom the ghost girl's sad story. Mom said that maybe the ghost girl had it good.

I know the ghost girl will vanish like always the moment I pull up to offer her a ride to wherever it is she needs to go. I pull up.

book five

FAMOUS
DANCING
OUTAW

SHOT THROUGH THE HEART

When Jessico White was four years old, his bed had been the back seat of a '47 Ford. His poor parents had passed him on to live with an old man they identified as his Grandpappy. Jessico had lived with his old Grandpappy in a garage where the '47 Ford rested up on cinderblocks. Jessico would sleep on the back seat, and his Grandpappy would sleep in front. Because he had long, spindly legs, Grandpappy would open the car door at night and put his feet on an oil can so he could stretch out. Then he and Jessico would lie there in the dark listening to the sweet sounds of the settling night. Sometimes Grandpappy would cackle and crack jokes Jessico didn't get. Or sometimes, whenever there was a working battery in the old heap, Grandpappy would croak along with tear-jerk country songs playing low and staticky on the radio, and maybe talk quietly about Jessico's Grandma, who was long gone. Those were the happiest times of Jessico's life.

When Jessico was older and living back home, he began huffen gasoline to get high and float beyond his life. His daddy, Donald Ray White (D. Ray), famous down in the Boone County beerjoints as a mountain dancer who would clog or tap-dance his heart out for a tall, cold one, would punish Jessico for getting high huffen gasoline by chaining him to a bedpost and whupping him with belts, tree branches, pieces of old tires, a plucked chicken oncet, the skinned body of a shot squirrel oncet, then there was that live rabbit oncet, or just aim empty beer cans at Jessico's head for a long, lazy, boring Sunday afternoon of target practice whenever the old teevee was on the blink.

Out of fifteen brothers and sisters Jessico once had, only a half dozen or so were still yet alive. Two sisters were killed in separate high-speed, twisty-road, drunken car wrecks. One sister followed her dreams up to Detroit, where she found work dancing topless in a hillbilly-ghetto bar. Her ex-husband hitchhiked up to Detroit to carry her back to the hills of home where he thought she really belonged. That ex-husband sat back in the dark of that smoky bar for hours, drinking whiskey shots straight and watching his wife when she came on to dance with her pretty titties bared and bouncing so beautiful. Finally he pulled his pistol out of his coat, and shot Jessico's sister straight through her heart.

Then a brother of Jessico's followed his own dreams up to Detroit, the way we West Virginians are wont to do in our hillbilly diaspora. One night he answered a banging on his first-floor apartment door to discover a biker revving his Harley right out there in the hallway, whereupon without warning the biker (who, according to Jessico's brother's girlfriend and only witness, they didn't know from Adam) pulled a pistol from out of his leather jacket and shot Jessico's brother straight through his heart.

The first time Jessico White got into trouble with the law was for breaking into a grocery store to steal a case of lighter fluid. Back in those teenager days, Jessico didn't care if he lived or died as long as he was happy and high sniffen gasoline, or huffen glue out of a sandwich bag, or soaken socks with lighter fluid to bury his face into and get lost in those heavenly fumes, anything to get that double-high super-buzz, talk about a warped mind, man, Jessico claimed he had one.

Once when he was on a super-buzz high, a lady from heaven came to visit Jessico, a beautiful lady with an angel's body and the shimmering shapes of diamonds in her long, beautiful, blond hair; but she had the face of a snake, the face of a rattlesnake whose forked tongue flicked out at Jessico while her snake's sweet hissy voice told him that if he wanted to, he could just go down and stand on them railroad tracks in the hollow without a care in the world, and when the old coal train came aroaring round the bend, all Jessico would have to do to bring it to a screeching halt was raise a hand up toward Elvis The King on high.

Jessico had ended up spending a lot of his younger days at the West Virginia State Industrial School for Boys in Pruntytown. As an adult, he'd spent his share of time behind bars too, where he practiced the steps his daddy had taught him, tap-dancing for store-bought cigarettes from the deputies. Jessico met his wife, Norma Jean, when she picked him up hitchhiking. His plan was to hit her in the head with a rock and rob her, but she had been wearing this real pretty pink sweater with silvery, sequined, angely shapes on its front that seemed to shine like diamonds in the dashboard light, and Jessico thought she was a rich woman with a running car who clearly liked his looks. Jessico and Norma Jean were married when he was nineteen and she was thirty-five. They never had any younguns. The reason Jessico never wanted any younguns was that younguns had a right to more in this life than he could ever offer them. Over the years Jessico had come to learn that there is love in marriage and happiness, but there is madness too. Like that one morning Jessico put a butcher-knife to Norma Jean's throat and told her that if she wanted to live to see tomorrow, she better start frying them eggs better than she had been frying them for nearly fifteen years. Jessico was real tired of eating them sloppy slarmy fried eggs.

The night the big White family tragedy went down, Jessico and Norma Jean had been up to his mother, Birtie Mae's, trailer in Prenter for her birthday, but when his relatives had got to partying hardy, Norma Jean convinced Jessico to go on over home to Peytona before things got out of hand. But when they got about halfway home, Jessico told Norma Jean that he had left his costly new sunglasses at his mother's, and he threatened to put Norma Jean in a coffin if she didn't turn the vehicle around right then so he could go back and fetch them costly sunglasses.

Earlier at the party, D. Ray had tossed Birtie Mae the keys to an old, running Dodge he had traded around to get her for her birthday, and she had climbed into it and gone acrosst the mountain for a drive, so Bertie Mae wasn't home at the time of the tragedy. When Jessico and Norma Jean pulled back up the hollow to the trailer, they found Jessico's brother Dorsey sitting out front on the stoop all forlorn. Both his eyes were black and his lips all split open like from a ass-whupping. Dorsey, who was about as articulate as a turnip, tried to explain that when he had come out of Ponty's trailer down the hill, where they had all gone to party (Ponty was the only other surviving White brother at that point), a couple of old boys had jumped him and took to whupping on him like they were crazy or on acid or something.

Soon after Jessico and Norma Jean had gone in the trailer to look around for his costly sunglasses, those same old boys showed up again out front and took to hollering around for Dorsey to come on down so they could finish making him answer up for that dope he stole. But D. Ray heard them, and he hurried outside the trailer to confront those boys. D. Ray came down off the stoop and told them if they didn't get on out of the hollow right then, he would go down to Harvey's and call the state police on them. Whereupon one of the boys, this Steve Rhodes fellow, shoved D. Ray and told him this wasn't between him and D. Ray, but between him and Dorsey. When Jessico saw Steve Rhodes shove his daddy on his own property like that, Jessico went crazy as a bat, and he ran out of the trailer and jumped Steve Rhodes and took to fighting with him down on the ground. Before long Steve Rhodes had hollered *Enough!* You done whupped me, Jesco, he allowed.

Jessico got up then out of the mud and the blood, figuring the fight was over, and he and Dorsey and D. Ray turned around to go back in the trailer. Suddenly out of the blue, Steve Rhodes had a shotgun in his hands, and he yelled *Get me now, you motherfuckers,* and he fired three times. The first shot got D. Ray square in his boney chest, and blew him backward into the mud. The second shot caught Dorsey as he ran for the trailer, a pellet popping his left eye out into his own hand like a grape. A ricocheting pellet from the third shot clipped Jessico in his throat, and he fell down choking and gagging on his own blood.

Birtie Mae, who folks down in the hollows call the Miracle Woman because of all the loss and grief and lingering sadness she has had to endure without losing her jolly sense of humor, returned home moments after the shootings, and she would relate later how her hands went clear up in D. Ray's blown-out back when she had tried to take the lifeless body of her husband into her arms.

Jessico was sure he was going to die. He had never been shot like that before, in the throat like that. And he was sucking for air. The last thing Jessico could clearly remember hearing that night before he blacked out was the deputy sheriff saying over and over, —Now, daggone you, Jesco, don't you go and die on us, old Jesco.

Jessico liked to think of himself as a "miracle child," for he was certain he had lived through death that tragic day. When he was lying there on the ground that day shot and bleeding, Jessico blacked out. And somehow even though he was unconscious, he knew his heart had stopped beating in his chest. Then it was like he had come awake in a pitch-black coal mine under the ground. But he could still see this little bitty light no bigger than the eye of a needle real far off, like at the end of a long, dark tunnel. And this little bitty light started coming at him, getting bigger and bigger, and then Jessico thought he could almost see somebody in that light, but real fuzzy like a figure on a bad teevee set. He thought that it was his daddy at first, it sort of looked like his daddy, but then he heard a voice and it wasn't his daddy's voice.

It was the voice of Elvis, *The King,* that Jessico heard, and The King told him, —Jesco, don't you go dying on us now, daggone you, don't you go and do it, you got to carry on in your daddy's footsteps, son, The King's voice said, and then suddenly Jessico woke up out on the cold ground in front of the trailer where his daddy was lying shot down like a dog, and the voice that sounded just like The King's voice then said, —Jesco, now you get up out of that ditch and get off them drugs and go on out and do what you have to do. Cause, son, now that your daddy is an angel tap-dancing up in heaven on them streets of gold, you are the last mountain dancer down here on the face of this old Earth.

THE PREACHER'S PORCH

I first heard of Jessico White in the summer of 1991 when my wife, Lindsay, and I were returning to our home in Pittsburgh after a hurricane named Bob had forced us to flee from Ocracoke Island off the North Carolina coast, where we had been vacationing. We had stopped on our way to stay over at my sister's lovely old renovated historical landmark doublewide of a home in Billville. No sooner was I out of my vehicle attempting to stretch my old stiff legs when my brother-in-law, that goat-bearded, beady-eyed, nearly bald, ugly fellow, began pestering me as he alone can pester me to get my fat butt indoors pronto so he could show me this bizarre videotape some old pal had sent him.

Perhaps I should make it perfectly clear at this point, gentle reader, that although one of the few goals in my brother-in-law's limited life is to goad me often beyond even my own famous forbearance, I have come to regard him, in spite of his enormous failings, like a brother. That day, I was much more interested in parking myself at the kitchen table while we sipped ice-cold Buds and batted the most recent central lies of our lives back and forth than watching any film. But in minutes I was watching a videotape made by this PBS filmmaker out of Morgantown, West Virginia, the aforementioned Jacob Young, who had done a famous series of documentaries about weird West Virginians, called *A Different Drummer*.

This particular documentary was named *The Dancing Outlaw*, and it turned out to be the outlandish story of a hillbilly character named Jessico White of Boone County, a fellow in maybe his mid-thirties just under six wiry feet tall, with long coal-black hair and a scruffy black beard and these torch-lit black eyes that looked out at you from a place you felt he inhabited alone, such as a blind alley or maybe a cave deep in the back woods, a place anyway where you never wanted to visit late at night nor linger. This Jessico character was apparently some sort of outlaw Elvis impersonator, and the last and self-proclaimed best of the old mountain dancers on the face of the Earth. I thought this Jessico character was basically a big joke, at the beginning.

But what this videotape eventually led to was a road trip my sister and brother-in-law and I took about a year later, when on a whim we drove over the hills into that spooky mostly uncharted country called Boone County, thinking to root out this Jessico White character for a lark. He had become something of a cult figure because of the documentary. He had become sort of famous. We didn't really believe we'd ever actually do it, locate Jessico White, that is, down in those lost dangerous hollows, down in dark forests of primeval dimension full of armed-to-the-teeth marijuana farmers and fabled mountain witches. We expected that day trip to be like the countless others we had taken together into the deep inner hills, my brother-in-law's huge Chevy van gassed to the brim, a cooler packed with ice and beer and my sister's famous braised-possum poor-boy sandwiches. We figured on driving around benignly in the hills and hollows, heedless, nurturing that sweet illusion of rootlessness, uninterested in debate or despair or destinations, sort of halfheartedly looking for adventure, meaning adventure more melancholy or amusing than grand or theatrical or remotely dangerous. What we figured on was searching out old graveyards to roam moodily through rather than seeking out any backcountry, low-slung cinderblock roadhouses to enter at our own peril, where I, for one, would surely sink my life into silly lovesick jukebox stuff, while I nursed cherished old pains and hoped some hillbilly would punch the wrong song.

We had all spent our fair share of time in the gloomy bottoms of Boone County over the years, as we had distant, undiscussed relatives around those parts. One of the abiding secrets in our family, a secret whose whole story my paternal grandfather carried to his grave, was that our branch of the family some four generations or so back had for some unknown reasons left Boone County more or less under the cover of darkness. Why anybody, especially a whole family branch no less, would have conspired to midnight-skulk out of Boone County, for God's sake, considering its reputation for moonshine and mayhem and murder, was a mystery to me. I mean, what act or event could have been so shameful or scary to warrant abandoning forever that place your people had, according to family legend, fought wild Indians and Yankees and criminal coal barons to call home? It was a mystery I always felt I needed to get to the bottom of some day, especially after I had become something of a lowdown midnight skulker myself, moving more often than not under the cover of darkness, both metaphoric and actual, as I drifted away from the place that for nearly twenty years I had called my own home.

My suggestion for making that old territory fresh and metaphoric for us somehow, so that we could play explorers transporting ourselves new into virgin country, was to follow the landscape as it had unfolded on the documentary film about Jessico White. My bright idea was to orient our passage not by whim or any homegrown memories of our own, but by points of interest on the mythic map of Jessico's documentary movie. A notion which led us eventually to that old cemetery on the hill above the tiny town of Twilight, where Jessico's daddy, Donald Ray, was buried.

Twilight was a town at the literal end of the line. You go over Williams Mountain on the Prenter Road down to a wide spot called Gordon and throw a left onto a narrow, crumbly blacktop and follow it maybe seven miles up the hollow until it just plain quits, and you have arrived in the tiny, dead-end town of Twilight, whose hazy rooftops we could see through the hovering wood-smoke in the bottoms from up in the old graveyard on the hill, where at one point my sister snapped a picture of me plopped down beside D. Ray White's gravestone for posterity.

In the photograph, I have a little swisher-sweet cigar stuck in my pie-hole, and I am leaning back on D. Ray's stone. I have this sappy smirk on my kisser, because just as my sister had snapped that picture, I suddenly felt like such an interloper lingering there. I felt like some sort of ghoulish tomb-tourist at the gravesite of a man whose son, Jessico, I had watched weeping his heart out on film for the whole world to witness at that exact spot, his daddy's grave, whereas I had never shed tear one for Charlie, my own dead daddy.

I could hear a couple of squirrels skittering about in the trees around us and the frail collapsed songs of autumn birds and the distant, faint hum of infrequent traffic on the road into Twilight far below. Otherwise it was hushed and still in the autumn glade, and time fell away. We wandered about the hillside, reading the old headstones. My sister, as is her wont, weeded the earth as she went, and righted any arrangements of dried flowers that had fallen over. My brother-in-law, whom sweet silence makes anxious, hummed and hummed and hummed under his breath. I wish I could report that I had been feeling religiousy and perhaps reflecting upon the hereafter, heaven and hell, sin, original and otherwise, responsibility and consequences, retribution, those things; but even among the dead, I moved about in my usual haze of horniness, and mostly I was imagining how my new young girlfriend Holly's bare smooth skin would smell with autumn air lifting from it, and the smoky taste of it when I licked under her arms. Whereupon, at one point, I tripped over a root and rolled down the hill like a fat old dog of romance.

My sister busied herself that day in the old mountain graveyard above Twilight brushing fallen leaves and broken branches off old D. Ray's grave, mottles of sunlight and shadows moving softly over her dear face, while humming "Amazing Grace" under her breath, and I wondered if she was being uncharacteristically ironic. Presently my sister had wandered about the hillside picking goldenrod and stems of Queen Anne's Lace and tiny purple asters, until she had enough for a lovely bouquet, which she positioned on D. Ray's gravestone. She then set about making a rubbing of the stone with a sheet of blank paper and blunt pencil she had brought along for that very possibility.

What occurred to me as I studied my sister bent to her solemn task over D. Ray's grave was that the last time we were all gathered in a cemetery together, meaning my sister and brother-in-law and me, was when we had buried Charlie over at Ansted in August of '88, as I mentioned earlier. There had been a multitude of mourners at Charlie's funeral, for he had been a man of lingering fame, and even beloved, I guess. At Charlie's funeral, my brother-in-law, who is considered to be about the most serious picker in his parts, with a good singing voice to boot, almost made it through "Amazing Grace," Charlie's favorite song, before his hangover and inherent sentimentality got the best of him and he high-pitched the final notes.

As I had stood there at Charlie's gravesite that steamy August day in '88, I attempted to cultivate my own sentimental memories of my old dad, and what I found myself recalling warmly was the last time he had punched my lights out. I was sixteen when one afternoon while I was flopped on the front hallway floor cooing dirt on the phone with Jenny Brown, the girl I loved with all my heart, Charlie suddenly stormed in the front door in a clearly agitated state of mind, demanding I get off the goddamn phone that goddamn second. When I tried to purr a simple good-bye, baby, to Jenny Brown, Charlie began kicking at me and swatting the top of my bobbing head. I dropped the phone on the floor and came up swinging. I had been boxing in the Golden Gloves a bit by then, not very successfully, true, but I felt I was plenty prepared to single-handedly confront John Wayne, not unlike the way Montgomery Clift had in that mythic western movie *Red River*. I could identify with Montgomery Clift in that movie when he decked his surrogate father, big John, and at last earned big John's grudging respect.

Because Charlie was so surprised and I was quick as a snake, I managed to get in a few glancing licks before he dropped me. I got back up, blubbering by then and yodeling with rage, and flew at him windmilling punches, but he nailed me again with a short left hook. This time when I pulled my tough-guy butt up off the floor, I skulked up the stairs wobbly and weeping and fell across my bed to blubber. Maybe five minutes later, Charlie knocked lightly on my bedroom door before opening it, instead of barreling on in as he usually did as though it were the swinging door of a saloon and he was the legendary butt-kicking sheriff.

Charlie simply stood there just inside the doorway, not saying anything. Through my teary, tough-guy eyes, I glanced at him and then gazed sullenly out my bedroom window into the back yard trees, whose autumn leaves were cupped like the frail golden hands of the dead. That's the exact image that popped into my young tough-guy poet's mind. I wished with all my heart that Charlie was dead as a doornail and six feet under, so that I could piss on his grave. Finally, Charlie said that he was real sorry, son. That he was between a rock and a real hard place, son. He had had to make a business phone call bad, son. But that was no excuse for him whipping on me, son, Charlie said. He was sorry, son, he said again, and then Charlie turned and closed the door quietly behind him. And that's about it, in the tender memory department for my old dad. Charlie had clearly learned his lesson that day, anyway, for he never attempted to tangle with me again. That day over in the little hilltop cemetery at Ansted when we had sent Charlie to his reward in that great Second World War in the sky, it was so hot and humid, the grass on the graves seemed to steam.

Presently that day in the Twilight graveyard, my brother-in-law came loping up the hill from down under the trees at the lower edge of the cemetery where he had been rooting around. He was carrying something on a stick, and when he got near enough I could see that it was a used condom. —Lookee what I found, my brother-in-law exclaimed with the exuberant leer of a boy who had just discovered the real flashy, criminal possibilities of his member. —I thought that you hadn't been here before, lover-boy, my brother-in-law said to me, wiggling his furry worm-like eyebrows suggestively. My brother-in-law was privy to too much trash about my shameful secret life. But who else did I have to bare my so-called soul to, except perhaps the world at large? —Shame shame, everybody knows your name, my brother-in-law intoned, cocking his brow and dropping his grizzled jaw to feature his favorite bug-eyed, dopey Larry-of-the-Three-Stooges look, which he must have imagined suggested significance. When I flipped him the bird, he merely laughed and made as though to launch the used condom back over the hill like some rocket-rubber to the moon, but my sister hissed —Don't you dare throw that awful old thing around here! We happen to be in a cemetery, so show some respect instead of your ass, my sister had hissily suggested. She then insisted that my brother-in-law cart the used condom up to discard in our day trip's environmentally conscious garbage bag of empty beer cans to carry back home.

My brother-in-law broke into a big-time whine (*rise and whine,* that is the motto that best describes how my brother-in-law begins every bald day of his life), but my sister hissily insisted. With his wormy lower lip sagged in a pout, my brother-in-law carried the used condom all the way back up the hill to the Chevy van. When my sister opened the top of the plastic garbage bag for him to deposit the used condom into, my brother-in-law had puffed up with all the dignity he could, upon such short notice, muster, and announced: —Well, okay, then, but when we get back to town, I'm the one who gets to toss it on the preacher's porch.

Elvis in the Land of Shadow Men

The hills and hollows we cruised through that day, as we meandered through the mountains, stopping occasionally to inquire after Jessico White's mysterious whereabouts, to maintain our pretense of purpose, were thick with eyes. A geography of eyes. Eyes of a sort anyway, meaning the countless satellite dishes, called by some folks the true State Flower of West Virginia. Consider the metaphor of flowers now, unfolded like huge metal blossoms in the yards of even the most tacky trailers, aimed at the cracks of visible sky in order to track television, blossoms that captured the leaked rumor of an outside world.

The yards were also thick with that ubiquitous southern West Virginia yard-art, garishly painted ceramic ceremonial creatures, frozen flocks of sacrificial chickens or ducks or gracefully contorted geese, which from a distance and at high speed looked momentarily as though they were real and rushing toward their destiny as dinner. Some of the yards, saturated with chemicals, were a brilliant, toxic green and full of miniature fountains and birdbaths and windmills and leaning shadow men. That was the land of leaning shadow men, life-size silhouettes of men in miners' or cowboy hats jigsawed from something thin like plywood, then painted pitch black. You saw those shadow men everywhere along the road, leaning against trees or the sides of houses or against fence posts, like leftover shards of nightlife. You just caught them in the corner of your eye as you buzzed by, gone in a blink, like an afterimage of good-old-boy beings emerging from the shadows of another dimension. They looked as though they were taking leisurely, philosophical shadow shits.

• • •

The fat jolly postmistress at the post office in the little town of Peytona just east of Racine back over on Route 3 turned out to be one of Jessico's cousins. She gave us directions to Jessico and Norma Jean's cabin over in a hollow at the foot of Drawdy Mountain. She then carried on and on about how proud folks was of Jesco, and not just because of the video that had made him famous as a mountain dancer, but because of the way he had turned his life around like nobody thought he ever could do. She claimed she couldn't even recall the last time she even heard about Jesco being in any old shooting or cutting or robbery or even being put under arrest for drunk driving or simply for beating the shit out of Norma Jean when she begged for it.

We passed the Drawdy Church of Christ traveling on Route 3 toward Madison along the Little Coal River. Then just after passing the Free Will Baptist Church, my brother-in-law pulled a hard left at the third road and we dipped down over the hill onto a muddy trail, which led up a narrow hollow. After passing a series of handmade signs tacked to the trees admonishing us to keep out and get out and bewear of dog and no truspassing, about a quarter mile down the road we came upon a tiny house perched up on the side of the hill, or *shanty* might be more descriptive, whose saggy front porch rose from the slope of the yard on wood poles, with steps on the far side rising to it. My brother-in-law pulled his van up in a wide space under some trees down the slope from the shanty, and parked there just a few feet in front of a long, black Cadillac limousine hearse. The old vehicle, which was tireless and resting upon cinderblocks in the rut of a front yard, was battered and bent and bore these vanity license plate tags that proclaimed: 1-ELVIS.

My brother-in-law turned off his motor and sighed deeply, and then he said: —Somehow I think we have arrived. For a few moments we all simply sat there listening to the Chevy van tick and staring up at the little cabin, which was covered with that tarpaper imitation red brick unrolled from bolts. About that time, two of the biggest, ugliest, meanest-looking turkeys I had seen in my life scrambled down around the side of the house, gobbling insanely. When I glanced back up at the little red shanty, I could swear I saw a curtain move in a front window.

—Holy moly, I said. —I vote, I said, —for finding a nice, friendly, family-sort of beerjoint that advertises clean restrooms and home-cooking and has a jukebox loaded with George Jones and Hag tunes and maybe a few oldie-but-goodies where we might pleasantly while away the rest of the afternoon.

My brother-in-law leaned forward and reached under the front seat. When he sat back up, I saw that he was holding his snub-nose .38 Detective Special, which he removed from its holster, and, leaning forward again, slipped under his belt beneath the back of his sleeveless hunting vest. What I haven't said about my pesty brother-in-law, by the way, is that although he is goat-bearded and nearly bald, he is also a burly, high-strung six-two, and about the last person on the face of the Earth one would want to fuck with. Plus when he gets a bee in his baseball cap he can be an incredibly hardheaded butt-hole. —I really do vote for a friendly, family beerjoint, I repeated. —We're here, my brother-in-law said, with this either sappy or insane grin on his face, I couldn't really tell which; and then he popped open his door and the next thing I knew he and my sister were striding purposefully up the hillside.

Suddenly I found myself out of the van and hurrying up the hill behind them toward the little red shanty and don't ask me why, but when I saw that curtain move in the front window yet again, I reached to pat my own pistol, before I recollected that I had foolishly sailed into this day utterly unarmed.

Due to acute paranoia and that basic hillbilly distrust of outsiders, the inhabitant of the cabin at first refused to open the bolted door when we clamored up onto the rickety porch out of the blue. But then I went into my sycophantic, two-step, big-fan shuffle, and bombarded the inhabitant with solicitous questions through the closed door concerning the documentary film about him, in case he was, indeed, the famous Jessico White. I told him I had watched that film maybe a hundred times and knew it like the back of my hand. I dropped that I was a writer who had published a couple of books and that I had driven down from Pittsburgh just to meet one of my favorite performers of all time.

After a spell, the heavy plank door swung slowly open, and peering at us from the dimness of that little room, like a rat in a hole, was, indeed, Jessico White, a.k.a. the Dancing Outlaw. He was black-bearded and fierce, and I gazed into his dark blazing mine-rat eyes with a shudder, clearly at my own peril. What I imagined I could see in the black bottomless pits of those eyes was a configuration of anger and madness and hurt and fear and suspicion and a childlike capacity for sadness and wonder and loneliness, and a flicker of what might best be described as tenderness, and shining somewhere back in those crazy eyes was a child-like capacity for fun, and a capacity for fame, and a childlike capacity for spastic violence so vast that it was plumb scary. They were eyes that I fancied reflected my own.

But shortly Jessico's wild, suspicious, trapped-animal eyes softened, and he was almost boyish in his surprise and joy at this unexpected visit from real-life faraway *fans*. Whereupon he could not have been more friendly, and, wiggling not unlike some happy puppy, he proudly gave us a guided tour of his four-room palace, including his *Elvis Chapel,* which was a dim backroom grotto of Elvis icons, a sanctum sanctorum of Elvis pictures and posters and a hanging rug that depicted a white-suited Vegas-vintage Elvis. There was also a rebel Elvis sewn into the center of a huge Confederate flag, and Elvis dolls and statues and Elvis plates. In a gold-gilded frame positioned upon a holy altar of a shelf between plaster-of-paris figurines of the Virgin Mary and Jesus Christ, there was a picture of Elvis painted on blue velvet.

In words that echoed comments he had made in the *Dancing Outlaw* documentary, Jessico said in a hushed holy voice that if it wasn't for this-here Elvis collection, he figured he would be dead by now or locked away in a crazy house until he died. —I was actually a animal, Jessico informed us, as he picked up the same revolving Elvis statue he had held in the video and set it in musical motion. —I mean a animal beast in the jungle, Jessico continued, his voice quavering with sincerity, that would feel like killing anybody for nothing but a drink, just for the pleasure of it; —but this here Elvis collection took that meanness out of me. It gave my mind something else to do than just being plain crazy. I don't have to feel that crazy way no more. Elvis was a loner just like me, and he didn't fit in 'til he got famous. Elvis liked sideburns and long truck-driver hair and sharp clothes like me, Jessico said, —and folks made fun of him 'til he got famous.

—Did you know, I asked Jessico, —that in high school Elvis's music teacher failed him and wouldn't let him in the Glee Club?

—Nobody knowed nothing, Jessico said solemnly, —'til Elvis got famous.

—Right, I said, then I said —Did you know that John Lennon once said that before Elvis, there was nobody?

—You don't say, Jessico said. —John who? he said.

—Just this dead English guy, I said.

Back out in the tiny cramped front room, which had dozens more Elvis pictures on the cluttered walls, plus a couple of pictures of Jesus and one of Marilyn Monroe and a rug with a depiction of James Dean on it wearing a cowboy hat, Jessico took a white jumpsuit with silver piping from a chest of drawers. He told us the jumpsuit had been handmade by his wife Norma Jean (who happened to be in the hospital that day because, according to Jessico, she had "got dizzy on account of her sugar condition and had fell down over the hill on her way to church and broke her nose"). Jessico held the suit up before him and tap-danced around the room for a couple of minutes, tossing his long hair and laughing. Jessico then carefully refolded the suit back into its drawer. Now don't you-all go tell Norma Jean I had my white suit out playing with it, he said and then he took out a wide silver studded belt with a silver buckle the approximate size of a hubcap. Jessico put it on around his waist over his patched, red-and-black plaid shirt, and he put on a pair of yellow-tinted aviator sunglasses. Then Jessico fetched a white dishtowel from the tiny kitchen, which he draped around his neck. He clicked on the big boombox on a table by a stuffed, half-collapsed chair with an Elvis throw-rug tossed over it, and he slipped a tape into its deck.

—Those of you-all, Jessico said, —who ain't never seen me before tonight will find out I'm totally insane. They just ain't caught up with me yet.

Jessico twanged this dented three-string dime-store guitar and danced wildly around the tiny room. He twirled and spun and belted out along with Elvis: You Ain't Nothing But A Hound Dog, Jailhouse Rock, Don't Be Cruel. Jessico threw karate chops and high-kicked like the madman he claimed he was, while singing along with Elvis on a dozen or more songs. He kept his black crazy eyes on my sister the whole time, for she is a very pretty woman. Finally the tape clicked off, and Jessico fell to the floor on one knee with his arms spread like wings. He tossed his head forward with his long, wet hair flapping over his flushed face.

I clapped like a maniac and whistled between my fingers like I was a madman too. I was a madman, by golly! I was wild and free and unafraid! And I loved the King, too, by golly! Clearly this famous Jessico character was another long-lost cousin of mine. There was no doubt in my mind that Boone County, backwoods, famous White-family blood flowed in my own hillbilly veins. My sister had joined me in clapping wildly. But not my anal brother-in-law, who grimaced and rolled his beady eyes.

Cousin Jessico jumped to his feet. He wiped the sweat that was running down his red face with the towel, and then, as Elvis had been wont to do for his own adoring female fans, cousin Jessico suddenly tossed the towel toward my sister.

My brother-in-law's hand flicked from nowhere quick as a copperhead to snatch that sweat-soaked dishtowel from the air. Whereupon my brother-in-law simply stood there frozen, holding that dripping trophy out before him with his fingertips as though he had just caught the snotrag of a leper. The tightlipped frown on his face suggested that one more funny move out of old cousin Jessico and the room would rain with hot lead. My brother-in-law was clearly convinced that cousin Jessico was truly crazy as a loon, but then my brother-in-law has always cultivated an abiding prejudice against the sanity-challenged (one of his main mottos being: *madness takes no prisoners*), while I, on the other hand, have always found a certain comfort among the crazy.

—God gave Elvis that-there voice, cousin Jessico told us that day down in Boone County, while he stood there strumming his guitar and talking in a quiet, churchy, recitation voice. —Nobody else can ever sing or talk identical to Elvis. Elvis was the number one king of rock and roll and he will be the king forever. He has made a lot of money even since he has been dead and he is famouser now than he ever was too. Elvis is supposed to be dead but he's not dead really. Some people think he ought to return and explain why he had to go play like he's dead, which he will do at a certain time. But like I say, we don't know when God is going to come back for the judgment day, that's just the day we're waiting on to see, but we don't know which day it's gonna be. It could be today or it could be tomorrow, we don't know. And that's the same way it is with Elvis. Elvis is gonna return some day and explain to all the people he didn't mean to hurt them, he just had to go do what he had to do.

THE SECRET LIVES OF ELVIS

L ike most Americans raised in the Age of Elvis, I know the basic facts of The King's mythic American life well. What I didn't know, until that day I first met Jessico White and began to suspect he was much more than just another mere Elvis impersonator, was that The King had lived many times before.

Cousin Jessico (whose given Christian name was *Jesse,* the same name as Elvis's twin brother who died at birth) informed me of this fact that autumn afternoon. To back up this assertion, cousin Jessico let me read documented proof that researchers who are studying the past lives of Elvis have discovered, employing the services of renowned mediums and psychics, that in one life Elvis was a Confederate soldier named Sergeant Travis Cox of the Fifth Mississippi Infantry Regiment, who was killed in action in the battle of Cold Harbor in Virginia in June 1864. Although information on Elvis as Sergeant Cox is sketchy, this much is known: he joined the Confederate Army in 1861 as a private, just like Elvis in his most recent incarnation, and fought in more than a dozen battles. He rose to the rank of sergeant, just as Elvis did in the U.S. Army. He enlisted in Jackson, Mississippi, but he was born on a farm near Tupelo, Elvis's own birthplace. He originally served as a bugler and a member of the regimental singers before he was promoted to squad leader. Elvis's musical talents are, of course, legendary.

But the most amazing discovery that cousin Jessico provided me with documented proof of that day was that Elvis Presley was the reincarnation of the Egyptian pharaoh Amenhotep IV. And among the incredible evidence was a recently uncovered painting of Amenhotep that bears a striking resemblance, including the sneerlike curling of the upper lip, between the ancient Egyptian ruler and The King of rock 'n roll. Said Dr. Antat Semnak, chief of artifacts for the Cairo Museum: "When we discovered the temple painting, the entire excavation crew let out a shout. Mr. Presley was one of the most recognizable faces in the world. Even the lowliest diggers knew it was Elvis."

Dr. Harold Tucker, a famed Egyptologist with the museum, headed an international team that studied conclusive evidence that Amenhotep and Elvis shared the same soul. He discovered incredible similarities between the lives of the Egyptian ruler and The King. Both men came into prominence in their late teens and both of them died at age 42. Both men were considered rebels. Egyptologists commonly call Amenhotep the first rebel against established religious order. Both men were leaders pushing controversial themes, Amenhotep the concept of a single divinity, and Elvis rock 'n roll. Both men lived for large parts of their lives in cities called Memphis. Strong movements sprang up to oppose both men's messages. Amenhotep's enemies, the priests of the old religion of plural gods, succeeded in destroying almost all references to him, even scraping his name from temple writings and smashing his statues. Elvis's enemies smashed thousands of his records in an attempt to curb the religious-like spread of rock 'n roll. Amenhotep worshipped the sun as the one god, and Elvis got his start recording at Sun Records. Legends about both men sprang up immediately after death. Amenhotep's mummy disappeared and has never been found, and many of his subjects continued to believe he was still alive. Hundreds of people have spotted Elvis since his reported 1977 "death." Both men built elaborate palaces. Amenhotep had the palace of Amarna constructed. *Amarna* translates from ancient Egyptian as "graceful," and Elvis owned Graceland in Memphis. "It's uncanny," said Dr. Semnak. "There's no denying the proof. Elvis Presley definitely lived before as Amenhotep. And we are sure that such a powerful presence has had many, many lives."

I informed cousin Jessico that day that I was absolutely fascinated by the theory that The King had lived many, many lives, and I was so duly impressed with his documented proof that I took out my little spiral notebook and recorded the date of that particular issue of the *Examiner* (March 6, 1990) he had given me excitedly to read aloud (it had become clear that cousin Jessico was not a scholar, could barely, in fact, read or write). And I told cousin Jessico I would look more deeply into this incredible matter of The King's many lives in the University of Pittsburgh's library, which I was certain had a whole wing devoted to research on The King, and I promised to get back to him with all the supporting evidence I could put my hands on.

What if Elvis had also been aware of this compelling evidence? it had suddenly occurred to me that day. What if Elvis had been aware of the startling parallels between his life and that of an ancient Egyptian pharaoh who died at 42? What if it had occurred to Elvis, as he approached the fateful age of 42, that perhaps there was a way to circumvent destiny: that if he radically altered his life in some way, disguised himself well enough, buried his real identity deep enough, he could make a clean getaway perfect enough to escape into a shadow-life and avoid his Elvis Presley fate? That is when I began to take a good, hard look at this so-called Elvis impersonator named Jessico White.

For, over the course of that afternoon down in Boone County, I came to suspect (and do not disparage this suspicion simply because of that tiny tab of acid I had tasted upon disembarking from the Chevy van, which had rendered me bold and mystic), that Jessico White was indeed, alas, *Elvis*. Elvis so perfectly disguised that he could impersonate himself without fear of ever being discovered on hillbilly high-school stages or in the parking lots of grocery-store openings or on local television whenever he could not bear that longing for some laughs and claps like in the old days. Elvis so perfectly disguised as an eccentric outlaw impersonator of himself and last mountain dancer that if he wanted to, he could grow old back in the pure, sweet isolation of the West Virginia hills, forever unfound.

At that point, cousin Elvis picked up a pile of photographs from a dresser, and after studying one for a moment he handed it to me. —Don't Norma Jean favor Elvis's momma? cousin Elvis asked me like a sly dog. —Some folks say Norma Jean could be Elvis's momma's twin sister, cousin Elvis said, testing me. I studied the photograph, and tried to recall pictures I had seen of Elvis's momma. Perhaps Norma Jean did resemble the mother of Elvis, if ever the mother of Elvis had worn a sweat-stained DANCING OUTLAW T-shirt, and had a frizzy halo of jet-black hair that looked as though it had been dipped in shoe polish, and the face of a suspicious angry dumpling. Norma Jean and Elvis's mom would be about the same age, anyway. —Holy moly, I gasped to cousin Elvis, —the resemblance is uncanny!

What had popped oddly into my mind at that point was this documentary I had once seen about Elvis, called *That's The Way It Is,* which had focused upon the production of one of his Las Vegas shows. One middle-aged lady with a blue beehive, who had been lucky enough to be positioned beside the runway and had caught one of the dozen or so towels Elvis had used to wipe his royal sweat and toss into the audience, had screamed so loudly with excitement that The King had also bent down to give her a quick kiss. Later, during an interview for the documentary, this lucky lady, so awash in blue and heavily bejeweled, had declared sobbingly that getting kissed by Elvis was not unlike being in seventh heaven and the high point of her whole entire life. And then they had interviewed another woman who had caught a towel. She had been middle-aged and frumpy, with frizzy jet-black hair, piled high, and I had suddenly recalled her as a dead ringer for Norma Jean, and when the interviewer had asked her what she thought about the rumors of Elvis's poor health, she had screwed up her scary dumpling of a face like a fist, and spluttered into the camera that she had done proved to Elvis last night that only her love alone could save him. Elvis, still yet wearing his sweaty white jumpsuit and spangled cape and yellow-tinted aviator shades, was captured on film backstage later joking around with his Memphis Mafia cronies when he said: —That old gal I was with last night, man, she could raise the dead.

Cousin Elvis then handed me a Polaroid picture of his daddy all dressed up in a suit like a preacher and poised to dance. —Look how handsome my daddy was, cousin Elvis said. —Even without his teeth in, cousin Elvis added. —Look at Daddy's eyes, cousin Elvis said, —don't it look like he lookin' for something out beyond all of us'uns? Out past the picture, out past Momma, or whoever was taking the peel-away picture, out past the mountains theirselves? Whenever I look hard at this picture, I feel like Daddy's looking for me somehow out here in the future, since here I am famous now and he never knowed me famous or even thought of it.

So I looked deeply into the eyes of cousin Elvis's own dead daddy, across that abyss between the land of the living, where cousin Elvis and I currently abided, to where both our fathers abided in the land of the dead, and what I saw were eyes that looked real similar to my own old dead daddy's eyes when I looked at them in old pictures, the manner they looked back out hard at me darkly alive, and angry and lonely and sad that they were the ones looking out from that side of things; and then every time, without fail, those eyes would try to fasten themselves to my own eyes and pull me to join them in the abyss. I looked hard into cousin Elvis's dead daddy's eyes for about a heartbeat. Not hardly long enough for light, which travels at about 186,281 miles per second, to reflect.

Down in the front yard, as we were preparing to pile back into the Chevy van for the long haul over the evening hills and then west up the Kanawha River Valley toward the Fayette Plateau and the perfect little peach of a town called Billville, my sister asked cousin Elvis if he would permit her to snap a few pictures for posterity. Cousin Elvis was happy to do it. He was pleased as punch. At one point, my sister posed cousin Elvis and myself in front of the long, black limousine hearse, whereupon, without prompting, cousin Elvis and I suddenly put our arms around each other's shoulders, as if to have a clear record in that photograph of what we had discovered in the course of that day about the kindred-ness of our restless and haunted, but fearlessly searching, wild bold spirits.

Old cousin Elvis was so perfectly disguised he did not hesitate a heart-beat for fear of drawing attention to himself with the I ♥ Elvis bumper sticker or the 1-ELVIS license plate on the front of that long, black hearse which had once been painted the purest white. I was utterly convinced that that was the hearse that had once led a mournful line of white stretch limousines through Memphis as seemingly endless as the broken white lines of a highway. We are talking here of a repainted Cadillac hearse that was once supposed to have transported Elvis on his last ride out of life, instead of carrying him upon the perfect clean getaway, and now there it was, parked in a hilly, rock-filled front yard on the Planet West Virginia, repainted and couldn't be traced.

After my sister snapped our picture, cousin Elvis jokingly lifted the front of his old plaid shirt to reveal the pistol he had been packing during that whole afternoon that I look back on now as being one of utter revelation. True, it was just a little .22 caliber piece of shit, but my brother-in-law was not amused, and for a blink I thought that my brother-in-law was going to whip out his own pistol and get the drop on cousin Elvis, maybe put cousin Elvis under some sort of citizen-fan's arrest for becoming so criminally enigmatic as to choose to abandon his old life of dimming fame and fortune and desperate fatigue simply to avoid his fate as a falling star.

As soon as we piled into the Chevy van, I hauled a tall cold one out of the icy waters of the Styrofoam cooler and popped it. Inch by inch, my brother-in-law began to eke his huge road-hog around in the only narrow level space available, in order to head back out of the hollow. As I took a long, icy pull of Bud, the idea descended upon me, as though from a suggestion in a dream, that I should return to this bottomland some day soon to convince *The King* that his perfect clean getaway story of escape and disguise and deeply hidden real identity could be the shadow-story of my very own sweet-and-sour secret life, and that he should let me write it down for the pure sake of posterity.

STRANGER STEW

The twisted perverted hillbillies portrayed in the film *Deliverance* were but your basic everyday Southern Baptist Sunday-school hillbillies, compared to the crazy cannibal hillbillies in the early Wes Craven horror film *The Hills Have Eyes*. The hills in that movie were thick with wild, idiot, feral children, with roaming packs of savage shadow-hillbillies you could only catch glimpses of in the corner of your eye until it was too late, and they were ravenously upon you. Stay on the main road, the old coot at the decrepit gas station had told the vacationing family from Cleveland who had gotten onto the wrong road, don't go down roads around here that are only dotted lines on the map. But the recently retired Cleveland cop tough-guy dad, who claimed to have dodged spear-chucking "coons" and dogs thrown off roofs at him by the hillbilly white trash who came up from places like West Virginia to work in the auto plants, knew it all.

The Cleveland law-dog, tough-guy spanker-dad soon enough discovers himself crucified to a tree near his family's silver Airstream trailer. Whereupon the patriarch of that clan of mountain monsters, who is your worst dream of a really big, bad, snarly, clearly ill-tempered, cannibal hillbilly, informs Dad that he intends to eat the heart out of Dad's memory. He douses the chagrined Cleveland Dad thoroughly with gasoline and leaves Dad to scream and wail and howl inconsolably from the night like something pure animal for the benefit of his family as he is barbequed alive. In this movie, things quickly go from bad to worse for the little lost family from Cleveland, and before the night is over several other members have had to deal with real unpleasantness at the hands of the hillbillies, who lope about in the dark drooling and slobbering and giggling, and who have walkie-talkies and are sometimes actually rather jocular as they coordinate their attacks using the call-names of planets, *Mars, Pluto, Saturn, Jupiter.* For the little bitty baby they kidnap, the hungry hillbillies have special plans. They are real tired of eating dawg, it seems. *Tenderloin,* is how they refer to the cute, cuddly, pink little baby, and the hillbillies make it clear that for their menu, tenderloin is done to a turn.

What I couldn't get out of my mind as I was driving around in the everlasting hills and sad dark hollows of Boone County hunting for my old cousin Jesco White, in order to begin my intended interviews with him for my book about weird West Virginians, was just how much that one bearded cannibal hillbilly boy, the one with the wild, black, bottomless eyes, the one who tore that chicken's head off with his teeth and sucked the blood and guts out of its neck as though it was a fat, feathery straw and those innards sweet as lobster, looked like old Jesco White. I was armed to the teeth that day, true, but not really looking at all eagerly for trouble as I searched high and low for that curious and no-doubt dangerous individual a.k.a. The Dancing Outlaw. The most recent report I had been able to find was a news clip in the *Charleston Gazette,* the mountain state's so-called "leading" paper, which read:

DEPUTIES REMOVE JESSICO WHITE FROM HOME
PEYTONA (AP)—The Dancing Outlaw is out on the streets.

Jessico ("Jesco") White, the former jailbird who danced his way onto primetime television, was removed from his home by Boone County sheriff's deputies Wednesday after a dispute with his wife.

Norma Jean White said her husband beat her and fired a gun at her because she did not want to take their dog for a walk in the rain, said Sgt. R.A. Miller.

There was no evidence of gunshots or physical abuse to Norma Jean White, Miller said. But she filed a domestic violence complaint anyway, which prohibits Jesco from coming home until a hearing December 8.

White, whose passion for Appalachian mountain dancing was the subject of a television documentary, recently appeared on ABC-TV's "Roseanne" sitcom.

I had written cousin Jesco a letter about my intentions that I wasn't even sure he had received or that anybody had read to him, in which I told him of my wish to write a chapter in my West Virginia book based upon him and his turbulent but finally inspirational life.

In the letter, I pointed out all the parallels I had found in our lives, which was why I had been so intrigued when I had first seen *The Dancing Outlaw*. You had trouble with the law when you were younger, and so did I, I informed Jesco. I told him about the summer I was seventeen when I had been involved in those seven armed robberies up in and around Atlantic City, which had been the basic subject matter of my second novel. I told Jesco that his talent for tap-dancing was in some ways akin to whatever talent I had for writing, that they were both forms of very personal expression that had made us both somewhat different from the people around whom we had grown up, and they had been ways we both had used to enlarge our lives, were even in some senses avenues of escape for us both from the limitations our early environments had placed upon us. His interest in Elvis and the inspiration Elvis had provided him was not unlike my interest in James Dean and the ways I had tried to pattern my own youthful behavior in his rebellious image. James Dean's picture was on the dust jacket of my second novel, I informed Jesco. I had been married to two women and I didn't have any children either, although not for the exact reasons he didn't. Still yet, there was a parallel.

Another parallel, and perhaps the most important one to me, was the complex, often painful, but finally loving relationship Jesco had had with his daddy, D. Ray. When Jesco had spoken bittersweetly of D. Ray on the video, bells of recognition had pealed for me, and I felt that I understood his mixed sentiments perfectly. I told Jesco that my own old dad had been a complex and often difficult man who I both loved and wanted to murder in some bloody manner with my own hands by turns.

When Jesco had wept while he was talking about his daddy in the film, I had envied him. I had wished I could feel such tears burn my own cheeks, for I hadn't been able to cry yet for my own old man, not at his funeral in August of '88 nor whenever I visited the little mountain cemetery over at Ansted where he was buried. I told Jesco that I thought his story was an important story to tell, and a very American story, a story about struggle and hardship, but also one of ultimate survival and more, *hope*, for instance, and even *triumph*, and, most of all, *renewal*, which I, for one, considered to be the sweetest form of revenge. I did not mention my suspicions of his perfect clean getaway into the secret shadow-life of Elvis.

I followed Route 85 east along the Little Coal River outside of Madison, passing through any number of wide spots in the narrow road called towns, until, directly past a small riverside park in Van, I turned east onto an even narrower road that wound along a hollow crowded with neat little frame houses and doublewides that constituted a roadkill of a town named Gordon. I then hit a fork at a boarded-up gas station and bore right and, a half mile up the crumbly road, I had arrived at the Gordon Grill, a long, low, windowless cinderblock building with a single big metal door in front that was riddled with the clear indentations of bullets, which, according to rumor, had once been Jesco's outlaw beerjoint of choice.

I pulled into the gravel and red dog across the road from that building of clearly bad intentions and studied it. There were several pickups and maybe a half dozen Harleys parked out front. I entertained the notion of having a couple of tall cold ones for the road within that dangerous establishment, while I made friendly inquiries concerning the whereabouts of the infamous Jesco White.

About that time, an ancient beat-up boat of a Buick pulled in and several longhaired, bearded, clearly armed-and-dangerous customers piled out. As they clomped along the concrete walk toward the big, bullet-dented door, they twirled and checked the chambers of their pistols.

When they pushed that heavy door open, I caught a serious beerjoint blast of blaring jukebox redneck music, and then when the door sealed shut behind them it was dead silent again, except for the soft cries of crickets by the creek and a distant car horn honking as randomly and forlorn-sounding as a hoot from an owl way back in the hills. About then, another rattletrap of a pickup pulled into the gravel lot across the road, and a rail of an old boy wearing that ubiquitous baseball cap and his seriously bovine babe got out and staggered arm in arm into the beerjoint, whose smoky yellow light flooded out about them like a halo in the moment they entered that roadhouse out of the eternal twilight of the hollow.

The urgent main adventure of my manhood might lie behind that bullet-blasted door, I reflected somberly, and then I pulled my own cap low over my steely eyes and slid out of my Red Ride. I strolled across the broken blacktop toward that roadhouse I imagined to be beyond any law, that smoky dangerous den of redneck moonshiners and mountain marijuana farmers and dope-dealing hillbilly bikers and gun-runners armed to the teeth, good old boys who woke up every morning feeling discarded and cheated and isolated, feeling proud and mean and full of outrage and violence and frustrated desire and as evil as the day is long.

I swaggered all the way up on the concrete porch and was reaching forward to push open the bullet-blasted door before I came to my senses. Zen-like, the realization had hammered me over the head like a baseball bat that no, I really didn't require another tall cold one for the road, nor truly need any unreliable, boozy clues concerning Jesco's hideout in the hills. A hand-printed cardboard sign taped to the door proclaimed: No Gunns—No Knifes—No Drugs.

I swirled to fling myself from that place, but hesitated. Whereupon I whipped my ubiquitous ballpoint from my shirt pocket, and, imagining myself quite the masked wag (as in, who was that masked wag, anyway? Why, that was the Lone Writer!), I inked in No Shues. Then I bolted wildly back across the blacktop to my Red Ride, not utterly unlike a bat out of hell.

• • •

The next thing I knew, I was high atop Williams Mountain, taking most curves on two wheels, until I spotted some letters arranged in the marquee before a little white frame Holiness of God church set back off the road in a stand of trees, whose message I slowed to read. It was the topic of next Sunday's sermon: SCABS DIE AND BURN IN HELL WITH THE GODDAM DEVIL. Whereupon I began a reflective, leisurely, twisting descent on a disintegrating road not on my map, drifting down and down sharply into bottoms where it was suddenly evening, and the dark coal-thick mountains rose up around me rugged and rocky and silent, and the submerged air of isolation in the narrow lonely hollow was palpable enough to cut with the old proverbial pig-sticker we West Virginians often carry purely for self-protection, such as my own German-made Kissing-Crane stiletto.

And then suddenly I found myself in the tiny town of Prenter, home of Jesco's mom Birtie Mae, the "Miracle Woman." I drove slowly down the one nearly deserted street that was downtown Prenter, maybe the saddest ruin of a town I had ever seen. The houses lining both sides of the road were these little, frame, mostly collapsed coal-company shacks, many uninhabited, windowless with fallen porches and paint long weathered away, and although the sun had come out and it had turned into a nice day, I didn't see a soul in that forlorn, hopeless place, not even a mangy dog or cat. I had the strangest creepy feeling that I was utterly alone, as I drove to the far end of what could have been a ghost town, where I pulled into a wide heavily rutted lot in front of the only store in town, called, appropriately enough, the Area Supply Store.

Across the road I could see a Peabody Coal Company sign, and I had passed another one just as I was entering Prenter, which was the sign I was pretty sure where, according to the sketchy directions I had gotten back at the Coal Miner's Kitchen (where I had stopped for a possum-burger and Bud brunch earlier), I was to turn back up into Birtie Mae's dark hollow. But to be certain, I went into the Area Supply Store to double-check, and to pick up a six-pack of cold Buds to suck for company, and for courage, sure, to become, as they say, *beer-brave.*

I piddled around, browsing back shelves while I waited for the two hard-core country boys who were hanging around up at the front counter sucking RC Colas and bullshitting with the maybe four-hundred-pound cashier lady to mosey on. But they appeared parked where they were for the duration, so finally I picked up a six-pack of Buds and a bag of barbequed pork rinds. I carried them up to the counter, smiling like a dope and bobbing my head obsequiously as I do perhaps in hopes of persuading the world at large of what a well-meaning human being I am at heart. But it was pure bashfulness on my part, and not fear, that rendered me hesitant and embarrassed around those—and all—strangers.

Both good-old-boys and the huge cashier, whose enormous bare arms looked like country hams tattooed with skulls and crosses and the countless names of men, eyeballed me with suspicion, checking out my limp ponytail and the tiny enigmatic tattoo of a sacred salamander on my right forearm and my sissy-looking sandals, as I put my items down and addressed my shyness enough to ask if any of them could give me the directions to Birtie Mae White's trailer.

The three of them looked at one other as though I had asked about a shortcut to Mars, a planet just past Kentucky, and they all grinned in unison, displaying mouths of uniformly sharp, pointy, brown teeth. I suddenly recalled a horror story I had read years before about this traveling salesman who gets stuck in a town of people with pointy, brown teeth only to discover to his chagrin that those residents were the descendants of a sea captain and his South Seas cannibal wife, and, yes, he ends up in a stew. And then, like a flashback, Wes Craven's crazy movie and its cannibal hillbillies with the names of planets returned to me. And then the huge cashier, who looked as though she alone could have supped upon every traveling salesman to pass through those parts in twenty years, said simply: —I wouldn't go back in there if I didn't have to go, mister. (*Stay on the main road!* the old man had begged the tough-guy Cleveland dad, don't go down no roads around here that are only dotted lines on the map.)

To my trained eye, the creatures before me were clearly only half-human, clearly mutant hillbillies, half-this, half-that, who had come down out of the mountains from their roaming packs of savage, cannibal relatives with the names of planets only to refresh themselves with a few RC Colas and check out any travelers passing through for potential stranger stew. And perhaps the drooling, idiot boy with long, stringy, black hair beneath his baseball cap and wild, animal eyes called his monstrous companion *Junior,* when they were discussing the directions to Birtie Mae's trailer, but to my trained-ear it sounded not unlike *Jupiter.* I thanked them for the sketchy directions and flung myself forthwith from that establishment.

Unfortunately, my modes of coping behavior are simple to the point of primitive. There is not much middle ground between my natural obsequious flighty tendencies and then, when something dangerous and dark clicks inside me, that mode driven utterly by the sort of adrenaline overload that once sailed that insane boy flying across a gym dressing-room back in junior high school to bury his fangs in the neck of that tough country boy named Charlie Wilkes.

Both of the clearly curious, cannibal hillbillies strolled out onto the front porch of the old Area Supply Store to watch me get into my Red Ride. In a moment of pure doper paranoia, I saw a look in their yellow, beady animal eyes that told me they wanted to eat the heart out of my memory. Those sons-of-bitches were clearly planning to follow me back into the middle of nowhere and cut off my return somehow and butt-fuck me blind, before they cooked me over a slow fire to a turn. Clearly those sons-of-bitches wanted to boil my dick for soup. Well, that sure wouldn't be very much fun now, would it? I reflected.

I run about six foot and two hundred myself, and when I suck in my beer-gut and puff up I am fucken Teddy Roosevelt, and Teddy had stalked around to the back of his Red Ride and swung open the tire rack and opened the rear window and lowered the tailgate and took his Brazilian-made Saucha-Iga twelve-gauge shotgun (which is sawed off to the point of being legal by maybe an eighth of an inch) out of its case. I cracked my shotgun open and popped Remington Long Range Express shells into its two chambers and then clicked my shotgun shut. I closed up the back of my vehicle, and, keeping the shadowy presence of the mutants on the porch in the corner of my eye in case of sudden moves, I swaggered back around to climb into the driver's seat like John Wayne.

I eyeballed the mutants meaningfully at that point, and placed my loaded shotgun within real clear easy reach. I pulled out slowly, keeping an eye peeled on the cannibal cooks on the porch. When I stopped to turn left onto the blacktop, I hollered back to those two humanly-challenged hillbillies, informing them in no uncertain terms not to let my ponytail or sissy sandals or yuppie-looking vehicle fool them, that if the truth be told my neck was evilly redder than either of their worthless assholes, and that if they knew what was good for them they would be well advised to keep their malformed members in their pants.

Whereupon, those mutant gentlemen had simply looked at one another and muttered in unison, *huh?*

TELL ME ABOUT IT

Just past the little white frame Free Will Baptist Church at the north end of Prenter, I threw a right at the Peabody Coal Company sign and headed up the narrow hollow. "A trailer on the right" was about the most cogent of my directions, and as soon as I came upon a trailer on the right I pulled up and stopped. The trailer didn't look anything like Birtie Mae's had in the *Dancing Outlaw* video, but I got out anyway and walked up a red dog driveway toward it.

I saw what looked like a face of fur at a window as I approached the front stoop. The screen door swung open and either a big, bareback, long-haired, bearded man or a bear stepped out. Its shoulders were shaggy and massive, and the thing stood there with its huge, hairy, ape-man arms folded across an amazingly hirsute chest and huge belly, observing me as though I had just walked down the ramp from a flying saucer. Take me to your leader, hairball, was what I felt like saying, but instead I managed to croak the question as to where could I locate Birtie Mae White's trailer.

The thing simply nodded toward the road and mumbled something about the trailer being up acrosst the creek a ways to the right, if that there was the place I was really wanten to go to, whereupon it turned abruptly on its heels and disappeared back into the trailer, shaking its huge head.

A fucken creek? I reflected. Back in my Red Ride, I found myself on a dirt road in moments which you can bet wouldn't be even a *dotted* line on any map. Then I came to the creek, which was unfortunately nearly dry, hence I had no good excuse not to roll down into its rock-filled bed and bounce across into what felt to my suddenly faint heart like an *alternate universe.*

The rutted dirt road wasn't much wider than my vehicle, and it wound into the deep woods. I buzzed up my side window to keep the low leafy branches of trees from slapping me in the face. There was an air of seclusion and secrecy and menace in the narrow hollow. I had a sudden image of the hollows between these hills as constituting an enormous labyrinth, as though they were corridors in a great maze of intricate passageways and blind alleys.

The great writer Jorge Luis Borges first discovered the idea of the labyrinth as a boy in an engraving in an old book he came across in his father's library, I recalled as I guzzled a cold Bud. And it became a lifelong symbol for Borges of being lost in life, of modern man's bewilderment in the world; but it was a symbol for Borges also of hope, even salvation. There is a presumed center to every labyrinth, and if we think of the universe as a labyrinth, as Borges did, then it must have a center, even if that center is horrible, or demonic, like the half-beast, half-human Minotaur, which was confined at the center of the mythic labyrinth Daedalus built for King Minos on the ancient island kingdom of Crete. It is nonetheless a center; and if we believe in it, we at least can believe in a chance for some kind of meaning. And we can at least hope that the center is holy, is divine. If there is no center at all, then the universe is chaos and we are up a river of shit with no philosophical paddle. I guzzled maybe three tall cold ones while I entertained these reflections, for all the good they got me in the bravery department, the reflections or the cold Buds.

As I drove on slowly down that narrow hollow deeper into the maze, I reflected upon what I might find at the secret center of my own labyrinth of life. Would I find my own future, or my past, waiting patiently for me in the present around the next bend? Whenever I begin to wax philosophical, I tend to get a chubby, as I did that day. I thought of Holly then, sort of out of the philosophical blue, a philosophical inkling, I guess one could call it, as my sixth sense kicked in, of the amazing pain I would feel months later when she would dish out the blow-by-blow details of how she had begun the New Year's with a bang, literally, biblically, with a forty-five-year-old handsome architect who had never had a serious relationship in his life, which made him the perfect man, of course, for her to philosophically fuck and drive me nuts as Nietzsche.

I rounded a bend in the dirt road and, instead of any secret center of answers, I came upon a trailer set perpendicular to the road, but on the left, so it could not have been Birtie Mae's, and I started to drive past it. I noticed what looked like a flock of huge ugly crows pecking about in the dirt yard. Then it dawned on me, they were actually these scrawny, ugly, black chickens. Really ugly, black, spastic, speedy chickens, who commenced to come scratching and jerking toward my vehicle, as though they were zonked on chicken-nip, or chicken-acid even, and I had this sudden picture of them pecking at their reflected, ugly images in the shiny sides of my polished Red Ride. I put the pedal to the metal.

In a blink I was barreling into a virtual tunnel of leafy branches that washed over my windshield like green waves. All I could see on the sides was a blurred impossibility of leaves and stems and vines and thorny runners. I slammed on the brakes, and began to inch along the bumpy trail until, after what seemed like ten miles of this wilderness confusion and gloom, I came to a yellow pole-gate across the road, with a Peabody Coal Company sign on it, bearing the warning not to trespass. I sat there quietly listening to the faint ticking of my vehicle in the otherwise deep silence of the surrounding forest. I couldn't even hear a bird. There was no sound of moving water. Insects didn't seem to buzz. The world had never seemed so quiet to me, so suspended, and the woods so dark and deep. I got a good case of the blues suddenly. I felt sad, old and empty, those things, and I had the crazy urge to simply get out of my vehicle, my cool Red Ride, even leave it running, leave its engine running deep in the woods up a dead end dirt road, and go climb over that gate and walk off to trespass into whatever secret country that trail would lead me into and not look back. Find a good secret place to fall off the face of the Earth from.

For a long time I had known that there was only emptiness inside me now in a place where hope and dreams used to be. I had to take a leak, but before I could do anything about it, I felt what I can only describe as a sort of shivering in the spooky woods, and rustlings, and the sense of something really big nearby, breathing heavily.

Over the years I have come to suspect that what we finally have to fear the most is carried in our hearts. But when I sensed something really bigger than me breathing heavily nearby in the dark Boone County woods that humid, drizzly Indian summer day, I threw my Red Ride into reverse and barreled backward out of that green hellhole. I was dripping with sweat and the muscles (such as they are) of my back and stomach felt like tiny fists opening and closing tightly, or a dozen spastic little heart attacks blinking on and off at once, from my twisting so intently around in the seat to steer frantically as I returned as rapidly as possible in reverse toward the world as I have always known it.

Those ugly black chickens, which looked like two-legged rats with feathers, scattered as I swung back into the dirt yard in front of the trailer to turn around. When a tall, rangy, ropy-muscled young man wearing shades and a baseball cap over his shoulder-length, greasy blond hair, who was bareback and heavily tattooed, came out onto the concrete stoop, and stood there looking me over, my first impulse was to gun my Red Ride on out of there, no questions asked.

But I opened the door and swung my sore, sweaty old butt out, then I sort of waved my open hands at him, instinctively I reckon, to demonstrate I wasn't an armed and dangerous sort of fellow. I took a few hesitant steps in his direction, at which point it dawned on me again that I was wearing my silly, sissy sandals and not packing a pistol. I had intended to wear my old Western shit-kicking boots that day back in the boonies, which always made me feel taller and tougher somehow, and helped me summon up my inner John Wayne if an occasion called for it, but the Indian summer day had been sweaty and sticky, so I was unfortunately wearing those flimsy, rubber-soled, sissy sandals, which had a tendency to flop off my feet. All of those amazingly ugly, black, evil-looking, feathery fowl were all around me, clearly real rat-curious about the taste of my naked toes.

The young half-human simply stood there on the stoop, his thumbs hooked behind his belt, clearly sizing me up for supper. He scratched a spot near his left nipple, which was covered with an elaborate tattoo of what appeared to be a bloody dagger plunged into a human heart. He spit a thin brown line of either snuff juice or blood out into the yard. Then he said: —What's happening, dude?

—Birtie Mae White, I gasped, as I took a few tentative kicks at one particularly black evil chicken that apparently had its heart set on my big toe, —where does she live?

—Jest back down the road a ways, the young mutant said, flashing his pointy brown teeth in a hungry smile. —They's a little turnoff left. She's back up in there a little ways, dude.

—Thanks a million, I muttered, and as I was turning and trying to kick at the increasingly encroaching chicken-rats my right sandal flopped off my foot and I stumbled. Those evil, black birds went wild, cackling like crazy, rolling their beady eyes, flapping their stunted wings, waiting for me to just hit the ground so that they could be upon me. I hopped around trying to get the sandal back on my foot, and finally banged backward against my vehicle breaking my fall, where I steadied myself and struggled with my sandal. At which point I noticed that the young hillbilly cannibal had come down off the concrete stoop and was hovering just a few feet from me. He nodded toward my vehicle and said, with blood dripping from the corners of his mouth: —Cool ride, dude.

—Listen, Pluto, President Teddy growled and pushed off his red Rough Rider and stood there all puffed up and jutting his manly *don't fucken tread on me* jaw, —or Saturn, or whatever the fuck your cannibal mutant motherfucken name is, I'm in possession of a sawed-off twelve-gauge shotgun that is primed and loaded and I'm not interested in any fucken invitations to dinner. Kill one of them ugly, fucken chickens, if you want a snack.

—Yo, dude, the young man said quietly and smiled, shaking his head as though bewildered, as though bemused and perhaps entertaining a vague pity. He lifted his shades off then, and his steady, curious eyes were gentle and blue, and what he said was: —You really oughtta chill out, Dad, man.

Tell me about it.

THE KING IS BACK

Most of Jesco's appearance on the *Roseanne* show ended up on the cutting-room floor; all, in fact, save for a short segment of him dancing at the very end of the program as the credits roll. Because of this, the Carsey-Werner Company, the producers of the *Roseanne* show, would not even permit Jacob Young to run Jesco's actual performance on the show in his documentary, *Jesco Goes to Hollywood*. Jacob Young had to settle for shots around the studio and those stage sets that constitute that parallel vision of the real world we call television.

So recorded there in the documentary was Jesco getting made up for the first time in his life, explaining his crude jailhouse tattoos to the attractive makeup girl as she dusts his nose with powder. She visibly flinches when Jesco tells her how his prison pals used a long sewing needle dipped in ink to pierce his skin, and then in something like a whisper, as though she is afraid of the answer, she asks Jesco where is it he is from now? Boone County, Jesco pipes up proudly, as though this will explain everything to that lovely, blond, incredulous California makeup girl.

What becomes real clear in the course of the documentary is: no. 1, Roseanne is genuinely pissed off about something, and, no. 2, Roseanne is truly a bitch. At one point during a break in the taping of the teevee show, we see her arguing furiously back in the kitchen part of the set with her then husband and producer, Tom Arnold.

After that performance the world at large will never get to see, Jesco goes around hugging the holy crap out of anybody who can't clear out of his path quickly enough. At one point, Tom Arnold peels bills off a fat wad to give Jesco to pay for having that crudely carved tattoo of a swastika on the back of his left hand covered. —I don't think he even knows what it means, Tom Arnold, who is clearly a dickhead himself, says directly into the documentary camera, while Jesco is standing there with his arm around Tom Arnold, asking somebody off-camera to take a picture of them together, him and his brother Tom, oblivious to what Tom Arnold is saying.

—Hey, Jesco, we're Jewish, Tom Arnold says to Jesco-The-Clueless, who simply continues to request that somebody take their picture together, while hugging Tom Arnold like a long-lost brother.

As requested by Tom Arnold, they take Jesco to *Tattoo Mania* on Sunset Boulevard to have the swastika tattoo on the back of his left hand covered by a cluster of two red roses and one deep blue blossom. While the tattoo artist is doing his work, with a small audience of heavily tattooed Sunset freakoids, Jesco explains that the swastika, which is, by the way, incorrectly drawn, was carved on him by a friend who was high on lighter fluid, as was Jesco himself, if the truth be told, and when Jesco came down from his trip he didn't like the tattoo, but he was stuck with it. The only thing Jesco had known about the swastika at the time was that it was a German sign of some kind, but he didn't know nothing about no German kinds of belief, or their religion. But he had asked a couple of his motorcycle gang pals what it meant, the swastika, and they told him this Hitler dude had killed hundreds and millions of people, even little babies, and baked them in ovens and bulldozed their bones into ditches, which Jesco thought was a bummer, and he got to thinking he was real sorry he had gotten that tattoo of a swastika if that meanness was what it stood for, so he was real glad to get it covered up with those real beautiful roses, which would always make him think of his good friend Roseanne Arnold, who it had been amazing to meet, because he didn't spect such a friendly and nice person as she was, how she had just come out and he had given her the biggest hug you could give a woman and she had hugged him back and

Jesco had known right then there was a real person just like him there and friendly and she had treated him like he was part of the family.

There is a great scene toward the end of *Jesco Goes to Hollywood* where Jesco walks along the foamy edge of the ocean, the waves flopping in from China behind him, strutting and boogeying in the sand while he holds a boombox to his ear and sings along with the lyrics *Let the world call me a fool*. Jesco is wearing that high-Vegas style of Elvis jumpsuit, which is red and tight with a high stiff collar and cape and decorated with golden half-moons and hearts and stars.

The King is back, Jesco announces to the camera, and he's having a ball. —I just want to tell you one thing, Jesco tells the camera, —I'm just a old hillbilly country boy from Boone County, but this cat done made it to Los Angeles, and the ocean by the beach, and he's here and having the time of his life. I said I'd have me a new life and this-here is it and it's really something. I'll cherish this good feeling 'til the day I leave this world, and I'll take this good feeling with me when I die, for the dream has come true for me.

THAT BRIGHT NEW SKIN
WE CALL FAME

What I observed through the screen door of the first trailer on the right up the next hollow was an old man sitting on a dilapidated green couch. He waved at me when I knocked, as though he were signaling for me to come on in and be a son to him. I called to him that I was hunting for Birtie Mae White's abode. Suddenly another one of those ubiquitous bareback good-old-boys stepped from out of the shadows inside the trailer to fill the doorway with his tattooed torso. When I got over being startled, I realized that it was Jesco White himself.

Cousin Jesco had a red bandanna tied around his head and he was wearing a necklace made of wooden beads, with what looked like a bear-claw pendant (Jesco told me later that Emmy Lou Harris had given him this necklace). He had a large elaborate multi-colored tattoo of what appeared to be a very hairy hippie on his smooth chest. It was obvious that Jesco didn't recognize me. Even through the screen door, I could see he had that old caught-in-the-headlights look in his eyes.

—Hey, Jesco, it's me, man, I said and stepped back from the screen door into the sunlight. —Chuck Kinder, the writer, from Pittsburgh. How you doing, man? I was, you know, in the neighborhood.

—Hey, dude, Jesco said and opened the door. I saw then that Jesco had other new tattoos, elaborate, big-bucks, artistic creations done in bright primary colors, blues and reds and yellows, as though little by little he was covering up his old jailhouse lighterfluid-buzz jobs of daggers and crude Confederate flags and crooked letters and misshapen breasts with a brand-new skin of designer skulls and roses with passionate petals and jewel-encrusted crosses and on his chest above his

heart was a fiercely praying Jesus who looked not unlike Robert DeNiro.
—Come on in, dude, Jesco said, seeming to be genuinely pleased to see me then.

—You got some cool new tattoos, dude, man, I told Jesco, finally employing some mountain manners.

—I got this-here one when I was out in Hollywood, Jesco said and lifted his left hand to show me the cluster of roses covering the swastika. He ran his hands over others and said —and there's this-here dude over at Madison what done most of these-here others since I got back from Hollywood real famous all over the world. Did you hear I was real famous all over the world, dude?

—Yeah, dude, I heard. Your new tattoos are great, dude. I only have one, so far, tattoo that is, I said and lifted my right arm to show Jesco the two-inch, solid-black tattoo of a sacred salamander on the back of my forearm. I told him how I got it up in Portsmouth, New Hampshire, a couple of summers back from a biker named Outlaw, and how my brother-in-law (—Do you remember him, Jesco, that big, nearly bald, goofy guy who sort of resembles a goat?) had busted my chops for not having something like a skull wearing a Confederate hat, or a hula girl with big tits, inked onto my arm instead of what looked like an advertisement for bait.

I proceeded to note that there were cultures where tattoos were considered signatures of the soul, as though you were wearing your own inner self on your skin, and your tattooed skin was considered a work of living, breathing, evolving art. There was nothing that Japanese gangsters, who often had full-body tattoos, enjoyed more than gathering with other Japanese gangsters to sit around sucking sake naked save for their tattoos, which often depicted the romantic stories of their lives.

It dawned on me that I was just jabbering to Jesco nervously, but that it didn't matter a whit, for he hadn't really heard a word of what I had been babbling anyway. Jesco had already launched into the story of the swastika and roses as though he were describing in detail the events recorded in Jacob Young's famous documentary, even repeating word for word what he had said on camera about his biker buddies' lesson on German history.

• • •

Jesco and I finally went into the trailer and sat down, me sinking into an old stuffed chair Jesco offered. Jesco, who was wearing cutoff jeans, sat with one of his legs up under him on a straight chair across the tiny cluttered room in front of the door. He introduced the old coot on the couch as his "uncle Harry by blood," and me to his uncle as Perfesser Kinder, his biggest fan from up at Pittsburgh.

—Pittsburgh? said the old coot, who looked about 110 and had his left leg cut off just below the knee. He then commenced to tell me how he had worked up in Pittsburgh maybe eighty or ninety years ago and did I know old so-and-so? The old fellow launched into a monologue about his days working up in Pittsburgh steel mills which droned on the whole time I was sitting there, little of which I could catch (although what I heard interested me), for Jesco continued on about his wild Hollywood excellent adventure as though the old man and his droned stories were a radio left on low in another room.

I sat and listened (trying to nod every now and then at the old man out of politeness, who didn't seem to notice anyway) while Jesco told me all about his trip to Hollywood as though he were watching the videotape on a teevee-screen behind his eyeballs and transcribing it for me, again repeating his on-camera riffs almost word for word, including how he had given his good friend Roseanne Arnold the biggest hug you could give a woman and she had hugged him back and he had known right then there was a real person there just like him and how h'it was really far-out, man, to meet different people out in the world. Dude, if you think they's nuts in Boone County, you ought to see L.A., dude, it's a whole nut-city. L.A. goes on all day and night, dude, and there was all these kinds of nuts or hippies or bums or winos or whatever you want to call those kind of nuts going day and night. But, you know, they're just the same kind of nuts there as anywhere else, I reckon, and I love everybody the same and they loved me too out there because of the way I walk.

Jesco then began to wax philosophical about the price of his worldwide fame. —Getting famous don't mean you're gonna get happy because of it, Jesco told me, solemnly. And you found out you couldn't really trust nobody when you're famous, because everbody wanted something out of you, take his wife Norma Jean for example.

—Yeah, I said, —I was sorry to hear about you-all having some troubles.

—That no-good old woman went and called the law on me for no reason that I know about, Jesco said. He got up and paced around the room, which meant he took about three steps one way and three steps back, amid the old overstuffed furniture and an ancient, console-model television set about the size of a refrigerator with a fishbowl screen. —And the law went and made me leave my own house. You shouldn't ought to make a feller leave his own house, and I'm the one payen the bills. Norma Jean even went out and bought a thousand-dollar tractor to mow the grass and I'm the one stuck paying that bill too, and we don't hardly have no grass no-how. And everybody thinks I done got rich but I didn't yet. All that money, for the T-shirts and cups and stuff, all that money has to go for taxes, my manager says, so I don't see hardly none of it, but I can't tell that to people. They don't want to believe it, but it's the truth. This feller is gonna make some Jesco White figurines and I'll get two or three dollars for ever one they sell. They're gonna make them over in China real cheap and sell them all over the place, worldwide, cause that feller said I done got that famous. That feller came around down here to see me and we went over to Charleston and had supper with my manager and we wrote up some papers and I signed them. But that's not gonna happen 'til round Christmas. There's a white stretch limousine what's coming up this holler tomorrow morning, and it's s'pose take me over to Charleston and I'm gonna judge a cowgirl dancing contest at a motel and they're gonna put me up in a fancy room upstairs and I don't know what I'm gettin paid but something. And then I'm s'pose to go to Nashville in August to be in a show and I'll get paid for that. But I've been thinkin I might not go do that, because I don't have no home to come back to and h'it's hard to tell you how much that hurts me inside. That little cabin is my favoritest home I ever had, and they done took me out of it on account of what my wife Norma Jean told them I done. She went and told them I told her to take the dog on a walk out in the rain and when she didn't want to do it I took shots at her and the dog. I told the deputy sheriff that was crazy to start with. I told him I wouldn't never do nothing like that. I raised that old dog from a pup.

The last time I saw Jesco, we were back outside Birtie Mae's trailer talking about the book I was going to write about him. I had decided on the spot that no chapter could ever capture cousin Jesco adequately. Only a full-fledged book could do his story justice. Jesco was the most famous person currently alive and living in West Virginia. And he wasn't some idiot blowhard politician or preacher or professional person of any stripe. He was a regular old redneck. He was the deepest essence of a real West Virginian. He was an old-timey mountain tap dancer and dead ringer for Elvis The King.

I had a copy of the letter I had written him a few weeks earlier, and since his own copy, which he had received after all, was over at the house on Drawdy Mountain, where he couldn't go on account of a court order, I left him my copy to give to his manager who would be arriving the next day with the stretch limousine. I wrote a note on it to tell her I would call her over the weekend and perhaps set up a meeting early the next week, for I wanted Jesco to feel secure about our book project. I also left her a copy of my first novel, *Snakehunter*, which had been recently reprinted, which, frankly, I used like a business card, not to mention trying to make an impression. I mean, she would read the dust-jacket praise various of my buddies had provided and know what a serious artistic type of fellow I was, who must clearly mean well.

Jesco loved my Red Ride. I told him we would do some serious four-wheeling around in it while we worked on the story of his life, and we laughed and high-fived on that. I told Jesco we'd cruise over to Madison and get tattoos together and we high-fived on that. I told Jesco, the plan was I'd call his manager over the weekend and come back over from Fayetteville the following Monday and we'd cruise into Charleston to get things settled to everybody's satisfaction. We'd have us a fancy supper somewhere, and have us some real fun. We laughed and high-fived on that too.

I told Jesco before we were through, the whole world would know who he really was. The whole world would know his story of flight and disguise and deeply hidden real identity. The whole world would know what really happened to the lost twin brother of Elvis, I told Jesco, for I had gotten the bright idea that Elvis's twin brother had not died at birth after all. Instead he had been kidnapped out of the hospital. Kidnapped by a nurse. A nurse named Norma Jean, say, and raised up in the dark hills of West Virginia unknown. That's the way I see your true story unfolding, anyway, I told Jesco. That's the basic plotline, anyway. I told Jesco that Elvis had been what they call a "twin-less twin." That Elvis had lived hard and fast and famous for two people, himself and his supposedly dead twin brother Jessie Garon, whose ghost voice Elvis heard echoing in his sad heart all the days of his life. I told Jesco that that had been his very own twin-brother voice channeling into the songs of Elvis, the songs that had made The King famous and great. And when I was finished writing the true story of Jesco's secret life, the whole world would know it. And we would work together night and day until we got his true story straight, is what I told cousin Jesco.

Jesco simply looked at me and said —Dude, you gotta get off them drugs.

None of the above came about. I called Jesco's manager over that weekend and after she had asked me what sort of money was involved in this so-called book business, and I had informed her none at this point, she told me Jesco wasn't interested in the book project at·all. She informed me that Jesco had told her I was this writer nut who thought he was a kidnapped baby or something. She said Jesco told her I was crazy as a bat. She told me Jesco said I had freaked him plumb out. Jesco wanted her to get him off the hook for anything I might try to hold him to. There's no hook to get Jesco off of, I told that woman. Then that woman wanted to know who I thought I was anyway, talking to Jesco about anything before I had talked with her first. And what right did I have to go scare that poor man who never did me any harm. Bye, I said to that woman, and hung up the phone.

So old cousin Jesco supposedly was not interested in having me lift the story of his life into that timeless realm we call art, I reflected. I reflected then upon the possibility that art was what you finally had to escape from in order to really live. Maybe me not having my way with the story of Jesco's life was the best thing that ever happened to him. As I have said, outsiders have come into West Virginia for generations and bought up the timber and mineral rights from good, honest, unsuspecting people who did not know what they really owned. Then the ruling-class cocksuckers exploited the natural resources, extracted what is valuable, something like coal you can burn slowly, and taken the real wealth out of the state. When it comes to something like story rights, what is ever finally fair? What, finally, is not up for grabs? Maybe it was for the best that I didn't mine Jesco's story and take it out of state like coal to burn.

The last thing I can remember Jesco and me talking about, as I had climbed into my Red Ride, was the news that Michael Jackson had just married Lisa Marie Presley. In fact, Jesco broke the news to me. I was flabbergasted. Jesco was pissed. Jesco was disappointed in Lisa Marie. How could she go and do such a sorry thing like that? Jesco wanted to know. What would The King think? How was that-there girl raised up, anyhow? —Well, The King would hear about it, Jesco said, —wherever he was, and you can bet your life The King will do something about it one way or the other. But maybe there was a bright side, maybe h'it would cause The King to come home. And here all the time I thought Lisa Marie was a-waitin' on me, Jesco said and laughed bitterly.

—But what about Priscilla? I said, and Jesco just looked at me. —I always figured you and Priscilla would end up together. Tell me the truth, I said, —Jesco, who are you really?

Jesco simply said —I told you, The King is back and he's having a ball.

I laughed and stuck my hand out the window for a final high-five, but Jesco looked away. As I pulled out slowly, I watched Jesco in the rear-view mirror all the time I bumped down the dirt road out of the hollow. I felt strangely as though I was leaving a part of myself behind there with him. Jesco looked just like that picture of essential sadness and isolation

I had watched fade from my sight in a rear-view mirror the first time I had seen him, as he stood there in the afternoon shadows.

Cousin Jesco would get back with Norma Jean in the coming months. Then they broke up again. And they did all that again and again. I heard that Norma Jean finally ended up in a tiny apartment in Charleston, living on disability checks. I heard that Jesco moved back into his beloved little mountain cabin and lived there with a certain amount of contentment until it burned to the ground along with his whole Elvis collection. I heard that Jesco ended up living all alone in a tiny camper back up on some deserted road. There would be a little piece in the paper about Jesco every now and then, like when he was tap-dancing for dimes at some grocery-store opening.

But that day I studied him in the rear-view mirror as I bounced down that dirt road out of the hollow, Jesco had looked so, so beautiful with Robert DeNiro praying fiercely over his heart, wearing that bright new skin we call fame.

book six

FAMOUS FAMILY LIFE

GHOST ROCK

Four hundred million years ago, the whole state of West Virginia lay in a long ditch beneath the tides of an ancient ocean. To the east rose a vanished continent named Old Appalachia. The ancient ocean left vast deposits of brine and rock salt and limestone from the fossils of marine life. Runoff from the highlands of the old continent caused rock strata beneath the ditch to repeatedly rise and fall, rise and fall. Millions of years later, the whole state of West Virginia was a lush swampland. Seventy million years ago, it was part of a vast windswept peneplain. Over time, the horizontal layers of deposited limestone and sandstone and shale and seams of coal were lifted and folded up, finally, into mountains.

Coal is a fossil fuel. It was formed when, millions of years ago, the great carboniferous forests settled slowly into their own marshes and marbled themselves there into the dark inner layers of those lifted mountains. Many sorts of fossils can be found in the shale partings of coal seams. Even the casts of whole tree trunks and root systems have been found in coal beds. Long ago, folks had the weird notion that fossils were made by magic forces deep within the earth's heart that had failed somehow to breathe their creations into life. The ancient Greeks had the bright idea that petrified bones were the remains of dwarves and giants who had once roamed the earth. Later yet, in medieval Europe, fossils were thought to be the relics of saints or, on the contrary, the skeletons of drowned, unsaved, pre-Noahian sinners.

Many years before I was born, a great-uncle of mine, an Uncle Jarvis, was unlucky enough to die young among sixteen or seventeen other coal miners in a big mine explosion over at Paint Creek. Because of the poisonous methane gas released by the explosion and because the explosion had ignited a fire in a deep coal seam, the rescue teams could not retrieve the bodies. Finally, the mine portals were sealed, and have remained so until this day. As was often the case in such circumstances, smoke from the fire began pouring up out of the mine's ventilation holes.

My paternal grandmother, Daisy Dangerfield Kinder, who told me this story and most all of the stories I can recall as equally informing and transfiguring my basically weird childhood, told me that Uncle Jarvis's wife, *Ant* Becky, took to rising at daybreak on each Sunday morning and dressing up in her best church clothes, whereupon she would walk over the ridge from her home to one of those smoke holes. Mimi, as we called my grandmother, told me that Ant Becky would sit there for the rest of the day talking down that thin pale column of smoke as though it was some sort of peculiar telephone line to poor old Uncle Jarvis, her beloved albeit squashed-as-a-bug husband. For many years, Ant Becky, that loyal, waiting, weird widow, did this, as though her dead husband's ghost was lifting up into eternity slowly from that hole like a thin, sad, curling stream of soul. Finally Ant Becky, who claimed she had begun to hear a busy signal, had to be put away for her own good, not necessarily a rare fate to befall kinfolks of mine.

What I recall wondering about in my weird kid way, when Mimi told me this story, was whether eventually over time Uncle Jarvis's bones would be petrified (I was the sort of kid who knew what "petrified" meant; I gobbled words like candy), and if they ever did, what if somebody some day would dig across his petrified bones? And wouldn't it be cool if his uncovered petrified bones would somehow rise up among the living again, like one of those neat zombies in the E.C. Comics, and move horribly among us? Or maybe somebody some day would open a seam of shale and find Uncle Jarvis imprinted there like an ancient fern. Maybe he would even be used as fuel, his fingers burned like black tapers.

Burning coal has a sweet decaying smell. Maybe, I recall thinking weirdly, after a while that was the way dead people smell, like burning coal. And on those days when I was a weird kid living in the lower end of Montgomery, while my hero daddy was off winning the Second World War like John Wayne, when the coal smoke was particularly heavy from the Alloy Plant's coke ovens up the river, and the air thick with the settling ghost dust of ancient plant life and dinosaurs (I knew all about dinosaurs), I recollect wondering weirdly if that was what the Second World War smelled like.

A tipple is a coal-screening plant, a place where loaded coal cars are emptied, literally, by tipping them, for the coal to be separated and processed. I worked once as an ironworker for a construction company that rebuilt tipples during the miners' holidays. Miners were required to take the same two-week group holiday each year, and during that time the coal company would shut down the tipples for repairs or recon-struction. The tipples I worked on over in the Kanawha Valley were these ramshackle, corrugated, sheet-metal buildings perched up on forked and jointed poles high on the hillsides, which made them look to my bud-ding poet's eye not unlike huge, hungry, black vampire-spiders hunched there sucking the juice of life from the veins of that sleeping prey we call the planet, which, I suppose, in a weird way they were.

I can recall climbing to the top story of the tipple at Harewood during my lunch breaks and hanging out of a door to look up and down the ancient Kanawha River Valley and reflect upon my legendary life up to that point. I can recall tipping my hard hat back off my sweaty, streaked handsome face and firing up a butt, either a cool manly unfil-tered Camel or Lucky Strike, and balancing myself precariously on the balls of my steel-toe-booted feet at the edge of that high open door and wondering what the rest of my life held in store for me, as the air rising from the old river far below felt as fresh as mist on my handsome face. I recall waiting patiently for Susie Robinson, the girl I loved with all of my heart, to drive her daddy's big Buick by on the road below and honk its horn and wave crazily up to her cool, destined-for-fame boyfriend posed like a picture on a dust jacket.

Over countless ages, the soft belts of the mountains of West Virginia were eroded away, so that by the time of the latest Ice Age, maybe a mere million years ago, a dramatic landscape of high-mountain hard-rock separated by a maze of gorges and narrow parallel valleys had been carved out, not unlike the little valley I find myself winding slowly along back down in Boone County one autumn afternoon. There is a faint drizzle in the air and mist rises up from the steep sides of the mountains into dark clouds that seem settled on the hilltops. When I roll down my window, I can smell the rainy road and the wet trees I pass slowly, and that special fresh odor of flowing water from a shallow rocky creek yonder, and then I catch the faint, somehow always melancholy whiff of distant wood smoke. So this is it, I suddenly reflect. This is what the future held in store for my legendary life. Driving around aimlessly in the hills and hollows on a drizzly fall day, dopey, primarily upon the perfume of time's passage.

As I round a sharp bend, I come upon a tipple, suddenly, like an apparition, there in maybe the only flat piece of bottomland in the hollow, with its narrow, windowless, corrugated sheet-metal buildings and chutes and pipes that rise up on arches of iron to disappear into the thick trees of the mountainside. The tipple I come upon in that lonely Boone County hollow is a Peabody Coal Company tipple, and it is nothing like the grimy, black, busy-as-a-beehive tipples of my memory. For one thing, the various buildings are so *pristine*, and painted in a sort of rose-colored pastel. Although it is only in the early afternoon, all the lights that line the buildings and the chutes and the surrounding chain-link fences and the spotlights in the parking area, where there are only a handful of pickup trucks, are blazing brightly, dim and pale in the light of day, but burning nonetheless with a light so yellow it is unearthly. And that is the weird general impression: There is just an absolutely other-worldly and oddly temporary look to the place, as though some giant spaceship has just settled down in this godforsaken hollow for a brief respite. Another thing that contributes to the spooky, lonely, abandoned feeling is that nobody is around. I don't see a soul. It could be a ghost-tipple for the lack of apparent human life, full of ghost miners pushing the buttons and pulling the levers of ghost machines somewhere deep inside those ghost buildings where coal, that ghost rock, is being prepared for the transfiguration of its ancient ghost plant and dinosaur life into television.

Then I understand. The giant spaceship is parked here in this lonesome hollow in order to refuel with ghost rock. That tipple is a coal-burning spaceship. Clearly an older model. And it is filling its tanks with the fuel of sickly sweet-smelling dead people like my poor old Uncle Jarvis and dwarves and giants and saints and sinners and dinosaurs and ancient plant-life pressed into diamonds of ghost rock before continuing its voyage to planets far beyond West Virginia.

Road-Kill Café

The old Dangerfield family homestead is back in the hills outside of Charleston, the state capital, on the Kanawha River. On Memorial Days when I was a kid, the family would usually caravan out to the old homestead to clean and decorate the graves in the cemetery on the hill above the log-and-fieldstone house where Mimi had been born and raised. That old house burned to the ground when I was about twelve. It was suspected that certain undiscussed, disreputable cousins had been cooking up a little moonshine in a *still* in the old coal cellar when things blew to high heaven.

Through the years, Mimi had bought and erected a rock garden of tombstones over the graves of her dead loved ones, including a large blue granite monument for her parents, Tom and Catherine. More than once, I tagged along behind Mimi over the hill to where her own sweet dead boy was buried in a far corner of the cemetery, and we weeded and cleaned off his grave together. Dennis, that is what Mimi named him, died one day after birth. Mimi had erected a small stone with a little lamb lying along its top on her son's grave. Dennis would have been Dad's kid brother. Every year, Mimi would lead me about the graveyard to ingrain within me the stories of those buried among the many mounds she might not live to raise stones above, which were marked only by small rusting metal signs. Mimi showed me where Aunt Fanny's little girl was buried. The little girl had caught her nightgown on fire from candles on a Christmas tree and burned to a crisp. The little girl had not cried out as she ran through the house flaming like a sparkler, and Aunt Fanny, who was back in the kitchen washing supper dishes, had finally seen the reflection on a polished hardwood door of the fire engulfing her little girl like a wick.

After some silly fight, Mimi had told her favorite sister Kitty that she hoped Kitty would up and die like a wormy-gut dog, and when Kitty did, from a ruptured appendix not a month later, at age twelve, Mimi never forgave herself. She understood then the power of words, of utterance, and she encouraged me to appreciate this power. A stone with the willowy angel of a lovely girl carved on its front stood over Kitty's grave.

Mimi showed me the graves where Aunt Julia and her only child were buried, the son who at sixteen had bushwhacked his daddy at the breakfast table, then had put the blood-splattered pistol into his mouth to scramble his own brains. Aunt Julia had spent the last sixty years of her life living with first one relative and then another, staying with each of them in turn until somebody was ready to shoot somebody else, whereupon Aunt Julia, her work done, reboarded the Greyhound and moved down the line.

Mimi is buried in another hillside cemetery over at Deep Water on the Kanawha River, a few miles downstream from Montgomery. Mimi had gone downhill ever since some teenage oaf had bumped into her at the cashier's counter of a Long John Silvers, where my Uncle Noyes had taken her for her eighty-fifth birthday dinner, and she had tumbled, broken her hip, and then gone into heart failure. Mimi had recovered, more or less, but was thereafter frail, and a few months later she had discovered a lump in her left lower abdomen. It was the "goddamn Big-C," as Mimi characterized the lump. As the lump grew, Mimi took to characterizing it as "that little shitass," and attacked it with old mountain remedies, such as miraculous moonshine enemas.

My wife Lindsay met Mimi in Montgomery the first morning we had arrived in West Virginia as a dubious couple back in 1972. I had not yet divorced my first wife, and Lindsay, who was traveling across country with me, was clearly a fallen woman. Lindsay was terrified of meeting Mimi, the family matriarch. I will withhold most of a story here, but suffice it to say that we arrived at Mimi's door that morning under a cloud. Both of my eyes were black and my hands were bandaged from a silly fracas I had somehow been drawn into in Bloomington, Indiana, the wrong town in the wrong state and wrong real bad situation I had blundered into more or less unconsciously. Mimi was mad. Mimi declared she intended to whup me with a belt for fighting again.

Then Lindsay broke into an account about how we had spent the previous night at an old funky riverside hotel in Charleston near the state capitol building, the first place we had passed in maybe a hundred miles on that foggy night with a *vacancy* sign blinking out front. After leaning on its buzzer for maybe twenty minutes, an old black gentleman had finally answered the door. He seemed astonished to receive actual travelers in the night instead of state senators with keys visiting their favorite whores.

In a shabby room that smelled like river, which had only cold running water and a bed that creaked as though in agony, Lindsay had refused to get into her nightgown until I arranged towels over a smoky mirror within which she swore she had glimpsed a face full of confusion and pain that she had not recognized. Lindsay told Mimi that the face in the mirror she had seen was not her own. They shuddered in unison at the idea of the face of a ghost whore, whereupon they cracked up.

Mimi herded us back to the kitchen hugging our arms, and she forced us to sit down for breakfast. At one point, while Mimi was scrambling eggs and squirrel brains with one spoon and stirring possum gravy with another, she gazed over at Lindsay with unbridled, intuitive affection, and announced that where the family had gone wrong with me from the day I was born was when they had made the big mistake of throwing away the baby and raising the afterbirth.

I flew in from San Francisco for Mimi's funeral. Throngs of folks were at the services, and family members and friends and complete strangers to me were falling apart on account of the death of that old woman, whom folks declared I was a male dead ringer for. I loved that old woman, but you didn't catch me wailing and crying around like those simple country cousins. I was busy making mental notes on all the bizarre amusing things about the proceedings that would have cracked Mimi up if she hadn't been the guest of honor.

During the services, some Methodist choir-granny the size of a beer barrel bellowed Mimi's favorite song, "Amazing Grace," a ton off-key. In a purely old-timey country-church and revival mode, poor old Papaw kept croaking out: —I'll be up there in heaven with you soon, Daisy, darlin', Praise Jaysus, amen. Mimi would have split a stitch, or maybe not.

The day had been appropriately drizzly and dreary and cold. Beads of rain sparkled on the bright chrome of old B. C. Hooper's polished hearse parked in front of the Montgomery Methodist Church where I had been married for the first time, and my sister for the only time. The shining black metal of the hearse hazed almost blue in the leaden morning light. When the cold wind shuddered into the trees along the street, leaves, sodden and dark, fell, pasting themselves onto the hearse's top and hood. —Don't you ever try to tell me trees don't shit, Mimi used to say as she furiously swept the leaves off her front porch, barking: —Tree turd, tree turd, tree turd. Long pools of dark water formed in the trenches that the vehicles' tires hollowed out in the wet gravel of the cemetery's winding road.

I returned to the Mayo Clinic for the third time in my life (out of four visits) when I was twelve and in the seventh grade. There was to be no surgery on that particular trip, only something of a general checkup of my condition, to determine, I guess, if that strange little surgically built bridge of skin that stretched between the top of my scrotum and the upper flesh of my left thigh, the little bridge that was supposed to tie my floating left testicle in its proper port, was doing its job, whatever that was supposed to mean to a twelve-year-old. I mean, the necessity of all that cutting and rearrangement was a mystery to me as a boy, and remains so.

Since Dad had been in the midst of another of his business breakdowns at that time, and Mom was forced to work midnight shifts again as a nurse in an emergency room during the course of that particular family downfall, Mimi declared that she would drive me herself across that seemingly endless midwestern distance to Rochester, Minnesota, in order that her beloved if somewhat gimped grandson, with the amazing aid of modern medical science, could continue to be rendered as testosterone-poisoned as any normal boy. I was the oldest grandchild and the apple of Mimi's eye, but we really bonded for the first time as potentially grown-up friends on that flat boring three-day trip west (and then our return east), when we had discovered with an intensity of understanding and a new immediacy of sympathy that one of our mutual fascinations and sort of hobbies was *road-kills*.

Mimi was an expert on road-kills, and she had seen them all, including a black bear hit by a coal truck and a Southern Baptist preacher run over by his own long-suffering wife. And Mimi was nearly psychic in the department of predicting the number of dead dogs we would pass per mile, depending upon the condition of the road, speed limit, traffic, and weather. Mimi knew enough road-kill recipes to fill a menu, canine cuisine such as Slab of Lab, Round of Hound, German Shepherd Pie, Pit Bull Pot Pie, Cocker Cutlets, Poodles 'n Noodles. (—You'll eat like a hog, Mimi would cackle, —when you taste my dog.) And then there was that old favorite pancake substitute, Flat Cat (—Served as a single, or in a stack), and Chunk of Skunk, Smidgen of Pigeon, Swirl of Squirrel, Snake Shake 'n Bake, Smear of Deer, and what she claimed had once been her real Sunday supper specialty, Center-Line Bovine, with all the trimmings, such as Critter Fritters and Road Toad A La Mode.

As we rolled endlessly across that great doze called Ohio, that wonderful, nutty old woman and I decided that some day her road-kill casseroles would make us rich. Some day, we decided, as we laughed and didn't think of doctors and hospitals and nasty nurses with enormous needles, we would open the Home Cooking Road-Kill Café and make a mint with gourmet hits like our daily takeout lunch sandwich special: *Bag 'n Gag,* meaning anything around handy, dead between bread.

Old-timers down in the hills of West Virginia will tell you that often animals once thought extinct sometimes wander out of the hills at night and attempt to drink at the pavement of roads as though it is the fresh water of a mountain creek that moves so slowly you can't see it passing, and being creatures from a forgotten time and place and sacrificial in their innocence, they look up unafraid and hopeful into headlights hurtling toward them out of the dark.

As I cruised along that twisty road that day down in Boone County in my private fragile dream of escape and renewal, I slowed often to consider the roadside smears of animals half-this, half-that, a creature that once could have been a huge cat with the face of a hog, a fawn with the striped fur of a zebra, a single remaining wing of enormous black feathers whose tips looked like tiny closed red fists that fluttered gently up out of bloody pulp in the soft wind of my passing, like a vague wave of hello and adios.

Guess That Mess, would have been another of the daily specials at the Road-Kill Café, meaning if the customer could guess the nature of that menu-item creature so ancient and rare that it was almost imaginary, that customer ate for free.

CARROT BOY

I was over at Mom's again one night when we were watching one of the hundred or so videos my kid brother had sent her over time from his home in Houston, Texas. This particular home video was mostly footage of my brother's three-year-old baby daughter, Amy Elizabeth, being relentlessly cute as she splashed around all pink and bubbly in her bath. She was playing and prattling on and on about important events in her perfect little-girl's life and her two pet kitty-cats, Patsy and Cline, and presents she wanted for Christmas. And then there she was laughing and singing and twirling about the tree like a Christmas sprite as she unwrapped her landslide of gifts, and there was my brother's lovely dark-haired wife, Rosaura, flitting in and out of the frame as she picked up discarded ribbons and wrappings. Behind it all was my brother's gently bemused voice, as he made wry comments about his darling daughter and wonderful wife and that mystery called a good life.

Because of this reason or that, neither of my two male Kinder cousins or I would ever have children. If my brother didn't have a son at some point, our branch of the Kinder name would die out with our lame generation. Mom had the home video virtually memorized, and would forewarn me excitedly of particularly cute Amy Beth antics to be on the alert for. Mom sat there misty-eyed but giggling like a girl and clapping her hands whenever her granddaughter would do something so precious it made us both gasp.

I'm about ten years older than my kid brother, so I was gone by the time he was a teenager. I do have a few crystal-clear, defining memories of him as a little kid, however. One of my chores was to watch after him during the day while Mom slept. I had to let him tag along with me everywhere. Like my great-grandfather Big Red, and Uncle Noyes, and later the Boy Red, my kid brother had inherited that random redheaded gene, and he had bright red hair and a freckled face, and I had felt as though it was my duty to remind him frequently that he looked like a little dumb Carrot Boy. Being a dutiful brother, I teased and tormented Carrot Boy relentlessly, but unless I actually pounded him to a pulp he seldom cried or whined or ratted me out. He was open and trusting, and the dumb kid loved me, his Big Brother.

Our house at that time was on an old road that circled back into the hills, and I recall one particular day when Carrot Boy tagged along with me as usual as I headed out that old road, vaguely on the lookout for any amusing minor trouble I could get away with. As we walked along the old road, I told Carrot Boy, for no better reason than meanness, that this was the road that took you out west like where the cowboys and outlaws and wild Redskins lived on teevee. I told him we were, in fact, getting pretty close to wild Redskin territory. I told Carrot Boy about how wild Redskins attacked white settlers and soldiers and cowboys, then scalped them, burned off their fingers, poked out their eyes, and pulled off their peepees, which they then fed like wienies to the dogs.

Every time Carrot Boy looked away from me, I gave a wild Indian yell or flicked a rock back into the brush and affected a bug-eyed look of sheer terror. I could tell by his bright red face and quivering mouth that Carrot Boy was about to shit his pants. At one of the points when Carrot Boy looked away, I jumped over an embankment into the thick brush under some trees. I screamed insanely as the wild Redskins scalped me. I thrashed about crazily as the bloodthirsty Redskins poked out my eyes. I gave a final blood-curdling cry when the wild Redskins pulled off my peepee. Then I was quiet as a dead cowboy.

Through the leaves of the low branches, I watched my horrified kid brother and snickered with glee. Carrot Boy stood beside the road calling for me and crying his little heart out. Carrot Boy had a bright beard of tears and snot, and finally he simply stood there blubbering and wailing like an animal simple with pain. After a time, and in my memory it could have been minutes or hours, depending upon my mood when I mull it over, Carrot Boy bent over and picked up a couple rocks from the roadside. Whereupon, still bawling his eyes out, and calling my name over and over, Chuckie Chuckie Chuckie, Carrot Boy came tottering down over the steep embankment.

TOTAL WRECK

The Boy Red wrecked the car late one Friday night out on the four-lane when he hit a slick spot and spun into the guardrail. He was banged up a bit, but nothing serious. The car, my sister's 1988 Le Baron coupe, was a total wreck and had to be towed. My brother-in-law was basically pissed because the Boy Red wasn't supposed to be driving that car in the first place, for he wasn't properly insured. Because of his horrific driving record, the speeding tickets and the DWI and that prolonged loss of his license, the Boy Red was difficult to insure at all, and to keep him on the family policy would shoot those premiums out of sight. But somehow my brother-in-law had scammed the Boy Red some insurance for his own old heap, which was the only vehicle he was permitted to drive dangerously.

I was spending the weekend at my sister's, as Lovelene and her daughter Cybil had come up from Charlotte yet once again, claiming her good intentions to finally clean the house out and do something about poor old Ike before some serious snow fell. From my bedroom out in the front of the house, I had overheard the heated words about why my sister had let the Boy Red use her car to begin with, her lame excuse being that the boy hadn't been able to get his own old heap started and he had a big date lined up with a nice girl more or less his own age for a change.

I waited until the din from this argument had died down before meandering out to the kitchen for some coffee. The Boy Red was sulking at the table with a couple of bumps and bruises on his head and looking uncharacteristically deflated. My brother-in-law was pacing the room trying to figure out what nature of lie to tell his insurance agent, who was a childhood friend. Also, they had to figure out some mode of transportation for my sister, now that her Le Baron was history. My sister kept repeating that at least the boy hadn't been seriously hurt, and that, thank God, he had been alone so nobody else had been hurt, and that they had to keep things in perspective.

About then, the phone rang and my sister got it. I saw her face go a whiter shade of pale. My brother-in-law and the Boy Red saw it too. Nobody said a word. I figured more complexity was about to hit the fan, and I was correct. On the phone was the mother of a boy who had been in the wreck with my nephew. She told my sister that, thank God, her son wasn't seriously hurt either, but she wasn't sure about the girls who had been with the boys. What goddamn girls? my brother-in-law was real curious to know, after my sister had tearfully repeated the conversation. At that point the Boy Red decided that perhaps it would be prudent to be more forthcoming with a few little details about the accident that apparently had slipped his mind.

Yep, the Boy Red finally admitted, there had been a couple of old girls in the car with them. He hadn't mentioned it earlier because they were old, trashy, scaggy girls he and his buddy had picked up out at the Pines, and not the nice girl he had told his Mom he had a date with. In fact, one of the scaggy girls, who was drunk as a skunk, had gotten mad at him when he asked her where she wanted to be dropped off. She had started hollering around that he was trying to dump her ass, which was true, of course, but beside the point. Then suddenly the bitch had reached over and grabbed the steering wheel, which was what made the Boy Red lose control of the car in the first place. The Boy Red had not had a single drop to drink, of course, because he was driving his mom's car. He hadn't even wanted to pick up the scaggy girls, but his buddy had egged him into it. It was dumb, the Boy Red acknowledged and hung his head, and he felt rotten about it, and he had learned a valuable lesson.

—It was like that time you told me about, Dad, the Boy Red said to my brother-in-law, —when that old drunk girl you once picked up stuck her foot over and, before you knew what she was doing, hit your gas pedal and you flew through that intersection up in Marlington and plowed through that car dealership's plate-glass window. You remember that story you told me, don't you, Dad? About that drunk girl and wreck?

At that juncture, I found myself surprisingly impressed with the Boy Red. In fact, I had always been somewhat impressed in a perverse way with the emotional mileage those kids could wring out of their parents, for the guilt trips they could lay on their parents. In fact, it occurred to me that perhaps my own bad behavior could in some convoluted way be blamed upon the fact that my dad had won the Second World War. The fact that I could never fill Captain Charlie's big bold heroic boots might also explain my proclivity for lying and my habitual unfaithfulness, and my patterns of self-destructive behavior. I had been a victim of my old man's blustery boldness, which in turn had blossomed into its fulsomeness because of the Second World War. I wasn't to blame for all the bad things I had done in my life. I wasn't to blame for my own youthful misbehavior full of criminal intent, which made the Boy Red's outlaw efforts pale by comparison.

The Second World War was basically to blame for everything, and why to this day I hate heroes and all they stand for with all my heart.

THE RIGHT TO STAND WITH MEN

Bring anything that cuts or shoots, my brother-in-law requested of me over the phone, and come on back down here quick, he added. It was that same Sunday afternoon. Lovelene and Cybil had headed on back to Charlotte. The place was still a mess. Poor old abandoned Ike was still chained up out back, not knowing what he had done wrong. Lovelene had ended up making the beerjoint rounds the night before with old Pete in tow, so the big cleanup hadn't exactly happened. But Lovelene had loaded up several armfuls of her more precious treasures that had been piled in the dining room, and I was pleased with that anyway.

I told my brother-in-law when he called that I had my heart set upon nursing my hangover the rest of the day, and did not look forward to any cutting or shooting. I simply wasn't in the mood to go out cutting or shooting, I explained to him. We're not going out anywhere, my brother-in-law told me impatiently, we're going to cut and shoot on the premises.

The story was that my brother-in-law himself had answered the latest phone call concerning more real bad news, not twenty minutes earlier. Now he and the Boy Red were armed to the teeth and waiting at the windows. Crazy Billy Canada had been on the horn. This Crazy Billy Canada character was a local burly bully, famous mostly because he was certifiably insane and proud of it. He was the infamous nutcase who a few years back had commandeered Jumpers' Rock in the New River, where many raft-trips stopped for lunch. Crazy Billy had decided that out-of-state Yankee weekend raft-trippers had no business or right to make the traditional, almost sacramental leap off Jumpers' Rock into the holy ancient West Virginia waters of New River. So one Saturday he had climbed down into the gorge and then clambered up on Jumpers' Rock with a bottle of bourbon and a pistola. He would not let any of that day's raft trips land on the rocky shore. At another time, my brother-in-law had personally seen Crazy Billy put a gun to his own head and play a private game of Russian roulette one night out at the Pines after a long losing streak at pool and being rejected by Harelip Harriet. Crazy Billy had been committed to the nuthouse up at Spencer on six different occasions.

This Crazy Billy was the doting daddy of the two scaggy girls who had been in the wreck with the Boy Red. Crazy Billy had called my brother-in-law to complain that the Boy Red had beat the shit out of his darling daughters and knocked their teeth loose. Crazy Billy told my brother-in-law that he knew his darling daughters were whores and he didn't care if they carried coal in their pussies, but he wouldn't abide any boy whuppin' on them, as that was his job and his job alone. So he was going to come on over and shoot the Boy Red down like a dog, and he had it coming. That was the code.

That *was* the code, my brother-in-law had agreed with Crazy Billy Canada wholeheartedly, except for the fact the Boy Red hadn't whupped on those girls. Those girls had been hurt in the car wreck, plain and simple, and they were coming up with that whupping story because one of them had caused the accident, and clearly she was afraid she'd get in trouble for it, but she wouldn't, for my brother-in-law wasn't out for anything, and, in fact, all they had to do to get their teeth fixed (teeth which were nothing but rotten stumps to begin with, according to the Boy Red) was to go to my brother-in-law's own dentist, who would take care of those bad teeth at no expense to Crazy Billy. My brother-in-law would pay for it all, he had told Crazy Billy. Well, Crazy Billy had retorted, both them gals say your boy done whupped on them. So I don't see no other way out except to shoot your boy down like a dog, and I was just a-calling you up to tell you to look for me a-coming, out of old-time respect for you. At that point, my brother-in-law had extended the invitation for Crazy Billy, that nutcase redneck sonofabitch, to just come on over, and we'll just see who in the fuck goes down around here.

What *code*? I was curious to know. I hadn't signed any code that said I had to arm myself to the teeth on a lazy, hung-over Sunday afternoon and wait around with an upset stomach and all tense for some insane hillbilly to come over and shoot it out. Well, my brother-in-law said somewhat haughtily, we are going to participate as a family in a gunfight at about any time, and if you don't want to be a part of it, then that's up to you. Jesus Christ, I grumbled when I got off the phone. God, I had a hangover, and I had looked forward to an afternoon alone lazily reading the various Sunday papers while I slow-sipped screwdrivers and abused myself at leisure. Grumpily, I loaded my snub-nose .38 Special and my shotgun. Daggone it anyway, but the last thing in the world I was in the mood for was a shootout.

The phone rang, and it was Holly. I tried to explain to her that I didn't have time to talk endlessly about the fact that I was twenty-two years older than her and diabetic and alcoholic and all the other multitude of good reasons we shouldn't be old coot and wife, because I was on my way out the front door to go back over to my brother-in-law's in order to engage some crazy person in cutting and/or shooting. What's the whore's name, Holly expressed a keen interest in knowing, before she hung up on me.

The Boy Red had a chair pulled up to a window in the picking room, where he sat with a pistola in his hand to cover the side door. Don't shoot until you see the red of their eyes, was the best advice I could offer the Boy Red as I passed by. My highly agitated brother-in-law was pacing about in the kitchen, a pistola in each hand. My sister, who was still in her church clothes, sat quietly weeping at the table, upon which there were at least a dozen guns loaded for bear, not to mention an array of sharpened knives. —Long time no see, I said to my distraught sister and I looked in the refrigerator for a cold beer and sandwich fixings. My sister wept and continued to admonish my brother-in-law to call the State Police before it was too late.

But, but, but . . . he couldn't do that, my brother-in-law attempted to explain, for this business was personal, and it wasn't the mountain code to call in the law for personal business. I threw together a baloney-and-mustard sandwich and popped a beer and sat down at the table. I asked if my niece was armed also and hovering at a window somewhere in the house. My sister sobbed out that they had sent her over to Mom's place to stay safely put, with the admonition to keep her big trap shut.

When a car pulled into the driveway, my brother-in-law cocked his pistolas and ducked down at the window over the kitchen sink. I crawled under the kitchen table. It was only my niece and Mom. —Dear God, what are they doing over here? my sister gasped. —Mom will drop dead of a heart attack. My sister started trying desperately to hide the guns, stuffing them in kitchen drawers, cabinets, lugging an armload out of the room, but too late. Mom was more nimble than usual, and scrambled in her wobbly, goose-like way up the stone walk and into the house. Mom quick-tottered on into the kitchen with the Boy Red sheepishly in tow. The poor, dear old woman was breathless and blue in the face from fear and alarm. What in the world was all this terrible business about? Mom gasped. She had heard that crazy people were coming over to kill her grandson. My niece initiated an elaborate whine concerning the fact that Mom had wheedled this information out of her. When my sister yelled at my niece, she stomped off toward her room upstairs, smirky and sullen.

Nobody, but nobody, was going to come over here and shoot down any grandson of hers, for she wouldn't allow it, Mom declared and picked up a pistol from the table and sat down holding it primly in her lap, an armed and dangerous church-lady. —Here, Momma, I said and offered her a dainty little .22 instead of the huge .357 Magnum she held balanced on her lap like a cannon. —Thank you anyway, dear, Mom said, still blue in the face but puffed up with determination and dignity, —I would prefer to use this big gun if somebody would just show me how it shoots.

What transpired then was an extended scene wherein my sister attempted to convince Mom to please put down her gun. To convince Mom that her granddaughter had blown things up all out of proportion per usual. That the Boy Red had had a tiff with another boy over some old girl, but that nothing had come of it. That all the guns were out was because my brother-in-law was going turkey hunting next week and he wanted to clean them. Especially, I told Mom, that .357 Magnum she was holding, for that was my brother-in-law's favorite turkey-shooter of all time, which perhaps helped explain why he had never managed to shoot one of those filthy creatures in his life.

My brother-in-law simply stalked about the kitchen rolling his eyes and flapping his arms as though he were some insane turkey himself, gobbling incoherently. Finally my mom seemed to let herself be convinced by my sister that all was well, and that my brother-in-law's agitated, red-ass behavior was based on his hemorrhoids, which had flared up again, and not impending disaster. Finally my sister offered to drive Mom home and she accepted, whereupon Mom placed her big-iron carefully on the table and, seemingly somewhat reluctantly, put her granny gunfighter days behind her.

As soon as they pulled out of the driveway, my whining, pouty, protesting niece in tow, my brother-in-law turned to the Boy Red and announced that they were done with just waiting around for the shit to hit the fan. —Boy, my brother-in-law said, —I don't know if you whupped on those scaggy girls or not, and I don't figure you'd tell me the truth about it anyhow, but you don't have to convince me, you have to convince that crazy sonofabitch Billy Canada. I won't let that crazy sonofabitch shoot you down or stomp you to death, but if you can't convince him you didn't whup on his girls, then you'll just have to fight him man to man. You're gonna have to give that miserable sonofabitch some kind of satisfaction or this will never end, and we can't go around with a crazy man at our backs. If this means you take a big-time ass-whupping, then you take it like a man. That's the mountain code, boy. I'll be there to keep it as fair as I can. You might have to bite and claw and gouge with the sonofabitch, but I'll make sure there ain't no knives pulled or brassknucks, my brother-in-law said as he stuffed guns into his belt.

The Boy Red simply stood there listening, nodding his head slightly, his eyelids at a movie-gangster, Robert Mitchum half-mast, his thin lips curled into a grin as tight and mean as a snake's. —I'll fight the old sono-fabitch, the Boy Red said. —And I'll kick his fucken redneck ass for him. I ain't getting my ass kicked over some scaggy old trailer-trash whores.

—That's my boy, my brother-in-law said and threw his big arm around his son's shoulders and hugged him proudly.

—Let's take the Red Ride, I suggested as I double-checked my .38, for I felt duty-bound to join my feudist family in this honorable endeavor. I swirled its loaded chamber, loving that sweet, oiled clicking, and I slid it back into its slick holster on my belt. Plus I sensed a mythic story in the making. —And I'll do the driving, I added, arching my eye-brows and wrinkling my forehead and looking out at my kinfolk through my own dangerous, hooded, feudist eyes.

As I drove my feudist kinfolk around that drizzly, darkening, early Sunday evening, searching beerjoint to beerjoint for a crazy man to confront, I took stock of myself. I was a fifty-something-year-old man. I was a uni-versity professor. Full of hope for the future, parents sent their children off to college to be educated by professors like me. They sent their nubile daughters. I was a tenured university professor who was on sabbatical leave in order to do research and reflect and write, and there I was, armed to the teeth, driving my redneck, ritual-feudist kinfolks around in rain that was becoming black and whispery. I was a fifty-something-year-old university professor on his way to what might be a ceremonial initiation shootout more bloody than the Battle of Matewan, and I was happy as a clam. Not even driving around casing joints with Morris Hackett, while I sipped beer from quart bottles and listened to sad, lovesick songs on the radio and longed for Ruthie and let myself imagine deliciously how she would suffer when they told her I had been shot down like a dog and died with her name issuing from my bloody, foamy lips, had I been happier.

We ran into Lovelene's ex-husband Fuzzy at Charlie's Pub out on Route 16. He was whiling away the lonely, rainy Sunday afternoon watching a boring Steelers game on teevee and sipping nonalcoholic O'Doul's beer. Fuzzy had been trying to turn his life around. He had been laying off the beer (he never did drink the hard stuff) and staying away from troublesome women who knew how to take aim. Fuzzy had already sworn off violence as a form of recreational activity after one night the previous summer, right there at Charlie's, when he had taken on four rangy, rough-neck river-rats (that breed of itinerant outlaws who drifted into the area during whitewater season to hire out as guides on the river and perhaps deal in dangerous items), and only managed to fight them to a draw, which was a clear sign that it was time for the old, wild, fierce Fuzzy to rest on his reputation. But when my brother-in-law informed Fuzzy of the Crazy Billy situation, Fuzzy ordered a six-pack of Old Milwaukee to go and declared he was coming the fuck out of retirement.

Out in the vehicle, my brother-in-law offered Fuzzy his choice of weapons, and Fuzzy selected the same monster .357 Magnum that had been so inappropriate for Mom. As we drove on out Route 16 to the Cinderella Inn, Fuzzy and my brother-in-law began recounting some of the famous fights that had become legendary in Fayette County over the years, not a few of which involved Fuzzy himself, such as that one night when Fuzzy was home on leave from his first tour in Nam (out of three), and he had briefly pounded on a couple of big redneck brothers out at the Pines over a pool game disagreement. But they had taken umbrage, and had shown up later that night with a car full of armed cousins out in front of Grandma Pearl's house, firing pistolas in the air and yelling for Fuzzy to come out and taste their hot lead. Whereupon Fuzzy, not utterly unlike a raving maniac, had charged out of the house in his boxer shorts barefoot in the snow, brandishing a beer bottle and screeching like a banshee. Those old boys had fallen all over themselves clambering back into their old Buick rattletrap, which they had fishtailed down the icy road with Fuzzy hot in pursuit.

So there we were, driving around in a rainy evening full of risk and peril and dark romance, a real feudist family, armed uncles and a dangerous daddy and the Boy Red in the back seat wearing shades with a black Harley-Davidson cigarette dangling from his thin, evilly smiling lips, looking like a young warrior-lion with his wild mane of red hair.

I vowed then that if it came down to it, I would be the one to streak the Boy Red's face with hot smoky blood, not unlike Faulkner's Sam Fathers had done to Isaac McCaslin, when at age sixteen the boy had submitted to the ancient ordeal of the *hunt* and had sought the wild and invincible spirit of the magic old bear with one trap-ruined foot, and in the process had proven his right to stand with men.

Hotel Angel

We checked out every beerjoint in that part of the county to no avail, and since Crazy Jimmy Canada had threatened earlier that he was coming over to my brother-in-law's house to settle the Boy Red's hash, according to the *code* we could now go pay that sonofabitch a little visit at his own abode. My brother-in-law was settled back in the suicide-seat quiet and grim, and we passed a pint between us. In back, the Boy Red drummed the seat in front of him furiously in time to the David Allen Coe shit-kicking cowboy-biker-killer tunes we had blaring. Now and then Fuzzy hung his .357 cannon out his side window and killed a road sign, the interior of the Red Ride filling with sweet thunder and smoke and wild redneck war whoops. I roared around every car we came upon, once tapping the rear bumper of an old Plymouth rattling along at a mere fifty for almost a mile when just before a dead-man curve I whipped on around it, pulling back into the right-hand lane just in time to miss a Chevy pickup whose brakes I could hear squeal, high and painful as a stuck pig's last lament.

Old Route 61 was generally called the Deep Water Road and wound its way down through the hills all the way over Page Mountain into the Kanawha River Valley at Fort Ancient. It was narrow and twisty and around every hairpin turn you came upon the face of a rock wall painted with prophecy and pleas to repent, plus the frequent news flash that JESUS SAVES.

My brother-in-law called for a piss break and I pulled off the road onto a shoulder of red dog and gravel. The rain had abated and there was now a streak of light high in the sky, but the hollows had filled with shadows. From somewhere down over the hill, I could hear a creek warbling in the dark. I felt the faint moisture of coming fog thickening in the cool air. My brother-in-law looked weary and worried and vaguely sad around his beady eyes as I studied him in the headlights. It occurred to me that maybe my basically bizarre brother-in-law was actually capable of some deeper human emotions and thoughts, although that seemed unlikely. Fuzzy blasted a beer can lying in the ditch, and then he fired off a couple of rounds to put an old abandoned car lying on its side among some trees off the road out of its misery.

I liked the way the whiskey was running in my blood, the way it wound to my head and cleared it, focused it, made me see exactly what I was capable of doing and making me ready. I slid my .38 from its holster and took dead aim up at the faint line of light in a night sky that domed above us like the inner dark shell of an egg. I fired once into that distant crack in the firmament.

Crazy Billy Canada lived about a mile past Beards Fork, and although it was almost two months before Christmas, his trailer was a miracle of blinking lights (down in southern West Virginia, folks often begin putting up Christmas decorations right around Labor Day, if they don't just leave them up all year). It was a doublewide down over the hill beside a narrow creek in a little community of trailers that you could reach by crossing a footbridge. It had been rested upon a cinderblock foundation with a poured-concrete front porch and room-additions built on both ends. There were strings of blinking blue and green and red lights lining the roof of Crazy Billy Canada's doublewide and its doors and windows, and a large cross secured above the front door was ablaze with silvery lights, and everywhere there was an abundance of angels, angels formed from wire of all shapes and sizes, their wings webs of lights, arranged like pure levitations of light all about the dirt yard. They looked like the glowing ghosts of angels, if even angels have ghosts. They looked like heavenly beings either lifting off or landing. They were lovely and amazing to my eyes.

We stood along the road beside the Red Ride for a time just gazing in a sort of hushed awe at Crazy Billy Canada's spirit of Christmas splendor and polishing off our beers. My brother-in-law shook his head and allowed as how he suddenly felt more like singing fucken Christmas carols than fighting. I asked him what the mountain *code* had to say about shooting up a holy doublewide. My brother-in-law said he didn't have a clue, for he didn't have the *codebook* in his back pocket or exactly memorized. My brother-in-law said he didn't see Crazy Billy's truck anywhere around, so what the shit? My brother-in-law put his guns back in the Red Ride. He said he was crossing on over that bridge to see what was what, but for the rest of us to stay put.

When my brother-in-law headed across the footbridge, the Boy Red and Fuzzy popped beers and leaned back against the Red Ride, but I put my .38 in the vehicle and followed him, not knowing what to expect. We walked down through that field of radiance toward the porch of the blinking doublewide purposefully together.

My brother-in-law's knocks on the front door of the doublewide were answered anon by a young, slack-jawed, pop-eyed, scaggy girl, whose mouth plopped open in surprise at our presence to reveal teeth as dark and mossy and toppled as Civil War tombstones. She spoke urgently over her shoulder to somebody back in the room, and then she turned and told us to come on in if that's what we had a mind to do.

We entered a small living room that looked like the site of an angel convention, or the lobby of an angel hotel, for there must have been a hundred or more doll-sized angels positioned on every square inch of flat surface in the place, shelves and shelves of angels along the walls, on top of the teevee, the coffee table, end tables, a congregation of little, filmy, winged angel-cherubs crafted from cloth and ribbons and gauze and dried flowers, but who had no faces. Where faces should have been, the angel dolls were featureless, blank and smooth as eggs.

Sitting there in what looked like a doublewide wheelchair in the middle of the room was a woman so fat that, like the little angels, she had almost no face. Her pinch of a face, such as it was, was almost lost in all those folds of fat. She had cheeks big as pumpkins and a waterfall of cascading chins. Even by southern West Virginia lard-ass standards, this woman was enormous. She was dressed in a flower-print smock as big as a circus tent, and maybe it was, for she was a circus freak of a fat lady, and she had no legs.

The fat lady must have noticed my downward glance, for she said to me in a voice I can only describe as sweet and girlish and musical: —I swand to gracious, if I had knowed we was gettin' visitors tonight I would have strapped on my company-legs. And then she rang the room with a laugh like bells and chimes and I laughed out loud along with her, I couldn't help it, for every single one of her chins looked like a grin. Even my brother-in-law smiled, and I could see the *red* drain right out of his neck. And the young, scaggy girl giggled sweetly, covering her mouth shyly with a hand.

—I lost my legs on account of sugar, the fat lady said then, bobbing her head resignedly. And I piped up then that I too had a touch of the old sugar. The fat lady and I nodded our heads together in mutual understanding and sympathy. The fat lady wiped the tears of laughter from her flushed face with a hand like a ham, then she daintily fluttered her stubby, sausage fingers to take in the room and commenced to explain the multitude of little angels with no faces.

During her life, the fat lady's beautiful twin sister had been an angel sent straight down from heaven above. But the good Lord had called the fat lady's twin sister home to heaven. The good Lord had accomplished this by having the fat lady's twin sister murdered by a crazy man. This crazy man had murdered the fat lady's beautiful twin sister from heaven with a type of big knife he used in his job as a butcher at a supermarket over in Mount Hope. In the statement he made after he was caught, the crazy man said he had seen the fat lady's twin sister in the store and asked who was she. Then he had gone over to her trailer right by the Paradise United Baptist Church out on the Kincaid Road one Saturday night seeking sex, which for him meant chasing her through the trailer while chopping her up with a knife. Later, the crazy man had hanged himself in his jail cell over at Beckley.

The death of her beautiful twin sister had left a hole in her heart so big, the fat lady had thought she would never get it filled up again. Now more than ten years had passed, and while she still struggled with the pain and heartache of her loss, making those angel dolls had helped guide her through her grief. What's more, at craft shows around the area those little, faceless angel dolls sold like hotcakes. Each one was different, save for that one feature, the blank face. The fat lady always left the face blank so it could be filled in by the memory of them who looked upon it. Now making those little faceless angels kept the fat lady busy twelve to fifteen hours a day, seven days a week, which was her way of making a living while she killed time waiting for Jesus to appear in the clouds to take her home to her beautiful twin sister. And she was ready, the fat lady said, to meet the Lord in the air in the twinkling of an eye, whenever the seven holy angels blew the seven trumpets at His glorious coming in the clouds, and the dead shall be raised incorruptible, and we shall all be changed and delivered up if we are worthy.

Then suddenly the fat lady told my brother-in-law she knew who he was and why he was there. She said her son Billy had crazy spells. She said it was on account of him drinking whiskey on top of sugar problems, and she looked at me for acknowledgement. I nodded vigorously that yes I knew what she was talking about when it came to whiskey and sugar and problems. The fat lady said that her son Billy had called my brother-in-law earlier today and made those mean crazy threats and he had regretted it the moment he hung up the telephone. She said that Billy had packed a bag and headed down to his sister's in Marmet to collect himself. He didn't want to go back up to the nuthouse in Spencer again, or get shot down himself, for he knew of my brother-in-law's own reputation for occasional craziness. He didn't want any more troubles than he already had. All her son Billy really wanted nowadays, the fat lady told my brother-in-law, was to be delivered up to heaven in a twinkling when the time came too.

My brother-in-law was looking down at his feet and shuffling around and mumbling. He mumbled that he was really sorry for any harm his own boy had done to her granddaughters. My brother-in-law told the fat lady that he would personally pay for any medical or dental bills the girls incurred. He told her to take the girls over to Billville to his own dentist, whose name and number my brother-in-law wrote down on a piece of paper, and get their teeth fixed as good as new. Tears came squeaking out of the fat lady's eyes, and they rolled down her red, pumpkin cheeks. What I was trying hard to picture was the fat lady rising up in the air like a big angely blimp to meet the Lord in the clouds.

The first angel doll I bought off the fat lady had a flowing ivory gown and gauze wings as light and delicate and as nearly transparent as a cobweb. And then I bought a bunch more. I couldn't help it. For Christmas presents, I told my incredulous brother-in-law. So my brother-in-law bought a few too. What the hell?

What a sight to behold, my brother-in-law and me, walking back across that footbridge, two old sappy sentimental redneck feudists with our arms full of angels with faces blank as bone.

KING OF PORK

Tourists in time and coalfield history one day, my sister and brother-in-law and I followed the Robert C. Byrd Drive south out of Beckley and then turned onto Route 16. Seven or eight miles down the road, we passed through Senator Robert Byrd's home town of Sophia, rolling slowly along three or four blocks of a main street of neat but sooty two-story brick buildings on our right and sets of railroad tracks on our left, with streetlights shaped oddly like question marks.

A self-made man, Bob Byrd had opened a little grocery store in Sophia after World War II, patriotically joined the KKK, and then turned his attention to local politics, progressing quickly up the political ladder from the West Virginia House of Delegates to the state senate to the U.S. House of Representatives, and then, in 1958, the U.S. Senate, where eventually he became the Democratic Whip and later, in 1976 under President Jimmy Carter, the Majority Leader, a powerful position he subsequently resigned in 1989 in order to become the chairman of the Senate Appropriations Committee, where he had secured his lofty position as the "King of Pork" in the nation's capital.

Senator Robert Byrd had made no bones about his intention at the time, which was to cop a cool billion bucks of federal projects for West Virginia by 1995, a goal he had already accomplished by 1992. While he was walking his dog one evening outside his modest home in Washington, D.C., Senator Robert Byrd was waylaid by some investigative reporters with cameras in tow. They bombarded Bob Byrd with spiteful, nasty, innuendo-filled questions about all the federal funds he was funneling into West Virginia. Senator Byrd hadn't blinked an eye. Senator

Byrd was unabashedly proud of that cool billion he had copped for his home state, a land that, after all, had been robbed blind for a hundred years by outsiders. You-all might call it pork, Senator Robert Byrd had patiently informed those idiot reporters, but we consider it long-overdue infrastructure in a land that time has long overlooked.

I can recall a time in my youth when I proclaimed embarrassment that a so-called redneck reactionary like Bob Byrd could be a senator from West Virginia. Mostly I proclaimed this at every opportunity to Charlie, who was a redneck reactionary Republican who loved Robert Byrd in spite of the fact that the senator was a redneck reactionary Democrat, while I, on the other hand, was a late-night, beer-loud, graduate-student, kitchen-table commie.

Once, directly before my parents were to arrive for a Christmas holiday visit to my first wife's and my little student apartment in Morgantown, I adorned the wall above the living-room mantel with huge posters of Ho Chi Minh and Che. This distressed my first wife, not simply because she knew it would bait Charlie, but also because I had hung the posters above the lovely manger scene she had so carefully constructed on the Christmas-card of a mantel.

Charlie hadn't batted an eye, though, basically because he didn't have a clue as to who the evil commies on the posters were. After I had educated Charlie smugly, however, we had spent that Christmas Eve around the festive blinking tree caroling our political differences of opinion at the tops of our lungs. At one point, Charlie jumped up and began waving his arms wildly in the air and stomping around the tiny living room, toppling the little Christmas tree, sending my first wife fleeing in tears from the room, which was simply his way of making a point in favor of capital punishment.

As a member of the Playboys, a rock-and-roll band for which he had picked guitar for nearly four years in his early twenties, my brother-in-law had played at Mark Twain High School's last senior prom before they shut it down in 1966. Since it had been the very last prom, all the schools' grades had been invited to attend, and alumni too. The high school's most celebrated alumnus, Senator Robert Byrd himself, had attended, according to my brother-in-law.

At one point during the night, Senator Robert Byrd had gotten up on the stage and played his fiddle, which he was famous for doing at the drop of a hat around the state at festivals of any sort, county fairs, funerals, political rallies, baptisms, grand grocery-store openings, ball-games, bar mitzvahes. For a laugh and to demonstrate what a good sport he was, Senator Robert Byrd even attempted to fiddle along with the Playboys when they did a Beatles number, "Can't Buy Me Love."

During a break, when my brother-in-law and a couple of the other band members were outside in back having a smoke and passing a pint, Senator Robert Byrd, having somehow shaken his entourage, which included two burly state cops, appeared out of the blue. While he had not personally taken a drink, Senator Robert Byrd had passed the pint on without comment when it came his way. When it came to music, Senator Robert Byrd had allowed at one point, as the band members and the United States senator stood out on the little concrete porch, shuffling about respectfully, well, he was just an old country boy who loved Old Timey Mountain and Bluegrass and Bill Monroe was his own personal hero in the music business, but he loved other kinds of music too you understand, especially gospel, or just any kind of church music, hymns and such, well, he held it all dear to his heart, Senator Robert Byrd allowed. He then asked the band members what they really thought about that Beatle business, those foreign boys with those funny clothes and all that long, girly hair that come over here from England and make all the little American girls act like they don't have good sense.

In southern West Virginia, we *are* the Beatles, my brother-in-law, who still had hair in those days, which was currently combed back into greasy all-American ducks, told Senator Robert Byrd. And it was true. The Playboys wore these shiny blue coats with the Playboy rabbit-head emblem sown on their breast pockets, and they had all let their hair grow a little longish and wore sideburns, and the little country girls down in southern West Virginia went nuts over them, as they had that night of the last Mark Twain High School prom, waving their sweet powdered arms in the air crazily and shrieking down in front of the stage, a phenomenon that clearly had not been lost on Senator Robert Byrd's keen political eye. Those little girls would be voters some day, and Senator Robert Byrd wanted to come to understand exactly what made them tick.

My brother-in-law had no idea how to explain what made those little girls tick in terms a United States Senator might understand. All my brother-in-law knew was that before this night was over, he was going to be the president of one of those little gals' pussies. In fact, when it came to the nooky vote, before this night was over, the Playboys planned to win by a landslide. —They're just real good music lovers, I reckon, my ugly brother-in-law, who was engaged, at that point, to three different ugly girls, had speculated.

—Well, boys, Senator Robert Byrd said, —I slipped out here to see a man about a dog. A fellow in my position enjoys a little more privacy than he can get in that little boys' room indoors. You never know when some reporter type with a camera might pop up. Senator Robert Byrd stepped spritely up to the narrow concrete porch then, and my brother-in-law immediately stepped up to join him.

When I pressed my brother-in-law, he admitted that he had, indeed, attempted to sneak a peek a Senator Robert Byrd's member, but not because he was feeling fairy suddenly. But because he thought he would probably never get another opportunity to see a United States senator's member, a sort of historical appendage after all, which, my brother-in-law admitted, he had wanted to measure against his own pork pirate. But without being too obvious a bug-eyer, my brother-in-law didn't get a really good look, and from his angle of vision could only see the enormous, rather knobby shadow of the senator's member as he and Senator Robert Byrd stood out there behind the little auditorium that night of the last prom of the Mark Twain High School and looked across the narrow valley to the lights of the tipple on the next mountain while they whizzed into the darkness. Whereupon Senator Robert Byrd, who didn't look the type, what with his pinched politician's face and a forelock that looked like a chocolate-dipped dairyqueen, had waxed sentimental for a few moments.

—This is sort of a sad night for me, boys, Senator Robert Byrd said in a philosophical tone while he whizzed, —what with the old school closing down and all. Being here sure brings back a lot of good, old-time memories. I miss it down here sometimes. Where I am now seems too far away sometimes. But I try to get back when I can. That's all a fellow can do, try to get back sometimes. I was kinda hoping a certain little Miss Somebody from the good old days might of showed up here tonight, but I reckon she didn't. Well, good luck to you boys. If you ever get down to Washington, drop by and see me. My door is always open to homefolks, Senator Robert Byrd said as he zipped up his fly, and then Senator Robert Byrd had disappeared back through the door into all of history.

Mark Twain High School was boarded up the next year, and then it burned to the ground a couple of years after that. That day we were driving around in those parts, when we passed where the old building had once stood over the hill a ways between the road and the railroad tracks in the bottoms, there wasn't a trace of it left. My brother-in-law insisted I pull over anyway, and we got out of the Red Ride and walked over the hill. Beneath the brush and weeds some of the old foundation could be seen. My brother-in-law found a slab of that concrete porch from which he had once whizzed with a United States senator, and had almost seized the opportunity of seeing a United States senator's historic member, clearly a high point in my brother-in-law's life. My brother-in-law asked me to take a picture.

—Of what? I was curious to know. —There's nothing left here to take a picture of, I told him.

—Well, Professer Know-It-All, my brother-in-law whined, —just take a picture of nothing left with me in it then.

BEAR IN THE WOODS

My brother-in-law was not famous in Fayette County as a great Caucasian hunter. My brother-in-law had been hunting both deer and turkey in season for over thirty years without bagging a thing save for dead-soldier cans of Budweiser he liked to toss in the roaring campfire and blast to smithereens. *Mister Noise,* was what his turkey-hunting buddies called my brother-in-law. Only a fellow named Mr. Smith, who was fabled for his patience and general bemusement at life and slowness of nature, would actually venture into the rough, mountainous terrain around Gaudineer Knob over in Pocahontas County to hunt with Mister Noise. Being noisy is a decided disadvantage when hunting wild turkeys, for they are not unlike huge chickens zonked on speed, with amazingly keen senses and survival instincts best described as paranoia in its purest natural state. But after years of effort and expenses, my brother-in-law finally encountered a turkey stupid or suicidal enough for even him to kill, hence my brother-in-law had returned from his annual turkey hunt triumphant for the first time in his life, which meant that for Thanksgiving dinner this year the family was going to be treated to about a three-thousand-dollar turkey, my brother-in-law's own most conservative estimate of what he had blown over the years on hunting gear and guns.

Because he wanted to return home early in order to strut about town and brag, my sister drove over to fetch him at his hunting camp north of Greenbank (where the Robert C. Byrd National Radio Astronomy Observatory and Alien Research and Angel Studies Center is located), and carry the great Caucasian hunter home from the hill. My sister found the fearless turkey killers roughing it at their hunting camp, which was a room in the Hermitage Motel, as they passed a bottle of Wild Turkey and warmed their hands in front of a *Debbie Does Dallas* flick on the VCR.

When we met at Billy Ray's roadhouse the following evening for the usual Friday night happy-hour hors d'oeuvres of chicken livers wrapped in bacon and rubbery deviled eggs, my brother-in-law presented me with a gift of one of the sacrificial turkey's feet. I looked my gift over carefully. It was reptilian, scaly, puke yellow, with three long, evil, yellow-nailed prehensile fingers and a thumb like a claw, in other words, perhaps the pure ugliest thing, outside of my own member, I had ever held in my hand. What was particularly unusual, though, was the fact that the horrible foot's middle claw-like finger was raised and frozen in that famous gesture of utter contempt known worldwide as, well, *the bird,* which, according to my brother-in-law, was exactly what that doomed creature's last expressed sentiment on the face of this earth had been. I thanked my brother-in-law warmly.

But what I noticed that evening was that my brother-in-law was not at all blustery with brave bullshit and heavy with stories of the mythic hunt, as I had expected him to be. He and my sister were both subdued. After hemming and hawing around and ordering a round of drinks, we all got up to avail ourselves of plates heaped with chicken livers wrapped in bacon and rubbery deviled eggs. When I told them that Lindsay had decided to come down to Fayetteville for Thanksgiving after all, they didn't say much, which really surprised me, especially the silence of my sister, who had pushed so hard for this hopeful reunion. Basically they both simply commented that that news was nice, and we all just sat there chewing chicken livers wrapped in bacon and those rubbery deviled eggs meditatively amid the beerjoint din.

I had seen my brother-in-law weep only once, and that was the night a few weeks earlier when old George Foreman knocked out Michael

Moorer to regain the heavyweight championship of the world. We watched the fight at my place, and my sister headed on home soon after we had hooted and hollered around about the outcome until we were dizzy and hoarse. I clicked the teevee off, but neither my brother-in-law nor I turned a lamp on, and we simply sat there doing shots of George Dickel in a room dark save for the slant of light from the kitchen. We had been absolutely elated at old George Foreman's knockout victory, and we were joking around about how old George had named all five of his own sons after himself, *George*, and what it would be like to have a world champion for a daddy.

Then, out of nowhere, for the first time ever in my presence, my brother-in-law began talking about his own daddy.

My brother-in-law's dad had died in a freak car accident. It happened on a Saturday when my brother-in-law was twelve. My brother-in-law had run and hid so that he wouldn't have to go to the store with the rest of the family that Saturday morning. His dad called around for him, but then gave up, and just climbed in the truck with Pearl and Lovelene to go do the big weekly grocery shop. My brother-in-law was pissed about the previous night, when his dad came home tired and broody from work, and had set a brown bag down on the kitchen table, a bad sign. Then his dad had fetched that particular mason jar down from the kitchen cabinet, the next bad sign. His dad then poured bourbon straight into the mason jar from the bottle in the bag. By ten o'clock, my brother-in-law's dad was weeping. By midnight, my brother-in-law's dad was yelling and breaking dishes against the wall.

That Saturday had been a rainy day and the roads were slick. My brother-in-law's dad had swerved to avoid hitting a dog and lost control on the wet pavement, and the truck slid off the road over an embankment. My brother-in-law's dad had not been driving that fast, but somehow the bumping of the truck jiggled the driver's-side door open and bounced my brother-in-law's dad out of the cab just as the truck struck a tree. The door slammed back shut on my brother-in-law's dad's neck and he was decapitated.

My brother-in-law allowed, that night of George Foreman's big victory, as to how he had "stuffed" (as he put it) his pain and anger and hatred for his father, and his guilt and sense of betrayal and confusion, because he had loved his dad so much too. His dad had been a quiet, gentle, good man when he didn't drink, and he didn't drink much really. He had been a Sunday school teacher type who only hit the bottle maybe one Friday night a month. My brother-in-law had stuffed these conflicting emotions about his dad over all these years, until he felt all eaten up inside by them, is what he told me.

My brother-in-law then commenced to bawl like a baby right there in front of me. I just sat there silently with an embarrassed, goofy grin on my kisser, thankful the room was dark, while I studiously looked away from the convulsive shadows of my brother-in-law's shoulders. Then I entertained an awful urge to giggle, but choked that dark impulse down. Finally I moved over beside my brother-in-law on the couch, and, not knowing what else to do, I sort of patted him. I patted him on his balding head. I patted my brother-in-law tenderly, as I might have a pitiful, bawling, bald puppy.

So I was basically dumbfounded when right there in Billy Ray's, suddenly, for no good reason I could see, or motive, my brother-in-law, sitting there at a table out amongst a packed Friday night honky-tonk crowd, commenced to weep. What I am saying is that my brother-in-law, a redneck killer of turkeys, was sitting in public munching on chicken livers wrapped in bacon with tears streaming down his face, not to mention snot shining like snails in his mustache. She's my little angel, my brother-in-law suddenly blubbered aloud as though explaining it all.

My sister reached across the table and took my brother-in-law by the hand, and then she looked over at me smiling and said: —Well, we have us a little announcement to make. We're going to have a wedding in the family in a few weeks. I said: —The fuck you say? You mean to tell me Momma went and caught her an old coot? I blurted out before it dawned on me how dumb that was. My brother-in-law would be pounding the table in joy and relief, not blubbering, at that prospect, and, besides, Momma had never been his little angel, to put it mildly. Then even before my sister said it, I knew the score. My niece was heavy with rug-rat, is what I knew before my sister said it. Her bright eyes shining with tears, her chin quivering, my sister took a deep breath and smiled and she said —Well, Angie is going to have a baby and she wants to marry the boy. He's a good boy, I guess.

—Good boy, my red ass, my brother-in-law opined. —I've never set eyes on the little sonofabitch yet, and when I do I plan to shoot the little sonofabitch down like a dog. I plan to break about as redneck as I've been in my life and kill the little sonofabitch deader than Hank Williams. And I'll kill his daddy and his brothers and uncles and cousins too, if any of those Gatewood white-trash sonsofbitches get in my way. I am talking here about big-time blood revenge. That boy's killed. Count on it. Take that dead boy to the bank. That's the mountain code. I'll shoot him and his kinfolks down and take to the woods and run wild as a bear. Are you with me, Chuckie-boy?

—Uh, shore, I said.

—You just hush up now! my sister hissed at my brother-in-law.

—Yes, dear, my brother-in-law said and hung his balding head.

—People are staring at us, my sister hissed at him and rolled her eyes around to indicate the nosy rednecks at neighboring tables who had stopped their own conversations cold and were leaning toward us expectantly. Under her breath, my sister went on to quietly relate that the boy's name was Billy, and she had met him twice. He was a little guy, my sister said and rolled her eyes, but he was sort of cute in a shrimpy way and clean-cut for a Gatewood boy. And he *had* graduated from high school, and he didn't have too many tattoos, and he didn't ride a Harley, unlike the last couple of criminal boys Angie had drug home. He worked construction with his dad and brothers when there were jobs, and he had a little piece of land near where his parents' doublewide was out on the Gatewood Road, and he had bulldozed a flat section off and hoped to run electricity out to it soon so he could put up a little trailer there for he and Angie and the baby to live in. Angie said she wanted to go back to school after the baby was born, so they were going to pay her tuition over at the Tech extension, and Angie would sign up for some computer courses. Or she might go to beauty school. And she wanted to get a little part-time job, just something out at the mall, so she could at least buy baby food and her own cigarettes, although she had promised to quit smoking while she was pregnant. And she wanted to get married around Christmas, but she just wanted a little wedding, just immediate family and a few friends. Over half of the girls in Angie's 1994 graduating high school class were pregnant already, my sister informed me, and only a couple of them are married. They hadn't told Mom yet, my sister told me, her eyes flushed with tears and her voice still a little shaky but holding. But they were going to tell Momma that evening before the story spread around town like wildfire and one of Mom's gossipy old biddy Baptist friends sprung it on her cold and Mom stroked out. We have to look on the bright side of things, my sister must have commented ten times in the course of her little announcement.

—Bright side? my brother-in-law mumbled around his mouthful of half-chewed chicken livers wrapped in bacon. —Bright side! Right. Sure. My baby is knocked up by a fucken wood-hick, and there goes her future down the toilet. Computers? Beauty school? Right. Why doesn't she just go on and go to brain surgeon school while she's at it? My baby is gonna grow old living out in some trashy Gatewood trailer pregnant year in and year out and on welfare half the time, and that's all she wrote for my baby girl.

—We'll just have to make the best of it, my sister said, as she smiled and waved at some people at the bar. —And that's all there is to it, she added with a quivery chin.

My brother-in-law sat there chewing on those chicken livers wrapped in bacon like the regurgitated cud of a cow, his shiny bald head all hangdog, his beady eyes wet and glassy, and he told me that my sister had given him the big news yesterday when she was driving him home about half-drunk and happy as a clam from the hunting camp in triumph. My brother-in-law told me he had been in the best mood he had been in years yesterday before the big news hit him like a Mack truck.

He had had a half-full bottle of Wild Turkey between his legs and another wild, three-thousand-buck, skinny Thanksgiving turkey in the cooler on the back floor, and stories of the great hunt were growing more clear and mythic in his mind by the mile (my brother-in-law always declares he sees no good reason in ruining a perfectly good story by sticking to the facts, to which I add amen). As was their custom when they were in that part of the country, they had pulled over into this little picnic area near the Cranberry Glades turnoff that was extra-special to them. It was extra-special because they had stopped there for the first time when they were on their honeymoon. Lordy but that had been a happy, carefree, long-ago day, my brother-in-law mumbled, his mustache yellowy with deviled egg and mucus.

My brother-in-law then commenced to tell me the sweet story of that carefree long-ago honeymoon afternoon. He told me that my sister had been trying to impress him, that happy carefree long-ago honeymoon day, with what a good, thrifty little wife she was going to make him. She had bought about five dozen of these dirt-cheap hot dogs on sale at a roadside market that morning. They stopped to have a little lovey-dovey picnic roasting wieners (after they had first roasted *his* personal wienie on a picnic table with traffic flowing right down the hill steady as a stream, my brother-in-law felt compelled to inform me, which clearly meant he and my little sister had had sex on at least *three* occasions!). Then they fired up the grill and put about a dozen of those thrifty-dog wienies on it. My brother-in-law had always really loved his dogs. And then my sister had slapped one of those babies on a bun drowned with ketchup and mustard, the way my brother-in-law liked his dogs. My brother-in-law had bit into that little devil like a concentration-camp starving person, whereupon he about gagged to death. Those fire-sale dogs my sister was so proud of tasted like dust. But my brother-in-law couldn't tell her that, his little bride, who was so puffed up and proud to be a brand-new wife, and thrifty and smart and a good cook and beautiful and the best piece of ass her husband had ever had, to boot (there my brother-in-law went again!). And they were so much in love. Lordy what a happy, carefree long-ago day that had been.

—Hey, my brother-in-law had gasped suddenly, that long-ago happy honeymoon day, and pointed over my sister's shoulder with his hot dog, ketchup and mustard running down his wrist, —hey, is that a fucken bear in the woods or what? When my sister spun around to take a look at the bear in the woods, my brother-in-law whipped that sawdust dog out of the bun and tossed it back over his shoulder into the bushes. When my sister spun back around and accused my brother-in-law of bad eyesight or untrustworthiness, he protested vigorously that he had too seen what he thought was a bear in the woods. Then my brother-in-law ate the rest of that ketchup- and mustard-slathered bun. And when he was done with it, my brother-in-law told my sister that that old hot dog was probably the best old hot dog he had eaten over the course of his life. My sister promptly fixed him up another one. —Hey, my brother-in-law said just before he took a big bite, look at the wild cat up in that tree!

My brother-in-law said he ate maybe a dozen of those godawful wie-nieless buns dripping with ketchup and mustard that long-ago day as his darling bride had made him one perfect hot dog after another with her own two sweet little wifey hands, and each time he had figured out a way to distract her enough to flip those barf-dogs back in the woods.

Well, that little roadside-park was the special spot my sister had chosen yesterday to tell my brother-in-law the big news that his sweet angel-baby-girl had been knocked up by a fucken wood-hick, my brother-in-law informed me with a caustic yellowy smirk and then shook his balding head. He got that goofy, grief-stricken look on his kisser again, and his lips began to quiver. Here we go again, I thought to myself, old embarrassment boo-hoo city. And out in a public, packed beerjoint to boot! Had he no shame?

My sister reached across the table again and took one of his big, hairy paws between her own little hands, and he looked up into her eyes. They simply sat there then, holding hands like that, that sappy lost look of love on both their faces.

book seven

FAMOUS LOST LOVE

LOST WORLD

Holly visited me twice during the time I lived in Billville, once in early October, when she drove down alone, and then later that same month, when she brought the kids for Bridge Day. When she had come down early in October, Lovelene's treasures were still stacked all over the house, but I ran the sweeper, dusted, waxed the kitchen floor, and put clean sheets on the bed. I drove out to Kroger's at the mall and got every goody I could think of that Holly craved, chocolate-chip ice cream, Dove chocolate bars, peach-nectarine-banana fruit juice, a dozen scented candles. There was no flat surface in the little bathroom for those scented candles save for the back of the commode, but, in my meticulous preparations, I transformed that throne of the white goddess into an altar of romantic innuendo.

Holly planned to take off work around noon that Friday (her mom was watching the kids), and she expected to arrive around five, which meant she would arrive at five sharp (she was as anal as I am about being on time). At 4:30 I fixed a George Dickel Ditch and went to sit in the living room, where I could peek out the curtains from one of the old stuffed chairs. I also smoked one of my little Swisher Sweet cigars. Holly always said she liked the mixed taste of whiskey and that sweetish tobacco on my mouth when we kissed. I sat there wiggling and jiggling and sipping and puffing and wiggling and jiggling, and at 4:57 Holly rumbled her rattletrap up in the gravel drive behind my Red Ride.

I tore back to the kitchen and flopped down behind my laptop on the table. I took a final puff and final sip and unbuttoned the top of my shirt and affected a frowny, theatrical look of intense concentration, squinting my eyes in a way I hoped suggested the anguished throes of hard-earned inspiration. I had left the front door open on that warm Indian-summery afternoon, and I heard Holly knock and come on in, as I had told her to do. I quickly fired up another little cigar and let it dangle from my lips with its smoke rising dramatically around my frowny face.

—Anybody home? Holly called out, and I heard her sandals clip-clop across the dining room's hardwood floor. The genius at work didn't look up at first when Holly stepped through the doorway into the kitchen. And when said genius did, he wrinkled his forehead and arched his eyebrows and looked up at her through the swirling smoke of that dangling cigar as though somewhat startled to see her, of all people, standing there with that sweet, suggestive, skeptical, crooked, complex, Ellen Barkin grin on her amazingly wide and generous mouth.

Mary McDonnell, the actress who would rise to stardom in *Dances With Wolves,* played a miner's widow-woman who ran a boarding house in the movie *Matewan*. In that role, Mary McDonnell had captured perfectly an Appalachian woman's way of walking, rolling her shoulders forward, with her arms held a bit before her, elbows bent slightly. It was a sort of direct, forthright, no-nonsense strut that suggested resolve and hard-headedness. And that was the way Holly walked when she had her mind set on something, such as exploring every nook and cranny of my little house before I got anything besides a basic hug and single soulful kiss.

Holly looked great that day. Her hair was newly permed and all electric and shaky, and her eyes sparkled and snapped and her breasts bounced as she sashayed from room to room. Her breasts appeared bigger, somehow, that day. Holly always complained that she had been built like a brick shit-house in high school, but that nursing her ravenous boy had ruined her breasts, which was nonsense of course. But that day her breasts did, indeed, seem, well, fuller, firmer, riper. —Holly, honey, I said, —your bosom sure is a sight for sore eyes. —Professor Honey, Holly said, winking and blinking, —I got one of those new, pushup, wonder-woman bras to make you my slave.

I followed Holly around the little house slavishly, while she opened drawers, peered in closets, glanced in the medicine cabinet, studied my mail thoroughly, checking everything out unabashedly and offering comments and suggestions about me needing order in my life and a sense of purpose, namely her, and then she commenced rearranging furniture.

I flopped down on the couch and waited for her to finish her rounds. Presently Holly strutted back into the living room and stood before me with her hands on her hips. She cocked her head and gave me that your-ass-could-be-grass look. —Where's your phone bill? Holly wanted to know. —Are you afraid I'll see how often you call your wife? —What? I said. —What? What phone bill? Oh, I haven't got one of those yet, baby. Phone bills, I mean. (I had hidden it, along with a few other little items, down in Ike's doghouse.) —Honey, I said, —you're the only one I call long distance, sweetheart, honest. I swear it.

There are over a thousand found caves in Greenbrier County, forming a vast network of interlinking passages and caverns like the maze of a great, fossilized root system spreading beneath the earth. Some of the "Greenbrier Group" of Mississippian limestone caverns are up to a thousand feet wide and form huge underground drainage systems and lakes and very long caves, for which the Greenbrier Valley is famous worldwide. There are twelve caves with mapped areas of more than ten miles each. Friar's Hole Cave System in Greenbrier and Pocahontas County has forty-four miles of cave passage. Organ Cave has forty miles, and Scott Hollow Cave has twenty-two. In Friar's Hole Cave there is a "Monster Cavern," which is filled with soaring stalagmites shaped like dinosaurs. There is a 168-foot waterfall in Cass Cave. In Lost World Caverns there are rooms the size of football fields, a thirty-ton white calcite chandelier, a gargantuan pillar called Goliath, and acres of gypsum flowers. There are whole underground river systems, such as Mystic River in Scott Hollow Cave. There are passageways sculpted in limestone the size of cathedrals, and in one there is an awesome calcite formation that looks just like an immense church organ. In this Organ Cave, eleven hundred of General Robert E. Lee's soldiers paused one

Sunday to have church services and seek solace in a torch-lit, religiousy respite from war.

A story that made national headlines in 1992 disclosed that in the 1950s, President Dwight David Eisenhower had secretly initiated the construction of a vast bomb shelter under the Greenbrier Hotel at White Sulphur Springs, utilizing some of the pre-existing caverns there, in order to serve as a reassembly point for the government in case of nuclear war. According to the report, this bomb shelter had been secretly built while the West Virginia Wing was being added to the famous hotel, and was completed in 1962. According to some rumors, virtually the whole resort complex had been duplicated underground, with one twelve-hundred-seating-capacity dining room just like the immense Colonial Hall in the hotel above. It was rumored that there were even golf courses in the caverns below. It was as though a whole vast underground resort existed like some mirror image, or movie-double, of the hotel resort above-ground, a hidden world simply waiting to be occupied and given a sort of underworld doppelganger life. Fascinated by that report, I had spent a couple of days in September skulking around over at the Greenbrier, in my capacity as an intrepid *Undercover Investigative Fictioneer*, while I sought to discover the secret door to that hidden part of my home state. And hence the Greenbrier over at White Sulphur Springs was the first destination on Holly's and my Saturday day trip itinerary.

An Indian legend explains the origin of White Sulphur Springs. Two young lovers came often to the wooded, secluded site to dally. The Indian maiden's father was a chieftain, and when he discovered their trysts, he was furious at their sneaky lust. He searched them out one day, and when he came upon them in the tangled coils of coitus, he shot two arrows. The first arrow found its mark, killing the brave albeit blindly horny young warrior. The second arrow barely missed the young maiden, and it pierced the earth. When she pulled the arrow from the ground, in order to stab herself in the heart with it, a spring of bitter sulphur water burst forth, which mingled with her blood when she sunk that arrow into her sorrowful breast. It was the spirits of the dead lovers that brought visitors daily to drink that foul but supposedly curative water. According to legend, the sacrificial lovers would be restored only when someone drinks the last nasty drop from the healing spring.

—No way am I gonna drink this smelly stuff, Holly had informed me. —But, but, but . . . , I implored her, —think of it as a gulp for the restorative sake of romance. Holly sniffed the murky, yellowish liquid in the small paper cup again. Holly was clearly dubious. After we had parked my vehicle and were walking through the grounds of the palatial, luxurious Greenbrier Hotel, we had stopped in the columned, domed pavilion amid the gardens which stood above those springs where one could partake of magical waters that might smell like rotten eggs, true, but were, after all, curative. —Curative of frigging what? Holly was curious to know. —But, but, but . . . , I told Holly, —the famous Greenbrier resort's guest register has included presidents from Andrew Jackson to Bill Clinton, exiled Bonapartes used to hang here, the Kennedys had all partied hardy here, the Duke and Duchess of Windsor, Princess Grace and Prince Rainier, they all dropped in, Ike frequently played golf on the championship courses here, Bob Hope, Bing Crosby, Jack Nicklaus, Sam Snead were all golfing regulars, and they all partook of these healing curative crappy-tasting waters! —Sam *who*? Holly was curious to know.

Holly sniffed the paper cup again and grimaced and made a barfing gesture. Holly said: —I will not drink this smelly stuff. And if you drink any more of it, Mr. Sulphur Rotten Eggs Breath, you can forget about any kisses from me for the rest of the day. —I see your point, I informed Holly, and flung that foul-smelling, crappy-tasting, albeit curative elixir far from me.

That day I led Holly about the grounds of the grand Greenbrier Hotel along obscure, narrow walks that circled through hidden gardens and around forgotten pools I had previously discovered, until we reached what had seemed to me to be a secretive back entrance that I had come upon skulking around there in September. Ancient Egyptians,

I informed Holly, as we stealthfully gained entrance to that stupendous establishment and ducked and dodged along endless hallways, ancient Egyptians believed that everything had a *ka,* which was an exact counterpoint. Gods and beasts, stones and trees, chairs, knives, you name it, and people, everything and everybody had a *ka,* a double. Hence not for a moment was it beyond belief that in a subterranean labyrinth of caverns beneath the Greenbrier existed a *double* of the vast hotel complex, its sort of *ka.* A sort of *ka* hotel awaiting the arrival of a ghost government, for ghosts were exactly who, after a nuclear war, would be left to govern in those Lost World caverns of doublewalkers. It had been the secret door to this double world I had been skulking about the Greenbrier in search of, but to no avail, I reiterated to Holly, as we ducked behind a plant upon encountering what appeared to my trained eyes to be a couple of security guards merely disguised as tottering, elegant, elderly ladies.

—Well, Professor Tut, we're never going to find any secret door sneaking around like burglars, Holly informed me, and, throwing caution to the winds, took off. —But, but, but . . . , I spluttered as I labored to catch up with her. And, although we were both wearing jeans, Holly brazenly ignored the posted dress-code signs, and she raced up broad carpeted stairs with me tripping and stumbling in her wake. Then we raced hand in hand through endless plush corridors and parlors and ballrooms and one three-hundred-foot dining room that could seat a thousand, for what did we care? We were young and old and in love. We managed to elude capture and, by a circuitous route I had committed to memory previously, we ended up in the bar area at the end of the Olympic-sized, indoor swimming pool needing refreshments mightily.

As I had discovered earlier, the bar happened to be named The Rhododendron Room, which brought a twinkle to Holly's eye. I ordered Holly the bar specialty, which was some sort of white rum and lime and white cocoa concoction called a, well, Rhododendron. Holly about blew our cover when, smiling coyly, she asked the bartender, who looked like Brad Pitt, if he had a key to the hidden door. —I'll sure look around for it, the utterly smitten, squirt son-of-a-bitch said, his eyes bulging at the sight of Holly's bosom, which that outrageous wonder-bra had transformed into a dashboard where one could rest one's Rhododendron.

I drug Holly over to one of the rattan couches lined along a wall of French doors, among huge potted plants and rhododendron bushes. The air in the pool room was as warm as hot breath, and I could hear the soft lapping of the pool water. The greenish, vegetal light had a trop-ical quality, and it reflected in shimmering ropy waves on the vaulted ceiling. I let myself imagine we were on a *film noir* nightclub stage set for some stylized dramatization of forbidden desires and repressed inner lives. In my best whiskey voice, I asked Holly how she liked her Rhodo-dendron, and I wiggled my eyebrows in a manner that I hoped sug-gested juicy bedtime stories concerning fondly recalled old fornications. Holly rolled her eyes, and she told me to put my tongue back in my pants, for she didn't have a single dirty detail left in her limited sexual history to jack me off with.

Holly looked lovely in that soft, liquid light. She gazed up into my eyes as she sipped her Rhododendron and grinned. There was a faint trace of freckles across her nose. The blond down on the backs of her arms looked moist. Some day this will be over, I reflected. Some day I will let this lovely girl slip away or lose her. I had begun to fancy myself as one of those uniquely American types who define themselves prima-rily in the loss and betrayal of themselves and what they love. For Proust (a somewhat similar European type), the only true paradise was a lost paradise, and love was not fully itself until it was lost, until it became memory, became the stuff of story. At its heart, every story is about a lost world, and that day Holly and I were alive and well in the lost world of our love story.

I sipped my George Dickel Ditch, and I got to reflecting upon what Holly's future lovers and maybe husbands would someday wonder about Holly and me and the sweet dirty-deed stuff we did during our love story. I wondered how they would feel when they read in my hillbilly book, assuming I would seek to have it published some day, that upon Holly's urging the previous night, we had gotten frisky in about every room of my little Billville home-place hideout. After doing our sweet, ritual bubble-bath business, during which we had about set the wall behind the commode on fire from all those candles, Holly and I had romped all about that house, bare-ass naked and dripping wet, running room to room, playing tag and touch and tackle, playing hide-and-seek, me *it,* her *it,* capturing each other time and again, collapsing together onto the living-room couch, the dining-room floor, onto the narrow stairs up to Peanut Heaven, onto the kitchen floor, rolling under the kitchen table, tickling, giggling, laughing crazily, rolling around on that old, cracked, but shiny waxed linoleum like playful albeit passionate puppies, licking, biting, barking, yelping, until we could hear poor old lonesome Ike howling along pitifully out back.

At some point, Holly and I had found ourselves entangled on the chair in the hallway by the red phone. I was blue in the face by then and sweating like a pig as I passed in and out of consciousness. Holly gave me mouth-to-mouth and beat my chest like a drum. When the phone rang, what was left of my damaged heart nearly popped in panic. Holly answered the thing before the second ring, and when the caller hung up, Holly had jumped up off me. She wagged the receiver in my face like a bloody organ she had just ripped out of my chest, whereupon Holly had been real anxious for me to tell all. To tell her who the whore was. But I said: —Wrong number, hon, wrong number, Jesus Christ, hon, wrong number, sweetie-pie, I whined. —I swear it.

THE UNKNOWN CONFEDERATE

DEAD

After we had made our perfect clean getaway from the Greenbrier,
Holly and I backtracked a couple of miles to Lewisburg, a little
historic hot spot of a town, where by my count there were 437 craft and
antique shoppes within its charming four-block commercial district.
Bypassing the Blue Moon Cafe, which described its luncheon experience
on a chalkboard out front, we ate down-home blue-plate specials upon
a rickety table by a greasy window at the locals' favorite restaurant I had
previously discovered, named Klingman's Meat Market, which was a
former, well, meat market.

At Klingman's Meat Market, you placed your order at a little counter
in back by pointing out your pleasure in the huge pots of stuff cooking
relentlessly on stoves in a tiny closet of a kitchen, anything anyway that
looked good from the doorway. After the polite if stolid church-ladies
piled your plate until it overflowed, you paid up front at an ancient contraption of a cash register, where Gwen Klingman herself, a wisecracking,
bent little old historic bird of a lady, charged a flat $2.95 for that drip-
ping platter of grub you had to carry with two hands.

All the conversation among the loafing, coffee-slurping old coots sitting around the dining room out front centered upon the ongoing trial
of the Six-Foot-Tall Attacker Beauty Queen, who, in late January of the
previous year, the day after she had relinquished her Miss Williamsport
crown at a pageant during which she sang *their* song, "The Power of
Love," with tears streaming down her face, directed at *his* vacant auditorium seat, the Attacker Beauty Queen had arrived in Lewisburg armed
with a 9mm pistol, a butcher's knife, a claw hammer, a syringe, lighter

351

fluid, a box of matches, and rubber gloves, entertaining the notion of murdering her faithless lover, her pregnant rival, and whomever else got in her way. The person who ended up getting in the Attacker Beauty Queen's way was her pregnant rival's dad. He had answered the door when the Attacker Beauty Queen knocked to request the use of the phone, claiming her car had broken down. Unfortunately for the Attacker Beauty Queen, her pregnant rival's dad happened to be a high school wrestling coach and former Secret Service Agent. Only a stunned heartbeat after she had clobbered him in the head from behind with a hammer, the pregnant rival's dad had subdued the Attacker Beauty Queen. He held her on the kitchen floor in a full nelson until the police arrived, whereupon the Attacker Beauty Queen had made comments such as: "The only thing I wanted to do was fuck up his car," and "I know I've ruined my life, and I'll get counseling if you-all think I should."

I knew all about this Attacker Beauty Queen business because I had driven over to Lewisburg from Billville when the trial started in order to check her out. The day I drove over, the Attacker Beauty Queen, wearing a simple all-white tunic suit-dress, had entered the courthouse with her lovely six-foot-tall blond head held high. As I was telling Holly the story, it dawned on me that the cad who had caused it all, that rat of romance, that two-timing, low-life, scumbag bullshitter ladies' man, might put Holly in mind of me, so I hurried to change the subject. I informed Holly that the trial was the most historic event to hit this quaint little town since the Battle of Lewisburg on May 23, 1862, when the Yankee forces under General George Crook, later famous as the captor of Geronimo, routed the local favorite Johnny Rebs.

Sticking to that Civil War subject, after lunch I drove Holly up to the old Confederate Cemetery on McElhenney Road at the edge of town. The mass grave was a large, cross-shaped mound that contained the remains of 95 unknown Confederate soldiers who were killed in the battle of Lewisburg or died of wounds thereafter. The mound was on a lovely bluff overlooking the valley and town below. It was surrounded by a rusting iron fence and a peaceful stand of old shade trees.

A strange thing occurred the day that Holly and I were there. I had attempted to take a picture of the cross-shaped mound, but I couldn't get my Polaroid camera to work right. So I threw the wretched contraption on the ground. Dumb, fucken twentieth century and the technology it rode in on, was my attitude. Holly picked up the cheap-ass camera and easily shot a picture of the mound. Dumb, fucken twentieth century, I opined, as we strolled back down the grassy path under the trees to the road. By the time we reached the Red Ride, the Polaroid pie was done to a turn.

Holly's photograph of the cross-shaped mound was a perfect composition, balanced and clear and quietly dramatic. With her artist's eye, she had captured the hazy slants of late afternoon light through the trees wonderfully too. She had captured the peace and quiet and old sadness of the place. But what we couldn't figure out, as we studied that picture, was this green effusia, this faint misty stuff that seemed to float above parts of the earthen cross like green gas, and which curled up into the air in places like the green, smoky shapes of—what? Men? Soldiers? And here and there in the green vapor were tiny yellow lights, like fireflies in the dusk under the shade of summer trees. It was clear to me immediately that Holly had just photographed the green ghosts of the Confederate dead. Holly could do things like that, psychic stuff, and her amazing flashes of intuitive insight kept me edgy. But there it was, a photograph that as far as I was concerned proved conclusively that there was some form of life after death for the unknown Confederate dead, albeit greenish in nature and gassy.

That night back at Grandma Pearl's house in Billville, I made a big bowl of buttered popcorn while Holly got into her blue flannel pajamas with the cute pink piggies on them. Those pajamas were so big and floppy on her that Holly had to roll up the pant cuffs and sleeves. I put on a video, *Four Weddings and a Funeral,* and we cuddled on the couch. We were both dead-tired but wired and happy. Holly loved the movie. It was funny and sexy and it had a happy ending. We fed each other buttered popcorn and then licked each other's greasy fingers while we talked about our day and the movie. In the movie, Hugh Grant played this bumbling but sweet young Englishman who fell in love with a gorgeous American girl played by Andie MacDowell, who had had over forty lovers as compared to his six or seven. In one funny scene, she counted her lovers off one by one with little sexual anecdotes about each one while Hugh's eyes got as wide and shiny as hubcaps. Their love affair seemed star-crossed at first, but after a series of touching, amusing mishaps, they ended up together, as they were clearly destined to do.

Are we going to have a happy ending? Holly asked me as I picked her up from the couch and carried her to bed. You can take it to the bank, I said and kissed her cheek and forehead and eyes. Holly snuggled up tighter to me and buried her face in my neck. The soft feel and fresh smell of those floppy flannel pajamas with the little pink piggies on them was like all of outdoors on a fall day. And that appley smell of Holly's hair, and the fragrance of her warm, sleepy skin made me gasp with desire and gratitude.

Holly nestled up against me and sighed and idly played with the gray brillo on my old chest. Holly was smart and strong and determined and brave, and she had all of life before her. The future was Holly's to capture in a mason jar like a firefly and watch blink. I lay there in the dark holding that lovely, sweet-smelling girl and I felt old and beaten down by my own devices, all that same sad, sappy, retro old-fart business.

—Are you sure you don't call your wife morning, noon, and night? Holly asked, and I answered that question with as much truth as I was capable. —And you don't know who hung up when I answered the phone last night? Holly asked, almost too sleepy thankfully to hear what I didn't say. —It's too bad your sister is out of town this weekend, Holly mumbled, —I really wanted to meet her. —I hope our love story, Holly said and pressed against me tighter, —has a friggin happy ending. Slowly caressing Holly's face with my fingertips, I whispered, —I know.

We lay there while Holly sleepily speculated about what our darling baby would look like. She wanted a boy first for us. She wanted my son to have my eyes, which she called *teal*, a sort of smoky, whiskey color, she said. (In truth, my eyes are the color of mud.) Holly wanted my son to have my nose and my (sagging) jawline, she said. What if, I asked, he's born with a graying mustache and a dick that creaked like a swing? Holly ignored me. Holly began spewing names. She rattled off dozens she had turned over in her mind late at night when she couldn't sleep. I had already told her that I would never name a kid after myself, as my old man had done to me, with all those ancient Spanish middle names that had somehow sailed down through generations of my basically Black German family, as though I was some chip off the old bullshit block. Holly still argued about this, but that night she ranged all over the place in the name department, until finally she somehow cuddled even closer against my old bones and began to drift off to sleep whispering the names of unborn boys warmly against my neck. —What about *Elvis*? I said. —I'd like to name the little sonofabitch *Elvis*. But Holly was asleep.

Holly always said I was too romantic for my own good, but that wasn't the truth. In my life, I have seen no romantic love that ever endured. When it came to romantic love, I finally harbored only dark ironies. Some day, if we were still together, Holly would roll over and wonder who was that old goat in bed beside her in the fresh bright light of the morning, and how had that old goat got there, and what was she, a steadfast and basically good girl, to do with him? Better to break your own old heart at a point you hoped you wouldn't die from it, was my basic philosophy, even if that meant giving Holly's own dear heart its tiny seizure. Holly was not a girl to linger in pain and self-pity. Holly was a girl who would not look back for long. Holly slammed doors behind her, and burned bridges. One of the names Holly conjured could well be the name of another son she would bear someday, but it would not be my son, for that son would never be born.

Trying not to disturb Holly, I reached over to turn off the bedside lamp. The Polaroid pictures we had shot that day were stacked on the bedside table. I flipped through them. I studied the photograph Holly had taken of the green gassy ghosts of the unknown Confederate dead in the lamp's soft light. I thought that it was the saddest picture I had ever seen. I could really identify with the unknown Confederate dead.

Sixteen Tons

When Holly brought her kids down to Billville on the third weekend in October for Bridge Day, I went all out. I got a bunch of Halloween crappola from Ben Franklin's and had a ball arranging it. I strung creepy cobwebs across the stairs all the way up to Peanut Heaven, and hung a huge cardboard witch on the back of the door. I carved a couple of spooky jack-o-lanterns and hung cardboard ghosts from the ceiling and hid trick-or-treat candy under both of the kids' pillows.

The kids barreled through the front door wired and wild. They scampered all through the house. They ran out on the back porch to see legendary old Ike, who smiled at them. They tiptoed up the haunted stairs to Peanut Heaven bug-eyed, as I surreptitiously made sounds like ghosts moaning from moldy graves or evil witchy crones cackling as they stirred their pots of bat-wing and toad-eye stew.

They had stopped for burgers on the way down, but the boy was already hungry as a little bear. Lucky for him, I had stocked up on anything I could even remotely remember either of them liking. Holly relaxed her healthful snack rules and I piled the coffee-table with chips and crackers and dips, and I popped in *Aladdin,* our fave video of all time, and we all piled on the couch and fed our faces. Later, after Holly had bathed the kids and got them in their pajamas, we all crept back upstairs to Peanut Heaven where Holly permitted me to tell two ghost stories, and then she read a Dr. Seuss story to them, while I stretched out on the end of the bed and listened with a swelling heart to my sweet girl's precious, sexy, albeit rather nasal Yankee honk of a voice.

We could hear the kids giggling upstairs for an hour before they finally conked out. We tiptoed up and peeked in on those beautiful babies. I turned the lights out in the living room, and Holly and I cuddled on the couch. You should have had kids, Holly told me. I told her I thought she was right. I had never really been around kids before hers. Kids were okay. Holly said: —Kids like you. You have a way with kids. I said: —I didn't know that until I started hanging out with your brats. Why do they like me? I asked. Holly said: —You act like a kid yourself about half the time, that's why they like to hang out with you. For you, Holly said, —acting dumb and silly is second nature. They understand that. You're fun to be around. I'm ovulating, Holly told me. —What would happen, Holly asked me, —if I got pregnant? —Well, in the first place, that would be something of a miraculous conception, I told Holly. —Me getting you or anybody else heavy with child, darlin', without a doc's help, is a pipedream, as you well know, I said. —I know, Holly said, —but we can pretend it's possible. And who knows, maybe we'll get the last laugh on medical science.

The next morning, at the friggin crack of dawn, Holly leapt from our bed when she heard the kids bounding down the stairs. She barely made it into the bathroom where she had hung her robe, before they were upon us.

I had purchased about six different kinds of cereal, Chocolate Coco Puffs, Count Chocula, Chocolate Cheerios, you name it, anything chocolate and surgary with prizes in it. The kids gobbled and slurped and, totally zonked out on chocolate and sugar, ran around insanely peeping their friggin little prize whistles. About 9:30, when I finally got everybody friggin focused, I drove us downtown, where I parked my vehicle, and we took a shuttle-bus out to the edge of town, from where we inched along amid the throngs of rubes up the closed-to-traffic northbound lane of the four-lane toward the Gorge Bridge.

Booths lined both sides of the closed northbound lane, where vendors hawked everything imaginable, from junky Hong Kong knick-knacks to lovely mountain crafts actually carved or woven by the hands of hill people, baskets, quilts, shawls, pottery, tree-branch canes, wooden toys, spinners, tie-dyed muslin dolls, broom dolls, bread-dough flowers, silk flowers, you name it. There were booths where kids could get temporary tattoos or have their faces painted while they heard a Bible story. Competing Christian bands blared from portable stages in front of gospel buses. One bus was a traveling rattlesnake terrarium. There was great greasy grub of all kinds, and before we had even reached the bridge, the boy had consumed a corn dog, a slice of pizza, a funnel cake, a Sno-cone, a candy apple, and a whipped pink cloud of cotton candy.

Before I knew it, I found myself clutching about ten balloons on strings in one hand, and holding the boy's tiny, sticky hand in the other, as we shuffled along in the crowd, with Holly and her daughter right behind us, one of Holly's fingers hooked over the back of my belt, a typical little family on a family outing on a splendid West Virginia fall day. Then I noticed a couple of old bats with the faces of ferrets, and eyeballs like boils, which were clearly focused upon the dirty old man and his young, inherited family, with looks of utter Christian contempt and fearsome ritual religious loathing. Habit being so strong, I twisted my face up into a look I hoped suggested to the little old God-fearing farts that my worst crime was, finally, confusion.

I affected my badass visage and elbowed the little family some space along the railing of the bridge between some fat rednecks. I winked at the boy, hawked from deep in my throat, and expectorated a great gob into the magnificent New River canyon far below. The boy's eyes widened and he glanced at his mom, who in turn gave me a wide-eyed, imploring look of disapproval, and wagged her lovely head at me. It's not nice to spit, the little fellow dutifully informed me, and I hung my head in shame. The kids giggled and Holly gave me a poke in my belly. I know, I know, I said, shamefacedly, that in the role-model department I am pond scum.

Then both kids gasped as not ten feet from us a fellow climbed up on the railing and jumped feet-first into the gorge. We watched over the railing as the jumper's rainbow-colored chute opened, and he floated down toward the raging river far below. When he hit the water, a motor-raft raced across the foamy current toward him. A moment later he was hauled aboard. The air below the bridge was thick with the descending blossoms of chutists. —They are called BASE jumpers, I told the lad. —At 876 feet, this bridge is the second-highest bridge in the nation and it is 325 feet higher than the Washington Monument, I informed the little fellow. —Are you going to spit again? the little fellow was curious to know. The name New River is a misnomer, I thought the tyke might like to know so I told him. —Actually, the New River is the second-oldest river in the world, I told him. —Only the ancient Nile River is older. The Nile River is over in, you know, Egypt, I told him. —Mom, can I get some more cotton candy? the youngster had been curious to know.

The bonding was just beginning. Next stop was the Youth Museum of Southern West Virginia over in Beckley, where an educational dinosaur exhibit was on display in a primeval landscape created painstakingly by the Youth Museum staff. As our little family strolled along a narrow path through giant lost world ferns arranged around Jurassic pools, I pointed this way and that, happily sharing tidbits of educational information. —That is a *Diplocaulus,* I said, indicating a boomerang-headed pond dweller. —*Deinonychus,* I said, pointing to a fearsome carnivore. —And that is the smallest dinosaur ever found, I said, nodding toward a *Compsognathus,* this dog-like lizard. Why had I always sought refuge within the arcane, I suddenly reflected, and solace?

—Mom, what are those things? the lad asked and pointed to a nest with the replicas of three brown dinosaur eggs. Eggs, honey, Holly said and knelt down beside her son and hugged him. Actually, I said, that is dinosaur poop. And the kids, as I had suspected they would, went nuts.

Adjacent to the Youth Museum of Southern West Virginia, in the New River Park, is the Beckley Exhibition Coal Mine, our next stop (In one of its promotional brochures, Beckley proclaims itself: *Beckley—The City with a Mine of Its Own*). The exhibition mine consisted of fifteen hundred feet of underground passages that had been restored from the old mine operated by the Phillips family in the late 1800s. It was an old, deep, low-seam mine of the hand-loading era type, and tourists rode an electric "man trip" car through the mine, guided by a veteran miner. Because we were a little early for the next tour, we got front seats on one side of the "man trip" car, right next to where the guide would sit.

The kids were excited, but subdued, as they looked at the pitch-black mine portal the tracks disappeared into. Holly's son climbed up on my lap, and her daughter squeezed in between us, as we all sat there wiggling in anticipation and gobbling homemade cream-and-butter fudge and black-sugar Coal Candy we had picked up in the gift shop. Our guide turned out to be a retired good-old-boy coal miner named Bill, who had labored dawn to dusk down in the mines for something like 87 years, I think he said, as had his daddy and his granddaddy and his great granddaddy and all seventeen of his brothers and innumerable cousins and any number of uncles and some aunts too of late, many of whom had died in cave-ins or gas explosions or from black-lung. To hear old Coalminer Bill tell it, he was serious hardcore *Coal Country* (not unlike myself, as I proudly pointed out to Holly and the kids).

The electric "man trip" cars filled up with tourists, and finally Coalminer Bill drove us into the darkness of the mine, which was not unlike entering a Haunted House ride at an amusement park. Holly's daughter put her feet up in the seat, and the boy clung to me. Holly had her arm behind her girl, and I could feel Holly's cool fingertips on the back of my neck. Coalminer Bill gave great tour, rumbling along in the cool dark of the tunnel until we reached various mine-faces, which were illuminated by mercury-vapor lanterns. Coalminer Bill would pull up and climb out and go from item to item at the working faces, explaining what they did and how they worked, Sullivan electric chain coal cutters, Harrison pick machines, old track-mounted cutting machines.

Coalminer Bill was full of statistics and mine history and lore and legends and personal anecdotes, and it all brought memories flooding back, is what I had whispered to Holly and the kids, of the days when I myself had to work for ten or twelve hours at a stretch at a mine face without once being able to stand upright in the low tunnel. But on a good day I could load maybe sixteen tons. —Just when exactly did you work in the mines, Alfonso, and for how long? Holly was curious to know. —I first went to work in the mines as a boy, I explained to Holly and the kids. You were just a little boy like me? the tyke was curious to know. —Well, actually I was a little younger than you, honey, I told him and Holly pinched the back of my neck. —That sounds like sixteen tons of you know what, Holly said. —What? her daughter said. —Of what? —Never you mind, Holly said.

Coalminer Bill told us tourists about the many dangers lurking in the deep mines for the miners. How if deep mines weren't continually ventilated or flushed with fresh air, mine gases, or *damp*, such as methane (swamp gas), carbon dioxide, and carbon monoxide, could build up, and miners would be in danger of poisoning or suffocation or explosions.

—Back in my day, I whispered to Holly and the kids, —we used little canaries to detect gas. The little birds were highly sensitive, I explained to them, —and would drop over in their little cages at the first hint of gas.

—You mean the little birdies would die? Holly's daughter asked, clearly distraught.

—Well, no, honey, they would just get sick to their tummies and barf, I explained to her.

Even in the dim lantern light, I could see Holly's daughter's big, blue, teary eyes. Holly hugged her daughter to her. —See what your sixteen tons of BS can do to people sometimes? Holly said to me.

—But but but . . . , I said, —that wasn't all BS, honey.

—Yeah, Holly said, —well, how can anybody tell what's what when it comes to your brand of stories?

—I know what BS stands for, Holly's daughter said and smirked.

BREAKING UP
IS HARD TO DO

Bright and early the next morning, I took everybody out to the Western Pancake House off the four-lane. There was a big fiberglass statue of a clowny cowboy out front, and Holly snapped a picture of the boy and me shooting fingers at one another and mugging for the camera in front of it. I got the Sunday paper out of a machine and we went in. I sat beside the boy and we looked at the menu together. Holly and her daughter launched into their usual battle about getting the girl to eat anything, for that child would live on lettuce and potato chips if you let her. The boy ordered enough grub for a couple of ranch-hands, a stack of blueberry pancakes, link sausages, two over-easy eggs, a side order of biscuits with sausage gravy, and a big glass of milk. Holly's daughter had settled on tea and dry toast. Well, I said to the girl, whatever you do, don't get the walnut waffles, cause that's what I want to get with all of my heart and soul and I never order what anybody else orders, I told her and stuck out my tongue. She stuck her tongue out at me in return, but still ordered the dry toast and tepid tea.

I read the funnies out loud to everybody, and tried to act out the various parts. I always saved my favorite comic strip until last, *Calvin and Hobbes,* and the episode that morning was amazingly serendipitous in its import. It opened with Calvin asking Hobbes if he wants to help write a book. Sure, Hobbes says, what's it about? Well, Calvin explains, you know what *Historical Fiction* is? This is sort of like that. I'm writing a *Fictional Autobiography.* It's the story of my life, Calvin continues, but with a lot of parts completely made up. Hobbes asks the obvious question: Why would you make up your own life? Calvin explains: Because in my book I get to have a flame-thrower.

When the boy blew some bubbles in his glass of ice water with a straw, I stuck a straw into my coffee and followed suit. —I can't take you boys anywhere, Holly said, only half kidding. Holly ran a tight table; she kept a tight rein on her kids, period. When it came to things like manners, when it came to anything as a matter of fact, Holly's kids had their marching orders. As soon as Holly's kids hit the front door after school, the running pitched battle would begin, especially with her daughter: Change out of your school clothes, pick up your stuff, get started on your homework, etcetcetc. It would sometimes rage until bedtime. But at least her kids wouldn't turn out like my sister's, I would reflect as I tried to ignore the clamor and high drama. Strife made me nervous. I avoided arguments, confrontations, turmoil and tumult. Holly could blow up in a heartbeat, rage and vent and then go about her business as though nothing had happened. But I couldn't. I seethed. I took my anger inside and held it there like something alive. I had never in my life hit anybody smaller than me, including some tough guys who just happened to be short, and who I would just wrestle to a draw as opposed to pounding the turds out of them as they richly deserved. But what I was really afraid of was what I was capable of doing in a fight, or even saying. I didn't fight fair. I aimed to hurt.

When the boy dropped his fork and it fell under the table, his face puffed up with embarrassment, and he glanced up at his frowny mom. Holly was in a bit of a frowny mood that morning anyway, but it had more to do with her own hurt feelings from the night before, when my sister had clearly snubbed her. I dropped my own fork and it fell under the table. I bet I can find my fork before you can find your fork, I told the tyke, and before Holly could utter a word of protest, the lad and I dove like submarines.

The night before, I had taken Holly out to Spearen Hollow to hear some picking. Carl and Pet Spearen were a retired couple in their 70s who lived in a white frame rambling Civil War vintage house on a hill at the end of a hollow out Laurel Creek Road. The hollow was filled with their own offspring and their grand-offspring, and hence the name Spearen Hollow. Carl was considered the best left-handed guitar picker in the county, and he played his old Gibson upside-down and backward, a rare, wondrous sight to behold. There was an open invitation on Bridge Day weekend for pickers and their families to congregate out at the Spearens', to set up camp and make themselves at home for two or three days of serious picking and plucking and partying on down. Folks traditionally rolled in from a two-hundred-mile-plus radius.

I had called my sister to see when they would be heading out to the Spearens, as was their custom. I had told my sister that Holly and I had broken up after her earlier visit, but that Holly had promised her kids a trip down Bridge Day, and I didn't see how I could get out of it. But that Holly and I were just friends now. —I still don't want to meet her, my sister had informed me in no uncertain terms. —Are you thinking about taking that woman out to the Spearens'? my sister wanted to know, when I called. —Shore, I said. She said: —I doubt that I'll be going out there tonight. I go out to the Spearens' every year, and it's something I look forward to, but I guess I won't be going out there tonight. So I asked my sister if I could speak to her daughter, for I needed a baby-sitter, and without another word my sister slammed the phone down on her kitchen counter.

By the time my niece and one of her hoodlum girlfriends showed up around eight, Holly had the kids ready for bed. I told my niece that there was a ton of leftover Chinese food from our dinner in the fridge (we had eaten at the area's only Chinese restaurant, called something like the New Peking Royal Golden Dragon Chop Suey Palace, and it wasn't half bad). I told my niece there were chips and dips galore, and Cokes, and for them to make themselves at home, but that they better not have any hoody tattooed boys in.

I drove out Route 16 past the turnoff to my mom's little house, past the Pines roadhouse, where I spotted Baddest Bill's Ford pickup in the parking lot, past one of the schools where my sister taught. We crossed over Laurel Creek at the Beckwith turnoff, and followed the narrow single-lane blacktop until it turned to dirt. I had only been out to

Spearen Hollow a couple of times, and the dirt road seemed to fork about every ten feet, and I have become basically night-blind as a bat in my dotage, but I was about half drunk, and that always helped my sense of direction. Then I saw the lights of the house up the hill through the trees, and began to thread my way through vehicles parked on both sides of the road. I lucked into a spot not fifty feet down the slope from the front porch.

The front yard was swarming with kids, and the front porch was packed with people sitting out on the swings talking and laughing. Pet Spearen met Holly and me at the top of the steps, and she gave me a big hug. Pet was a white-haired tiny bit of a woman who had the energy of a teenager. She was gracious and warm with Holly. She led us into the house chattering away and, when Holly spotted an antique curio cabinet in a corner and raced to it, that's all it took to become one of Pet's dear friends for life. Then it was time for the grand tour of the wonderful old house, room to room, treasure to treasure, story to story. I had been through it before a couple of times, so when they headed upstairs, I begged off to grab a beer.

I stood on the back porch and looked over the yard that spread out under old trees toward a sloping field and forests on up the hill. There were trucks and campers and tents arranged everywhere around a dozen different blazing campfires, sparks and smoke rising into the cool autumn air. Groups of people were standing or sitting in folding lawn chairs around the various fires, picking and singing. I felt as though I was looking out over the campfires of a wagon train circled for the night. I climbed down off the porch and strolled across the yard to the nearest campfire, where old white-bearded Carl Spearen was plucking his ancient battered Gibson guitar backward and upside-down, playing along with my brother-in-law on his own Gibson.

I stood there at the edge of the group just listening to that old-time Appalachian music lift into crisp night mountain air tinged with wood-smoke toward a fat, full, yellow pumpkin of a moon. One of the Spearen boys was playing along with his old dad and the others, and I saw one of the Spearen girls sitting on a picnic table over under a tree with one of her own kids leaning back between her legs, listening to them play "Home Is Where The Heart Is," and then play "Homeward Bound," "Walkin' the Dog," "Stone Cold Heart," and then one of my own personal favorites, "Whiskey Before Breakfast."

The dark under the trees seemed to deepen. A wave of laughter carried down from a campfire up the hill. A cloud shaped like a hand moved across the yellow harvest moon. A mild wind rustled in the crisp leaves of the fall trees. What I had come to find out was that the more I tried to uncover about my life, the more I found there was left to conceal, and the less I understood still. If I kept it up, I knew I would lose everything. All I could do was remember what I could, always at a distance, remember things always vanishing, always there. I would never catch up with my past, even though my life was slowing down to a crawl. It was going. I could feel it. Then they were playing "Breaking Up Is Hard to Do." We can't keep pretending, and living a lie, my brother-in-law sang softly. I don't want to say good-bye, I don't want to see you cry, I'll never forget you, and the sweet love we had, this is breaking my heart, breaking up is hard to do, they sang.

I felt Holly's arm move around my waist, and I lifted my arm so that she could slide in under it beside me. I hugged her to me, and we stood there in the night listening to the sad song. Holly tugged on my sleeve and I bent down toward her. —Where is your sister? she asked me. —My sister got sick, I said. —My brother-in-law just told me. They think she got some kind of food poisoning. Right after dinner, she got sick as a dog, I explained to Holly and I could feel her stiffen under my arm. —You haven't told her about us really, have you? Holly said, looking up at my face steadily. —Shore I have, I told her. —Don't be so paranoid, I suggested. —My sister is sick, that's all. We stood there listening to the people play. —Let's go, Holly said. —Say what? I said. —I want to friggin go, Holly said. —Shore, I said.

THE SECRET INNER LIFE
OF WEST VIRGINIA

That Sunday afternoon, I took the little family down to the historic Fayette Theatre to see a children's play, *Jack and the Giant*. We all laughed our heads off at the talking cow, and when the old troll ran up and down the aisles growling, the tyke clambered onto my lap. We walked back up Maple Avenue to Grandma Pearl's old house in the warm autumn sunshine, everybody holding hands and trying to sing the silly lyrics to the songs we had heard. Holly fixed the kids snacks and then sent them outside to play.

Holly and I sat at the kitchen table and talked. —I know you're worried about finances, Holly said, —but we could manage. I know you want your wife to keep the house. I know you, you'll walk away without anything. But I don't care. I don't want anything you have over there. Okay, let's put our practical caps on, Holly said and got up from the table to find a piece of paper and pen. —Okay, with my salary, sucky as it is, and my child support, here's what I survive on each month, Holly said and wrote some figures down, which made me real nervous. —Okay, even if you keep making the bulk of the house payment, and the utility bills and general maintenance and all the rest, what do you have left over each month? Holly asked, as she tapped the end of the pen against her tongue and looked at me expectantly.

What I couldn't remember right then for the life of me was exactly how much I had told Holly I made. And she had a head for figures. It was not unlike that time when I had forgotten what I had told her my IQ was. Her IQ was 142, she had told me, and I had told her mine was, what, 156, 169, 210? Who could remember a thing like that, except maybe Holly, and she had nailed me on it later. *What* had I told her I made a year? 80, 90, maybe 100 grand? Who could remember a thing like that? —Honey, I said, —money is not the question here. Old age is the question, darlin'. Holly said: —But you said you would marry me if I got pregnant. I said: —And I would. I mean, that would just cancel all my doubts and fears. —Oh, you're so friggin noble, Holly said, —to be willing to do the *right* thing by me, just like my pathetic ex-husband. Jesus, Holly said, —you assholes are all the same. —I reckon so, I said.

Deep in that exhibition coal mine the day before, old Coalminer Bill had talked about the dangers the miners faced working alone down in the hole. One big danger for the miner was running out of fuel for his carbide lamp before his shift was up, and being left in darkness so total and palpable you could rub it between your fingers like oil. To demonstrate how utterly dark it could get down in the mine, Coalminer Bill had pulled a switch in a box and plunged us into a darkness unlike any I had ever experienced. I felt entombed in that exhibition blackness. I tried to imagine what it must have been like for miners to daily make that perilous, dream journey down into that hole. The ghosts of miners *were* down in that haunted hole. I could feel and hear them, and they were awake in their way and waiting patiently in the dark for deliverance. This was the true inner life of West Virginia, a place where all caves were connected. The hidden, secret inner life of West Virginia was a vast maze of mines and caves and long caverns that were all interconnected and haunted.

So there I had been in the damp and dark of a hole deep in a West Virginia mountain with the dear son of another man on my lap. Beside me in the dark was the dear, dramatic daughter of another man. The sweet-smelling mother of these children had her cool hand on the back of my neck. I had taken this wonderful woman's love away from another man. Could I take his children's love away from him too? And then what? What in the world could I teach this boy? What in the world could I give these dear children of value?

I could hear water dripping somewhere in the dark, and faint rustlings along unseen walls, and, from deeper in the mine, sounds like faint sighs, like the soft breath of dreaming bats. I could feel my old lungs filling slowly with dinosaur dust. I felt old and sad and empty, and I had the crazy urge to lift that boy from my lap and settle him safely beside his sister, and then to simply walk off into the pitch blackness and not look back, to walk off into that dark dizzying labyrinth of divergent and convergent and parallel passageways and blind alleys that constitute the lost inner world of West Virginia, never to be seen again. I would slip through some strange ring into another realm, far from the surface of my life. And over time, the memory of the outer world of light would begin to fade away from me like some dim dream of childhood.

As Holly and her dear kids drove away from Grandma Pearl's little green house that Sunday, honking her horn and everybody waving and calling out good-byes, I knew deep in my heart that we would never be together as a family, and I felt amazingly lonely. I felt a sense of loss and regret unlike any I had felt before in my life. I felt a sense of loss for important things I had never really had, nor would ever have.

When Holly drove off that day, she was full of high hopes, and so was I, until her little rattletrap disappeared over the hill, and the reality of who I was and who I had been and who I could never be came rushing back over me like a wave of unutterable sadness. So I did what I always did whenever I was deep in despair and doubt and sappy with self-pity: I moped forlornly back into my beloved little hideout of a house, fixed me a stiff one, and, trusting serendipity, turned on the television, where on channel 69 Sigourney Weaver battled zealots and monsters to the death in the subterranean tunnels of a Prison Planet.

It was pretty to imagine my own inner Sigourney Weaver battling zealots and monsters to the death deep in the dark tunnels of my own Prison Planet.

book eight

FAMOUS MYSTERY TOUR

KNOCKED UP

When Lindsay was thirty, she divorced her first husband, this jerk who fancied himself an emerging American author and dangerous outlaw-biker to boot, after three real pitiful years of marriage. For a time after her divorce and before her remarriage to me, Lindsay lived as though she welcomed grief and ruin. In moments of sustaining illusion, she told herself that she, the *Lindsay*, was living legendary. In moments of less illusion, Lindsay saw her life as lost. A dead-end job selling real estate was a far cry from that glimpsed golden ideal of her future she had had as a girl going east to Vassar College (she had been the first scholarship girl from Montana to ever attend Vassar). Although men now told Lindsay she was beautiful, she could only see herself as she had been in high school, a fat girl with pimples who played tuba in the marching band, was editor of the yearbook, and was brilliant in Latin. She had to admit, however, that after she had supposedly blossomed into a beauty in college, her life had been full of romantic events, if not love. But where had they led her?

Lindsay's father had walked her onto the train that early morning she had first departed for Vassar, put up her carry-on luggage, and at the last moment had hugged her good-bye, the first time Lindsay could remember him hugging her since childhood. Lindsay's father had then told her out of the blue that if she slept with a boy, he would know it. That night, somewhere in the darkness hours east of her father, Lindsay had worked up enough nerve to go out and smoke on the open platform between cars like an adult, the first time she had smoked like that, a real grown-up puffing in public. The vague sweep of the Western landscape felt so distant and dark and daring, and Lindsay imagined herself a mysterious woman in a veiled hat smuggling her life east. Lindsay's cigarette smoke trailed that train moving away from her father like a ghost too thin to haunt.

Back inside, Lindsay's acned face had rubbed raw against the train seat as she stared at endless, oily horizons, or tried to sleep, and by the time her train pulled into Poughkeepsie days later, her face was a bloody mess. Lindsay's roommate was tall, thin, blond, and as beautiful as the pale girls whose pictures Lindsay stared at in *Vogue* magazine. Lindsay's beautiful roommate wore a pastel-print McMillan blouse, wrap-around skirt, loafers, and a clunky bracelet of gold charms depicting crowning achievements in her life. As she had felt her beautiful roommate giving her the once-over, Lindsay had tried to smooth her straight, bright-red corduroy skirt over her bulging hips.

As the months passed, Lindsay would sit for hours at her darkened window overlooking Davidson Hall's front door and watch the endless moonlight French kissing of girls and the boys who loved them with all of their hearts.

Rolf was Lindsay's first true love. A dark, handsome German boy, he was a Yale student Lindsay had hired her freshman year to tutor her in German. Soon she dreamed of doing anything Rolf asked of her. She dreamed of his hands on her breasts, her nipples rolled gently between a thumb and forefinger while being licked like her one and only high-school boyfriend used to do, that pimply, big-hipped boy who was the marching band's drum major and always stuttered when aroused.

One spring Saturday afternoon when Rolf came to campus to tutor Lindsay, he caught sight of Lindsay's beautiful roommate and fell head over heels in love with that blond vision. The beautiful roommate took a fancy to Rolf, such a dark, intense, handsome boy. He amused her. One weekend, the roommate announced to Lindsay that she planned on shacking up with Rolf in an apartment he had borrowed near the Yale campus. She was curious to see if he was as full of fire as he appeared. The beautiful roommate modeled her new blue nylon nightgown for Lindsay. The beautiful roommate danced a slow bump and grind about the room while Lindsay stared through that soft, flowing film at erect nipples red as blood. A few weeks later, the beautiful roommate swore Lindsay to secrecy, then announced that their old friend Rolfie boy was full of fire all right, for she was knocked up.

What was Rolf to do? A scholarship exchange student, he had little money, but Rolf did the honorable thing just as Lindsay had expected him to do: He begged the beautiful roommate to marry him. They could quit school, find jobs of some sort, manage somehow to make a future for themselves and for their son. When the beautiful roommate told Rolf she might abort, he begged her to bear his baby for the sake of the future, if nothing else. The beautiful roommate quit taking Rolf's calls. She began leaving campus early on Fridays for weekends in New York with other boys. Rolf began coming to campus during the week, lurking about, following the beautiful roommate around between classes, begging, begging her. She threatened to tell authorities. Lindsay would sit in her darkened window and watch Rolf pace below, smoking. He was growing so thin. Lindsay was even losing weight with worry. Why wasn't she the one knocked up? It should have been her knocked up. She would carry Rolf's child, his son, his baby boy under her heart, gladly. Even if Rolf didn't love her at first. Rolf would learn to love her.

Perhaps Lindsay could talk the beautiful roommate out of the abortion! Perhaps if she offered to take the baby herself! Even if Rolf would not want the baby that way, without the beautiful roommate in the bargain, Lindsay didn't care. She would adopt the little baby as her very own, name it some beautiful name. Lindsay hated Vassar. She would leave Vassar in a heartbeat, get a job, disappear somewhere nobody would dream to look—Hoboken, say—and hide out there until her boy was a fully grown man. Lindsay sat at her darkened window and imagined a brand-new love story. It was full of rescue and escape, and it had a happy ending. She would somehow rescue her baby boy and escape with him into a lifetime full of love, beyond worry, free from regret and guilt. Lindsay imagined the features of her son's handsome face, its shape, his lean, perfect, maturing body, his tender feelings and thoughts for her, his love for her, the words he would come to speak to her full of gratitude. One night, as Lindsay gazed out her window, a beautiful, dreaming baby appeared before her. It floated in mid-air, luminous among the dark leaves of the trees. Lindsay realized that that dreaming baby's life was her mission on Earth.

That night, the beautiful roommate told Rolf the whole thing had been a dumb hoax, that she had never really been knocked up at all, that it was simply a dumb, bad joke (even she had to admit that!), which had gone too far. Rolf beat his fists bloody against Davidson Hall's front door and ran off into the dark. Lindsay went searching for him. Hours later, she found him in a Poughkeepsie bar drunk. While Rolf wept quietly, Lindsay downed three brandy Alexanders and two pink squirrels to catch up. Lindsay got drunk as quickly as she could, and she mourned along with Rolf for the loss of their son. —A hoax, Rolf cried, and looked up at Lindsay through his tears. —A despicable lie! Why would she tell a story like that? Somebody that beautiful.

That night would be like no other for Lindsay, full of events so new that she would alternately attempt to re-imagine or forget them all the rest of her life. In a drunken delirium, Lindsay and her beautiful German boy circled back to a campus transformed in moonlight, whose old stone, ivy-covered buildings loomed lovely to Lindsay for the very first time. They found themselves lost on some dark path in the heart of Shakespeare Gardens, a park on campus containing every plant mentioned anywhere in Shakespeare's poems or plays. Rolf stumbled off the path. He pulled Lindsay down beside him, into a secret chamber, beneath an oak. That night the air of Shakespeare Gardens was like spice, thick with things nearly forgotten, faint melodies, lights in the leaves, a flickering lantern of moonlight that fell over Rolf's dark handsome face. If Rolf fell asleep, Lindsay would cross his lids with love's oil, and he would wake with her charmed in his mind. She would pluck the wings of butterflies, and she would fan moonbeams into his dark eyes. Hiding in this palace-wood, she would carry his changeling under her heart. She would. She would. She would run away with Rolf. Anywhere. Hoboken.

Germany. Marry him in a heartbeat, take his name as her own. Would she be worthy?

Rolf unbuttoned Lindsay's blouse, lifted her bra. Rolf took Lindsay's left breast in his hand, kneaded it a bit, rolled her nipple between his thumb and fingers just the way she had hoped he would, but then he suddenly just squeezed her nipple as though it were a giant zit. —Ouch, Lindsay said, jerking back and banging her head against the oak. —I beg your pardon, Rolf said. He unzipped his pants and pulled out his penis, which, even through the glooming, Lindsay could see was limp as a worm.

—Look what she did to me, Rolf said, wagging his limp member for emphasis. —This tragedy is all her work. Touch it, Rolf said, and wagged the thing again. —Please touch it. Help me. Please help me.

—Sure, Rolf, Lindsay said and took Rolf's limp penis in her hand. It sure didn't feel like any of the other four members she had held before.

—That awful blond bitch, Rolf said. —I am a ruin now. Now I can father no children for the future. There is no future for me now.

—Sure you can, Rolf, Lindsay said. —You'll see.

—Nothing can ever make it work again, Rolf said and sobbed once. —I can never be a father now, thanks to that blond bitch and what she did to me.

—Sure you can, Rolf, honey, darling, Lindsay said and wagged Rolf's limp member for him. —Really, you will. You just don't feel like yourself right now, honey, darling.

—Did I ever tell you about how I was wounded seriously during the war? Rolf said. —Well, I was. I was just a little boy, but no matter. In Dusseldorf. One hundred yards from the Rhine. I have this scar. If you wish, I will let you look at it some time. I let the blond bitch see it, for all she cared. My own grandmother was killed in the war. Well, she died. An uncle was killed by a bomb. I know history first-hand. Please pull on it a little more, please. There. See what I told you? Nothing will ever make it work right again.

—I'm sure it will work again, honey, Lindsay said. —Darling. Sweetheart, you just don't feel well right now. Who would? Put your faith in us, Rolf, darling, Lindsay said. Lindsay pulled Rolf's limp penis up and down as rapidly but gently as she could. Then she tried wagging it quickly but gently side to side.

—See there, nothing doing, Rolf said, and sighed deeply. —I am the only child. I don't have any brothers. My brothers are all dead. All killed in that war.

—That's awful, Lindsay said, as she alternately rotated Rolf's limp dick clockwise and then counter-clockwise, but to no avail. —How many brothers did you lose, precious?

—Eight, Rolf said. —Do that other thing for me, please. Please, for me.

—What other thing, darling? Lindsay said.

—The next base, Rolf said. —Please, for me. Go to the next base, please.

—What next base, Rolf? Lindsay said. —Sweetheart, darling?

—More like this please, Rolf said, and he placed a hand on the back of Lindsay's head, his fingers in her hair. Had she washed her hair that morning? Lindsay thought. The night before? Rolf slowly pressed Lindsay's face down toward the limp penis she was currently whipping gently about in a path that vaguely resembled a figure-eight.

—I don't know, Lindsay said. —I've never done that before.

—Please, more for me, Rolf said. —The blond bitch would never. Not once even. Which proves she never loved me.

—She wouldn't? Lindsay said.

—Please, for me, Rolf said. —Oh, see! Look! There. Look, it is working almost again. Please. Yes. Oh, thank you. Thank you for the sake of my future, honeybunch. Please. Thank you, yes. Please. Oh, yes indeedy. Please. Oh, please, honeybunch.

Rolf's damp crotch smelled like wet leaves. Lindsay had thought of rain, how it smelled, and how it might sound in the oak tree's leaves above the secret chamber. From somewhere in Shakespeare's Gardens a cat yowled, and for all the world it sounded to Lindsay like the soulful cry of an abandoned baby. And then, in Lindsay's mind's eye, the bald little heads of babies pressed up out of the earth in slow motion, like mushroom caps after a rain.

. . .

When Lindsay was a little, lonely girl living at a wilderness ranger station at Red Feathers Lakes in Colorado, where her father was a forest ranger, and her artistic mother spent whole days alone in the woods sketching scenes from nature, Lindsay had started a butterfly collection. Her father had given her a *Book of Knowledge,* and she looked up each butterfly she caught. She pinned the butterflies down on a wooden display board, and beneath each one she carefully printed both their English and Latin names. What Lindsay hated, though, was putting the lovely little creatures to sleep. First she put them in closed jars and just waited for them to go to sleep, but the butterflies beat the powder from their beautiful wings against the glass, and it had occurred to Lindsay they might be going to sleep in pain, which troubled her tender heart. One day, Lindsay captured a beautiful swallowtail butterfly with black and yellow wings, a bright blue-and-red body, and a lovely smell like her mother's perfume. Thinking it might go to sleep more peacefully, Lindsay simply pinned this exquisite, flawless, delicate creature down alive on her display board, thinking its heart would be an impossible target to miss. This swallowtail did not die for a whole day and night at the end of its pin, and Lindsay simply could not make herself touch it again. Each time Lindsay looked at it, this butterfly would try to flutter up as though it remembered her friendly face, and first tender touch. During that long night, Lindsay lay awake hoping she would somehow be able to hear the butterfly's last breath. Was it her own heartbeat she heard pounding fearfully in the dark that whole night?

Many years later, in a rundown motel in Miles City, Montana, Lindsay would suffer through a horrible abortion (her first of four). An old Flathead Indian woman, wearing black, her eyes like burning coals, had fit a ring onto Lindsay's uterus, something that Lindsay had prayed would make her quickly and painlessly abort, make that problem go away like magic, but did no such thing. All Lindsay did was begin to bleed and cramp so badly she could not stand up. Lindsay lay in that darkened motel room hour after hour, watching the soundless television's light flicker on the water-stained ceiling. Hour after hour Lindsay bled. Was it her own heartbeat she heard echo in that dim room? Whose last breath was she listening for, anyway? This dying baby was not imaginary. This dying child was not luminous, and it did not float in mid-air among leaves.

From a childhood fairy tale, Lindsay knew that somewhere there was a pond where all human babies lie in waiting, until the storks came to fetch them and fly them to their waiting mothers. A secret pond where the pretty little babies lie asleep, dreaming sweet dreams, sweeter than any they will ever dream afterward in this life. In this pond, though, were many dead babies, babies who, before they could be born into this world, had dreamed themselves to death, but due to no fault of their mothers who loved them, such as Lindsay's own baby, the baby who had dreamed too much for its own sake before it could be born.

Lying there in that dim motel room, Lindsay had thought of Rolf for the first time in years. Somehow it was easier to think of Rolf than the man who she had thought loved her. Could she let herself imagine that it had taken all these years for Rolf's swallowed semen to magically reach her womb? Could she let herself imagine this blood leaking from her body as the long-overdue death she owed Rolf? Poor Rolf. There was still no future. Drawing upon her dream life, Lindsay imagined the closed air of the small room thick with the perfume of the beautiful black-and-yellow wings of the soul of her baby. Lindsay imagined the color of her pinned heart as bright blue and red, a bruise draining its dark blood between her spread legs onto the old, crummy sheets. At some point during that long night, Lindsay decided to name this leaking part of herself *Rolf.*

INTERIORS IMPOSSIBLE
TO SPEAK OF

One night, a month or so before I was to move down to Billville to live and work on my hillbilly book, Lindsay and I were hanging out, watching nothing in particular on television, she perched on her blue couch and me sofa-sailing on my red couch across the room. I was deep into my fable of embarkment. I was sipping ice-cold vodka straight like a seasoned hardboiled ironist and vaguely wondering if my upcoming self-proclaimed voyage of self-discovery would be in truth simply another frivolous fiction of self-invention. Steadfastly true at least to my inconstancy, I sat there in the monastery of myself thinking that the only thing I ever knew for sure was what I made up.

Lindsay was sadly studying X-rays of her teeth. Lindsay had experienced a very grim time that day at a visit to her sadistic dentist, who had informed her that only with immediate and intense treatment and perhaps some luck could they save her teeth. Lindsay kept picking up those X-rays and holding them up to the lamplight to examine.

—I just wasn't ready for this, Lindsay said. —The worst thing I can imagine happening is putting false teeth in some fucking glass every night. I'm not that old. I'm just not old enough for that, Lindsay said. —Well, if it happens, then I swear I'll get goddamn golden, diamond-studded dentures. I will. I'll have a smile that will blind people. Until it turns green, anyway, Lindsay said and took a long pull on her cigarette. She tapped it lightly on an ashtray, tending to its tiny campfire. Lindsay narrowed her gray eyes in the languid updraft of smoke and studied those X-rays. Her valentine of a face had this soft golden glow in the lamplight. In recent months, she had let her hair grow thick and long again, like it was when we first met back in Missoula, Montana. And it was reddish again, like in the old days. In the lamplight, her glossy hair shimmered with coppery saloon-girl highlights. She looked like Miss Kitty from *Gunsmoke*. She looked like the old gunmoll of my heart.

Lindsay had always been so proud of her smile. It was a great wondrous smile, with these flashing white teeth that seemed to snap the tails off sentences, and she had a wonderful laugh that could literally ring a room like a bell. So Lindsay studied those grim X-rays and cracked denture jokes instead of crying her eyes out, for while she is the most tenderhearted person I have met in my lifetime, she is also one of those tough-minded Montana women who cut their losses with laughs. She would refuse under any imaginable torture to cry in her beer for the world to watch, most of all a faithless husband of nearly twenty years.

Seemingly out of the basic blue that night when Lindsay was mourning the imminent loss of her great glorious smile, she got up and fetched our old wedding-picture albums from a bookcase and began gazing through them picture by picture, with a slowness like winter. I sensed the beginning of some great evening sadness. I felt like I was coming down with something. I felt frozen in the enormous *now* of a still life, each breath, each moment, a pointillism of permutation. I braced myself for a tortured melancholic round of waxing nostalgic, which I decided to attempt to tune out, or I'd fall fucken apart myself.

Instead, Lindsay simply spoke to me in a hushed but cracked voice, without looking up from the album, as she continued to turn its pages slowly. Lindsay said that she was aware we had some serious problems. But that she didn't want to see all we had shared and known together over nearly twenty years simply come to an end. Lindsay told me that night that she still loved me, though admittedly ours was not a perfect relationship. But no couples have a perfect relationship over time. We change, reinvent ourselves, and retreat into interiors impossible to speak of. She knew that. She knew too, Lindsay said, that so much had to come out into the open if we were to survive. And, God, she dreaded the knowing. But she dreaded even more the doubting. The asking inside every time I looked at her as if I wished she were somebody else.

Of all the pains, Lindsay said, that had to be the worst. Lindsay told me the last few months had been a living hell.

Lindsay reminded me of that evening years ago back in Missoula when we were walking down by the Clark-Fork eating melty ice-cream cones, how I had told her that I wanted to marry her so I could grow old with her. Lindsay told me that had been the most beautiful thing anybody had ever said to her, and she had truly believed me and she knew then she loved me more than I could ever imagine. And she told me that she still loved me and she wanted to grow old with me still, but that I seemed so unhappy any more. And then Lindsay said now she was going to probably lose all her teeth. And she couldn't blame me now for not wanting to grow old with an ugly old woman with a mouthful of gold teeth that would finally go green.

—Hey, I said, —we're doing it, aren't we? Growing old. You and me and that mean old cat, Miss Lulu. Hey, I said, —look on the bright side, if they pull all your goddamn teeth we'll save the sonofabitches and put them under your pillow at night one at a time, and that'll mean a lot of loot from the fucken tooth fairy, or was she too old to believe any more in the fucken tooth fairy?

Lindsay lifted little Lulu from her lap and placed her on a pillow. She stood up and walked from the room without comment. I heard her opening drawers in the mud room, and then back in the butler's pantry, and I didn't know what to think. Then Linday passed in the hallway and went into my front-room office and my heart skipped a beat. Had I turned my Sony off? What was the last thing I had up on the screen? I heard her opening my desk drawers. Jesus-H-Christ! I almost jumped up to go stop her before it was too late, before she had found clear evidence that I could never take back. But then Lindsay shuffled by in the hallway again, smoking like a stove, her bedroom slippers swish-swishing as she walked back toward the kitchen, with imperious Miss Lulu, our little Siamese princess, like a tiny shadow on her heels.

I began clicking the remote madly. I didn't know what I wanted to watch at a time like that. Some innocent animal show. Some program about ancient Egypt. Divorce Court. I looked around the living room of our wonderful old yellow-brick haunted house of a home, taking it all in as though for the first or last time. All the framed prints and paintings on the high pale rose walls, each with its perfect personal history, how this dear old friend or that had given each of them to us on this very special occasion or that. Arranged on the altar-piece of a stone mantel above the fireplace were exotic items from the four corners of the Earth, Mexican pottery and pots and a clay-baked Mayan holy jaguar figurine, a carved stone fish from the west coast of Africa, an iron goat-god from Greece with horns and an enormous cock of iron, objects ancient people had maybe prayed to for rain or corn or fertility, gifts all. Our living room was a marriage museum of accumulated treasures and history. It was a monument of us, an ark.

I heard the wind rise up and branches of the big oak out front squeaking against the high broad windows of our living room. There was a flash of summer storm lightning. Or was our living room some sort of cemetery of tombstones, not trophies? In the gloaming of the soft yellow living room light, the antique toys on the table by the front window looked like the mystery organs of aliens. The wind-up metal chicken that dropped little plastic eggs out of its butt as it clucked and wobbled like a drunken sailor could have been a yellowy disembodied birdheart of some giant hen race. That's how my mind was working right then. Everything old and comfortable and dear to me was transfiguring before my eyes into tortured images and struggling metaphors, refusing to be still.

Old mean Mister Thunder boomed and little Lulu came scurrying around the corner, her nails scratching madly on the hardwood floors. She jumped up onto my sofa and buried herself in my beer gut and shivered there. Little Lulu was not a brave kitty. Little Lulu was a birdheart. Little Lulu hated old mean Mister Thunder. When I was a kid I had a multitude of imaginary friends. I talked my heart out to my imaginary friends. I told my imaginary friends everything, and I made up stories for us in which we always won and were safe at last. I didn't have a single intimate friend any more in my life who I could talk my heart out to, imaginary or otherwise. But I had Little Lulu. I told Lulu all.

And Little Lulu knew absolutely that I would never let old mean Mister Thunder get her.

When Lindsay returned to the room, she set a tall glass on the coffee table in front of her blue couch. Her mother, a renowned artist and woman I adored, had made the coffee table for us, a Christmas gift years ago, its top a free-form mosaic of inlaid agates that looked like the smooth colorful pebbles from the bottom of a mountain stream. The tall earth-tone ceramic lamp at one end of my red couch, her mother had made that also, all beloved items maybe lost to me now. There was something floating in the glass on the table, but I couldn't tell what it was. Lightning flashed again behind the big blue windows of our living room. I had a sudden image of some unspeakable bone baby floating in formaldehyde.

—Hey, hon, what's in that-there glass? I asked Lindsay.

—Oh, just a little vodka, Lindsay said and took a sip, which gave me the shivers. She gazed at me with eyes like dark pools of perplexity and sadness with no end.

I said —Hey, there's something weird in that-there glass of vodka. That ain't no olive in that-there glass of vodka.

—You want a little drink?

—I reckon I do, I said.

It was a pair of those plastic vampire teeth, which Lindsay had sported last Halloween when she had dressed up as Vampira and gone around all night biting guest goblins on the neck.

I took a long pull on that glass of vodka and vampire teeth. They bounced enigmatically against my lips as I drank. I had a strange flash-back to what passed as my childhood.

On summer days when I was a kid, Mom would often make a big pitcher of iced tea and forgetfully leave it sitting out somewhere around the kitchen instead of putting it in the refrigerator. On my periodic treks through the kitchen, I would frequently hoist the pitcher up for a few quick gulps. One day I spotted it sitting out on the stove and as usual I picked it up to drink. Eyes closed, head tilted far back, I gulped deeply. At first I thought that the object bouncing against my mouth was an ice cube, but then I realized that it wasn't cold. Apparently, the mouse had climbed over the back of the stove and had fallen into the tea and drowned. Later in the afternoon when a couple of neighbor ladies stopped over to visit with Mom, I had offered to serve them up something refreshing to drink. Mom, delighted with my unusual display of manners, thanked me warmly.

—I just remembered something funny, I told Lindsay. —A funny story from what passed as my childhood.

—The last thing in the world I'm interested in right now, Lindsay said and took the glass from me, —is one of those dumb funny childhood stories you use to change the fucking subject when things get scary.

—But, but, but . . . it's sort of funny. It's about a drowned mouse.

—See, zee dentures in zee glass zare the real future, Lindsay said in her best Vampira voice. She lifted the glass up and gazed into it like a fortune-teller's globe. —Zee dentures zare tragic. Zee fucking future ees tragic.

WISHBONE

The air about that Thanksgiving Day table was redolent with the odors of an old-fashioned family feast, and thick with things left unsaid, all those gathered family innuendos of silence. We ate my brother-in-law's three-thousand-dollar tom-turkey, which he had smoked, and although that wild bird was a touch gamey, it was not utterly unchewable. I sat there at the table at about two in the afternoon already half drunk, having had my share of whiskey before breakfast, after a mostly sleepless night. I looked around the long table at my relatives, my family, my kinfolk, and I felt a flood of emotions and a network of sympathies and connections that took me by surprise. I had been reflecting a lot recently upon the fact that the more I thought I had come to know as I labored on my coming-of-old-age book, the less I understood. All my pursuits seemed finally to be forms of evasion. I sat there at the table and brooded about my various roles in life, as son, as a brother, and brother-in-law, as an uncle, and, most of all, as a husband, all of which left me with a sort of unspecified longing and shame.

As always, Lindsay was the life of the family, a wise-cracking live-wire ringing the rooms with her wondrous laugh (her great smile had been salvaged!). She and my sister and Mom scurried to and fro from the kitchen toting the platters of Thanksgiving vittles. Lindsay had brought my niece a bright red baggy sweatshirt whose logo read: I'M NOT PREGNANT—I'M A WATERMELON THIEF, which effectively broke the ice on that issue. It occurred to me, as it had before, that my family liked, if not loved, Lindsay more than they did me, and I didn't blame them one bit, for so did I.

Lindsay and I had treaded so tenderly about one another ever since she had arrived the previous evening. It was as though we had given each other painful permission to hold back on some unspoken but shared regret, to be silent and comforting with each other, to avoid any effort at this point to get to the painful heart of the matter.

Lindsay looked lovely. Her hair was even longer and thicker than when I had last seen it in August, and a deep rich coppery auburn. Her hair had felt so soft when I touched it in bed the night before while I watched her sleep, this woman I had been married to for nearly twenty years. I knew I had lived most of my life on the edge of things, on a personal fuckup frontier, a border town of bullshit, a receding shoreline of life and love. I orbited around that gravity we call love, drawn and repelled, and I could never land for long. I didn't know if I had lost something deep and important inside myself, an ability to truly love, or if I never possessed that art to begin with. This was my wife of nearly twenty years, I told myself as I had watched Lindsay sleep, after she had earlier touched my shoulder tenderly with her fingertips in the dead of the night, earlier when she thought I was sleeping, and then she had rolled over to face the wall and weep. I knew I loved her deeper than understanding. The utter tenderness I felt for her had made my eyes flush with tears. The art of empathy was what I treasured most in Lindsay. It was an art I bitterly envied. In an interview I had read with Jeanne Moreau, that wonderful French actress in whose liquid eyes you could see an eternity of pain and understanding, she stated that she had come to believe that love and passion don't go together, that love is constant, not consuming, not jealous, not the flip side of anger and hatred, lines I had copped and used on occasion. She was post-passion, Jeanne Moreau had announced, laughing and tossing her head, and she was happy and content and had come to know at long last how to love deeply.

As we had sat around my sister's table grazing that Thanksgiving feast like starving war refugees, a feast we had consumed, including seconds and some thirds, in maybe eight minutes, I reflected upon what all of us, a little, typical, Gothic American Family, had to be thankful for that day.

We were all thankful that Fuzzy, who was sitting directly across from me, had recently collapsed into an alcoholic coma at a probation-officers conference. Fuzzy, who was supposed to be on a panel discussing the role of alcohol in juvenile crime, had literally toppled over while sitting at a table on a dais after two nights of no sleep and partying. We were thankful because Fuzzy was on the wagon again, seriously it seemed this time, and he was amazingly sweet and polite and solicitous, especially to Mom, who he always called Mrs. Kinder ma'am. After about every other bite old Fuzzy took, he turned to thank my sister with great profusion for including him. And although my brother-in-law popped beer after beer, the cans hissing like wet cats, Fuzzy, with hands that shook, only downed about a dozen cans of that godawful nonalcoholic O'Doul's beer.

My brother-in-law was thankful for that dead deer, his first and only buck in over thirty years of hunting, which was swinging slowly from a tree out back in the chilly wind, its long tongue hanging from its mouth like a black flag. What with the wild turkey on the table, this had been a banner year for my brother-in-law, the great, noisy, Caucasian hunter, and both Big Game stories became more funny and mythic as he retold them, puffed up with pride and thankfulness, blabbering with his full mouth open. My brother-in-law did allow as to how the rack of his deer left a little to be desired in the antler department, meaning the horns of his trophy looked more like those of a goat than a buck, which might explain why the pathetic, suicidal creature had practically tapped my brother-in-law on the shoulder, who had been snoozing under a tree, begging for a bullet.

We were all thankful that the Boy Red had not, in accordance with the code, been shot down like a dirty dog, and that the thirty-six-year-old bleached blond Pines beerjoint babe with the tattooed tits, who the Boy Red had invited over for Thanksgiving dinner in order to meet his mom, had regretfully declined.

We were thankful that my knocked-up niece had decided not to marry the wood-hick daddy of her unborn child, for the time being anyway, and move out to that trashy Gatewood Road into his trailer with no running water or electricity, this latter having been the deciding point, for she could not abide life without television and her soaps. My niece's latest plan, as of about 10:30 that morning anyway, was that she would have the baby and live at home and go back to school and study hard and some day fulfill her ambition to become either a beautician or brain surgeon.

Mom was just basically thankful that she still had not been sexually assaulted in the middle of the night by Mike Tyson.

I personally was thankful that somebody had finally given Fido, my sister's big, hairy, usually amazingly smelly sheep dog, a bath, as he was ensconced under the table at my feet, intent upon practicing autoerotic activities with his tongue.

Everybody was thankful that Lindsay had decided to come down for Thanksgiving after all, especially me. I had missed her terribly, which at last I confessed to myself. I missed her and our big, old, yellow-brick barn of a house, which she had slaved on tirelessly over the years to make into a home. I missed that little princess who was only disguised as a puss and who ruled Lulu Land. When Lindsay had finally fallen deep asleep the night before, I had slipped out of bed and searched around in her briefcase until I found her current journal, which I had snuck into the bathroom and locked the door.

In the harsh overhead light, I had read about how much she had struggled with the decision about coming down to Billville for Thanksgiving. That she was unutterably angry with me for my unfaithfulness and the bullshit and alibis. That her heart was broken. That she wouldn't wish her life on anybody. That she needed to start withdrawing from my family. That she knew that they all knew, my family, they all knew, and they deceived themselves about the kind of person I was, a *Kinder* art form, and they would have her buy into the Big Lie that was my life, which she would refuse to do.

And then I had read her most recent entry, one made while I was on a late errand for Mom the previous evening. Clearly my wife had snooped into my manuscript while I was gone, as I was at that moment snooping into her journal, which had become our closest means of communication, snooping, when sometimes we did approach the heart of the matter. Lindsay wrote that she would rather be hated than liked but unloved. She wrote that she failed in her shell of silence. She wrote that she couldn't stand to be referred to as the "wife" in my hillbilly book and not by name. She wrote that her successor had a name that apparently ran riot throughout the narrative. Her successor had a reality, while she only had a role. Her successor had emotion, passion, while she was merely a cardboard character, a weeping obligation. Lindsay Lindsay Lindsay Lindsay Lindsay, I had whispered urgently over and over again as I sat there on the commode smoking a joint.

After his second and third helpings, the Boy Red jumped up from the table, tipping his chair over backward in his haste, in order to bolt to his aged tattooed girlfriend's for dessert (a big *piece* of something or other, I reckon, he had told me and winked, when I inquired), which meant my sister might not see him again for days. A moment or two later, my niece threw her napkin onto her plate and promenaded out, for she planned to eat yet another Thanksgiving dinner (she *was* eating for two now, after all) with the daddy of her unborn baby at his parents' doublewide out on Gatewood, and she was followed soon thereafter by Fuzzy, who first insisted upon stacking every sopped clean china plate on the table in his shaking arms and rattling them out to the kitchen, before he went to join his girlfriend Pattycake at Shoney's for his second Thanksgiving repast of the day also.

When my brother-in-law waddled out to his reclining chair in front of the teevee to become unconscious, I followed him and flopped down on a couch, farting and belching like a beached Pilgrim instead of helping the women clean up in the kitchen, which in southern West Virginia would have been politically incorrect of me. At some point while I slumbered through the ballgame on teevee, Lindsay had arranged the tines of the wishbone in my nostrils. Everybody thought it was the height of hilarity when I awoke with my heart pounding crazily, and jerked that bugger of bone from my nose. Although by mountain code it was his right as great hunter and host to snap that wishbone, my brother-in-law allowed as how he would not now touch it on a bet, considering where it had recently resided, so Lindsay and I made our silent wishes and pulled it apart with our respective pinkies to see who would end up with all the luck. Lindsay won. When I asked what she had wished for, Lindsay simply looked at me with those big gray eyes without making comment.

POINT OF HONOR

The first time Lindsay had ever been in West Virginia was the fall of 1972, when she had driven her old rattletrap Cutlass across country to come and fetch me back to Montana, where we had decided to launch our life together. That previous summer, we had had a big blowup about her rich supposedly ex-boyfriend, who I had discovered she was still seeing behind my back, and about her abiding feelings for Ray Carver, my best friend and another of her supposedly ex-boyfriends.

I was going to return to them-there hills of home where I truly belonged, I had told Lindsay, as we waited in the early morning at the station for my bus to board. I figured I'd go back to work down in them dark dangerous coal mines, I informed her. I mentioned that I had had three uncles, two cousins, any number of childhood friends, and an aunt die in them coal mines, squashed down there in the dark like bugs, or blown up in explosions, or choked to death by mine damp. —Well, baby, Lindsay said and patted my cheek as they announced the departure of my bus over the loudspeaker, —you be careful now, promise?

But long distance, we had decided we were actually in love, Lindsay and I, on the horn at all hours, sending hairy love letters thick as phonebooks, meaning letters stuffed with locks snipped from our heads, from my chest, from under my arms and pubic area (at her request), snipped from her pubic area at my request, a wondrous bit of bush she perfumed and tied with a tiny red ribbon. The plan was that she would set out driving east from Montana, and I would travel west on a Greyhound, and we would rendezvous in the bus station in Bloomington, Illinois, midway across America on our maps.

On my way west to meet Lindsay in Bloomington, Illinois, I had barely managed to return to consciousness as the bus pulled into the station in Indianapolis. I was about as sad and shaky with a moonshine hangover as I had been in my life. My wild, bold self was collapsed inside me. My heart was speeding into fear and self-loathing. I couldn't think of a single real friend I had made in my life, much less being able to believe in the love of that beautiful woman driving across America for my sake. When I stumbled off that bus, I could hear my bones creak. My red eyes were thick with the black glue of the midnight roads. When I splashed cold water on my face in the restroom and then glanced in the greasy mirror, I looked like a blurred mug-shot of myself, numbers under my quivery chin and all. Thank God the bus station bar was open. By the time, not two hours later, somebody with a speech impediment mumbled over the loudspeaker that the bus to Bloomington was now boarding at gate such-and-such, I had recovered my slick heart of romance. I fell asleep promptly on the bus though, and then we were in Bloomington in a heartbeat, and I was astounded about how far ahead of schedule I was in this new life of mine.

I had hours to kill before my babe hit town, so I stuffed my suitcase in a bus-station locker and loped down the street feeling that old real thirsty fellow rising inside me. Home, home, I knew it entering the first bar I found, where I sat nursing a tall cold one while I watched my favorite soap, *General Hospital*, which was fortuitously on the big teevee above the bar. Then I had noticed a Hoosier football schedule on a poster beside the teevee and checked it out. The Hoosiers didn't play the West Virginia Mountaineers, I observed, which was the only college team I gave a rat's ass about, outside of Stanford. *Hoosiers*! it had suddenly hit me. Fucken *Hoosiers*! *Indiana*! I was, alas, in the really wrong Bloomington! I was in the wrong state!

We would laugh about this in years to come, I promised Lindsay, when I finally reached her on the phone in the Bloomington, *Illinois*, bus station hours and hours later. We would laugh about how I had gotten drunk on moonshine and somehow got on the wrong bus to the wrong Bloomington in the wrong state. We would laugh about how

Lindsay had to drive through a surprise early-autumn blizzard in the Bitterroot Mountains, got a speeding ticket outside of Billings, got hit on by a drunken Native American in Sheridan, and had had the shits for the last two hundred miles, and now, blind with fatigue and utterly road-weary, she would have to find a place to spend the night, and then drive on alone into Indianapolis the next day and find the fucken bus station, where I suggested we now rendezvous in order to launch our new life together.

When Lindsay first observed my black eyes the next morning, she asked me about the condition of the doors my face had encountered this time. —Isn't that what you're going to trot by me? she said. —That you ran into a tough door in the dark. —Some insane guy jumped me outside a bar last night, I explained to her. —What guy? she was curious to know. —Just some insane guy, I insisted. I explained that I had felt so bad about how upset she had been on the horn, I had gone out to a bar for a little nightcap. —And then for no good reason, some insane guy jumped me. That's all there was to it, I swore and crossed my heart. Whereupon Lindsay had debated out loud and long about turning around and speeding nonstop back to Montana alone like a woman with good sense. —I think, Lindsay said, squinting her eyes at me in the smoke of the cigarette she was furiously puffing as though I were some pathetic specimen she had to dissect in order to understand back in high school lab, —that I would prefer to grow old as a single, once-divorced woman than a widow. Whereupon I had, in effect, begged Lindsay to place her bets on me after all, please, please, give me a chance, pretty please, I had whined, and finally, against her better judgment and in spite of all the bad omens, Lindsay caved.

The closest thing to a honeymoon Lindsay and I ever had was that trip west back across country after she had conquered the utter approval and love of Mimi and the rest of my family and had ignored all their heartfelt entreaties to please please reconsider her decision to share her life with me before it was *too late*! We had stopped at her sister's in Nebraska, where we crashed in sleeping bags on the living-room floor after a long night of beer drinking. At about three in the morning, I was awakened by Lindsay's brother-in-law, Rob, as he crawled in the hallway without his artificial lower legs to the bathroom in order to barf.

At an exceptionally lowdown cowboy & Indian bar in a little town outside of Denver, which we were detouring toward in order to meet Lindsay's paternal grandmother and the old lady's paramour, we drank a multitude of longneck bottles of Lone Star beer and fed each other Rocky Mountain oysters from a platter the size of a hubcap.

In Sheridan, Wyoming, I had cruised a strip of low-rent bars looking for the Native American asshole who had given Lindsay a hard time when she had stopped for a drink on her way east. But things had ended up with us peacefully skinny-dipping in a fancy motel's indoor pool at about two in the A.M. Later I fell fast asleep during a scary movie starring Ray Milland called *Frogs,* leaving Lindsay alone to face the horror of crazed cannibal amphibians running amok, which Lindsay took as another bad omen about our chances in life together.

Lindsay and I drove Momma home about three or four o'clock that Thanksgiving Day afternoon. Momma led Lindsay down the little hill beside her house to show off her compost heap around back. I waited in the vehicle out front, smoking and sipping from a Bud. When Lindsay finally reappeared, I suggested we take us a little drive in the pretty day, and Lindsay, lighting a cigarette, said: —Why not?

It was a cool, beautiful November day, the sky tender with a high, frail, bruised, blue light and that ubiquitous hint of wood-smoke in the fresh mountain air that rushed through the open window over my face. Lindsay put a Cowboy Junkies tape into the deck. She picked up my turkey-foot totem from the dashboard and pretended to pick her nose with its extended middle finger. I drove north on the four-lane, and Lindsay commented upon the lovely fall wildflowers the state had planted along the highway. I whipped over beside the road on a dime, and we got out to pick bunches of goldenrod and dried Queen Anne's Lace and purple asters. I told Lindsay that in *The Rating Guide to Life in America's 50 States,* this asshole of a so-called author named G. Scott

Thomas had ranked West Virginia in 45th place in terms of a good place to happily reside. —What an asshole, Lindsay agreed. —I, for one, love the pants off West Virginia, she said, and added, —especially in the fall. It had been fall the first time she ever visited West Virginia, Lindsay reminded me. I told her I knew that. I told her if I ever got the chance, I'd whup on that so-called author asshole named G. Scott Thomas.

Lindsay and I were carrying our bunches of fall flowers back up the bank to the Red Ride that Thanksgiving Day, when out of the basic blue she had asked me: —Who did you get in a fight with that time?

—What fight? What time?

—You know what time. Back when I drove across country to retrieve you. And I was on the cusp of returning to my carefree single life in Montana.

—Like I've always told you, some insane guy jumped me outside of a bar.

—Was the fight over a girl? Were you trying to sneak in a last outlaw lay?

—No way, Jose!

—You bet. I wonder what my life would be like now if I had turned around and gone back to Montana alone.

—Is that what you wish you'd done?

—That's a good question. That's a real mystery.

—Well, why don't you answer it? Do you wish you'd driven back to Montana alone when you had the chance? That's my question.

—I don't think you answered mine. That fight happened twenty years ago. Somehow I've always suspected that you haven't told me everything. For one suspicious thing, you don't brag about that fight, like you tend to do about every other tiff you've been in in your tough-boy life. I don't see what difference it makes now. So why not simply tell me the truth?

Okay. Okay. So Lindsay wanted the real story. So I told her the real story. I told her that after we had talked on the horn that night years ago, and she was so pissed at me and all, I went out and bought a bottle for company and solace. I didn't go out to any bar, like I had told her earlier. Instead, I had stayed in the motel room and drank by myself. I was jumpy. I was rattled. I felt stupid and desperate. I had the radio blaring hillbilly beerjoint music, and I was sort of dancing around the room by myself to let off steam. I started shadowboxing in the mirror at some point. Then, and I don't know why exactly, I really don't, I told Lindsay, I had punched myself in the face while I watched in the mirror. Then I did it some more. I would pick a spot on my face in the mirror, then aim a punch there. I started making up a story in my mind about being in a big fight, a legendary fight over a point of honor. I imagined telling Lindsay about the fight, about how she would react. I didn't figure she'd get so pissed. I had figured that she would feel a little sorry for me somehow, and not be so mad. Maybe kiss my wounds. I also thought she would be impressed somehow. At what a tough guy I really was. At how far I would go over a question of honor. At one point in my imaginary fight in that mirror, I was taking on six guys at once. I was taking on Frazier, Foreman, Ali, all the great fighters of that time, and all for a point of honor. My inner Sigourney Weaver had emerged that night and relentlessly battled the demons in that mirror. My inner Sigourney kicked ass. But then I ended up just telling her that some insane guy had jumped me. Which in a sense was true. Only I was the insane guy who had jumped me. And, strictly speaking, I guess I did do it for a girl. For Lindsay.

—Your inner Sigourney Weaver? Lindsay said. —Jesus. You beat yourself up? That's what you're asking me to believe now? That you gave yourself those black eyes while watching in a mirror? You want me to believe that? That your, Jesus, inner Sigourney Weaver beat you up?

—Pretty please.

MISSING ANGELS

This was the message on the billboard, along with blown-up pictures of the five missing children:

ON CHRISTMAS EVE, 1945, OUR HOME WAS SET AFIRE AND FIVE OF OUR CHILDREN (ANGELS AGED FIVE THROUGH FOURTEEN) KID-NAPPED. THE OFFICIALS BLAMED DEFECTIVE WIRING. ALTHOUGH LIGHTS WERE STILL BURNING AFTER THE FIRE STARTED.

THE OFFICIAL REPORT STATED THAT OUR ANGELS DIED IN THE FIRE. HOWEVER, NO BONES WERE FOUND IN THE RESIDUE AND THERE WAS NO SMELL OF BURNING FLESH DURING OR AFTER THE FIRE.

WHAT WAS THE MOTIVE OF THE LAW OFFICERS INVOLVED? WHAT DID THEY HAVE TO GAIN BY MAKING US SUFFER ALL THESE YEARS OF INJUSTICE? WHY DID THEY LIE AND FORCE US TO ACCEPT THOSE LIES?

I had thrown a left off the four-lane at the Billville lights onto Route 16, the Laurel Creek Road. The idea to take my wife of nearly twenty years on a *mystery tour* had suddenly come to me. Maybe sharing a few West Virginia mysteries with my wife of nearly twenty years would be like sharing a few mysteries of my own interior landscape. But it would have to be a short mystery tour, considering all the weird things there are to see in West Virginia. Our marriage had been something of a mystery tour, it occurred to me.

A quarter of a mile before you reach the Pines roadhouse traveling northeast on the Route 16 two-lane, you come upon the old Sodder compound. I pulled over in the short, steep driveway in front of the compound's metal gate. The compound was surrounded by a high wooden whitewashed fence, and we could see the rambling, one-story main house through the gate. At the top of the driveway was the billboard with the blown-up photographs of the five Sodder children who either burned up in a Christmas Eve fire in 1945 or were kidnapped never to be seen again.

George Sodder, the father of the missing children, later admitted that he had been very outspoken in his hatred for Mussolini, and that he had had many heated arguments with other Italian people in the community concerning his opinions, which were not shared by many of the local Mafiosi. At one point, he had even received a slip of paper with a black hand drawn on it. But could the local Mafiosi, who were mostly retired stonemasons infamous primarily for their fixed bingo games and bootleg red table-moonshine, who more or less dabbled in petty crime for a pastime, could they have been powerful enough to buy or cow county officials, who declared the fire accidental and the missing children burned to ashes?

All of the children were handsome or pretty, with dark hair and dark Italian eyes. The blown-up, black-and-white photographs on the billboard were of Maurice Sodder, age 14, his brother Louis, age 9, and their sisters Martha, 12, Jennie, 8, and Bett, age 5. Above the row of photographs on the billboard in bold, black letters was the admonition: AFTER THIRTY YEARS IT IS NOT TOO LATE TO INVESTIGATE.

We sat there for a short spell while Lindsay read the billboard in a hushed voice. —That is the saddest thing I've ever seen, Lindsay said. —Why did you bring me here? Why did you show me this? Lindsay said.

I pulled back onto the road. —It's a part of West Virginia lore, I told Lindsay. —It's a West Virginia story. I just wanted to share it with you. And then I commenced to tell Lindsay the rest of the story, as best I knew it. How at the same time he had erected the billboard, George Sodder had covered his entire yard with concrete and surrounded it with an eight-foot-high fence. How after George had died, Jennie, his widow, withdrew into their compound and refused to ever leave the house again. How she took comfort in the belief that although her children were beyond her reach, and she had never solved the mystery of their disappearance, they were alive somehow. For if they were dead, as a mother, she would know it. A mother would know if the children she had given birth to were dead or alive. A mother would know if her children were angels in heaven or not. If they were angels, a mother would feel the soft wind of their wings. A mother would hear the golden angely voices of her children in her dreams if they were dead, is what that poor old woman believed with all her heart.

As I drove along, I could feel Lindsay's perplexed gentle gaze upon me, and I assumed she was upset about the disappeared children and why I had carried her there to see that billboard. Or maybe she was still dumbfounded with my latest story about those black eyes of twenty years ago, and I was getting edgy. What other old stories might she want to get to the bottom of?

But then, seemingly out of the basic blue, as always with Lindsay, she brought up the four abortions she had had as a young woman, what they had cost her in self-respect and abiding sense of loss. Lindsay wondered out loud what her life would be like now if she had let even one of those four babies live. Lindsay wondered out loud what would have become of them, her children who were never born, who they would be today. Lindsay wondered out loud what our lives would have been like if we had ever had a child. We had once talked seriously about adoption, Lindsay reminded me. Lindsay then told me that she believed Jennie Sodder's children were alive somewhere. Lindsay told me that she believed a mother *would* have heard the angely voices of her children in her dreams if they were dead and in heaven.

I was getting nervous about the too-personal direction of the conversation. That conversation was getting too close to scary things concerning past choices and lost opportunities and the sad dominion of regret better left unuttered. I did what I always did when conversations began getting too close to scary stuff: I brought up our cat, our princess, little Lulu.

Where we lived was Lulu Land. We admitted it. Most other people hated our precious princess. Most other people were of the opinion that our precious princess was a fur-covered piece of shit. Lulu didn't like to be petted by anybody but her mom or me. Lulu hissed a lot. Lulu puked a lot, and usually in perfect puke-traps where, barefoot in the dark, one or the other of us would slip and slide. After Lulu took her morning poop, she would race insanely about the house screeching like a banshee, having lost about half her body weight. Lulu was a terrific nighttime mouser, and she would tote her treasures back to bed. Lulu would deposit them upon the pillow next to her mom's nose. More than once in the nearly seventeen years of Lulu's life, Lindsay and I had clutched one another as we hopped up and down on our bed exclaiming in unison eek eek eek.

Safely back in neutral, Lindsay and I batted cute Lulu tidbits back and forth while I followed Route 16 the half dozen twisty, dizzy miles to Chimney Corners, where I turned east onto Route 60 toward Hawks Nest and Ansted. Just up the road around a couple of big bends, I pulled over into the little gravel parking lot in front of an old Quonset hut with a Volkswagen Beetle embedded in its corrugated side. There was a huge fiberglass gorilla perched on the Quonset hut's roof.

MYSTERY HOLE

Willie R. Wilson had been a thirty-year Navy man. During the Second World War he had served as a chief hull technician on board a destroyer escort. Although he had always missed the mountains of home, Willie Wilson came to love being a hillbilly on the high seas. When he returned to West Virginia after retiring from the Navy, he found that now he missed the sea. Willie Wilson missed that disorientation that frightened him so at first, that had made him dizzy with odd angles, but had also given him an illusion of lightness, of suspension, and, whenever a particularly huge wave sent him sailing, an illusion of strange, clumsy flight, as though, freed from the gravitational laws of land, he became at sea some sort of holy staggering angel. What Willie Wilson dreamed of doing when he returned home was to somehow recreate in the hills his religious high-seas experience of flight. He also had big dreams of becoming a magnate in the roadside souvenir market.

When Willie Wilson had come upon the old Quonset hut for sale beside Route 60 only a few minutes east of Hawks Nest, which not only resembled the hull of a boat but also had once been used as a temporary tabernacle by a local Hardshell Baptist congregation, whose own church building had finally burned to the ground after being struck eleven different Sundays in a row by lightning, Willie Wilson took it as a sign from God.

Willie Wilson also took the manner in which he had first arrived at the old Quonset hut as a sign from God. He had been drifting around the narrow mountain roads day in and day out in his old Volkswagen Beetle in search of the dream spot for his career in roadside souvenirs, when he rounded a particularly sharp curve in that road that coils like a snake on a hot rock through the hills. As though drawn by an enormous magnet, Willie Wilson had run his out-of-control vehicle headlong into the corrugated wall of that enlongated metal igloo. But instead of crunching like an accordion, his car's front-end simply disappeared without a trace, vanished, vaporized, as it were, as though he had plowed into another dimension, with the front-end of that old Beetle inexplicably embedded into the side of that curved, corduroyed surface and invisible to the naked eye, where that vehicle remains even unto this very day, a tourist attraction.

What Willie Wilson also discovered, after he wobbled out of his old Beetle and looked dizzily about, was that there was something particularly weird about that wide spot in a West Virginia road. As he explored that otherworldly for-sale property that day, Willie Wilson discovered a strange spot on around the Quonset hut down over the hill a ways, where, upon a little level area, he had experienced such a sudden singular lack of gravity that he had thought he was lifting off the face of the Earth, not unlike in his old days of roly-poly religious flight upon the high seas. When Willie Wilson had recovered from the whirly-bird holy staggers, he had fallen upon his knees in thanksgiving and had wailed worshipfully and holy hollered and shouted praises at the top of his lungs unto Jaysuuuuus on high amen.

Lindsay and I sat there for a few moments in the Red Ride checking out the enormous fiberglass gorilla on the roof and reading the homemade signs plastered on the front of the building that extolled the thrills awaiting within that mountain tourist mystery mecca.

DONT MISS THE INCREDIBLE ASTOUNDING UNBELIEVABLE MYS-
TERY HOLE! AN EXPERIENCE THAT WILL HAUNT YOU THE REST
OF YOUR NATURAL LIFE! IF YOUR HEART CAN TAKE IT! YOU
WONT BELIEVE WHAT YOU SEE! SEE THE LAWS OF GRAVITY
DEFIED! SEE THE BALL ROLL UPHILL! FEEL YOUR BALANCE

UPSET! MIND BAFFLING! INTRIGUING! UPSETTING! SEE FOR YOUR-
SELF! NATURE'S LAWS GONE PLUMB BESERK! MANY THEORIES HAVE
BEEN OFFERED! WE WELCOME YOURS! GUIDED TOURS EVERY 15
MINUTES! SOUVENIRS-GIFTS-NOVELTIES FOR SALE!

I had been blowing past the Mystery Hole for years, when one drizzly
day while I was drifting around the mountain roads with no clear intentions or destination in mind, hung over and with a shaky stomach after
eating three hot dogs with secret sauce down at the Have Ya Et Yet Cafe
in Chimney Corners, I pulled over on a whim.

Willie Wilson was this little bit of a white-haired, cherub-faced fellow
with thick Roy Orbison shades, who wore a Western bolo tie and had his
pants hiked up under his flabby old-man tits. I liked his looks on the
spot. We took to jawboning as I had browsed among the bins of amazing
Hong Kong and Jap gyp junk inside his little souvenir shoppe. I spotted
some tiny colored glass bottles shaped like fiddles two for a buck, and I
bought all twenty for my sister's collection, plus I picked up a couple of
bumper stickers proclaiming SEE THE MYSTERY HOLE and ALMOST
HEAVEN—WILD, WONDERFUL WEST VIRGINIA. I also bought a pair of
purple parafoam dice for my rear-view mirror, and for the radio antenna
of the Red Ride a black pirate flag with a skull and crossbones, and I
bought the bushy tail of a squirrel. Touching my twenty had clearly been
close to a religious experience for Willie Wilson, and, from that point
onward, Willie Wilson and I had been like brothers.

Willie Wilson's roadside Mystery Hole was open for business even on
Thanksgiving Day, of course. Lindsay was dubious that day about
entering the Mystery Hole with her husband of nearly twenty years who
she had learned not to truly trust. Lindsay was not certain she was in the
mood to be baffled or astounded or have her balance upset or to entertain an unbelievable experience that would haunt her for the rest of her
natural life. Lindsay was not certain her heart could take a Mystery Hole
tour that day, not to mention her tummy, for she was still yet trying to
digest the world's toughest turkey. Plus I had foolishly told her earlier
about my own first time through the Mystery Hole when I had, upon

returning to the surface of the Earth, lost my lunch. But my entreaties to trust me one last time prevailed, and before long Willie Wilson led my wife and me, hand in hand, like a spelunker bride and groom, down into the depths of the Mystery Hole.

Taking tourists into the Mystery Hole was more like a mission for Willie Wilson than a business. He used it as an opportunity to preach about that Religious Rock named *Jaysus* to folks disoriented at best. At the chainlink gate to the Mystery Hole, Willie Wilson had handed Lindsay and me a highly interesting brochure concerning the religious life of the Hardshell Baptists. Tomorrow may be too late, was the Hardshell Baptists' general drift, with which I had to agree. As we started down the narrow wood ramp into the Mystery Hole, Willie Wilson asked us this: —Do you-all know that some day, and it may be soon, Jaysus will actually and really come back and appear in the clouds?

To which I vigorously nodded *yes siree Bob* and opined: *amen*! But I was simply being agreeable, for where the story of Jesus is concerned, and that resurrection business, I entertain suspicions.

Willie Wilson walked slowly backward as he led Lindsay and me down the descending twisting maze of dark hallways toward the Mystery Hole, preaching as he went and pointing out amazements through shadowy doorways, including what appeared to be the preserved bodies of three local beauty queens, Miss New River Gorgeous, Miss Gauley Mountain Ghost, and Miss Mystery Hole. Now some might say those were merely mannequins made up to look like the preserved bodies of local beauty queens. Some might say that the other horrific fun-house figures and marvels and monstrosities in that congress of perverse wonders were fake, the Chicken Boy, say, and the Patagonian Mermaid and the Two-Headed Hog and the Hairless Jackanapes and the Five-Legged Calf. Not to mention that family circle of Hillbilly Cannibals we viewed through an open doorway as they sat like zombies about a kitchen table apparently dining upon a platter of what for all the world looked like human organs. Some might say those wonders owed their misbegotten, arresting peculiarities to roadside gyp tourist-trap poetic license, but not I. I had learned to enter Willie Wilson's storied interior landscape willingly. Wholeheartedly I let myself sink into the inner chambers of Wilson's dark imagination and die unto myself there.

When Lindsay and I arrived at the end of those descending corridors, and emerged into a knotty-pine room of yellow shadows and utter distortion, where balls rolled on tracks toward the ceiling, bright plastic birds on strings swung backward, and reflections reversed themselves before vanishing into the watery surfaces of curvy mirrors, Lindsay had stumbled hard against me, startled and, it seemed to me, scared. We had arrived at that subterranean place beneath the realm of the real where gravity held no sway, and I put my arms around my dear wife of nearly twenty years and pulled her to me.

—Do you-all know, Willie Wilson Bible-babbled at us, —that when He comes, all those who are saved and looking for His coming will be caught up to meet Him in the air?

A-fucken-men, I mumbled and held my dear wife against me tightly lest she fall or fly away. What is the nature of love in the absence of gravity, is the thought my dear wife and I shared purely by mental telepathy, as we clutched one other, Lindsay and me, to keep from lifting off from these pages forever.

Lindsay thought that the Mystery Hole was a trip that day. We felt like kids playing in a carnival fun-house hall of mirrors. Plus Lindsay did not toss her cookies over the hill as I had done my first time through. Lindsay was amazed by the Mystery Hole, and smitten with old Willie Wilson. I swear she flirted with the old fart. When the services were over and we had finally holy-staggered back to the surface of the Earth as we had always known it, Lindsay insisted upon taking some pictures of Willie Wilson and me arm in arm before the entrance of the Mystery Hole, with that huge fiberglass creature looming above us in the branches of the trees like the hairy ghost of some gorilla Goliath.

Lindsay and I were dizzy and goofy and in high spirits when we emerged from the Mystery Hole that day. We were giddy and silly and enjoying that little adventure like we hadn't anything in a long time. I felt a sense of renewal about us. For a short time that Thanksgiving Day, I had risen above confusion and regret. And I was just plain old-time happy. Lindsay and I had shared a West Virginia story that day. We were making a West Virginia story as we went along, one that we would later relate, detail by amusing detail, to friends and relatives around kitchen tables late at night. We would interrupt one another with new details, recalled and otherwise, for our story. There would come a time when I would swear on the Bible that old Willie Wilson had performed a mysterious ceremony down in the Mystery Hole that day. I would claim that Willie Wilson had remarried Lindsay and me. In fact, he did that very thing. Lindsay and I had exchanged special rings old Willie Wilson had taken from his pants pocket and given to us for the special occasion. When I kissed my bride in the Mystery Hole that day, we rose up from the slanted floor. We floated up arm in arm toward the star-filled ceiling.

When Willie Wilson had holy-hollered: —PRAISE JAYSUS, BROTHER AND SISTERWOMAN, as we greased his palm for our armloads of mystery-souvenirs, tacky and holy and made in Hong Kong, I felt almost religiousy amen.

—PRAISE JAYSUUUUS, BROTHER! I had holy-hollered back at old Willie Wilson.

But that rare spasm of religiosity and hopefulness had lasted for about as long as it took me to roar around the next bend in the mountain road. The moment I lost sight of old Willie Wilson waving in the rear-view mirror, I was right back where I started that day. I was stuck somewhere in the lonely interior landscape of my private West Virginia story again.

STORE-BOUGHT ANGEL

Unlike me, Lindsay had bawled like a baby when we buried Charlie at that little mountaintop cemetery in Ansted. In the hot, cramped chapel of the local funeral home where the services were held, the family members were seated in rickety folding chairs on the front row before Charlie's open casket. When some local, country preacher, who save for old-timey heroic reputation clearly did not know Charlie from Adam, began his spiel about what a good father and husband and War Hero and onward Christian soldier Charlie had been, Lindsay simply lost it for no good reason I could see. Well, she and Charlie had gotten along famously, I guess. Lindsay had uncharacteristically wept and sobbed in public and I had whipped out my handkerchief for her to clutch against her fountain of a face. She was crying enough for the both of us, was the way I saw it.

Lindsay had not been back to the Restlawn Memory Gardens since the day of Charlie's funeral. I threw a left off Route 60 into the cemetery's driveway, pausing for a moment, as I always did, to gaze at one of old Bernard Coffindaffer's trio of crosses just past the entrance. I parked in front of the long concrete walk that led up the little knoll among the graves. I fetched a small paper bag out of the glove compartment, and then Lindsay and I walked slowly up the slope, hand in hand like newlyweds.

The metal vase attached to the marble slab at Charlie's gravesite was still full of flowers from the last time I had hauled Momma over to decorate graves. Lindsay knelt down and ran her fingers over the raised brass letters of Charlie's name on the plate that had cost me an arm and a leg.

The letters of my own name. Lindsay removed the old flowers from Charlie's vase, and then began to arrange the wildflowers we had picked beside the four-lane.

—Do you ever miss him? Lindsay asked me.

—No, I told her truthfully. —But I think about him all the time.

But what I didn't tell my wife of nearly twenty years was that I had begun to suspect that I was becoming more like Charlie every day, at least the way he had been as he grew old, with his dark moods and unspecified anger and his quiet hopelessness and sense of loss. And his profound loneliness. What I didn't tell my wife of nearly twenty years was that what I often brooded about was when, in their long married life, my father and mother had been in love, and when had they stopped being in love, and what had held them together over the long years after their love was dead as a doornail.

Only one memory came to mind whenever I tried to imagine my parents when they might have been in love. In that memory, the three of us, Mom and Dad and me, are walking home from the movies at night in one of those small southern West Virginia towns where I was so successfully disguised as a child. I roam ahead of them down the dark, quiet streets, but never far. The trees along the walk, the maples and old oaks, are thick with summer leaves that rustle in a warm breeze. I run ahead from tree to tree, hiding within that strange dark the trees seem to shed like pools beneath them. As I run toward each tree, I try to titillate my fear by imagining that there are creatures back in the shadows, werewolves with quick wild eyes, who are just dying to eat me raw. I hug tightly to a tree's trunk, pressing my cheek against the rough bark, deliciously anticipating the first bite. And there walking slowly toward where I wait in the darkness are my parents, my beautiful mother and huge, handsome father, swinging their held hands slowly in time to a song my father is singing low under his breath: *Good night Irene good night, good night Irene.* Over my mother's beautiful face the shadows of leaves move, and light from a streetlamp trims her dark hair like a thin encircling flame. As he sings, Dad looks at Mom with an expression on his face I can only describe as awe. As I watch Mom and Dad walking toward me holding hands in the soft quietude of that sweet night, I sense a warmth and longing between them that must surely have been love.

When I looked down at Lindsay on her knees arranging flowers on Charlie's final resting place, I saw that tears were streaming down her face. I gently pulled my dear wife up beside me and held my dear wife in my arms for the second time that day. I glanced around the little mountaintop cemetery to see if there were any witnesses to this public display of tenderness. But we were alone.

I had seen my wife weep more in the past year than I had in the previous eighteen or so. But she had never ever been a weeping obligation. I almost cried myself. What I had begun to understand was that I had always best found the pathway to my own pain through the pain of another person. I hadn't cried at Charlie's funeral, which was somewhat understandable, I guess, but I hadn't cried at Mimi's either, somebody I imagined I loved. But I could be brought to tears watching other people, perfect strangers even, on television news reports, say, grieve openly over loved ones burned beyond recognition or mangled in car wrecks or found murdered in the woods. Cheap sentimentality was another thing I shared with Charlie.

I held Lindsay tightly. We stood there clinging to each other in that mountaintop cemetery, as she blubbered her heart out. She wasn't bawling simply for the waste of Charlie's life, of course. She was grieving for us, for what we had lost somewhere along the line. For the "death of love," maybe, which is how Lindsay had put it in another short entry in her journal I had read at some point and committed to memory: "Still more notes of lament. Cold winter day. Both of us trapped inside. Both of us retreated into our inconsolable interiors for privacy in our pain. Death of love. Death of love."

—Now, now, I had mumbled and patted my wife's back. —Now, now. Lindsay pushed out of my arms and fumbled to light a cigarette. She stood there smoking and looking around the little mountaintop cemetery and at the dark woods beyond the fence.

—I just want to make one thing clear, Lindsay said. —I am officially, as of now, finished with all that boohoo bullshit. I don't plan on being the victim any more. I'm finished with feeling pathetic. I am not the perpetrator here, and I will not be the fucking victim. I don't know what your plans are. I don't know if you're coming home or not. There's nothing I can do about what you do. But if you are still seeing that woman, just don't come home. If that's over, then maybe we can try again. But, frankly, I'm not certain this marriage is going to survive. I'm not sure I care.

When we reached the stone planters three quarters down the walkway, I led Lindsay left across the grass, until we reached the grave of little Joshua Feltzer, who had died in 1988 in his only year of life.

Beside the ground-level grave-marker-plaque, somebody had placed a yellow Tonka truck, with JOSHUA'S CONSTRUCTION CO. hand-painted on its door, and a yellow Tonka earth-moving machine, both of whose beds were filled with blue Easter-basket grass. In that blue grass were positioned a dozen or more of those tiny plaster-of-paris angels, many of which I had put there myself over the past months.

I had been coming out to the Restlawn Memory Gardens at least once every week, and I had gotten in the habit of sometimes stopping at the Ben Franklin's general store in Billville to buy a little angel, at about six or seven bucks a pop, which I would place among the other angels Joshua's regular mourners had left him, along with the blizzard of cigarette butts you could always find around the gravesite.

I took the latest store-bought little angel out of the paper sack and handed it over to Lindsay.

—I wondered what you had in there, she said as she turned the little angel over in her hands. I told her about the time I had brought Mom and my sister out to decorate graves when I had first spotted the Tonka vehicles packed with angels over Joshua Feltzer's grave. When I had started to pocket an angel for a sort of symbol souvenir, my sister had convinced me to put it back where it belonged, you jerk! I mean, what was I thinking, my sister had wanted to know. Stealing an angel from the grave site of a little dead baby. Since then, for reasons I couldn't explain,

I had been hauling little angels out there now and again and leaving them, I told Lindsay.

—You certainly have some peculiar hobbies, Lindsay said. She vaguely gestured at the cigarette butts littered about the gravesite, and then lit one of her own. I fired up a joint. I loved the scorched smell of dope-smoke in fall air.

Lindsay said —I wonder what they think about the proliferation of little angels. When they come out here to mourn for their little boy and see all the extra angels.

I had also wondered about that myself, I told Lindsay, about what the person, or persons, who came out here to smoke like stoves over Joshua Feltzer's grave thought about all the extra angels. I had wondered if they thought it was a sign of some kind, some message from the beyond, some small miracle maybe? Did it fill them with wonder? Did it give them comfort? Or did they think it was some sort of cruel goofing on their grief? I knew myself it wasn't the latter. I sure wasn't making fun of them, I assured Lindsay. But I wasn't sure why I had been doing it. It was a mystery to me, that's what it was, like it was a mystery to the mourners, I said. It just seemed like an interesting, enigmatic thing to do and then write about doing.

—Like the mystery of why Sigourney Weaver beat you up in front of a mirror over an imaginary point of honor?

—Remember the time when little Lulu . . . , I started to say, but when I saw the glint in Lindsay's eyes, simply shut my trap.

—So why did you get so sappy about little boys' graves and little angels? Lindsay asked.

—I don't know. It seemed like something somebody would do in a country song.

—You always have tried to live your life like a country song. Full of fucking melodrama and cheap sentimentality. I hate dumb country music.

—In my book, there's nothing like a High Lonesome soundtrack for the story of a good-old-boy's life.

Lindsay simply shook her head and said —So, where are you going to put this one? She kept turning the new store-bought angel over in her hands. I couldn't read Lindsay's expression. I couldn't tell if she were getting teary or pissed again. I bet teary, standing as we were over a dead baby's grave, for Lindsay was such a softie when it came to country-song items like dead little angely babies. But maybe pissed.

—I don't know where I'll put it, I told her truthfully. The blue grassy beds of Joshua's vehicles were piled with angels, jam-packed, angels tumbled on top of angels, as though the business of Joshua's Tonka vehicles was hauling angels off to some angel-fill. One of the angels in the back of the truck was broken, I saw, its little head knocked clean off. I bent down and picked its headless body up, holding it in the palm of my hand, the cups of its tiny wings framing the chubby, sexless, bone-white body, the hole in its neck like the gaping mouth of a baby bird sprung wide open for a worm, or to sing or scream. I bent down again and fingered through the blue grass until I found its head, whose hair looked like a glittery, golden helmet, and whose eyes, these painted blue dots, gave it a startled look. It was almost too good to be true, as far as symbols go. It couldn't have been better if I had made it up out of the blue.

—Poor little angel guy, Lindsay said and took a long draw on her cigarette.

—What should I do with this broken guy? I said.

—Why don't you keep it for a symbol souvenir, Lindsay said. —Isn't that what you really want to do?

I shrugged, but I accepted this as a sort of permission, and I put the little broken angel and its golden head in my pocket for further consideration and appropriate use.

Lindsay bent over and stubbed her cigarette out in the grass, and then held the butt in her hand.

—Just toss it with the others, I suggested. I put my roach out on my tongue and swallowed it.

—The little angel? Lindsay said and lifted her level gray gaze to my face.

—No, I said, —your butt.

—I'm not a graveside litterbug, Lindsay said.

I said —Nobody would know the difference.

Lindsay said —What about little Joshua? What if he's riding up on one of those clouds looking down at us right now? That could happen in a country song, couldn't it?

—You bet, I said.

Lindsay put the store-bought angel down on the ground and took a tissue from her suitcase of a purse. She knelt and began picking up all the cigarette butts around Joshua's gravesite and folding them into the tissue, which she then put in the purse. Lindsay picked the store-bought angel back up and looked at it again; then she said —I get the picture. You're writing all this up right now, right? As we go along, right? And if I do something interesting enough with the little angel, if I put it in a place that is full of symbolic import, meaningful with metaphor, well, then, lucky me, I get a mention in the book, right? I get a line in your stupid country song, right?

—That's not what I'm doing, I said, getting edgy and scared and huffy. I tried to keep my mind clear as a bell. I needed to remember everything in this scene down to the last detail.

—That's what the fuck you are always doing, dear, Lindsay said softly, and looked at me with her wide gentle gray eyes, like I was a glass tower-of-turds.

—Okay, mister symbol-man, Lindsay said and knelt down. She slipped the little store-bought angel through the open side window of the yellow Tonka truck. She maneuvered it behind the steering wheel. —There you go, Lindsay said and stood up. —Now you've got a little truck-driving angel-man. So tell me, is that enigmatic enough for me to make the book?

—Jesus, I said, really impressed, committing her every word and move to memory. —I wonder what in the world little Joshua Feltzer's mourners will make of that.

—Just spell my name right, Lindsay told me.

—I wonder, I said, —what a little truck-driving angel's handle would be.

—Elvis? Lindsay speculated, and I was really impressed by that too.

—You haven't even said you're sorry, Lindsay said. —What did she mean to you, Chuck? Tell me.

—Not much really, I stammered. —It was just a thing. I was flattered. She made me feel like I wasn't a fat old guy.

—You bet. How can I ever believe anything you say? Ever again. Ever.

—But, but, but . . .

—Or anything you write. How can anybody?

—Okay, in a way I really loved Holly. Giving Holly up was the hardest thing I ever did.

Lindsay turned from me and began to stride down the slope. I stood there for a moment watching her go. Then I hurried after her. When I caught up with her, I took Lindsay by the hand, and we walked like that, my wife of nearly twenty years and I, my bride and I, hand in hand, on down the hill to my vehicle, like we were at the end or the very beginning of some dumb country song.

book nine

FAMOUS LAST DANCE

GHOSTS OF THE HEADLESS COEDS

The ancient, haunted hills of West Virginia are abundant with weird lights and apparitions and ghosts, those sad, lost spirits of the restless and unhappily dead. The famous Greenbrier Ghost even has her own state historic roadside marker, which reads: "Interred in nearby cemetery is Zona Heaster Shue. Her death in 1897 was presumed natural until her spirit appeared to her mother to describe how she was killed by her husband Edward. Autopsy on the exhumed body verified the apparition's account. Edward, found guilty of murder, was sentenced to the state prison. Only known case in which testimony from ghost helped convict a murderer."

Other famous West Virginia ghosts include the Ashton Ghost, and the Ghosts at Brigadoon, and the Ghost of the Blue Light, and the Ghost of the Lost Girl of Grafton. Then there is the Ghost of the Boy Crying in the Rain, and the Ghost of the Lost Hand at Prickett's Fort, the Ghost Wagon of the Seven Loops, the Conscientious Ghost of Meadow River, and the Ghosts of the Lost Ladies of Sunrise, who were two Confederate, camp-following, beautiful young women captured and shot as wanton whore spies by jealous, spiteful, horny Yankees. Then there is a cave in Raleigh County haunted by two drunken ghosts of Confederate soldiers who stumble around while eternally singing "Dixie."

But the saddest ghosts in the state of West Virginia are the Ghosts of the Headless Coeds.

On the Sunday night of January 18, 1970, Mared Malarik and Karen Ferrell, two freshman coeds at West Virginia University, made plans to see the movie *Oliver* with some friends at the Metropolitan Theater in downtown Morgantown. It was a cold mountain night and Mared, a pretty, 5'6" brunette from Kimelon, New Jersey, wrapped her slim body warmly in a brown fur coat. Karen, a petite blond girl from Quinwood, West Virginia, wore a black fur coat and brown slacks. The movie let out about 11 P.M., and the girls decided to hitchhike back to their rooms in Westchester Hall dormitory, which was located across town from the main campus. The girls' friends saw a cream-colored Chevrolet pull over at the intersection where Mared and Karen were hitchhiking, and they watched the girls climb in and the car pull out heading in the direction of the dorm, and the friends didn't give it a second thought.

When the girls didn't return to their dorm that night, their disappearance was quickly noted and reported to the state police, whereupon a state-wide bulletin was issued with their descriptions, and an intense search was launched, but to no avail. Then on the first of March, six weeks after the girls' disappearance, a thirteen-year-old boy looking for empty pop bottles along US 119 near Morgantown found Mared's purse. At that point, Governor Arch Moore (the aforementioned elected outlaw who in later years would languish in a Texas federal pen) directed two units, about a hundred men, of the National Guard to join with state police and an army of volunteers to search the rugged area inch by inch.

Shortly before noon on Thursday, April 16, several National Guardsmen were combing through a thick wilderness area up a narrow hollow about a hundred yards from a dirt access road to an abandoned coal tipple near the old Weirton Mine. They were joking about all the used rubbers they had found around the deserted secondary road, which was clearly a local lovers' lane. One of the guardsmen, a fellow named David Noble, an old buddy of mine, was halfheartedly poking a stick into a large hole in a tree checking for discarded weapons or body parts, or, more hopefully, hidden contraband, jars of moonshine or bags of marijuana, say, when he happened to glance up at a scurrying sound. Noble lit a joint and just stood there for a moment gazing around the rough terrain, wondering how long this tramping about the woods would go on. Then Noble spotted a gnawed human foot sticking from beneath a pile of brush not ten feet away.

As the authorities began uncovering the bodies, it became clear that the murderer had taken a great deal of time and effort to hide them. Six or seven slabs of heavy stone had been hauled from a creekbed thirty feet away and placed over the corpses of the coeds, and then the stones were in turn covered with logs and limbs and more rocks and then leaves, until a small mound had been formed over the dead girls. Under the debris, both girls were found lying on their stomachs in something of a cruciform position, with Karen Ferrell's legs crossing those of Mared Malarik. Both bodies were badly decomposed. Also, both girls had been decapitated, and their heads were nowhere to be found.

My buddy Noble showed up that evening at the Washington Café, or Auggie's, as we called it, where all the hip, doper college kids and long-haired professors hung out in those days in Morgantown. Noble was still dressed in his muddy National Guard camouflage fatigues, something he was way too cool to normally do. I could tell something was bothering him. He was uncharacteristically quiet, for one thing, and didn't strut about babbling and boasting as he usually did, anything to be the center of attention. Rooster-boy was Noble's nickname back in those days. Noble gulped down a couple of beers not saying anything, and he kept running his hands back through his shaggy dirty-blond hair and shaking his big, oddly shaped head. He was clearly rattled about something, and it occurred to me that he had finally strangled his beautiful, faithless wife Sally (a woman Noble would divorce and remarry four times over the years to come), but was just too cool to admit to it. When the local evening news came on, Noble asked Auggie, this little bit of an Italian fellow who owned the place, to turn up the sound on the big set above the bar. And, lo and behold, there was Noble being interviewed on television about finding the bodies of the dead girls in the woods.

During the interview, Noble had a cigarette coolly dangling from his thin lips, and he talked in a low but steady voice as he described in detail seeing the half-eaten foot of a dead girl sticking out from a pile of debris deep in the dark woods. —This is it, Noble had said directly into the

421

television camera and took a deep, dramatic drag off his cigarette, while shaking his craggy, wolfish face. —This is the end of ordinary life, Noble said, as he flicked the cigarette toward the trees. This town would never be the same for him, Noble said, now that he had discovered the headless bodies of those dead girls in the dark heartless woods. Those dead girls had been some kind of cruel signal for him, Noble said, some kind of evil sign of the times. Life, even in a small, university, mountain community like Morgantown, Noble intoned meaningfully in his best baritone, could never be sweet and innocent and ordinary again. Noble was clearly stoned out of his mind at this, probably the high point of his life, in terms of attention and recognition anyway. At Auggie's you could have heard the proverbial pin drop. Until I started snickering.

A month or so later, Noble took a notion to return to the scene of the crime, and I tagged along. After a half-hour ride over twisty blacktop two-lanes, we finally pulled over and parked alongside of that old dirt mine-access road in the hills south of town. There was another car parked a ways up the road from us. I noticed it had New Jersey tags, and I recalled that Mared Malarik, one of the murdered coeds, had been from New Jersey. The vehicle was empty, unless some couple was doing it down in the seat. Noble was subdued, and so was I. Instead of heading down the brush-filled slope into the shadowy woods to search for the scene of the crime, we both just hopped up on the warm hood of the car and fired up joints, while we listened to country music on the radio and didn't have much to say.

Ever since the bodies of the girls had been found, those woods had been packed with people in search of the lost heads, for which the girls' families had offered a hefty reward. Most of those searchers had been sincere, sad and serious, but some were carloads of drunken, idiot frat-rat louts, the kind of punks who topple tombstones for a prank, and to whom dead girls simply meant a little less nooky in the world but some potential reward money. Those frat bums had taken to running through the hills with flashlights for fraternity initiations, hooting and screeching insanely, as though those woods were their own to haunt like evil, angry spooks. Finally some carload of drunk dopes had roared back to town one night with the story of the headless ghosts of the girls, who the wasted witnesses claimed they had seen stumbling silently through the trees exactly like what they were, namely the headless ghosts of girls without eyes to see or tongues to cry out, their slender, smoky arms outstretched as they groped and clutched and waved hands like haze before them.

Unlike the stories of the Lovely Ghosts of the White Ladies of Powell Mountain, or even the Drowned Ladies of Cheat Lake who rose from mist and fog full of sad grace and beauty, the Ghosts of the Headless Coeds were awkward and gangly, goofy and comical somehow in the recounting, like the funny old stories of the headless English ghost of Anne Boleyn lurching and weaving in and out of stone walls and walking out of windows to be blown about castle battlements like a tiny cloud.

We sat on the hood of the car smoking as the arriving spring evening settled as gently as a warm fog onto the mountain, the shadows down the slope spreading and thickening like slick, black pools of oil. The damp odor of the woods hung in the clean mountain air like fresh wash left out all day in the sun. The fresh smell of resin rose from a stand of pines at the edge of the trees. The sure, comforting sounds of cicadas began to click from the brush and from the trees down the slope and from around the darkening shapes of rocks that looked like big black eggs scattered about the hillside. A few early lightning bugs blinked like small hot eyes in the darkening air. Although the sky was clear and I could see the evening star and the pale, rising, cat-grin moon, there was a light breeze with the clean feel of coming rain in it. Ordinary words cannot capture the profound sense of sadness, of the presence of such a vast unhappiness, I suddenly felt there alive at the edge of those sweet woods.

Noble fired up another joint, and after holding a big toke until he was bug-eyed, he began babbling about that loss of ordinary life again. Those poor girls would sure never return to their sweet, young ordinary lives again. The only world those dead girls had now was all of death, all of evil. And the families, the moms and dads and friends of those murdered girls, they would be haunted by the lost faces of those young girls forever. Boyfriends would grow old remembering the sweet scent of those girls' summer skins, the springwater taste of their mouths, Noble muttered, emitting probably the most poetic words of his turbulent life.

I was twenty-seven that year. What came to me that evening by the woods was that my own ordinary life, such as it was, was over for me. At that point I didn't have idea one about how or exactly when, but I knew I was on a bus out of my own ordinary life. And in August of that summer I did it. I left my first wife and punted my promising teaching position. I got aboard a Greyhound bus and rode it west, wide-eyed with fear and hope to San Francisco, that gateway into the Age of Aquarius, to start all over again, maybe reinvent myself as some kind of flower child, another endeavor I failed at utterly.

The stars came out over those woods where Noble had found the bodies of the dead girls, and the pure, tender, mountain air of that spring night was cool and calm and unconcerned. I trembled suddenly, and tears sprung to my eyes. I felt like such a fucking sap. I glanced over to see if Noble had noticed my momentary sentimental collapse, but he was just smoking and looking off into the night woods.

I flipped my butt sparking toward the woods, hopped down off the hood, and hauled out my hog for some relief. But just as I started to let fly, aiming my golden arc toward the dark line of trees, the hair on the back of my neck suddenly bristled. I had a sudden feeling that Noble and I were not alone there at the edge of the woods. I had a terrific, almost instinctive sense of another presence. The night around us was full of that feeling, shaky with that awareness, the grass and bushes and trees down the slope almost crackling with it. When I looked into the dark woods, I saw something moving through them. But it had not been a sad, goofy, stumbling ghost of a headless girl. What I saw was a single, small, round roving light. It was a flashlight. The flashlight of somebody searching high and low for things lost in the woods. Somehow I knew it was somebody from New Jersey, the owner of the car up the road from us. Some father or brother, or boyfriend, from New Jersey searching for things lost in the woods. And just what would they do, I wondered, if they actually found them, those lost heads of their dear murdered girls? That light moved slowly among the trees within the dark woods like a little yellow lost moon.

GHOST MAYOR

I ritually drive the five or six miles south past the Billville turnoff to where I ritually turn off the four-lane left onto old Route 16. I duck low in my seat as I pass the Skyline Drive-In at Hilltop, although I don't see Baddest Bill's blue Ford pickup parked in front anywhere, nor catch a glimpse of the lovely Mary X through the steamy windows. Just a piece down the road, I throw a ritual left off the two-lane onto the Red Star Road shortcut and twist over the hill a country mile or so until I come to the Dunloup Creek Road, where I throw another ritual left. I am headed for maybe the one hundredth time deep down into the New River Gorge to the legendary ghost town of Thurmond, which John Sayles had used for the location of his movie *Matewan*.

Thurmond had been a turn-of-the-century railroad boomtown founded by Captain William Dabney Thurmond, who had made a fearful reputation among local Unionists as the Confederate leader of the Thurmond Rangers during the Civil War. The bearded, hawk-nosed Thurmond was an upright Baptist, and he ruled his town with the unforgiving iron hand of a patriarchal, Bible-thumping bluenose. The town thrived upon the serious and respectable business of making money in a new industrial era; yet, ironically, because of the sin-filled surrounding area, the town had acquired, over time, the legendary reputation of an outlaw community. Diagonally across the New River, at the mouth of Dunloup Creek, like the town of Thurmond's dark twin sister, the wild and glamorous community of Glen Jean rose up, with its dazzling array of saloons, dance halls, and houses of ill repute.

Upstream and across the river from Thurmond proper, Thomas McKell, the coal baron who had founded Glen Jean, had built the one-hundred-room showpiece Dunglen Hotel, a rambling, frame, three-and-a-half-story architecturally eclectic building surrounded by double-decker porches, its name proudly displayed in giant electric light-bulb letters on the roof. It was an establishment for the coal-rich ruling-class cocksuckers, famous for its freewheeling nightlife of beautiful imported fallen women and a hotel bar that never closed its doors a moment from when it opened in 1901 until state prohibition took effect in 1914. It was famous also for high-stakes gambling, which included one game of poker that was recorded in *Ripley's Believe It or Not* because it continued nonstop for fifteen years. For those were the wondrous old days when, as one journalist of the time described them, "champagne flowed like water at the Dunglen Hotel and hardly a night passed that robbery or murder was not done down by the railroad bridge."

After crossing the narrow bridge over the New River, I park beside the boarded-up wood-frame two-story train station at the end of town. I stroll back to the bridge and walk out on it and lean against its iron railing to watch the evening settle as gently as a curtain down over the shadowy mountainsides of the steep gorge. The bridge is an iron railroad bridge, with a set of train tracks along one side and along the other a single-lane motor-vehicle crossing with iron-mesh grates for a surface, as opposed to pavement. I watch as the light lifts like fog from the gorge and clings to the mountaintops briefly before seeping into the aperture of darkening evening sky. Below, through the iron mesh of the bridge's bottom, I can see the black foamy water churn, and the ripples of the swift shallow river are lambent in the fading light. I once brought Holly and the kids down to this place, and her boy and I had practiced spitting through the iron grates into the river rushing dizzily beneath our feet, until Holly had barked at us to behave.

In the old days I could have seen the electric lights sparkling on the verandas of the elegant Dunglen across the water, where handsome rich folks would have been parading before supper, and I could have seen the smoky yellow lights of the saloons along the river bank yonder, and their long shivery reflections on the dark current. The Dunglen burned down in 1930 under suspicious circumstances, and that pretty much ended the old high life in the gorge. I breathe deeply in the air rising off the river and feel it clean to the bottom of my lungs. I love this old ghostly gorge, and for all the time I have abided in Billville, I have come out to this place often to enjoy the company of the departed where I feel at peace.

Years back, a very drunken Italian fellow had attempted to prove he could fly like an angel by leaping from the center of this very bridge, but he had fallen like a rock into the river, whose strong undercurrent had washed his drowned body up an hour later downstream at Rush Run. When old Mayor Leo Schaffer was duly called upon for a death inquest, he had summarily fined the dead Italian on the spot the eighty-one dollars and gold watch they found in his pockets for the misdemeanor of committing suicide within the town limits. When a burly relative of the fallen Italian angel had complained, Harrison Ash, the sheriff and a man of legendary easy conscience, beat the turds out of the big Italian and threw him in the lockup for un-American attitudes. Harrison Ash, who was six-foot-four and weighed 275 pounds, wore a Western Stetson and reputedly had eighteen notches on the pearl handle of his pistol. Sheriff Ash was able to maintain a semblance of order in the wild town by basically terrorizing the lawless. Law and order clearly broke down within his own family, however. For when his wife, Mrs. Isabel Ash, stood trial for murder in 1910, it emerged that she had accidentally shot the wrong party while out gunning for her husband, the legendary sheriff.

I stroll down the railroad tracks toward the ruins of a town where spirits were known to walk abroad by whim, day or night. Thurmond had also been mentioned in *Ripley's Believe It or Not* as a town with no streets. The train tracks ran within feet of the front of the main business block, and Berry Mountain rose like a wall of dirt from directly behind the row of brick buildings. I can see distant window lights from the few cabins still occupied high up on the ridge of Berry Mountain, but that is all there is left of human life around here, those dozen or so souls whose little houses hang to the side of the gorge above town. When I stroll past the old post office, another building which has not yet joined the disappeared, I stop to peer within its windows, my reflected face in the ancient wavy glass like a wanted poster of myself from another lawless life.

What's actually still left of the town of Thurmond, which was once called "The Dodge City of West Virginia," is a row of several three-story stone or brick buildings, their window-fronts mostly boarded up or broken out. At the east end of the block is the old Mankin building, which once housed J. Ward Mankin's drug store and the New River Banking & Trust and marked the city limits. Next to it is a handsome stone building where the Standard Dry Goods used to be and Mrs. McClure's restaurant, whose windows were filled with flags and portraits of local GIs during World War II, and where soldiers in uniform ate free.

On down the block is the entrance to the Banker's Hotel, and then the National Bank of Thurmond, with its stately granite-block facade and twin Grecian pillars. Further down the tracks is a large, house-sized coaling tower, where once coal cars were filled, the same tower a flock of birds lifts from in Sayles's movie *Matewan,* and sweeps up as a body into the blue sky just moments before the final big gun battle breaks out. When John Sayles made his movie in 1986, he found that with only a few alterations, such as awnings and benches and polished windows filled with signs and goods for sale, the ruins of the old town made a ghostly movie-double for the Matewan of 1921. For a time the sounds of gun-shots once again rang out along the banks of this river.

I mosey on out between the two sets of tracks still running through town to a place I have concluded was the site for the shootout scene in *Matewan.* Upon that spot, I take out my blue snub-nose .38 Detective Special. Upon a post at the far side of the tracks near the bank of the river, I position a dead soldier named George Dickel. I commence quick-drawing my .38 and firing at George, the sounds of my shots cracking the evening silence of the narrow river valley, their echoes reverberating back through the darkening hills like the distant barks of dogs. On maybe the fourth try, I plug George. I blast George to smithereens. I blow smoke from my gun barrel, and then with a fancy gunfighter twirl I holster it. I am the last man standing. I am Sid Hatfield. I am the real sheriff of this movie.

In my mind's eye, I can see those bloody moments in the movie *Matewan* unfold at this very same site when the scene explodes into mayhem, as Sid Hatfield and the Baldwin-Felts draw and fire and shots ring out from the miners ducked back in the doorways and the gun-thugs on the tracks open up and Sid stands there blazing away with both barrels as he backs toward the cover of a building's corner and the air is heavy and thick with white smoke in which the gunfighters disappear and reappear like ghost dancers in some desperate death-and-resurrection ritual.

No, in my imagination I am the mayor of this movie. I am Mayor C. C. Testerman, and I grab my betrayed, spilling, doppelganger guts and spin around dramatically and fall onto the tracks to die like a shot-down dog. I lay there like a fallen, fat, heroic, betrayed, gut-shot mayor. I lay there waiting for my sweet Jessie lamb to rush to me and take my fat head in her lap as I leak to death in the dirt. Even in the midst of my death scene, I somehow know that ten days hence, in the land of the living, Jessie will be in the strong, fast arms of my best friend, Police Chief Sid Hatfield. But because of the kind of mayor I have always been, I will try not to haunt them in the land of the living.

I am a ghost mayor now, of a ghost town. Now there is a notion I can embrace. As a ghost, I will enjoy the privilege of passing through walls. I can haunt through the wooded hills about town, keeping people awake until all hours. I let myself imagine my old friends telling affectionate, amusing ghost stories about me. I can imagine fading into nothing but a pale set of sad eyes and weak smile in the darkness. I can imagine my ghostly voice sounding like a call from a deep well. I can imagine, on long dark nights when I can finally no longer abide it, floating in through Jessie and Sid's bedroom wall, and invisibly farting like thunder. Could ghosts, I wonder, get boners? Could ghosts jerk off? What I cannot imagine is a tranquil peace for myself in these hills, my ghost boner and I. Nobody can ever imagine successfully a quiet slumber for the dead in this ancient agitated landscape.

DIFFERENT CREEK

I am cruising through a series of neat little towns down on Route 16 as I follow along the shallow coal-darkened waters of Slab Fork Creek. I pass through Helen and Amigo and Allen's Junction, all little communities full of well-kept shingled houses with wire-link fenced yards. I pass businesses like Billy Bob's Feed & Hardware and Betty Lou's Beauty Shoppe *For Gal's Only* and Tucky's Bar, and an old barn of a beerjoint called the Hillbilly Hot Spot. I pass any number of those ubiquitous southern West Virginia Baptist churches, one with a sign in front announcing NO CHURCH SUNDAY NITE DUE TO BIG FUNERAL, and below that HAPPY BIRTHDAY BABY JESUS. I count a dozen or more drained above-ground swimming pools beside doublewides with poured-concrete front porches. I have come to suspect that any of those little towns was the sort of place where I can put down roots and fit in. I can pleasantly imagine how a doublewide with a little poured-concrete front porch and an above-ground pool beside the Slab Fork Creek, with the Hillbilly Hot Spot right down the road, can become almost heaven for a good-old-boy like me.

All along the twisting road I am traveling down this particular day in early December, the neat little houses drip with Christmas decorations. Their fenced yards are full of jolly Santas being pulled in sleds by prancing plastic reindeer. And angels, angels are everywhere, clusters of angels gathered in yards, tiny angels perched on fences like the frail ghosts of doves, as though a congregation of angels, a company of angels, has descended through the smoky air like Christmasy grace upon the little towns along the Slab Fork. Southern West Virginians and their goddamn angels!

Sappy with stoned sentimentality this drifting December day, I have the sudden notion that maybe those legions of angels have descended to serve as witnesses, little angels with wings like haze whose gentle vision has settled upon the closed, solitary lives of the people in the hollows like a sort of holiness. Or maybe you could think of those little interlopers as heavenly spies, undercover Baptist preacher angels, little right-wing mealy-mouthed moral midgets descended to rat out the irreligious, the drunks and fornicators and other local fun-lovers. In my own book, angels are purely problematic dream creatures, either hip new-agey beings or backwoods religiousy riddles, but the sort of riddles that can cause even a hard heart to quicken with metaphor, which is the first blink of belief.

I have gone on record, though, that as a genuine West Virginian-American I believe in ghosts. And I believe in alien life forms, who come down in the dark to fornicate with cows and sheep and homecoming queens and politicians and preachers of every stripe and just plain old folks throughout West Virginia. And I am gathering the evidence. It is my essential mission in life these days.

As I round a slight bend just past Allen's Junction, I spot a grizzled old coot wearing a shabby overcoat and a red Santa Claus hat sitting in a green metal lawn chair on the far bank of the shallow creek. He has a scraggly white beard and long shaggy white hair. He is holding what looks like about a half-full fifth bottle of either hair tonic or possibly whiskey in his lap, and he is simply sitting there famously on the bank by the creek, his legs crossed and sort of tipping back in the chair, as he gazes at the slowly flowing, cold, dark water, grinning like Willie Nelson.

An eccentric old-coot character, surely locally beloved and famous, wearing a red Santa hat, is simply sitting there drinking either hair tonic or whiskey beside that winter creek as though it is the most natural and satisfying thing in the world to be doing.

Well, maybe it is. To my trained eye, it's clear that that old coot is a philosopher. Even if the current of that creek shrinks to no more than a thin trickle like a slowly overflowing sink, it is a form of transport for the old-coot philosopher I can readily appreciate. That old-coot philosopher lives to sit there beside that thinly flowing water even in the dead of winter, because every moment it is a different creek.

Even from where I am passing slowly in my vehicle up on the two-lane blacktop, I am sure I can see tiny blue shapes darting in the shallow water at the old-coot philosopher's feet, flashing in that cold tiny flow. For me, that famous old coot wearing a red Santa Claus hat settled philosophically upon a green metal lawn chair beside a creek in the dead of winter is my ghost of Christmas future.

With any luck, I reflect, that famous old philosopher coot could be me some day.

GHOST GEOGRAPHY

The summer after my sabbatical, I returned to Billville for my brother-in-law's big Five-O birthday bash, which was a blast. So that my sister would not have to be burdened, all the local ladies had brought countless covered dishes, and Charlie and Emily Mahood were cooking a couple of pigs in pits in the yard. There were kegs in every corner of the vast back yard, and endless mason jars of moonshine made the rounds. The Boy Red's group, The Rock Garden Bluegrass Band, blasted away all the late afternoon and early evening from the side porch. Later, when they had to pull out to do a nighttime paying gig out at the Pines, my brother-in-law's own group cranked it up. Lovelene was up from Charlotte, and she and my brother-in-law harmonized like in the old days. All of Lovelene's old lover-boys, Doublewide Ron and good old Pete and her ex-husband Fuzzy, circled one another warily, itching to draw.

When my brother-in-law's band took a break, Fuzzy got behind the microphone to make a drunken sentimental speech and raise a toast to the birthday boy. As soon as my sister had led Fuzzy and my brother-in-law away arm in arm weeping profusely, the Squire got up to make another speech. Then a line formed, and the speeches didn't conclude until disrupted by a fairly good dog fight. Finally Duffy Boyd and his bluegrass boys began picking and everybody began rocking out around the yard again. It was a great old-time party, and the sheriff wasn't called even once, which would have been a waste of time anyway, seeing as how he was there and drunk as a skunk himself.

I absconded with a jar of shine and strolled down through the back field past the big vegetable garden to the apple tree at the edge of the woods. I slid into the old tire swing and began to push myself up and back slowly and sip the shine and watch from a distance that great community of my sister and brother-in-law's family and friends celebrating. There was a crescent moon in the cloudless sky and an infinite field of those particular constellations you can see nowhere else on the face of the Earth save in the heavens above West Virginia. Fido, my brother-in-law's old, dumb, shaggy dog, had followed me down the hill. I fired up a joint and blew smoke into his smiley face.

Up the hill, I heard the clang of iron and gunshots, the sounds of men playing serious horseshoes drunk in the dark. I heard my brother-in-law give a Rebel yell, which probably meant he had received still yet another present he appreciated mightily. Earlier he had been trying to teach his new grandson, Jacob Lane, how to give a Rebel yell, a lesson that had not succeeded perhaps because the boy was a month old. My brother-in-law had put a pair of oversized cool shades not unlike his own upon the bald tyke, and had toted him proudly about the yard for an hour like a beloved joke on himself. My niece had turned out to be a wonderful little mom. My niece had a job up at the Comfort Inn as a receptionist, and she had moved into Grandmaw Pearl's little house when I left town. She wanted to go back to school and learn computers and maybe someday move down to the good life in Charlotte. My niece was dating maybe the sweetest, best, hardworking boy I had ever met, whose name was Kenny Baire.

The Boy Red had a hard winter. He and a buddy were caught cold, spotlighting deer. They had their guns confiscated and were fined big-time. They had also spent ten hard days in the Braxton County Jail, which was a regional jail, and very unlike a regular county lockup where you can pull your time yawning and jerking-off. Up at Braxton, you had the opportunity to wear yellow uniforms and were transported in leg irons and handcuffs and waist chains, and you were in the company of hardened, older men who winked at you dangerously. So it was, however, according to my brother-in-law, that the Boy Red took his can of whuppen without whine one, pulled that jail time cool as a copperhead, and even duked out a couple of tough horny convicts in the showers.

Somehow the Boy Red had also managed to carry, and pass with flying colors, sixteen hours at Tech, which meant he had only a term to go before he headed for Houston where my kid brother had a job waiting for him. My kid brother had spotted the Boy Red's business acumen from that time years ago when the Boy Red had pumped up his dad's joke-gift Inflatable Naked Lady life-sized sex-balloon, and had pimped that pocket-pussy to his little pals for a quarter a pop.

Things in my family could have been worse. I sat there swinging slowly on that old tire and sipping shine and studying my fate in the stars without great trepidation at that particular moment, nor understanding, for that matter.

Presently I moseyed back up the hill to find Mom, who I had promised a ride home. I found her sitting on the front porch all alone. —Hey, Momma, what's happening? I inquired of Momma. Mom was in one of her moods, clammed up and ready to roll. Mom's knees were bothering her bad, and she held onto my arm as we made our way around the road side of the house to avoid any random gunfire and the raucous partyers, who were taking no prisoners as they celebrated their hardcore country lives full-tilt and without excuses.

By the time we arrived at the Red Ride down by the barn, I was practically carrying Mom. As I drove her over to her little house out Lindberg Road, she simply sat there gazing out the window, sighing now and then loud enough so that I would surely hear her. But when I asked her what was wrong, Mom snapped: —Nothing. Nothing at all, Chuckie. I asked Mom if she was upset with me in particular about something, and she had snapped —No. I knew what Momma was upset about. She was upset and sick with worry about Lindsay and me. Mom was upset about the fact that I had about everything I thought I might need for the rest my natural life loaded in the back of the Red Ride. I was traveling into my high lonesome sunset light. But I didn't study on talking about it. And if Momma brought it up insistently, I'd have to smack the sweet little old church-lady. You bet.

436

I walked Momma up onto her porch and waited while she unlocked her door. I saw the old nosy bat next door in her window, but I didn't flip her anything. At Mom's request, I searched throughout her little house, looking in her closets and under her bed and behind every door. But neither that O. J. killer nor Iron Mike was home. I gave Mom a big goodnight hug and kiss and shared a semi-sob with her at the door for both the past and future and who knows what. I was sappy with sentimentality, a real dangerous emotion for me, daredevil and teary. As I peeled out, I hammered the horn and gave a Rebel yell to provide the nosy old bat next door with something to take to her grave.

For no good reason, I threw a left north when I hit the four-lane as I hunted for the perfect exit from these pages that had dictated what I did, had done, was going to do, for way too long. The traffic was too heavy for me to stop in the middle of the Gorge Bridge as had been my late-night custom, in order to piss into the abyss and brood and barf. For no good reason, I rolled on out to the Route 60 Midland Trail turnoff, and swung west toward Ansted with Roy Orbison singing "In Dreams" on the tape deck. In no time I was at the entrance to the Restlawn Memory Gardens cemetery, the Bernard Coffindaffer cluster of crosses rising like mystery totem poles in the moonlight. The gate to the graveyard was closed, so I sat there sipping from my mason jar of moonshine for a spell and listening to Roy Orbison singing "Blue Angel."

I drove on over ghostly Gauley Mountain down Route 60, passing through Victor, where on a bluff to the right Papaw Parsons's old rambling frame farm house once stood, before he burned it to the ground for the insurance. A few years later, he was found dead on the floor of that trailer he had set on the old house's foundation, a half-empty fifth bottle of Old Crow just out of his reach. I cruised slowly through Ansted, where the mother of Stonewall Jackson is buried. It took all the character I possessed not to pull over at that friendly tavern at the edge of town, with its soft yellow light falling through the open doorway into the warm summer night, where Papaw Parsons is recalled to this day as the best wrist-wrestler in the county ever. I cruised past the Paddlers' Paradise Motel, which brought pleasantly to mind a particular night there and old sweetie-pie.

It took all the character I possessed not to pull over at the little white-frame Lovers Leap Baptist Church, ablaze on the hillside. The sounds of joyful song and holy shouts were soaring through its opened doors. I could easily imagine myself in that tabernacle, being swept up into a delirium of deliverance. I could easily imagine myself becoming a foot-washing fool and flinging copperheads high into the air to catch coming down with one hand.

I passed the old stone buildings and parking area of the Hawks Nest State Park picnic grounds and scenic overlook, from where you can see the mouth of Hawks Nest Tunnel, which was built to divert the turbulent current of the New River from its broad, rocky channel that meanders around a bend through the mountain to a power house where four huge turbines generate electricity for United Carbon Company plants down the river.

Here's another West Virginia ghost story to take home with you. The tunnel, which was begun in 1930 and completed in 1933, and is 16,252 feet long, was drilled through a mountain of almost pure silica. While digging Hawks Nest Tunnel, hundreds of miners, mostly migrant blacks, had dropped so regularly of deadly silicosis that their shack community was called "Town of the Living Dead." At least 476 workers had died, and over a thousand more suffered from silicosis. Of those dead miners, 169 were buried in a field at Summerville, with cornstalks as their only grave markers. A Nicholas County undertaker had been given a contract to bury the black miners at $55 a head. Sometimes a man would be buried within an hour after he died. The graveyard is in a little valley this side of Summerville, and to this day not a single grave of the victims is marked.

Around a couple of hairpin turns, I drove beneath the shadow of the old Hanging Tree, where, according to local legend, outlaws used to be strung up ritually and left for crow-bait and passersby to ponder. Dad used to pull off the road there on our way to Mawmaw and Papaw Parsons's farm for us kids to pee and reflect. I can still recall Dad's story of being a boy and seeing a naked black man swinging from a limb of that tree. I can recall seeing the secret totems hung like gifts to the dead in that ghost-tree, polished bones and bits of glass strung like Christmas decorations on fishing line that glittered in the sunlight.

I rounded the bend where, over the hill, they had found the dismembered body parts of poor Mike Rogers, and later of Sammy Smith, two of the many mysteriously disappeared in Fayette County, including all those unfortunate fools who dared to hitchhike over Gauley Mountain on this very road at night. It may have been the reflection of my lights in the mountain mist, but for a moment I swore I saw the ghost of poor old Mike Rogers's head rising up from over yonder by the road like a ghost balloon, still in that clear plastic bag, his eyes wide open as though with wonder.

Braking around a sharp bend, I pulled the Red Ride over at the Mystery Hole wide spot, which was closed for the night. There was a chain strung across the entrance of its little roadside parking lot. I sat there while I smoked a joint and listened to Dwight Yoakam sing "A Thousand Miles From Nowhere." I gazed up at that enormous fiberglass gorilla perched on the roof of Willie Wilson's holy Quonset hut among the overlapping, shady branches of trees, its mighty King Kong arms raised as though in rage or worship, its eyes wide and white and its white-fanged mouth frozen in an arrested roar or hymn. I sat there in my vehicle smoking a little dope and sipping a little shine and listening to the Mavericks sing that sad blue neon song about the memory of a red dress hanging on a door.

Lindsay had not deserved any of it. Like my home state, Lindsay had been cheated and robbed blind and plundered. No other diamond, save for Lindsay, has ever been discovered in the coal seams of my home state. Our marriage, dying deep in my mine and abandoned there, like the imprint of an ancient rose, had made Lindsay's candle-flame condemned eyes look a billion years old. The long hole behind Lindsay's life was my mine. In the Mystery Hole, where the dust of old-time oceans hangs thick and dangerous, they used to send in canaries to try the air. Take a deep breath, honey, I should have said to Lindsay the day I married her, try your wings.

I sat in the Red Ride that night outside the Mystery Hole sipping shine and listening to the gritty whiskey wail of Waylon Jennings, memory eating at me. I looked up through clouds faint as ghosts at the crescent moon, that scary old grin. This world looks different from up there. All this cold blue. Living on the moon would be lonely, small-time to Earth's big-time, no beerjoints of blue neon. That night, I could feel the moon's pull and didn't know what to make of it. I could feel myself spinning, dizzy, giving, I guess, in to gravity. The passing of Old Mister Time cast sorrowful shadows, like great slow wings, over the old hills. In my home state the air is full of ashes, the hills thick with snakes. West Virginia is that state famous for its solitude and isolation, not to mention all the trapped dead and disappeared. In my home state, some nights are long enough to have two or three moons.

Dressed up in her elegant pain, Lindsay had looked so lovely and full of grace that evening in May when she informed me she was really considering going it alone. Lindsay had been poring over a map of Montana, her own home state, spread out on the kitchen table. Lindsay was talking about new starts when last I set eyes upon my wife of over twenty years, my bride who, I had come to realize maybe too late, I loved with all my heart.

STARS AND BARS

I threw a left at Chimney Corners onto Route 16, the Laurel Creek Road, and headed south back through the night toward Billville. At each suicide curve in the twisting switchbacks, my headlights swept those ubiquitous silvery spray-painted admonitions high on the faces of cliffs that rose like curtains of rock at the edge of the road to REPENT, and that old news flash that JESUS SAVES.

I rattled across the narrow, rickety, Charles Rogers Memorial Bridge. Charles Rogers, one of Fayette County's most illustrious sons, was a black soldier who had won the Congressional Medal of Honor and had risen to the rank of general. Below his collapsing memorial bridge in the New River bed were rocky islands where my first dear wife and I had once picnicked when we were dating. On a towel spread over warm stone, I had finger-fornicated with her for the first time, sealing the fact of our true love and disastrous future. I dipped in and out of pockets of fog, and, even over the sound of my tires on the damp road, I could hear the rush and waterfalls of Laurel Creek tumbling down its rocky course off the mountain.

I roared past the old Ball's Mill and the ghost beerjoint, which, before its interior burned up and then its river-rock walls were leveled, had been called the Canyon Lodge. To this day, on particularly dark moonless nights you can still sometimes hear the spooky strains of jukebox music and faint laughter and echoes of what sound like distant gunshots.

I hit the straight stretches at Beckwith blaring David Allen Coe outlaw-biker, shit-kicking tunes while I burned rubber up the empty nighttime two-lane. The occasional lights from little houses or trailers back off the road were about as blurry as my life. Then I spotted the blinking yellow lights of the Pines roadhouse coming up on the left, surrounded by pickups and Harleys and clunkers, and spelled out on its sign in front was the name of the night's house band, THE ROCK GARDEN BLUEGRASS BOYS, the Boy Red's group. Not seeing much selection in the matter, I slammed on my brakes and slid into the river gravel and red dog of the little parking lot.

The big low-slung cinderblock barn of a beerjoint was packed with rowdy river rats and ridge-runners and bikers with their tattooed trollop babes. It was rank with the smell of sweat and cheap perfume and sour beer and barbeque pork rinds, plus suffused with palpable clouds of blue smoke. In the flickering lights of fancy beer signs around the walls, shadows of the dancers at the back of the room jerked like old-timey movies. Above both pool tables in the middle of the room, where balls cracked sides and spun on green that burned your eyes, lights slung low from the ceiling settled soft yellow pools of illumination wherein skin looked startled and new.

Mary X was real easy to look at in that soft yellow light, as she stood over there in her wide-legged, swell-thighed, full-hipped, doomed but asskicker Appalachian-Woman-Attitude stance. Her wet red mouth was as petulant and resolute as ever. I hadn't set eyes on that woman in six months maybe. Mary X stood there chalking her stick reflectively, apparently not spotting my entrance. When she took her shot and sunk it, she didn't whoop like she used to do in the old days, which made me wonder if she still longed for me yet.

I eased my way into a place at the bar and ordered a Bud from one of the Spearen boys, a friend of the Boy Red's, who was a new part-owner of the Pines and respectfully called me Mr. Kinder when he served up the beer, a result of my minor fame due to local write-ups, not to mention my advanced age and the fact that I always tipped him with an affected extravagance. I guzzled that cold, longneck bottle of Bud and tried to sharpen my perceptions in the fuzzy room, tried to make faces and memories, regrets and excuses, seem clearer in the flickering neon night.

The Boy Red's band was on a break, so I figured he was probably out back smoking dope. I guzzled another longneck Bud while I slouched down at the bar and kept my eyes off Mary X. I kept my back to that long-legged, wet, red-mouthed woman. Somebody started punching tear-jerk country songs on the jukebox. In the blue-tinted mirror behind the bar, I watched as couples across the big room collapsed into one another's hungry arms and began to slow-dance and commence some serious sucking of necks. Mary X was now a redhead, I couldn't help but notice in the mirror, and the backs of her long legs were silky in that sweet pool-table light, as her short black leather skirt lifted when she bent over to make a perfect shot. When she straightened to chalk her cue one time, our eyes met in the blue-tinted mirror.

Almost at the same moment I saw Mary's blue-tinted reflection sashaying across the room toward me, out of the corner of my eye I spotted Baddest Bill hulking through the front door. Old Baddest hadn't changed much, I observed in my shivery peripheral vision. He was still about the meanest-looking motherfucker I had seen before in my life. He looked like a black-bearded, tattooed, evil, fierce killer-refrigerator. I pretended as though I had dropped something important on the floor, such as my false teeth or glass eye. I dove down among the stools and boots before the bar. Peeking out from under my arm, I observed that Baddest Bill made straightaway for Mary, intercepted her beeline to me, as a matter of fact, and to my trained eye it looked as though they took to fussing. At which point I considered crawling rapidly from the room, but on second thought figured that might draw even more attention than if I simply tried to skulk out.

Pulling my cap as far down over my face as I could, I stood up and as nonchalantly as possible picked up my wad of beer-wet bills from the bar. —Hey, thanks for coming on out, Mister Kinder, sir, the Spearen boy boomed above the room ruckus. Jesus fucking Christ, I reflected, automatically waving my hand at him to pipe down, which the Spearen boy took as an offer to shake, and he crunched my paw in a grip of iron and pumped my arm like he was jacking up a car, all the time booming out —Thanks, Mister Kinder, thanks, man, sir! I kept my eyes on the blue reflections of Baddest Bill and Mary, as they stood there while she wagged a finger in his huge ugly face and he shook his massive head in some sort of desperate denial. I observed the Boy Red come in the back door with the rest of his rhinestone redneck band buddies, and truck on over to a distant corner where their instruments and stools waited within a wire-mesh cage.

I peeled off a twenty from my wad and handed it to the Spearen boy and told him to buy my nephew and his band a couple of rounds on me. The Spearen boy waved the bill in the air like a little exultant flag hollering across the room to the Boy Red, hey, looky here, his Uncle Mister Kinder Sir is here. Hey, Uncle Chuckie, the Boy Red called out, and pumped his fist in the air in clear delight that his self-righteous uncle, who had been treating him like the nephew from fuckup-ville for the past year, had come out to hear his band cook. I waved back and pointed frantically at my watch and fluttered my hands like shot birds flopping to death in deep grass, hoping to convey that I had just remembered a pussy appointment so important that I had no choice but to shoot out of that beerjoint like a bullet fired from a gun, and then, tripping and stumbling in my haste, I attempted to fling myself from that establishment with a modicum of dignity.

When I hit the door in a dead heat I figured that even if I couldn't make it all the way across the lot to the Red Ride, where I could fetch my .38 from under the seat and lock the doors before it dawned on Baddest Bill to do me bodily harm, perhaps I would at least have time to crawl beneath a nearby vehicle. I was ten giant, hopping steps out the door before my legs went watery upon hearing that old growl that passed for Baddest Bill's voice inquire of me: —*Whar ya goen, fuckface?*

I made a sort of hopscotch stop, and then turned slowly to gaze upon his great, bearded, meaty face, wherein no light of the human soul shone through eyes flat and blank and cold as ice on a winter river. Hey, old Bill, I said and waved and bobbed my head in greeting as obsequiously as an old hound caught eating a pet chicken. Baddest was wearing a sleeveless leather vest and leather pants, which squeaked when he took a couple of steps toward me and stopped. I saw Mary standing in the doorway behind him and other faces huddled there like a bizarre bouquet of blinking flowers. There was a smirk on Mary's tired, pretty face. Baddest stood there looking me up and down with stony eyes for a couple of moments, as though measuring me for a coffin, his tattooed tree-branch arms folded across his chest, before he reached up and took the cigarette dangling in the midst of the black bush that passed for his lower face. After blowing lightly on its ember, Baddest flicked the glowing butt like a comet at my own face.

I flinched like it was a flaming arrow, and then, laughing uproariously and wagging my head at my old buddy's joke, that old cut-up Bill, I slouched back toward Baddest holding my hand out to shake. In the heartbeat I got close enough, I planted a perfect sucker-kick in the motherfucker's balls, the best one I ever landed. Baddest blinked once and made a little puffing sound and then simply stood there looking at me with those eyes like mossy stones underwater. Uh-oh, I reflected, this is not good. I flew at him winging combinations, and two things occurred to me in the next furious moments, one, how easy the big, slow, dumb sonofabitch was to hit, and, two, how it didn't make a dick of difference.

I saw his first punch coming at me like a program I had circled to watch in the *TV Guide*. That didn't make much difference either, except that I managed to duck just enough so that instead of breaking my face into pieces, it plowed a trench along the top of my head, the air about which began to sparkle. The fighting style of Baddest Bill was simple enough to figure out, he merely stepped forward one flat foot at a time, windmilling haymakers. My own fight plan was simple too, duck and dodge and scramble about until hopefully Baddest Bill either ran out of gas before I got killed or he was magically transfigured into that rare Southern Baptist full of forgiveness, pity, and mercy. Then he clipped me a good one alongside my jaw, and I could feel blood explode where my teeth dug into the soft flesh inside my mouth. Then a hook caught me low in my right ribs and I went down on my knees, the bloody, swollen knuckles of both hands grinding into the gravel. I pushed up and, as Baddest lumbered toward me, I sort of tried to tackle him, which was about as smart as tackling a tree. I did manage to pin one of his tattooey, thug arms to his body, so he simply commenced to somewhat languidly hammer the back of my head with his free, ham-sized fist. The next time I went down, I knew I wouldn't get back up in this life. I scrambled around in the red dog and gravel on my hands and knees, trying to dodge or absorb with my arms the kicks Baddest was aiming at my head, while the crazed beerjoint yahoos encouraged him to stomp me like a bug.

Just as I had rolled up in a ball beside the front tire of a Ford pickup, offering Baddest my back, the sacrificial shit-kicking suddenly ceased. Meaning the kick I expected that would smash my spine to smithereens and render me a cripple for the rest of my natural life didn't arrive. The ruckus of boots scuffling in gravel and shouts and hoots and Rebel yells seemed to suddenly sweep away from me, and I scurried under the truck and peeked out from behind a tire. The mob was moving away from me in a body, like the clumsy dance of a bunch of old circus bears. When its ranks parted for a moment, I saw the Boy Red wailing away, his fists and feet a blur of bad intentions upon a stumbling, dumbfounded, formerly Baddest Bill. The boy's long, red hair was as flaming and wild as the mane of a young lion in the yellow jungley parking lot lights.

Then the crowd closed about them again, and I crawled from beneath the truck and tried to get to my feet. I kept collapsing against the side of the truck, and then I commenced to regurgitate. When I looked up again at the crowd of bloodthirsty beerjoint baboons, I saw that things had degenerated into general mayhem, a serious fracas with thrashing figures all around the parking lot grunting and throwing punches and pounding and stomping joyfully upon any poor devil who went down. I knew that I, for one, was finished with fisticuffs for the evening, but the Boy Red was still deep in it. My one thought was to make it to the Red Ride and get my gun. I was wobbly as a baby, and I kept falling and barfing and getting back up. When I tumbled on my ass once again not ten feet from my vehicle, I felt somebody grab me under my arms and hoist me up. It was the Boy Red. His eyes were yellow and wild and he was panting. A stream of blood ran down the side of his flushed face from a gash at his hairline. His lips were split and bloody.

—You okay, Uncle Chuckie? the Boy Red gasped at me. I could only bob my head like a goofy puppet missing some strings *golly, sort of, gosh, I reckon.* He helped me the rest of the way to my vehicle and we both fell back against it. The fight was still yet raging all around the parking lot, but most battlers had more or less squared off with a particular partner and had settled down to trading punches like squabbling family members at a picnic reunion. The din had died down, and it was strangely quiet, just grunts and the dull thuds of fists thumping flesh.

—You gotta get out of here, Uncle Chuckie, the Boy Red said and spit blood into the red dog, as did I. —Somebody has bound to called the lawdogs, he said.

—What about you? I managed to croak.

—I'm cool, the Boy Red said and spit bloodily again and looked back toward the struggle with eyes of fever. —Plus I ain't done here yet, he said and gave me a big, bloody grin.

The Boy Red tapped a light punch on my shoulder. —Don't tell Mom, he said.

The Boy Red tilted his head back and shook out his mane of hair, and he stood there quietly with his fierce eyes closed for a moment or two. Then he roared a Rebel yell and charged back across the parking lot toward the dead center of that profound necessity of lost causes, his long, red freak-flag flaming with stars and bars.

A Part of This World and a Part of Another

Three cop cars, one city, one county, and one state, sirens singing, had roared past me by the time I reached the Route 19 four-lane, where for no good reason except circularity and custom and ceremony I turned back north and drove the couple miles to the Gorge Bridge. I pulled up and parked in my usual spot in the middle of the span of the longest arch bridge on the face of the Earth. I took a swig of the moonshine left in the mason jar, which was about as smart as licking lava, and I sat stunned with the new relationship I had with my raw bloody inner left cheek.

I opened my car door and sat on the edge of the seat, bent over with my feet planted on the pavement. Blood kept filling my mouth and I kept spitting it out onto the bridge, not to mention entertaining the recurring barfs. At that time of morning, there was no traffic at all, not even long-haul trucks, and I just sat there for a spell with my thumped head in my bloody hands. When the shivers and pukes finally passed, I flicked on my flashers, turned the tape deck up to extremely loud, and tumbled out of my vehicle.

Here's where I get vague. I know I was still hunting for an exit sign. I had been driving around in the hills hunting for an ending to this book, a way out. But when I wrote myself out of this book, what then? Had I been trying to write myself out of the real world, or into it? For so long now, a part of my life had been about writing the stories of this book, and another part about trying to live them fully, the stories about my home state, this land of strip-mined lives, and the failed sad facts of reclamation. But now which was which? Which was my real home state, and which was the parallel world of my memory and imagination?

I tell my students good endings must surprise the reader but seem inevitable. Perfect endings will also reflect the author's own surprise at how things turn out. As I've mentioned previously, I always tell my students about how Flannery O'Connor recalled that she herself had no idea until several sentences before he did it, that that itinerant Bible salesman in "Good Country People" would steal that poor woman's wooden leg in the barn loft, and run off out of the story with it, which reflects that magic moment in a great story where the characters take over their own fictional destiny, rise up off the page into full-blown real lives of their own, and do just what they must for their own sake and for the sake of the story, sometimes in spite of any earlier other ideas or intentions of the author. But I am talking about the special truth of fiction here and not history, where they say every word is supposed to reflect that special, more elusive, truth of facts.

The writer Richard Brautigan once said that he always wanted to end a book on one of his very favorite words, *mayonnaise,* and so he did, the final word of his masterpiece *Trout Fishing in America* being the mystery word *mayonnaise.* It was, after all, his book and he could do what he wanted. Now that's fiction for you.

These days I spend mostly drifting around the hills of southern West Virginia, little mountain town to town, where I seek out clean quiet rooms in modest motels or hotels. I find me a down-home diner that has daily blue-plate specials, like meatloaf and mashed potatoes with possum gravy and where I can get me a wilted lettuce salad, the kind Mimi used to make when I was a kid, which is cut-up garden-fresh leaf lettuce, yellow onions, and crumpled fried bacon, with the hot bacon grease from the frying pan, cut with a little vinegar and sugar, used for the salad dressing, stuff that will eventually stop your heart, but so what?

I seek out homey roadhouses with good country-music jukeboxes, where I can while away my evenings sipping longneck bottles of Budweiser and watching the Pittsburgh Pirates on the teevee set above the bar, and maybe shoot a little shit with a fading beerjoint beauty, whispering in her ear that my name is Hank. I have been living the High Lonesome life of a loner, a stranger passing through every town. My life has become the slow-motion dream of a drifter, a way of life perfect for sappy country songs, which I really wouldn't highly recommend to anybody.

I am still yet trying to decide who or what I can't live without. In the mountain beerjoints, I've met any number of lonely old men with their own blue secrets, who offer up no laments or apologies and in their essential solitude call themselves happy enough. Old coots who have learned to live their lives according to their own limits. My main alibi has always been that my most destructive inclinations rose out of some deep inability to live with who and what I was. But what I have come to know is that sometimes you just have to learn to live with what you can't rise above.

I call my old Momma often, and my sister too, check in so they won't worry that I have disappeared off the face of the Earth. I call Lindsay too, all the time, and sometimes she will talk with me. She hasn't headed back to the Big Sky country of Montana yet. I do not, for her own sake, whine and beg for her to take me back. Deep in the lonely nights I am often tempted to call little Holly, but I never do it. Then I sip whiskey and write all night on my trusty little laptop, still trying to solve even the simplest of mysteries about my home state. When I heard wild rumors that Cousin Jesco had finally shot Norma Jean down like a dog, I spent a few days driving around the hills and hollows of Boone County trying to find out the truth of that story, but what I found was that Jesco was by now as mythic as the mountains, and all stories about him are essentially true.

I wake up some days with the feeling that I am only a poor reenactor of myself. But I have come to admit everything. I have come to admit that I am my failed father's son, little John Wayne Jr., and the beloved outlaw son of Morris Hackett's too, little Bogie-Boy. I watch *Alien* movie reruns every chance I get, late at night in those various motel rooms I call home. Sigourney Weaver is a wonderful actor, the way she never gives up and keeps on kicking that deep demon butt on one forbidden planet after another. I'm going to write her a fan letter one of these days. If they ever make a movie out of my wretched life, I'd like for Sigourney Weaver to be the star.

450

If and when I ever drive back North, I don't know what I'll find there. I don't know if I have anything to go back to any more, except a job that I'm beginning to miss. Presently I am holed up at the Poca-hontas Motel on Route 21 north of Welch, where I am writing these last paragraphs. Clearly I got off that bridge alive. Clearly this isn't the longest suicide note, at 500-plus wrinkled manuscript pages, in the history of the world after all.

Sure, that last night I stopped on that bridge, I was hovering between one world and another. Sure, I thought about going over that low rail into the second-oldest riverbed in the world. Sure, I thought about joining that sad dentist and his pissed blind dog down in that great gorge of ghost towns. Who came to mind that night was old Sid Hatfield. I reflected upon Sid Hatfield's untimely death. I wondered if Sid Hatfield had realized, with a sort of sudden, final, omniscient clarity, that he had been betrayed when he heard those apocalyptic explosions. I wondered if Sid Hatfield had realized that to have been lured down into that clear deathtrap was simply a real stupid failure of imagination, and that now all he had left to do in his life, as he felt the impact of the first of his own beneficent bullets, was to die purely impenitent. Who Sid had finally betrayed was himself. Charlie had done that too. Count me in too. But so what?

Old Willie's song about regret had come on the tape deck. I under-stood what old Willie meant about being able to cry for all the time he had wasted, except that that would be a waste of time. Not to mention tears. Sure, I was full of regret, but there was nothing I could do about it now. And I pretty much knew what I would change if I could go back in time somehow, but there was nothing I could do about it now. I had no excuses, and somewhere down deep in me I was basically impenitent. Some say the dead, like yesterday, are nothing but lonely, useless ghosts. Some say the dead are angels, and death is only the abandonment of soli-tude. I don't know. You tell me, brother.

Say I had hopped off that bridge, and after I had exploded on the sur-face of that water at an estimated hundred miles an hour, what was left of me had floated far downstream over the rocks of the New River to where it merges with the Gauley to form the Kanawha, and then I had floated on down that Indian ghost-river, before I managed to finally climb that other shore, drying my wings, only to discover that I was back in Montgomery, my own home town, where I was born, and that I had to begin again, buy another ticket on that same old last bus out of town.

That night, I leaned over the railing and took to praying, as genuine West Virginians are wont to do. Jesus, from loneliness spare us, spare us from feeling maybe we are not special, give us a breather, put a song in our hearts, a fable, a joke, a good story to tell, and grant us a courageous sense of irony, and a sense of when to split, and oh Lord save our sorry asses from ridiculous deaths.

And, lo, a sensation of well-being passed over me, a sense of old-timey strength and purpose, together with a sense of anticipation, ineffably sweet, and of happiness, strange, mysterious happiness, and for a few heartbeats life seemed enchanting, miraculous, imbued with exalted significance. For a few heartbeats I felt like a young, beautiful Elvis, on the verge of it all.

Elvis, that ultimate alien-angel, who makes guest appearances in this world and God knows how many others, and whose ghost-wave voice rose serendipitously from the Red Ride's tape deck just then that night singing "Love Me Tender" (I love old Elvis; but, if the truth be told, I have always aspired to be the Jerry Lee Lewis of American Letters). I recollect that same old sadness and sense of loss grabbing me suddenly by the short hairs. So what else was new? Plus I recollect I had to take a leak bad.

Through the rising fog, I saw the high beams of a long-hauler halted up at the lights at the Billville turnoff. I leaned against the Red Ride and tilted my head back over its top to gaze up at those constellations of summer stars unique to the skies above West Virginia. I unzipped my jeans and led Trigger out of the barn. Elvis was singing Hound Dog now and I danced in place. Holy moly, but the tip of that handy albeit hoary appendage stung like the dickens each time its old head tapped on the pavement.

I found myself humming along with Saint Elvis, and then singing out loud there in the middle of the New River Gorge Bridge, not unlike

Saint Elvis a part of this world and a part of another. I whizzed and watched the high beams of that truck advance through thickening fog toward where I holy-hollered along with Hound Dog at the top of my lungs, and did a sort of staggery tragi-comic two-step behind my vehicle's flashing red lights, just a poor old mostly imaginary rhetorical being dancing with his mythic dick.

ACKNOWLEDGMENTS

I am not a historian, nor am I an academic. I am a storyteller. And for the purposes of this book, I was a story catcher. I drove around the hills of home in West Virginia and talked with folks, listening to stories they had to tell me. I visited places of interest to me and looked around. And I read. I read everything I could get my hands on that concerned my home state, from old newspapers to tourist brochures to history books. I did not do any really systematic research; my reading was way too haphazard for that. I didn't even take many notes, except perhaps for the names of people and places and the dates of important events, so that I could try to keep things straight anyway. I simply immersed myself in the narratives, took those stories down deep within myself, deep within my own imagination and memory, made them my own, and then more or less regurgitated those factions as they fit into the history of my own interior landscape. I wanted to finally feel as though I was writing from my own living memory about people and events long past.

I can't count the times, for instance, down in Welch, when I would sit on the third step up from the landing in front of MacDowell County Courthouse, the very stone step that Sid Hatfield's head had come to rest upon when he was gunned down decades ago on that spot, and I would read the section over and over again from Lon Savage's book, *Thunder in the Mountains,* about that bloody event, and I would look up from those vivid pages and gaze around. I swear there were times when I thought I could see Sid and the lovely Jessie strolling my way across the street toward all of death and legend.

So, here are some of the books that affected me the most like that, that became a pure part of my own living memory and imagination.

The aforementioned *Thunder in the Mountains: The West Virginia Mine War 1920–21* by Lon Savage is one of the best books I have read in my lifetime. I must have read that book cover-to-cover a half dozen times at least. Why nobody has made a movie of that great West Virginia warrior saga and mythic love story I don't know.

There was a series of pictorial books by Fayette County historians and authors Melody and George Bragg that I found fascinating and invaluable, which included *Unsolved Mountain Murders, Volumes I and II*, and *Windows to the Past, Volumes I and II*. I sat up into the wee hours many times pouring those true tall tales into myself along with a little brown stuff.

West Virginia, A History by John Alexander Williams was a first-rate book that I found very smart and absorbing. Then there was *West Virginia, A History* by Stephen W. Brown and Otis K. Rice (who was an old professor of mine at W.V. Institute of Technology). A few others that come readily to mind are *Historical Highlights of Southern West Virginia* by Shirley Donnelly; *Tales and Trails from the Fayette Tribune* collected by Dale Payne and Bob Beckelheimar; *Bloodletting in Appalachia* by H. K. Lee; *Hatfields and McCoys—True Romance and Tragedies* by Willis David Staton; *The West Virginia Mine Wars, An Anthology* edited by David Alan Corbin; *The Autobiography of Mother Jones* by Mother Jones; and finally the sundry wondrous writings of John A. Keel, including *The Complete Guide to Mysterious Beings* and *The Mothman Prophesies*.

I need to also thank a bunch of mountain brothers who shared their stories and thoughts with me regarding this hillbilly book. First and foremost let me thank this ugly, bald, goat-bearded old boy named Jon Kemper, who is perhaps the best bullshitter and storyteller I have known in my life. I want to thank my old West Virginia friends John O'Brien (author of the wonderful book, *At Home in the Heart of Appalachia*) and David Noble and James Lee Handloser for being my old friends. My old W.V.U. professor John Stashy was an important person in my life, but he is utterly blameless for this hillbilly book. I want to thank my brother, David Kinder, who remains a West Virginian at heart although he has repaired to Houston in order to be rich. The late great writer Neale Clark was very helpful to me when I lived in Billville. The genius filmmaker Jacob Young was somebody I stole a ton of stuff from (thanks to the idiotic political powers that be in West Virginia, who are attempting to promote image over art, you can no longer purchase a copy of any of Young's brilliant series of films depicting weird West Virginians). I owe much to Jessico White, the true Last Mountain Dancer, whose mythic story was the seed of this book. Who I can't really thank enough for his wisdom and wily ways with a good story is my twin cousin (we were separated at birth) Doctor Mike Newhart. And I better mention my best outlaw buddy Lee Maynard, author of those scandalous tomes, *Crum* and *Screaming with the Cannibals,* which were actually banned in Beckley for tarnishing West Virginia's ready-for-prime-time reputation by calling a hillbilly a hillbilly. I envy Maynard bitterly for this distinction. Finally, I'd like to thank my house band, The Deliberate Strangers (Tom Moran, Stephanie Vargo, and Jon Manning), who along with the aforementioned Lee Maynard and myself, made it back safely from the infamous Outlaw Writers Tour down in the dark, dangerous hills and hollows of West Virginia.

ABOUT THE AUTHOR

Born and raised in West Virginia, Chuck Kinder has worked as a coal miner, moonshiner, bartender, bouncer, bandit, professional boxer, circus performer, tango teacher, cook, and college professor. As a young itinerant professor he taught at Stanford University, the University of California at Davis, and the University of Alabama at Tuscaloosa. He is now Director of the Writing Program at the University of Pittsburgh.